# Contents



## UNDERSTAND



## SURVIVAL GUIDE



## SPECIAL FEATURES

# Welcome to Rarotonga, Samoa & Tonga

*Adrift on these daydreamy South Pacific islands – deliciously remote and unhurried – it's easy to get back to the simple pleasures of eating, sleeping and succumbing to holiday whims.*

## South Seas Dreaming

Perpetuated by Hollywood, the paradisiacal reputation of this part of the South Pacific can be traced back to the tales of returned European explorers. These nations have modernised since then, but their allure is undiminished: you'll still find gin-clear waters and gardenia-scented air. But what's most amazing is how untainted by tourism most of the islands are. Blame it on remoteness, blame it on air fares, but few people who fantasise about the South Seas ever actually make the journey. This is the true gift of these Polynesian isles: here's your chance to get right off the tourism grid.

## Polynesian Ways

These cultures are so idiosyncratic that almost every encounter yields a memorable moment. Locals burst into song in public, and on Sundays the singing in church raises the roof. Villagers casually swing bush knives by their sides as they walk along; kids sit on the scuffed tombs of their relatives as if they were outdoor furniture; and games of rugby and volleyball erupt with gladiatorial intensity on threadbare patches of grass. Locals sell traditional handicrafts such as tapa cloth, woven mats, baskets and carvings by the roadside, as hotted-up cars scoot past with Polynesian hip-hop blaring.

## Island Time

Through the conduit of snorkelling, diving, sailing, swimming, hiking, drinking, feasting and talking about nothing in particular with loquacious locals, visitors to these islands quickly change down a gear or two and slip into island time. Indeed, time here is a flexible commodity, and days roll in and out on the tide. One day you're exploring vanilla-bean plantations, snorkelling with tropical fish, swimming in sunken caves and dancing at a bar, and the next a plane is waiting to jet you back home. The trick is to go with the flow – don't stress too much if things don't happen precisely when you expect them to.

## Dinner Is Served

These South Pacific islands don't have a great rep for fine food and wine. But sidestep the Westernised resort restaurants and be adventurous: you'll find hearty local stews cooked with coconut milk, fabulous fresh seafood (how's that lobster?) and even the odd peppy Chinese noodle soup. And who needs shiraz when the weather is this humid? Sip a cold local lager instead – it's the perfect thirst quencher as the sun sets on another day in the promised land.

## Why I Love Rarotonga, Samoa & Tonga

By Charles Rawlings-Way, Writer

Sure, you've got the palm trees, the seafood, the hypercoloured reefs, the sweet scent of hibiscus on the evening breeze... But the best thing about Rarotonga, Samoa and Tonga is the pace of life here – or rather, the lack of pace. I spend most of my time careening around Australia's big cities, drinking too much coffee and talking a lot. Every slowed-down trip I make to these islands is an antidote to the mayhem, extending my allocated time on this lonely planet by unknown years.

**For more about our writers, see page 256**

Above: Samoa (p98)

# Rarotonga, Samoa & Tonga

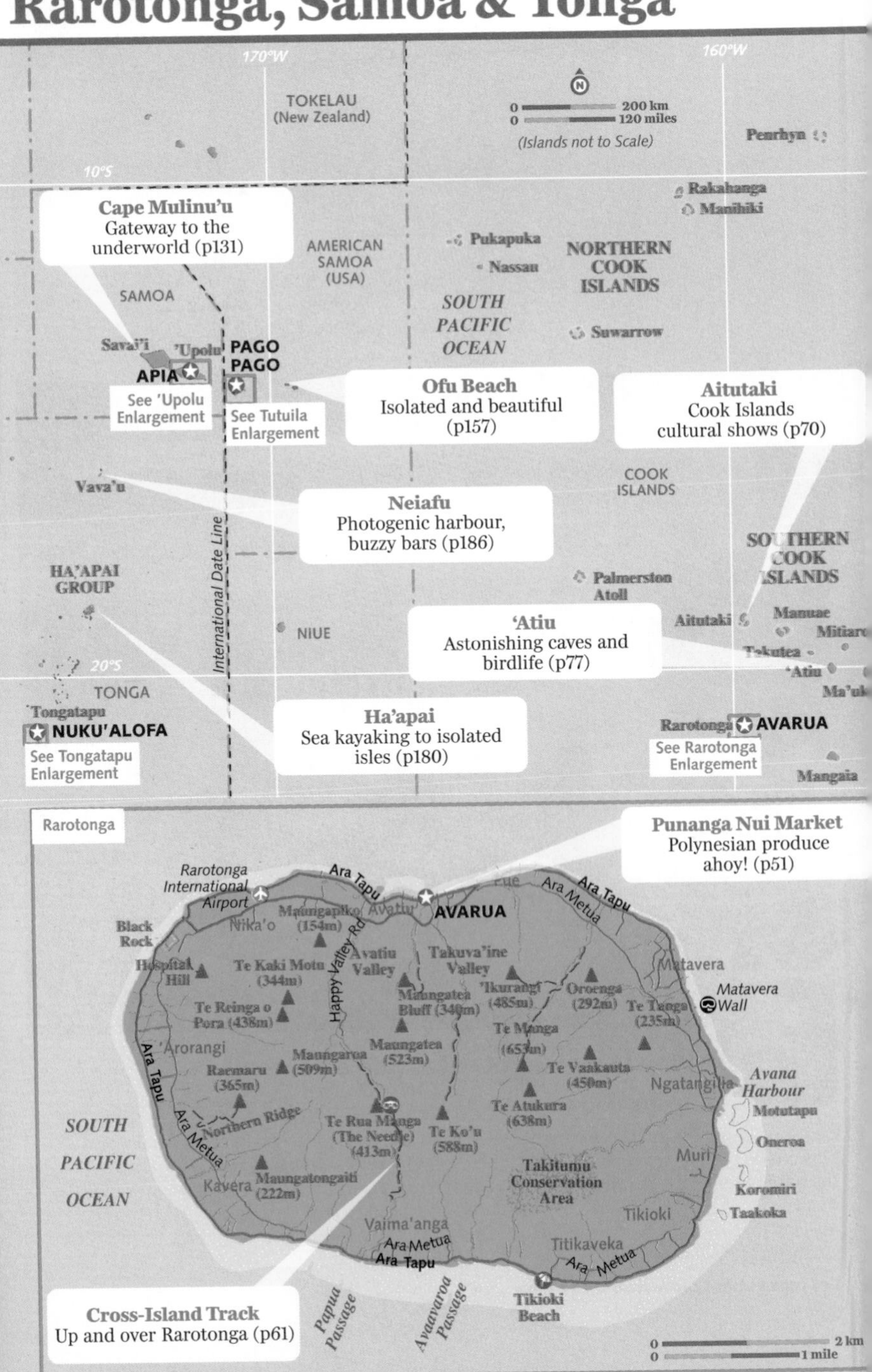

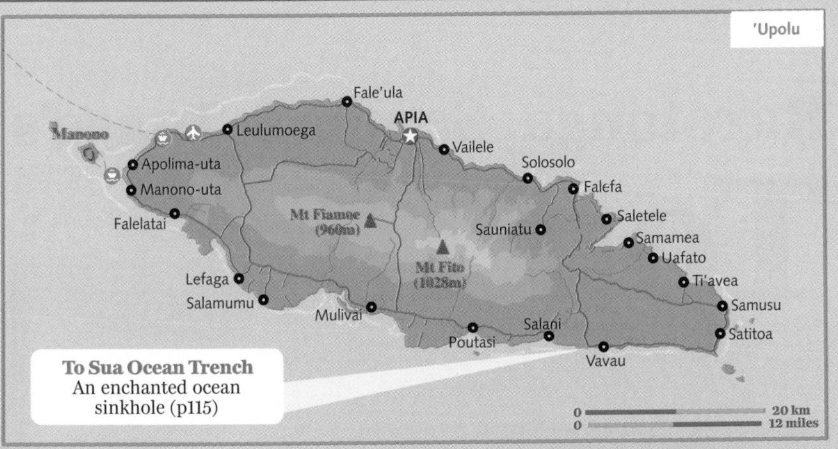
'Upolu
Manono
Fale'ula
APIA
Leulumoega
Vailele
Apolima-uta
Solosolo
Manono-uta
Falefa
Falelatai
Saletele
Mt Fiamoe (960m)
Sauniatu
Samamea
Mt Fito (1028m)
Uafato
Ti'avea
Lefaga
Salamumu
Samusu
Mulivai
Salani
Satitoa
Poutasi
Vavau
To Sua Ocean Trench
An enchanted ocean sinkhole (p115)
0 20 km
0 12 miles

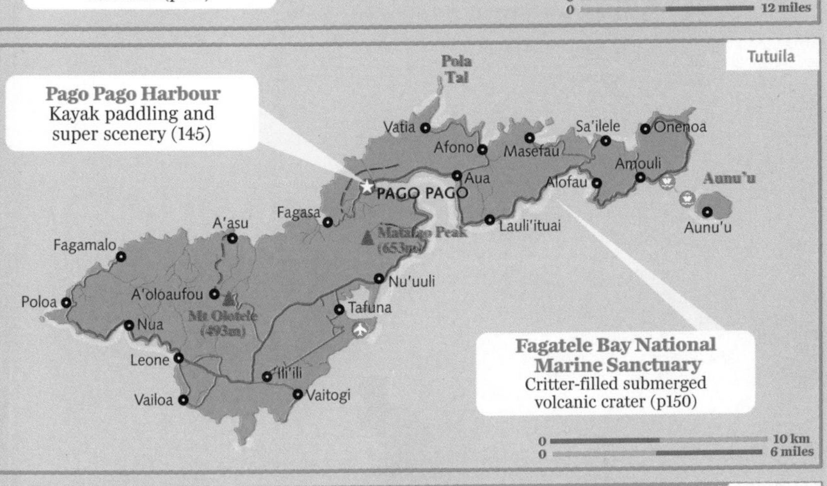
Tutuila
Pola Tal
Pago Pago Harbour
Kayak paddling and super scenery (145)
Vatia
Sa'ilele
Onenoa
Afono
Masefau
Amouli
Aua
Aunu'u
Alofau
PAGO PAGO
Fagasa
Lauli'ituai
Aunu'u
A'asu
Fagamalo
Nu'uuli
Poloa
A'oloaufou
Tafuna
Mt Olotele (493m)
Nua
Leone
'Ili'ili
Fagatele Bay National Marine Sanctuary
Critter-filled submerged volcanic crater (p150)
Vailoa
Vaitogi
0 10 km
0 6 miles

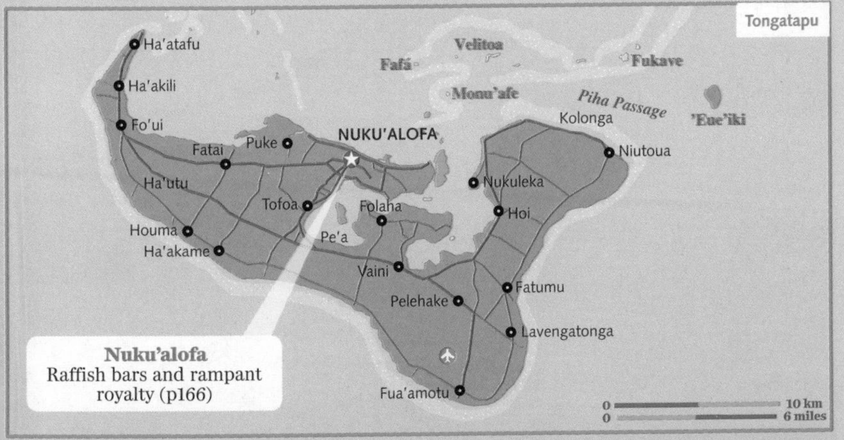
Tongatapu
Ha'atafu
Velitoa
Fafá
Fukave
Ha'akili
Monu'afe
Piha Passage
Fo'ui
Kolonga
'Eue'iki
NUKU'ALOFA
Puke
Niutoua
Fatai
Ha'utu
Nukuleka
Tofoa
Folaha
Hoi
Houma
Pe'a
Ha'akame
Vaini
Fatumu
Pelehake
Lavengatonga
Nuku'alofa
Raffish bars and rampant royalty (p166)
Fua'amotu
0 10 km
0 6 miles

# Rarotonga, Samoa & Tonga's Top 15

1

## South Seas Surfing

**1** Every surfer worth their wax knows about the big waves in Tahiti, where the Billabong Pro comp happens every year. But intrepid wave hounds are gradually exploring Rarotonga, Samoa (p105) and Tonga, and finding brilliant uncrowded scenes in warm, crystal-clear tropical waters. Cyclone season (November to April) brings gnarly waves from the north, while during winter (May to August) low-pressure systems in the Southern Ocean and Tasman Sea bring big swells to exposed southern coastlines. BYO board is the norm.

## Hiking the Cross-Island Track

**2** A Cook Islands sojourn usually involves lots of good eating and drinking, and long, lazy days on the beach. Offset all this tropical indulgence with a jaunt along Rarotonga's challenging Cross-Island Track (p61). The three- to four-hour hike via the 413m-high Te Rua Manga (The Needle) immerses walkers in some of the island's most eye-popping scenery. Starting from Rarotonga's northern coast, the terrain includes tangled tree roots amid tropical forest, meandering, rocky streams and waterfalls.

MARK TIPPLE / GETTY IMAGES ©

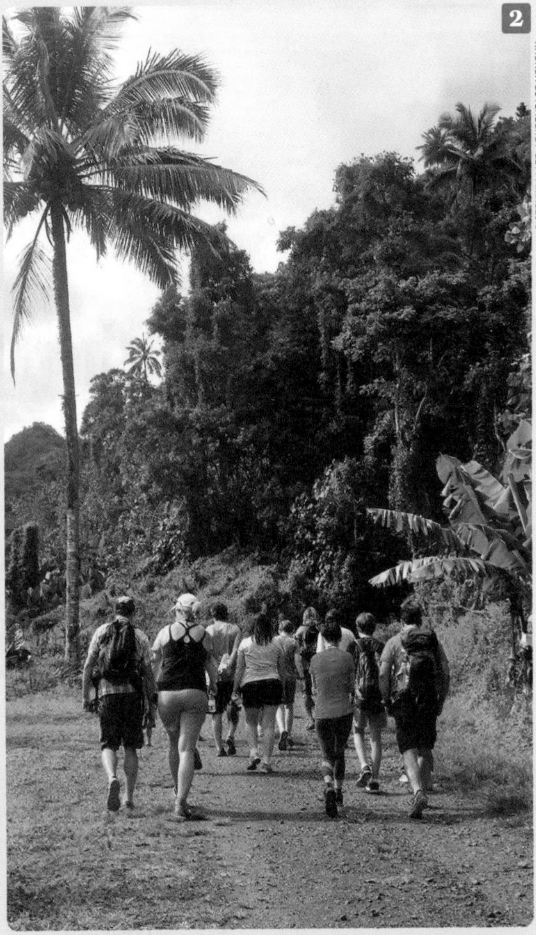

2

RHONDA GUTENBERG / GETTY IMAGES ©

## Pago Pago Harbor

**3** In American Samoa, Pago (p145), as it's affectionately known, is a gritty working town full of fisherfolk and canneries. But that's what makes its backdrop so surprising: vertical green peaks with jagged silhouettes, plunging dramatically into an elongated bay of dark teal. Launch a kayak to experience the bay at its best, ideally at sunrise or sunset when the light plays off the mountains. You're just as likely to paddle past children playing on the beach as to pass stacks of shipping containers.

## Beach Fale in Samoa

**4** These elongated, open-air huts on stilts (p227) hover over Samoa's trademark white sands, taking in panoramic vistas of turquoise seas while the cool breeze blows through. Few other South Pacific countries have retained their traditional architecture to the point that it's what they offer tourists, without design or modern fanfare: in Samoa, guests sleep on the *fale* (house; pictured) floor and privacy is found by pulling down thatched louvres. *Fale* are basic and budget, but the views are worth a million bucks.

5

6

## Sea Kayaking in Tonga

5 One of the best ways to see the aquamarine waterways and remote sandy islands of Tonga's Vava'u (pictured) and Ha'apai (p182) groups is to take a guided multiday kayak tour. There's plenty on offer, from single-day trips to week-long packages: get some exercise, camp on beaches or in *fale,* and meet villagers on outer islands that are usually next to impossible to access. And there'll be plenty of time for swimming, snorkelling and beachcombing along the way.

## To Sua Ocean Trench

6 Once you've descended the 20-odd metres of wooden ladder into the crystalline waters of this fairy grotto (p115) in Samoa, you'll experience an odd sense of being totally removed from (and yet at one with) the world. It's not so much a 'trench' as a sinkhole with sheer rock walls adorned with greenery. You can swim under a broad arch of rock from the larger pool, teased by droplets of water hitting the surface, to a second wide opening to the sky.

PETER HENDRIE / GETTY IMAGES ©

## Fagatele Bay National Marine Sanctuary

7 This impressive submerged volcanic crater (p150) in American Samoa is fringed by Tutuila's last remaining stretch of coastal rainforest. Its cliffside depths host more than 140 species of coral and innumerable species of colourful tropical fish – parrotfish, damselfish, butterfly fish, you name it – plus other sea creatures such as lobsters, crabs, sharks, octopuses, turtles, giant clams and, between June and September, migrating southern humpback whales. Snorkel or chase some hiking trails around the coastline. Green sea turtle

## 'Atiu's Caves

8 One of the Cook Islands' smallest and rockiest outer islands, 'Atiu is an ecotravel hotspot. Sign up for a birdwatching tour to spy an endangered *kakerori* (Rarotongan flycatcher), then descend into the cathedral-like arches of Anatakitaki Cave (p79; pictured), the only known home of the elusive *kopeka* ('Atiuan swiftlet) – listen for its distinctive echo-locating clicks. Don't miss Anatakitaki's other main attraction: a candlelit dip in the cave's sequestered subterranean pool. You can also visit Rima Rau burial cave here.

## History & Archaeology

9 The great Polynesian migration that populated the South Pacific from the west took place around 3000 years ago. History is alive and present here, with all sorts of significant sites remaining. Check out 'the Stonehenge of the Pacific' – Tonga's Ha'amonga 'a Maui Trilithon (pictured), lonesome in a field – or the Pulemelei Mound (p132) in Samoa, an abandoned pyramid lost in vines that's the largest ancient structure in Polynesia.

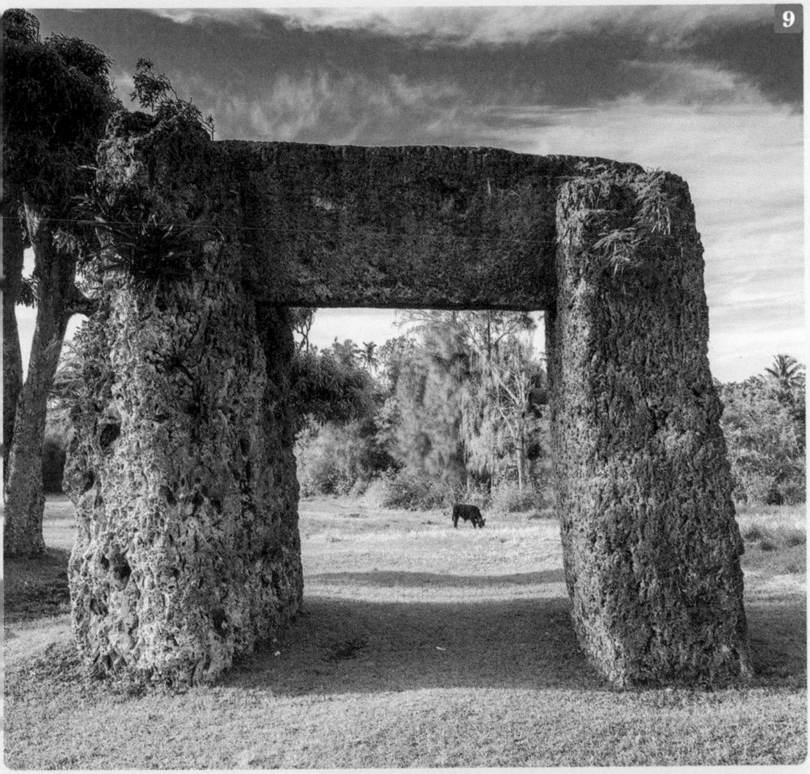
9



## Cape Mulinu'u

**10** At the western tip of Savai'i island you'll find the beautiful outlook of Fafa O Sauai'i, considered one of ancient Samoa's most sacred spots. According to tradition, this gateway for souls into the next world has two entrances: one for chiefs and another for commoners. One entrance is through a cave near Cape Mulinu'u (p131); the other is on the trail made by the setting sun over the sea. You mightn't reach the afterlife, but don't pass up a swim in the rock pool here. Coconut plantation, Cape Mulinu'u

DOUGLAS PEEBLES / ROBERT HARDING ©

10

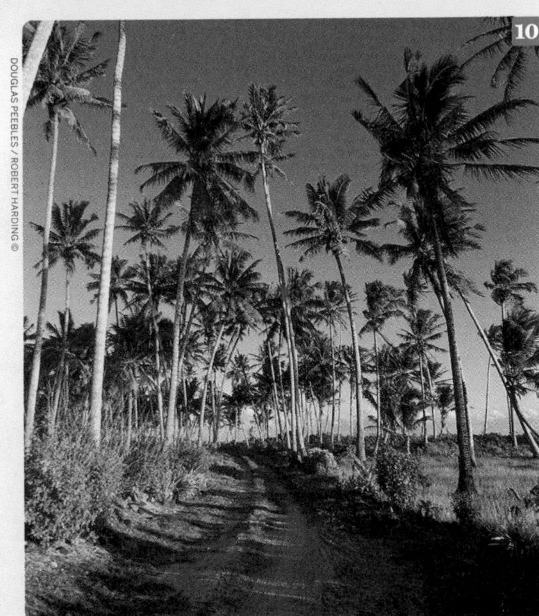

## Ofu Beach

**11** Surely in line for nomination as one of the world's top beaches, Ofu Beach (p157), on the island of the same name in American Samoa, is 4km of shining, palm-fringed white sand flanked by ridiculously picturesque jagged peaks that rise behind it like giant shark's teeth. Part of the Manu'a group, it's not easy to get to, but sometimes the best things in life require a bit of effort. You may be the only person there...

## Cook Islands Culture

**12** An accessible way to experience some Cook Islands culture (p220) without having to venture too far into the wilderness is to check out an 'Island Night' show at a resort or restaurant in Rarotonga or Aitutaki. Yes, they're prepackaged and often lacking in spontaneity, but the traditional dance, close harmony singing, fire-throwing and drumming displays are certainly authentic. When you're (inevitably) asked up on stage after the big buffet dinner, just go with the flow, smile and shake it out. Bottom: Cook Islander dancers perform at the 10th Festival of Pacific Arts

11

MICHAEL RUNKEL / ROBERTHARDING ©

12

VINCENT TALBOT / GETTY IMAGES ©

HOLGER LEUE / GETTY IMAGES ©

MICHAEL RUNKEL / ROBERT HARDING ©

## Punanga Nui Market

**13** On Saturday mornings in Avarua, Rarotonga, skip the hotel buffet and make tracks to Punanga Nui (p51), one of the Pacific's best markets. In between the colourful *pareu* (sarongs), handcrafted ukuleles and local buskers is an entire morning of foodie discoveries. Kick off with organic island coffee and a still-warm coconut bun, then move on to fresh-fruit smoothies and crepes crammed with tropical fruit. Leave room for a few local specialities such as *rukau* (steamed taro leaves) or *ika mata* (marinated raw fish).
Above: Lei (flower necklace), Punanga Nui Market

## Downtown Nuku'alofa

**14** Signs of Tonga's intriguing 'never-colonised' monarchist history are everywhere in the dusty capital, Nuku'alofa (p166), from the impressive waterfront Royal Palace (pictured), encircled by casuarinas and manicured lawns, to the fenced-off and flower-covered royal tombs nearby, and smiling King Tupou VI on the newly printed plastic banknotes. Nuku'alofa is an appealing spot to decompress for a few days, with some good cafes, restaurants and guesthouses, some raffish waterside bars and the amazing produce-lined aisles of Talamahu Market.

## Drinking in Neiafu

**15** In Vava'u in Tonga's northern reaches, Neiafu (p186) fronts onto one of the world's most photogenic natural harbours – a safe haven for yachts in a storm. Prop up the bar at one of the old town's harbourside booze rooms and sink a few cold beers. The conversation drifts between moorings, weather charts, trade winds and destinations – there might even be a South Seas duo strumming and harmonising in the corner, a kava session on the go...or at least some classic rock on the stereo.

# Need to Know

For more information, see Survival Guide (p233)

### Currency

**New Zealand dollar** (NZ$) Cook Islands
**Samoan tala** (ST) Samoa
**Tongan pa'anga** (T$) Tonga
**US dollar** (US$) American Samoa

### Languages

English is widely spoken, along with local languages – Rarotongan, Samoan and Tongan.

### Visas

Short-term visitor visas issued on arrival. New Zealanders don't need a Cook Islands visa; American citizens don't need an American Samoa visa.

### Money

ATMs and money changers in most large towns; cash only on most outer islands.

### Mobile Phones

Local SIM cards or global roaming are available in all countries. Reception is variable but available, even on remote islands.

### Time

Tonga is GMT plus 13 hours, Samoa GMT plus 14 hours, the Cook Islands GMT minus 10 hours and American Samoa GMT minus 11 hours.

## When to Go

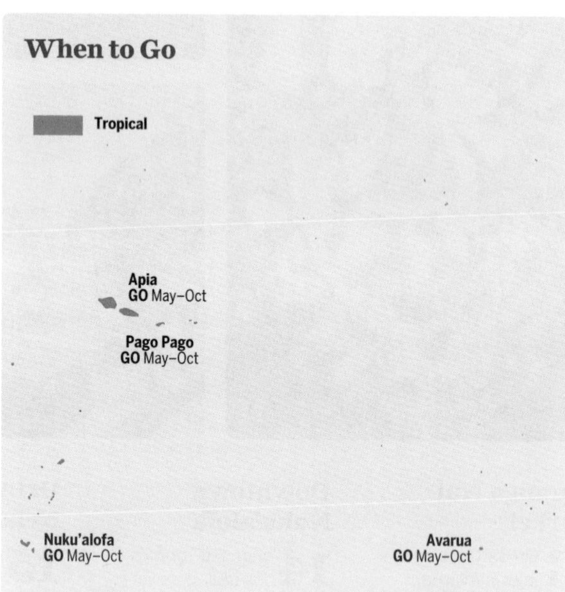


### High Season (Jun–Aug, Dec & Jan)

- Many islanders living abroad come home to visit family.
- Book flights well in advance.
- June to August is dry; December and January are humid and wet. Cyclone season is November to April.

### Shoulder (May, Sep)

- Trade winds lower the humidity and keep temperatures pleasant.
- Flights are cheaper and less likely to be booked.
- Travel with company but very few crowds.

### Low Season (Feb–Apr, Oct & Nov)

- Expect hot temperatures and high humidity.
- Scour the web for deals on resorts looking to fill empty rooms.
- Diving visibility can be reduced due to heavy rains.

## Useful Websites

**American Samoa Visitors Bureau** (www.americansamoa.travel)

**Cook Islands Tourism Authority** (www.cookislands.travel)

**Lonely Planet** (www.lonelyplanet.com/pacific) Destination information, hotel bookings, traveller forums and more.

**Pacific Islands Report** (www.pireport.org) News from across the South Pacific.

**Pacific Region Headquarters** (www.prh.noaa.gov) Pacific weather.

**Samoa Tourism Authority** (www.samoa.travel)

**Tonga tourism** (www.thekingdomoftonga.com, www.tongaholiday.com)

## Important Numbers

International country codes:

| | |
|---|---|
| **Cook Islands** | ☎682 |
| **Samoa** | ☎685 |
| **American Samoa** | ☎1-684 |
| **Tonga** | ☎676 |

## Exchange Rates

| | | |
|---|---|---|
| **Cook Islands** | NZ$1 | US$0.70 |
| **Samoa** | ST1 | US$0.39 |
| **American Samoa** | US$1 | US$1 |
| **Tonga** | T$1 | US$0.44 |

For current exchange rates see www.xe.com

## Daily Costs

### Budget: less than US$100

- Guesthouse bed: US$15–50
- Basket of fruit at a local market: US$3-10
- Bicycle rental per day: US$15-25

### Midrange: US$100–400

- Double room in a boutique hotel or small resort: US$100–250
- Main course in a local cafe: US$10–20
- Snorkelling or glass-bottom boat trip: US$30–60

### Top end: more than US$400

- Night in an over-the-water bungalow: from US$500
- Dinner at a restaurant with international chef: US$75–200
- Two-tank scuba dive: US$150

## Opening Hours

Following are some generalised opening hours – time is flexible in the Polynesian realm! In many places, everything closes on Sunday; see country directories for details.

**Banks** 9.30am to 3pm or 4pm Monday to Friday.

**Bars & Pubs** 11am to midnight or later.

**Cafes** 7.30am to 8pm.

**Post offices & government offices** 9am to 4pm Monday to Friday.

**Shops** 9am to 5pm Monday to Friday, to 1pm Saturday.

## Arriving in Rarotonga, Samoa & Tonga

**Rarotonga International Airport** (p45; Avarua, Cook Islands) Shuttle services and taxis to anywhere on the island; many hotels provide transfers.

**Faleolo Airport** (p141; Apia, Samoa) Taxis and shuttles into Apia (35km); many hotels provide transfers.

**Tafuna International Airport** (p156; Tafuna, American Samoa) Buses and taxis into Pago Pago, 15km away.

**Fua'amotu International Airport** (p166; Tongatapu, Tonga) Local taxis meet all flights, or organise a direct accommodation transfer into Nuku'alofa, 21km away.

## Getting Around

**Air** The most efficient (and sometimes the only) way to island hop; flights can be expensive.

**Car & motorcycle** Hire available on large islands; in remote areas it's usually not an option. Bring a current international driving permit and home driver's licence. Drive on the left in Rarotonga, Samoa and Tonga, and on the right in American Samoa.

**Ferry & boat** Ferries ply short distances between main islands; cargo ships make longer hauls. Or if you're lucky, hop on a yacht!

For much more on **getting around**, see p235

# If You Like...

## Beaches

**Ofu Beach** (American Samoa) In the remote Manu'a Islands, this is a palm-fringed white-sand stunner backed by ridiculously picturesque jagged peaks. (p157)

**Uoleva** (Tonga) The west coast of this island in the Ha'apai Group has a spectacular leeward coast of white sand lapped by surely the clearest water on earth. Oh, and did we mention the humpbacks breeching offshore? (p184)

**Aitutaki Lagoon** (Cook Islands) The 15 palm-covered *motu* (islets) that ring Aitutaki's mind-boggling lagoon all get a vote for their beaches. One Foot Island is the best known. (p72)

**Lalomanu Beach** (Samoa) This beauty at the eastern tip of Upolu island has it all – white sand, turquoise waters and offshore islands. (p115)

## Castaway Islands

**Niuafo'ou** (Tonga) Also known as Tin Can Island, Niuafo'ou is in Tonga's northern extremes. It's shaped like a floating doughnut, with an enclosed lake 23m above sea level. (p196)

**Suwarrow** (Cook Islands) In the Cooks' northern group and the country's only national park, Suwarrow was home to hermit Tom Neale. Read up on his adventures in *An Island to Oneself*. (p91)

**Tofua** (Tonga) The mutiny on the *Bounty* took place offshore of Tofua in the Ha'apai Group in 1789. More recently, Swiss snowboard champ Xavier Rosset spent 10 months alone here to test his mettle! (p187)

**Ta'u** (American Samoa) At the eastern extreme of American Samoa, Ta'u features some of the world's highest sea cliffs, dense rainforest, inactive cones and craters, and numerous bird species. (p159)

## Diving & Snorkelling

**Vava'u Group** (Tonga) A diver's delight, sites in Vava'u range from coral gardens and encrusted wrecks to sea caves and other geological marvels. (p185)

**Samoa** Many travellers use Samoa as a place to gain their diving certification and there are quality operators on the main islands. Popular spots include Tialipi's Heaven off Savai'i and Anganoa Wall on Upolu's south coast. (p98)

**Aitutaki** (Cook Islands) There's fantastic diving to be had in Aitutaki, with great visibility and features such as drop-offs, multilevels, wall dives and cave systems. (p70)

**Muri Lagoon** (Cook Islands) Snorkellers, rejoice: pristine waters and sheltered coves. (p59)

**'Eua** (Tonga) 'Eua is fast becoming known as an untouched paradise for divers. The Cathedral Cave complex is said to be Tonga's biggest sea cave, with amazing light shows. (p178)

## Hiking

**Cross-Island Track** (Cook Islands) The most popular walk in Rarotonga, taking in some impressive scenery, including the Needle. It's a sweaty three- or four-hour effort from one side of the island to the other, over the peaks in between. (p61)

**'Eua day hikes** (Tonga) Choose from a raft of day hikes on Tonga's 'forgotten island', a growing ecotourism hotspot that deserves a decent visit. (p179)

**Lake Lanoto'o** (Samoa) Take a guide to hike to this pea-green crater lake full of wild goldfish in the central highlands of Upolu island. (p115)

**National Park of American Samoa** Hiking is one of American Samoa's biggest drawcards, with well-maintained trails through extraordinarily pristine rainforest and coastlines providing plenty of options. (p149)

**Top**: Ta'u (p159), American Samoa

**Bottom**: Robert Louis Stevenson Museum (p114), Samoa

## Sailing

**Port of Refuge, Vava'u** (Tonga) An impossibly photogenic, protected harbour with everything a visiting yachtie could ask for. Turn up on your own yacht, charter one here, or offer to crew on Friday-afternoon races. Cold beer and conversation flow at day's end. (p186)

**Pago Pago Harbor** (American Samoa) This deep, sheltered harbour beneath towering Rainmaker Mountain almost slices Tutuila in half. (p145)

**Muri Lagoon** (Cook Islands) Plenty of options here, with Rarotonga Sailing Club rentals, day trips, sunset cruises and 'learn to sail' courses. In AD 900 the great ocean-going *vaka* (canoes) set off from here to settle New Zealand. (p59)

**Samoa Adventure** Head out on a catamaran adventure. (p105)

## Modern History

**Robert Louis Stevenson Museum** (Samoa) Inspect where the great Scottish author lived out his last days in Samoa as Tusitala (Teller of Tales). (p114)

**Abel Tasman Monument** (Tonga) See where the Dutchman became the first European to set foot on Tongatapu, in 1643. He called the island Amsterdam! (p177)

**Massacre Bay** (American Samoa) Hike to where 51 died in a skirmish between French sailors under de la Pérouse and Samoan villagers in 1787. This was the first European expedition to set foot on Tutuila. (p150)

**Aitutaki Lagoon** (Cook Islands) This protected lagoon was used in the 1950s as a refuelling stopover for Solent flying boats on the 'coral route' across the Pacific. (p72)

# Month by Month

**TOP EVENTS**

**Heilala Festival**, July

**Te Maeva Nui**, August

**Teuila Festival**, September

**Oceania Sevens**, October

**Vaka Eiva**, November

## January

**Flights are full, with expats coming and going, taking advantage of extended Christmas holidays.**

### New Year's Eve

Celebrated with fervour, as in the rest of the world. Tongans always claimed to see the New Year first, but there's been plenty of debate since Samoa shifted itself west of the International Date Line in 2011!

## February

**It's still hot and humid, and it might be raining. Head for the resort pool (if there is one...you'll possibly have it all to yourself) or get some Chinese food on your plate.**

### Chinese New Year

The date changes each year (it's based on the Chinese lunar calendar), but this two-week-long celebration on islands that have a Chinese community usually includes dancing, martial arts, fireworks and loads of food.

## March

**The weather remains stinking hot, but that doesn't worry those who are in the water. Visibility is good for divers right through the summer.**

### Penrhyn Gospel Day

In March the tiny island of Penrhyn in the Cooks has its Gospel Day (www.cookislands.org.uk/gospelday.html), celebrating the arrival of Christianity through dramas that re-enact aspects of the event. Expect some highly original and modern approaches.

## April

**The rainy season lasts until late March or early April and then things start to cool down (a bit!). Tropical-cyclone season is over and the first of the yachties start to turn up later in the month.**

### Te Mire Kapa

The Cook Islands' annual Dancer of the Year competition is held throughout April. There are events for all ages, from juniors to 'Golden Oldies', enticing hip-swingers from right across the islands.

### Flag Day

American Samoa's main public holiday on 17 April, Flag Day (www.samoagovt.ws/tag/american-samoa-flag-day) commemorates the raising of the US flag over the islands in 1900 with an arts festival and much traditional fanfare.

### Samoa International Game-Fishing Tournament

Get in a boat and wet a line at this very fishy festival (www.sigfa.ws), which attracts people from all over, keen to snag a marlin, sailfish, tuna or giant trevally. Fortunately for the fish, the vibe is very 'tag and release'.

## May

**The southeast trade winds (all-natural air-**

conditioning) start to pick up in May – the perfect time to windsurf, kitesurf or jump on a yacht for some island-hopping.

### International Siva Afi Competition

Feel the heat and the flames as Samoa displays the finest fire dancers in the world, in what is claimed to be the world's second-longest-running Fire Knife Competition (who keeps track of these things?).

## June

**The stable weather of June marks the start of the busy tourist season, with Australian and Kiwi visitors fleeing the southern winter. Many islanders gear up for July's festivals: there are drum rehearsals and sport practice aplenty.**

### Samoa Independence Celebrations

Full-on fun as Samoans celebrate their 1962 independence from New Zealand (NZ). There is all sorts of entertainment, from a flag-raising ceremony and firework displays to concerts and exhibitions (www.un.int/samoa/event/independence-day).

### Pacific Nations Cup

Tonga and Samoa join Fiji, Canada, the USA and Japan in a condensed program of play-offs for this annual rugby prize (www.worldrugby.org/pnc). The games are held from May to late June in all the participating countries.

## July

**Warm and dry July is festival time for many island groups, highlighted by sports competitions, beauty pageants, traditional song and dance, and plenty of partying. You can also expect booked-up hotels – reserve early.**

### Heilala Festival

Celebrating the flowering of the *heilala,* Tonga's national flower, this is Tonga's biggest excuse for a party, with music from hip-hop to church choirs on block-party stages. Dance performances, talent shows, parades and the Miss Heilala Pageant also make the grade.

### Miss Galaxy Pageant

This international *fakaleiti* (men dressed as women) beauty pageant held in Nuku'alofa, Tonga, is riotous fun and always sells out. The three-night celebration usually kicks off with a float parade.

## August

**The July festivities spill over into sunny and dry August, with music festivals and cultural happenings. This is the height of the tourist season, so you'll enjoy it all with plenty of company.**

### Te Maeva Nui

Originally called the 'Constitution Celebrations', this festival's new name translates to 'The Most Important Celebration' (www.cookislands.travel/temaevanui). Marking the Cook Islands' shift from NZ governance to self-rule, festivities include traditional song and dance, a parade, and arts and sporting events.

### Samoa Swim Series

Over three days in early August, the 'SSS' comprises three swimming races in Samoa's warm ocean waters (www.samoaevents.com/samoa-swim-series.html). For each swim you can tackle a long (4km) or short (2km) course. Either way, there's a big feed waiting afterwards!

### Kingdom of Tonga Military Tattoo

This three-day muso-military spectacular sees performances from military units from all around Tonga. It's a chance for the highly drilled outfits to show off their musical and military chops. Pomp and ceremony aplenty.

## September

**September is lovely in the Polynesian realm. School holidays are over, the trade winds keep humidity down, the cyclone season hasn't ruffled any rooftops yet and tourists are few.**

### Pacific Games

Every four years, the Olympics-like Pacific Games feature 4000 athletes from 22 Pacific nations competing in around 34 sporting events. Epic! The 2019 games are slated for Nuku'alofa, Tonga's capital (watch this space – financial factors may send them elsewhere).

### Regatta Vava'u

Held in early September each year, Regatta Vava'u (www.regattavavau.com) is a blossoming party week with all sorts of action for yachties and landlubbers alike.

### Teuila Festival

Samoa's capital, Apia, reels in the crowds with canoe races, food and craft stalls, traditional dancing and a beauty pageant (www.facebook.com/teuilafestivalsamoa).

### Tongan International Billfish Tournament

Held annually in Vava'u and into its third decade, this sea-going tournament (www.vavausportfishingclub.com) sees fishers from all over the world turn up and try to hook the biggest possible marlin. Very macho.

### Miss Samoa Fa'afafine Pageant

Frock up and head to Apia to watch Samoa's most glamorous *fa'afafine* (third gender) whirl and twirl in a flamboyant celebration of tradition, tolerance and taffeta.

## October

**You never know what kind of weather you'll encounter in October in these parts. The cyclone season officially kicks off now, but they're rare at this time of year, and temperatures aren't too high.**

### Samoana Jazz & Arts Festival

Local and international artists criss-cross between venues in Samoa and American Samoa over a weekend packed with music and other performing arts (www.samoanajazz.com).

### Palolo Rise

Time to celebrate procreating coral worms (*palolo*) rising from the reef at midnight! The worms are netted and eaten – 'the caviar of the Pacific'! Observed in Samoa and Fiji in October or November, seven days after the full moon.

### White Sunday

Celebrated in Samoa, American Samoa and Tonga, White Sunday is when kids rule the roost. Women and children dress completely in white, with biblical-story re-enactments and creative dance performances throughout the day.

### Oceania Sevens

Featuring teams from the South Pacific nations (including the Cook Islands, Tonga, Samoa, American Samoa, Fiji, Tahiti, Australia and New Zealand), this annual rugby comp (www.oceaniarugby.com) features as much dance and celebration as collisions between massive men.

### Tisa's Tattoo Festival

Traditional Samoan *tatau* and modern-day needlework are on display – and on offer – at Tisa's (www.tisasbarefootbar.com), a chilled-out beach bar just outside Pago Pago in American Samoa.

## November

**Pessimists call this the beginning of the rainy season, but Pacific islanders know it as the beginning of the season of abundance. The fishing is great and most fruit starts to come in season.**

### Vaka Eiva

Held in Rarotonga, Vaka Eiva (www.vakaeiva.com) is the Cook Islands' big-ticket sporting event. Outrigger-canoe races take centre stage in a week-long paddle fest, featuring around 1200 breathless canoeists.

## December

**Celebrating Christmas is serious stuff for Polynesians, and – as in many places in the world – December is defined by lots of shopping and churchgoing. Flights are heavily booked.**

### Mahina Arts Festival

A week-long arts party (www.tongaholiday.com/tonga-events/mahina-arts-festival) in Tonga's capital, Nuku'alofa, this festival features dance, poetry, storytelling, theatre, film and visual arts, with lots of workshops. It sometimes starts in the last week of November, before straying into December.

# Itineraries

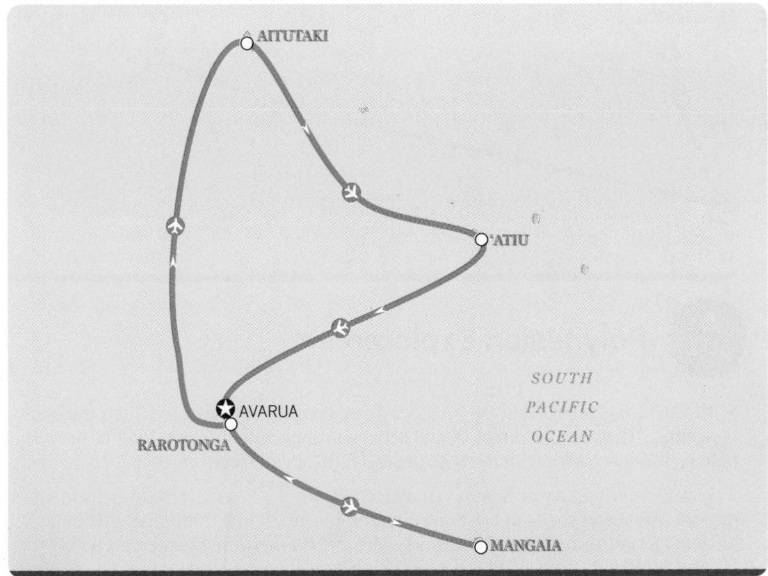

## Southern Cook Islands

The Cooks' Southern Group is a hop, skip and jump from Rarotonga. Even if you haven't got much time, you should still be able to tackle the whole route in two weeks – you won't regret it!

Start your trip with four days on Rarotonga: time enough for a stroll around the island's capital, **Avarua**; a hike up the Cross-Island Track; a day's snorkelling in Muri Lagoon; and a visit to the BCA Art Gallery. Don't forget to check out an island night while you're here.

Hop on a plane for the 45-minute flight to **Aitutaki**, then hire a scooter and explore the island. A lagoon cruise is essential, but you could also consider hiring a kayak to explore some of the deserted *motu* (islets) around the lagoon's fringe.

Then it's another short hop to **'Atiu**, where you can visit Anatakitaki, the cave of the kopeka ('Atiuan swiftlet); sample the island's home-grown coffee; and take an ecotour.

Wing back to Rarotonga and hop on another quick flight to **Mangaia** – the Pacific's oldest island – and see its extraordinary caves and vast cliffs, perhaps the most dramatic sight anywhere in the Cooks.

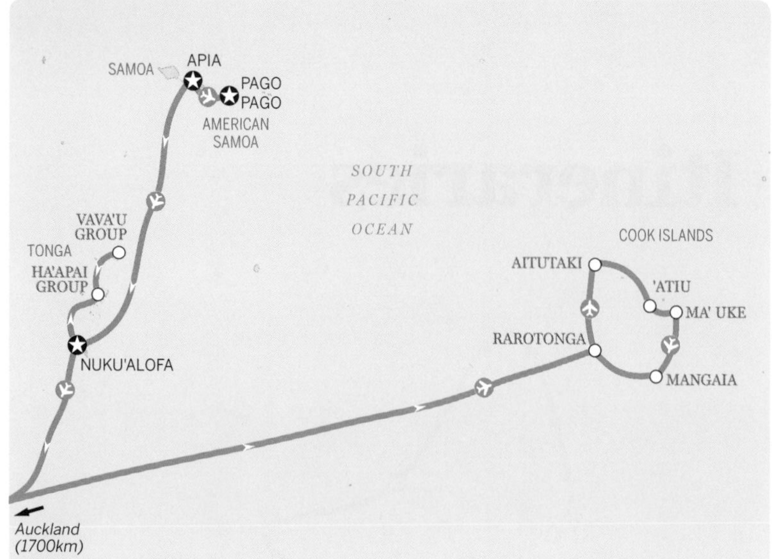

## Polynesian Explorer

With a month of island time up your sleeve, this part of Polynesia will deliver a bounty of delights. There are no direct flights between Tonga and the Cook Islands, but a short detour through Auckland in New Zealand is far from an inconvenience.

Kick things off in **Apia**, Samoa's capital: check out the Robert Louis Stevenson Museum, explore Upolu and spend at least one night on the beach in a traditional *fale* (house). Take the ferry to Savai'i for cave tunnels, lava fields and white beaches, then visit the forest-engulfed Pulemelei Mound, Polynesia's largest ancient monument.

From Apia, fly to the American Samoan capital, **Pago Pago**. Backed by steep mountains jagging down to green-blue Pago Pago Harbor, it's one of the most improbably scenic cities in the South Pacific. Go for a sea-kayak paddle, or hole up for a few days and work on your epic South Seas novel.

Fly back through Apia to scruffy-but-charming **Nuku'alofa** in the ancient Kingdom of Tonga: eyeball the Royal Palace en route to buzzy Talamahu Market. A short flight north, the **Ha'apai Group** offers beachy living in thatched *fale,* sea kayaking and kitesurfing, while the **Vava'u Group** delivers more sea kayaking, plus diving and sailing. A night or two bending elbows with the yachties in the bars along Neiafu's harbourfront is a night or two well spent.

Wing back into Nuku'alofa, then jag through the duty-free shops at Auckland Airport en route to the Cook Islands' capital, Avarua, on **Rarotonga**. Hike the Cross-Island Track, snorkel at sublime Muri Beach, and don't miss losing a few hours wandering around Punanga Nui Market (the fruit smoothies and roast-pork rolls are a knockout!).

From Rarotonga, catch a plane to exquisite **Aitutaki**, where you can chill out lagoonside for a few days. Boat-trip out to Tapuaeta'i (One Foot Island) and get your passport stamped. From Aitutaki, further short-hop flights will deliver you to the Southern Group islands of **'Atiu**, **Mangaia** and **Ma'uke**. Give them a few days each to explore the eye-popping caves and cliffs, then jet back to Rarotonga for your flight home.

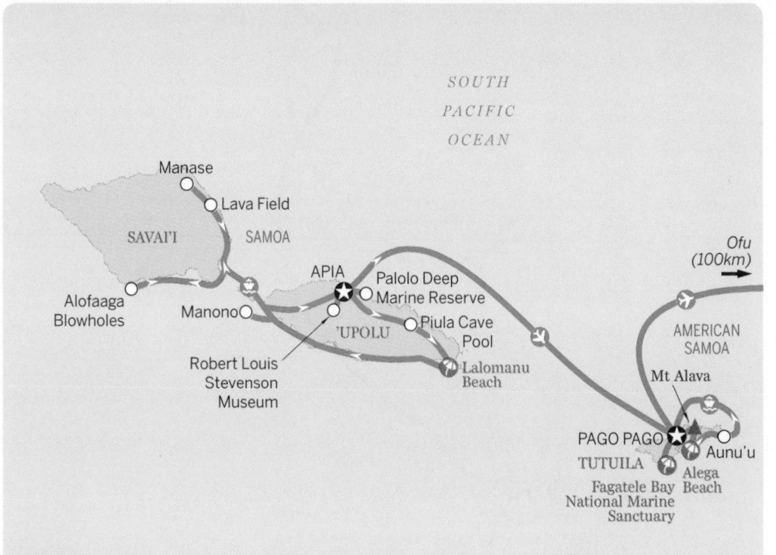

## Samoan Island Hopper

From the Samoan capital city **Apia**, start your island-hopping experience with a visit to **Palolo Deep Marine Reserve** and the endearing **Robert Louis Stevenson Museum**. Next, head east to seductive **Lalomanu Beach**, with a pit stop at **Piula Cave Pool**. Meander along the south coast, peeking into To Sua Ocean Trench, then take a boat out to the island of **Manono**.

Return to Upolu to ferry to Savai'i. Check out the wave-surging **Alofaaga Blowholes**, the desolate **lava field** and the sands at gregarious **Manase**.

Catch the ferry back to Upolu and return to Apia. From here, fly to **Pago Pago**, American Samoa's picturesque capital. Travel east to scale **Mt Alava** for spectacular views, then maroon yourself on **Alega Beach**, detouring for a close-up of Rainmaker Mountain. Wind along the coast to Au'asi and take a boat to the small, wild island of **Aunu'u**, before the slow ride back to **Pago Pago**. Alternatively, head southwest from Pago Pago to explore the pristine **Fagatele Bay National Marine Sanctuary**.

If there's still time, fly from Pago Pago to the island of Ofu to experience the amazing isolation of **Ofu Beach** – 4km of footprint-free white sand.

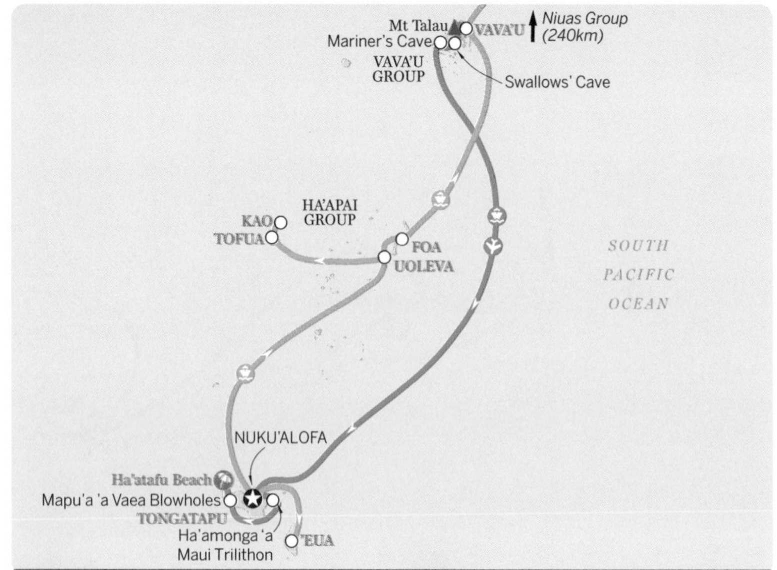

## Tongan Highlights

Hit the highlights of Tonga on a two-week island jaunt.

Head straight to the paradisiacal Vava'u Group, Tonga's activities hub, either by plane or ferry. On Vava'u, clamber up the peak of **Mt Talau** for some awesome island views, then join a chartered or bare-boat yacht and set sail around the islands of the group. Change your anchorage each night and jump into the brine each day to snorkel and swim. A multiday guided sea-kayak tour is another superb option. Don't miss swimming into **Swallows' Cave**, or experience the underwater wonder of **Mariner's Cave** before moving on to idyllic islands further south. Arrange your charter to sail through the Ha'apai Group (grab a beer at Mariner's Cafe in Pangai if you do) en route to Tongatapu. Alternatively, catch a short flight back to the main island.

On Tongatapu, have a quick look around **Nuku'alofa**, visit the **Ha'amonga 'a Maui Trilithon** ('the Stonehenge of the South Pacific') and check out the **Mapu'a 'a Vaea Blowholes**. Then get yourself into holiday mode by spending a day or two snorkelling, swimming and lazing around **Ha'atafu Beach** (a great family option).

## Slow Boats Around Tonga

Sure, you can fly around the Tongan island groups...but everybody does that! Boats are much more interesting.

Spend a little time pottering around Tongatapu and acclimatising to the tropics in **Nuku'alofa**, then ferry out to nearby **'Eua** and spend a few days hiking through the island's lush rainforests and exploring caves and sinkholes. You'll sometimes have to climb huge, tangled banyan trees to get out.

Once back in Nuku'alofa, clamber aboard the ferry and chug north to the coral charms and serenity of the low-lying Ha'apai Group. Shack up in a beachside *fale* on **Uoleva** for a few days, or at the other end of the cash spectrum there are a couple of wonderful resorts on **Foa**. If you have the inclination, charter a boat to take you out to **Tofua** and **Kao**.

If time is not your scarcest commodity, ferry on to the magical distractions of the **Vava'u Group**, where there's almost too much to do: sailing, diving, swimming, eating, drinking... The remote **Niuas** beckon a few hundred kilometres to the north – three volcanic islands where you'll find lava fields, pristine ridges and laid-back locals (and unscheduled ferries).

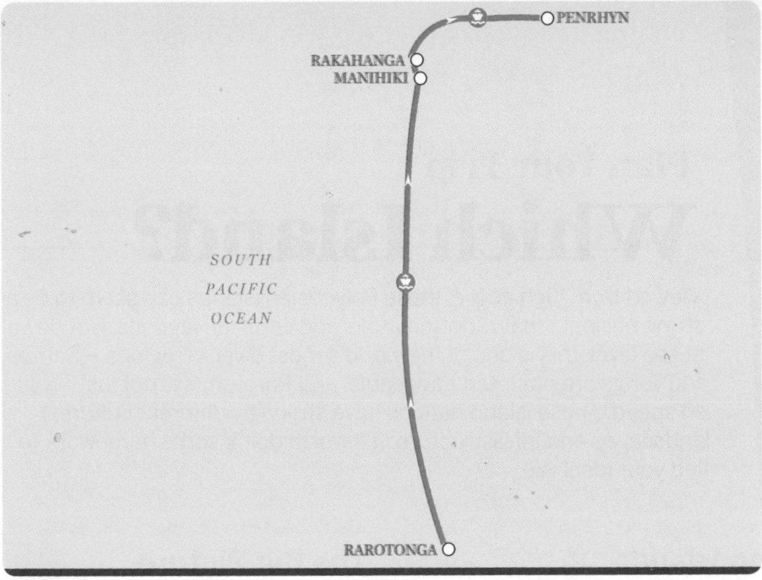

PENRHYN
RAKAHANGA
MANIHIKI
SOUTH PACIFIC OCEAN
RAROTONGA

## Northern Cook Islands

The Cooks' Northern Group is a long, long way from busy Rarotonga – it's a fantastic place to experience traditional Cook Islands culture. Only the hardiest and most intrepid of travellers ever make it out this far, but if you can surmount the logistical challenges, the rewards are sublime.

From **Rarotonga** you could catch a plane all the way to the Northern Group islands, but it's astronomically expensive. The most adventurous way to get there is via inter-island freighter all the way to **Manihiki**, the black-pearl capital of the Cook Islands, with its tiny coral atolls and massive natural lagoon.

With a bit of luck there will be a boat moving on to isolated **Rakahanga**, or if it's not stopping there, straight on to **Penrhyn**, where life is still lived very much along traditional lines. Back in Manihiki, boat it back to Rarotonga.

This is not the trip to take if you've got any time constraints! You'll have plenty of time to get to know the islanders and practise your fishing skills – but don't plan on going home too soon, as the next boat might not be along for a while...

Plan Your Trip

# Which Island?

Viewed from high above, these Polynesian islands can seem to be a string of similar palm-dotted atolls and cerulean lagoons. But down at sea level, this is one of the world's most diverse regions – Samoa and Tonga are not interchangeable, and Rarotonga is not just Tonga on speed. These island nations have strikingly different cultures, landscapes and infrastructure: it's worth doing some homework to find your ideal isle.

## Top Islands

### Rarotonga & the Cook Islands

**Rarotonga** Gateway to the Cooks, capital city, families, activities, sightseeing by scooter

**Aitutaki** Spectacular lagoon, history

**'Atiu** Ecotourism, caves, coffee

### Samoa

**Upolu** Gateway to Samoa, capital city, mountains, beaches, blowholes

**Savai'i** Mythology, pristine nature, volcanic scenery

### American Samoa

**Tutuila** Gateway to American Samoa, capital city, Pago Pago Harbor, national park, marine sanctuary

**Manu'a Islands** Ofu Beach, impressive scenery

### Tonga

**Tongatapu** Gateway to Tonga, capital city, history

**'Eua** Outdoor and underwater adventure, wild landscapes

**Ha'apai** Exploring, history, activities

**Vava'u** Turquoise waterways, islands, sailing, fishing

## The Big Picture

### The Cook Islands

The Cook Islands can cater for everybody, from those requiring a bit of resort-style pampering to families to the independent traveller. Adventurous types will also have a great time, especially if they make the effort to get to some of the less-visited outer islands.

Rarotonga is picturesque and small enough to circumnavigate in an hour or so, while Aitutaki has arguably the world's most beautiful lagoon. Both have slick marketing to go with good facilities and infrastructure.

Officially, visitors are required to have booked accommodation before arriving, although you can usually arrange a hotel when you arrive at the airport. Many places to stay on Rarotonga are booked up in advance: plan ahead.

### Samoa

Samoa offers a lot for visitors. Not as 'compact' as the Cooks' main island of Rarotonga, Upolu and Savai'i are big, mountainous islands that allow independent types to explore without running into other travellers all the time. There are remote hiking trails, lakes, waterfalls, swimming holes, caves, beaches and blowholes. Resorts mostly cater for packaged tours, but there's plenty here for the independent traveller too. It's relatively easy to travel around

**BOOK YOUR STAY ONLINE**

For more accommodation reviews by Lonely Planet authors, check out www.lonelyplanet.com/rarotonga-and-the-cook-islands/hotels, www.lonelyplanet.com/samoa/hotels, www.lonelyplanet.com/american-samoa/hotels and www.lonelyplanet.com/tonga/hotels. You'll find independent reviews, as well as recommendations on the best places to stay. Best of all, you can book online.

under your own steam, and Samoa has a growing number of facilities for visitors.

### American Samoa

American Samoa delivers some truly spectacular scenery and is often said to be the prettier of the two Samoas. Many of the folks who fly in here are business or government travellers, but American Samoa also offers a lot to independent travellers, especially those who explore some of Tutuila's more remote spots or make it out to the Manu'a Islands. And a kayak paddle around Pago Pago Harbor must surely be one of the most scenic and culturally curious experiences you can have in the South Pacific!

### Tonga

The 'never-colonised' Pacific kingdom of Tonga offers something unique to visitors – most Tongans don't seem to care whether you're there or not! As the country has been supported by foreign aid and remittances sent from Tongans living overseas, there has never really been a need to worry about earning money from tourism. While a lot of the aid is still there, particularly from China and Japan, worldwide economic problems mean that remittances are dwindling. Of late, the government has begun to realise that tourism earnings could benefit the economy.

There is a significant *palangi* (Westerner) population, which has been keen to establish a tourist industry. Developers are recognising the opportunities presented by the kingdom's amazing environment, especially the waterways of Vava'u and, more recently, Ha'apai. Big investors aren't really here, though – after all, this is a kingdom and if the king or nobles want their land back, who's to say they can't have it? There's a saying here – 'For every beach in Tonga a *palangi*'s dreams lie buried in the sand'.

Most visitors come from New Zealand and Australia, fewer are on packaged tours. Many come to take part in specific activities: sailing, fishing or sea kayaking. There are awesome opportunities for independent travel, especially if you head to the outer islands. Tonga is, however, not really the place to head to for a pampered vacation.

## The Resort Experience

Despite the stereotypes, luxury resorts take up only a small fraction of the accommodation roster. Mostly you'll find a selection of charming boutique outfits that blend local style and warmth with a degree of comfort and opulence. A 'resort' may not meet your image of what a resort should be: the word is used somewhat loosely here. Swimming pools, for example, are far from mandatory – but you'll usually be able to eat your meals in-house if you want to. Note that some resorts (and hotels) have no-children policies (especially under 12s), but others let kids stay for free – always ask when booking.

**BEST UPMARKET ACCOMMODATION**

**The Cook Islands**

**Etu Moana** (p75; Aitutaki)

**Pacific Resort** (p66; Rarotonga)

**Sea Change** (p65; Rarotonga)

**Mangaia Villas** (p89; Mangaia)

**Samoa**

**Coconuts Beach Club Resort** (p120; Upolu)

**Seabreeze Resort** (p119; Upolu)

**Lupe Sina Treesort** (p120; Upolu)

**Samoa Tradition Resort** (p109; Upolu)

**American Samoa**

**Moana O Sina** (p152; Tutuila)

**Tonga**

**Sandy Beach Resort** (p184; Ha'apai)

**Fafá Island** (p178; Tongatapu)

**Matafonua Lodge** (p184; Ha'apai)

## The Cook Islands

There is a good mix of international standards and boutique charm on Rarotonga and Aitutaki. Families are well catered for and there are plenty of activities and fun nightlife. If you're looking for an upmarket holiday in the region, head here.

## Samoa

There's nothing too luxurious here, but the beaches are dazzling, the atmosphere authentic and stress nonexistent (with or without the swanky spa).

## American Samoa

There's not a lot going on here in terms of luxury resort accommodation. It might be a small part of America and it just about matches the scenery, but Hawai'i it ain't!

## Tonga

Head out to the Ha'apai or Vava'u groups for a scant number of eclectic, though not necessarily fancy, resorts in remote settings. Many have an eco bent; none have swimming pools.

### BEST FOR A LOCAL EXPERIENCE

**The Cook Islands**

**Kura's Kabanas** (p64; Rarotonga)

**Aremango Guesthouse** (p64; Rarotonga)

**Gina's Garden Lodges** (p74; Aitutaki)

**Atiu Villas** (p80; 'Atiu)

**Samoa**

**Namu'a Island Beach Fale** (p118; Upolu)

**Regina's Beach Fales** (p130; Savai'i)

**Lusia's Lagoon Chalets** (p126; Savai'i)

**Satuiatua Beach Fales** (p133; Savai'i)

**American Samoa**

**Le Falepule** (p152; Pago Pago)

**Tonga**

**Port Wine Guest House** (p190; Vava'u)

**Treasure Island Eco-Resort** (p195; Vava'u)

**Nerima Lodge** (p171; Tongatapu)

# The Local Accommodation Experience

If you want to travel independently and experience the culture up-close, go local and you won't be sorry. Each country has its own version of mid-level and local accommodation: small boutique hotels and guest houses are becoming increasingly popular throughout these islands. Forgoing the 'resorts' allows you to get more bang for your buck, meet the locals and explore some remote islands.

Note that many smaller family-run places don't take credit cards and don't have air-con, but most can provide airport transfers if arranged in advance. On remote islands you may encounter faulty plumbing, cold showers, unreliable electricity and 'rustic' vibes. If you need wi-fi, check in advance.

## The Cook Islands

On Rarotonga and Aitutaki, stay at midrange motels or in good-value, self-contained holiday rentals. Expect to pay for views and location. On the Cooks' smaller outer islands, go local at family-run homestays.

## Samoa

Midrange hotel, motel and resort accommodation here ranges from the slightly dilapidated to well-maintained rooms with all the mod cons. Some beach *fale* (huts) also enter into midrange territory.

## American Samoa

A sign of American Samoa's reliance on US government support rather than tourism is the limited accommodation choice on Tutuila. That said, there is a handful of interesting and quirky midrange places to stay here.

Tapuaeta'i (p72), Aitutaki, the Cook Islands

### Tonga

For an immersive cultural experience with a midrange price tag, stay at a Tongan-run guesthouse or B&B. Decor might be a tad shabby, but the experience will certainly be authentic.

## Going Budget

If you are on a limited budget and where you lay your head really doesn't worry you, there are some intriguing options in these tropical paradises, ranging from beachfront shacks to hostel dorms.

### The Cook Islands

On the budget side of the tracks in Rarotonga and Aitutaki, stay at laid-back backpackers or guesthouses – complete with activities aplenty.

### Samoa

Samoa's signature budget-style accommodation is the beach *fale*, a simple structure that comes in a variety of styles. At their most simple and traditional, *fale* are just a wooden platform with poles supporting a thatched roof, surrounded by woven blinds that can be pulled down for privacy. These are found on some of the best beaches.

### American Samoa

There's a dearth of budget accommodation on Tutuila, reflecting the fact that most visitors are there for business rather than tourism.

### Tonga

If spending your *pa'anga* on accommodation isn't why you're here, Tonga has something for everybody. There are plenty of options, from rambling guest houses to semi-permanent tents, beach-bum shacks and basic backpacker joints.

## BEST BUDGET OPTIONS

### The Cook Islands

**Tiare Village Airport Motel** (p50; Rarotonga)

**Amuri Guesthouse** (p74; Aitutaki)

**Aremango Guesthouse** (p64; Rarotonga)

**Matriki Beach Huts** (p74; Aitutaki)

### Samoa

**Anita's Beach Bungalows** (p118; Upolu)

**Vaiula Fales** (p122; Upolu)

**Dave Parker's Eco Lodge** (p115; Upolu)

**Joelan Beach Fales** (p127; Savai'i)

### American Samoa

**Tisa's Barefoot Bar** (p153; Tutuila)

### Tonga

**Mafana Island Beach Backpackers** (p195; Vava'u)

**Flying Annie Moa B&B** (p190; Vava'u)

**Hideaway** (p179; 'Eua)

# Independent Versus Prepackaged Travel

## Independent Travel

Outside high season (June to October) you could arrive just about anywhere in the South Pacific without any idea of where you're going or what you're doing tomorrow and still have an amazing trip. During the seasonal rush, however, the better places book out fast, so it's wise to plan in advance. If you can, avoid the Christmas and New Year period, when expat islanders head home to visit friends and family.

## Package Tours

The South Pacific lends itself to the package-tour market. Given the high price of flights to and within the region, and the often inflated price of accommodation once you arrive, a package tour can be a financial godsend. On the downside, packages don't give you much leeway to explore independently. Also, you usually have to prebook a hotel or guest house for each destination before departure, meaning you can't swap resorts halfway through if you're not happy.

Good places to get a feel for pricing are the websites of the airlines that service the region. But if you want more than a straightforward combo package, a good travel agent is essential – they can negotiate better prices at the larger hotels and handle internal flight bookings. Most packages quote double-occupancy pricing; solo travellers have to pay a single-person supplement (it's not just half the double rate). Extra people can usually share a room, but there's a charge for the extra bed, which varies enormously from resort to resort.

### Diving Tours

Diving package tours are another option; they typically include flights, accommodation and multiple days down in the deep blue.

### Surfing Tours

Several operators specialise in surfing holidays in this neck of the South Pacific, including the following:

**Perfect Wave** (www.theperfectwave.com.au) Packaged-up surf holidays in Samoa.

**World Surfaris** (www.worldsurfaris.com) Samoa and Tonga – the best breaks on surf trips, customised by those in the know (Australians).

## CAMPING & HOSTELS

Camping options come and go, but generally these are provided by small hotels and local guest houses that allow campers to pitch a tent on adjacent land and to use the bathroom and kitchen facilities. There are few real hostels. Locally owned budget guest houses that offer simple rooms with shared bathrooms do a good job of filling this gap, although few have dorm accommodation.

Plan Your Trip

# Outdoor Adventures

Plenty of people come to the South Pacific in search of low-key R&R, but if you're feeling active there's plenty to keep you busy here too, both on/in the water and on dry land. Give it some thought before you go.

## Activities

### On the Water

Millions of square kilometres of warm tropical sea, picture-perfect lagoons and long swathes of beach are the most obvious attractions for travellers in this part of the South Pacific. Almost everyone comes to this region to get wet – diving, snorkelling, surfing, swimming, sea kayaking and sailing all have their devotees, and the fishing is among the world's best.

#### Boat Trips

We're talking day trips on a boat here – not plush, month-long cruises on a liner. There are all sorts of options throughout the islands, from glass-bottomed boats peering down on marine life to day tours on small boats, big boats, yachts and catamarans. Many will offer stops along the way for swimming and snorkelling, bushwalking, fishing or beach barbecues. Make sure you know what's included (lunch?), check if there's a toilet aboard, then head out for the day and enjoy. Don't forget your sunglasses, hat and sunscreen.

A lagoon cruise is a must if you're visiting Aitutaki in the Cook Islands, as is a day sailing if you're in Vava'u, Tonga.

## Top Island Activities

### Rarotonga & the Cook Islands

**Rarotonga** Water sports, hiking, exploring, fishing, diving

**Aitutaki** Water sports in and around the lagoon, diving

**'Atiu** Cave explorations, birdwatching

**Suwarrow** Yachting, birdwatching, exploring the national park

### Samoa

**'Upolu** Hiking, water sports, fishing, slipping down waterfalls at the Sliding Rocks

**Savai'i** Hiking, exploring waterfalls and lava overflows, diving

### American Samoa

**Tutuila** Water sports, sea kayaking, hiking, exploring the marine sanctuary and national park

**Manu'a Islands** Swimming at Ofu Beach, hiking

### Tonga

**Tongatapu** Cave exploring, sea kayaking, surfing

**'Eua** Hiking, birdwatching, diving

**Ha'apai** Sea kayaking, water sports, diving, kitesurfing

**Vava'u** Sea kayaking, fishing, water sports, sailing, diving

## Diving

This neck of the South Pacific is as much a Garden of Eden below the waterline as it is on land. No doubt you'll impress your friends when you get home with stories of awesome walls, high-voltage drift dives, close encounters with sharks and manta rays, luscious soft and hard corals, shipwrecks and gorgeous reefs replete with multihued tropical fish. Visibility is mostly excellent, waters are warm year-round and most dive centres are first rate. Each island has its own underwater personality and distinctive assets, conspiring to create a seemingly endless diving repertoire.

Diving is possible year-round, although conditions vary according to the season and location. Visibility can be reduced in the wet season as the water is muddied by sediments, and areas exposed to currents might also become heavy with particles. On average, visibility ranges from 15m to 50m.

Though it's possible to dive without a wetsuit, most divers wear at least a Lycra outsuit to protect themselves from abrasions. A 3mm tropical wetsuit is entirely appropriate.

In most places you'll find professional and reliable dive centres staffed with qualified instructors catering to divers of all levels. The majority of dive centres are affiliated with an internationally recognised diving organisation – eg PADI, SSI, NAUI and CMAS. They are mostly hotel based, but they do welcome walk-ins. It's a good idea to visit the centre before you sign up, to get the feel of the operation. Most places have websites: do some homework before you go.

Dive centres are open year-round, most of them every day – but it's best to reserve your dive at least a day in advance. Depending on the area, centres typically offer two-tank dives (usually in the morning) or single dives (one in the morning and one in the afternoon). Many sites are offshore and involve a boat ride.

Diving in the South Pacific is expensive in comparison to most destinations in Asia, the Caribbean or the Red Sea. Set dive packages (eg five or 10 dives) are usually cheaper. Gear hire may or may not be included in the price, so it's not a bad idea to bring your own equipment if you're planning to do a lot of diving.

If you're a certified diver, don't forget to bring your C-card and logbook with you. Dive centres welcome divers regardless of their training background, provided they can produce a certificate from an internationally recognised agency.

## Fishing

For many anglers the South Pacific is a dream destination, with super local fishing and even better big-game ocean fishing. Common catches include yellowfin and skipjack tuna, wahoo, barracuda, sailfish, and blue, black and striped marlin.

### DIVING FOR THE FIRST TIME

These warm Polynesian waters with their prolific marine life provide ideal and safe conditions for beginners. Arrange an introductory dive with a dive centre to give you a feel for what life is like when you can breathe underwater.

Your training will begin on dry land, where the instructor will run you through basic safety procedures and show you the equipment. Under the guidance of the instructor, your first dive will take place in a safe location (sometimes a swimming pool) and will usually last between 20 and 40 minutes. You'll practise breathing with the regulator above the surface before going underwater. Then the instructor will hold your hand if necessary and guide your movements at a depth of between 3m and 10m.

There is no formal procedure, but you shouldn't dive if you have a medical condition (including acute ear, nose and throat problems); epilepsy or heart disease (such as infarction); if you have a cold or sinusitis; or if you are pregnant.

If you enjoy your introductory dive, you might want to follow a four- to five-day course to get first-level PADI (Professional Association of Diving Instructors) certification. This will allow you to dive anywhere in the world – it's like a driving licence (minus the 'r').

## DIVING & FLYING

Most divers travelling to these South Pacific countries get here by plane. While it's fine to dive soon *after* flying, it's important to remember that your last dive should be completed at least 12 hours (some experts advise 24 hours) *before* your next flight to minimise the risk of residual nitrogen in the blood, which can cause decompression injury. As so much inter-island transportation is by air, careful attention to flight times is necessary.

Deep-sea fishing charters are available throughout the islands. If you're feeling sporting, the Samoa International Game Fishing Tournament in April draws a crowd, or there's the Tongan International Billfish Tournament every September in Vava'u (billfish are marlin).

### Kitesurfing

Kitesurfing or kiteboarding has a growing legion of fans, and Rarotonga and Aitutaki provide a couple of great options. Aitutaki even hosts an international kitesurfing contest in late June. In Tonga, you can kitesurf on Uoleva in the Ha'apai Group.

### Sailing

Sailing through the South Pacific is a dream come true for yachties. Every year during the May-to-October dry season, hundreds of trans-Pacific yachts harness the east-to-west trade winds and cross the central South Pacific, checking out some of the most remote islands on the globe. The yachties are usually gone by the end of October as the November-to-April cyclone season approaches.

Never fear, however, if you don't have your own boat, as hitch-hiking across the Pacific is not out of the question…especially if you've got a bit of experience. Many yachts are looking for extra crew. Check noticeboards at yacht clubs and yachting hotspots such as Vava'u in Tonga. Vava'u's picturesque Port of Refuge is one of the planet's best safe anchorages.

Chartering a yacht is also an option, especially if there is a group of you: once again, Vava'u is the place to go. There are 61 gorgeous islands with spectacular turquoise waterways to explore here. Keep in mind that you'll need to have enough experience to meet the charter company's requirements and that it won't let you head out of Vava'u or further afield.

But even if you don't have any experience, you can still go sailing here. Take a day cruise on a yacht or catamaran, learn to sail in Rarotonga's Muri Lagoon, rent out a small sailboat or play around on a windsurfer.

### Sea Kayaking

Almost every island resort or visitor destination in the region will have kayaks or canoes for guests to use. These will range from simple family float-arounds to sophisticated high-tech sea kayaks designed for multiday adventures. The former are generally free for guests, or rentable by the hour, half-day or day. The latter are usually for use on guided tours.

For those who are keen to head out on an adventuresome guided paddle, there is a growing number of options, from half-day paddles to 11-day whoppers. Tonga is the place to go, with myriad islands, lagoons and stretches of sheltered water. There's a day-trip kayak operator on Tongatapu, with longer trips available in the Ha'apai and Vava'u island groups.

Kayaking, Namu'a Island (p118), Samoa

### Surfing

Polynesians invented surfing, with the first recorded observations of boardriding made in Hawai'i and Tahiti in the 1770s. Nevertheless, surfing in most Pacific islands is still in its infancy. Increasingly, however, surfers are seeking uncrowded waves in Rarotonga, Samoa and Tonga. There aren't many easy-going beach breaks here: surfers need to be intermediate at least, and should always talk to a local before hitting the water. Waves break outside coral lagoon reefs, so the paddle out can be long and enervating – and these reefs can be very unforgiving if you get that take-off wrong. Also, few islands have surfboards for sale, so surfers must come equipped – but surfing virgin waves in these warm, vodka-clear waters is an incredible experience.

### Swimming & Snorkelling

Everyone loves to splash around in warm tropical water, of which there is no shortage in these central South Pacific countries. To enrich the experience, there's so much underwater marine life to look at here that you (and especially your kids) won't want to come to the surface. A mask, a snorkel and a pair of flippers may be all you need to make your visit entirely memorable.

If you take your snorkelling seriously, BYO gear, especially if you're heading out to somewhere remote. If you're going to a tourism hotspot and snorkelling is just something you want to try, you should be able to rent equipment or buy it cheap locally. Resorts often have snorkelling gear available free for guests to use.

### Whale Watching

Migrating humpback whales head to these central South Pacific waters for the southern-hemisphere winter, generally arriving in June and staying through to October. They give birth in shallow, warm waters around island groups, with myriad whale-watching tours there to bear witness, especially in Rarotonga and Tonga.

These tours attract considerable controversy, opponents suggesting that operators disrupt breeding cycles and exploit these creatures when they're at their most vulnerable. See p193 to help you make an informed decision.

#### TROPICAL CYCLONE WATCH

In the Atlantic they call them 'hurricanes' and in the northwestern Pacific they're known as 'typhoons', but in the South Pacific they're called 'tropical cyclones'. These massive weather systems rotate around a centre of low atmospheric pressure and bring torrential rains, massive seas and sustained winds of up to 200km/h that can totally devastate low-lying Pacific islands.

Summer is danger season, whether you are in the southern hemisphere, where cyclone winds rotate clockwise, or in the northern hemisphere, where hurricane winds spin anticlockwise.

Cyclones often track further west than these central South Pacific nations and they often miss land, but when they do turn up they pack a serious punch. November to April is cyclone season here: yachties generally head either to the northern hemisphere or south to Australia or New Zealand to sidestep the danger.

## On Land

### Caving

Because of the geological and volcanic nature of these islands, they are blessed with all sorts of caves, sinkholes, blowholes and depressions that will keep spelunking types entertained forever. But organised caving experiences here aren't particularly hard core, usually involving a guided walk into accessible, safe caves, without anything more complex than a torch in your hand.

### Cycling

Atolls tend to be flat and are excellent for cycling around. But all South Pacific islands are not atolls, however, and loftier islands produce a lot of ups and downs to be negotiated. Road conditions may not meet your expectations (once you get off the main road, in many cases it's dirt tracks with lots of potholes) and unexpected obstacles (kids, pigs, chickens, dogs...) may slow your progress. Dogs in particular can be a bit outspoken and intimidating, so give them a wide berth (there's no rabies in

Top: Snorkelling, Tongatapu (p166), Tonga

Bottom: 'Atiu caves (p79), the Cook Islands

## CORAL ATOLLS

The central South Pacific has two types of island: 'high' ones that are mostly the peaks of volcanoes, extinct or active; and 'low' ones, aka atolls, that are formed by coral growth on sunken submarine volcanoes.

Basically, the ocean floor has many submerged volcanoes. Some rise above the sea's surface to become islands, and corals begin to grow around the edges. If subsequent tectonic-plate movement causes the volcano to sink, the coral continues to grow in order to stay close to the sunlight. As the central island sinks, a fringing lagoon forms between the island and the reef. A coral atoll is formed when the island finally sinks completely, leaving a ring of coral encircling an empty lagoon. Charles Darwin was the first person to recognise this phenomenon.

The long conversion of these coral islets to inhabitable islands begins when coral sitting above the sea's surface is broken up by waves, eventually forming a coarse, infertile soil. Seeds blown along by the wind, carried by the sea or redistributed by bird droppings can then take root. Initially, only the most hardy of plants, such as coconut palms, can survive in this barren environment. Once the pioneering coconuts have established a foothold, rotting vegetative matter forms a more hospitable soil for other plants.

The people of the South Pacific have learned how to eke out an existence from even the most modest of coral atolls. Vegetables brought from other islands, such as taro and *kumara* (sweet potato), supplement what grows naturally, and fish from the sea and the lagoon provide protein. Atoll populations, however, live a precarious existence, as resources are scarce and the atolls are vulnerable to droughts, storms, tsunamis and rising sea levels.

this part of the South Pacific, if that helps ease your fears).

Renting a bicycle on these islands can definitely be a cheap, fun adventure though, and most places where tourists show up in any numbers will have some sort of bicycle-rental outfit. Ask for some local advice before you hit the road; test the brakes, gears and tyres, and ask for the newest bike.

### Hiking

The weather may be hot and wet and distances far from epic, but there are plenty of opportunities for hiking on most of these islands. Rugged coastal areas, sandy beaches, lush rainforests and volcanic islands all invite exploration on foot. The main challenge is that not all trails are well maintained, and they can quickly become obscured because of the lush, fast-growing tropical environment. Combine this with the effect heavy rain can have on tracks and there's a good chance of getting lost (or at least covering yourself in mud). So, for more remote treks, it might pay to organise a guide to go with you.

The cost of guiding can vary enormously. Sometimes villagers will be happy to accompany you for nothing, but mostly they'll be interested in cash. In remote places you may have no choice but to pay a lot for a guide.

Even on short walks, the sun and the almost perpetually hot and humid conditions can take their toll. Be sure to carry insect repellent to ward off mosquitoes, antihistamines to counter wasp stings if you're allergic to them, plenty of water and salty snacks to replenish body elements lost to heavy sweating. A hat, sunscreen and good walking shoes are also essential.

The Samoas have a number of excellent hikes – American Samoa even boasts a fully fledged US national park with US funding and well-maintained hiking trails. Rarotonga's Cross-Island Track is legendary, and the Tongan island of 'Eua has a growing reputation as an excellent hiking hub.

## Plan Your Trip

# Travel with Children

Few regions in the world are as family friendly as this part of the South Pacific. With endless sunshine, boundless beaches, and swimming and snorkelling on tap, there's plenty to keep kids engaged. Family is profoundly important and children are cherished in these island cultures – your kids can expect plenty of cheek-tweaking attention!

## Best Regions for Kids

### Rarotonga & the Cook Islands

Beyond the beach there are fruit smoothies aplenty, and activities from lagoon tours and snorkelling to gentle back-road cycling and exploring Rarotonga's reefs on a semisubmersible boat.

### Samoa

Shallow, protected beaches make for good swimming and snorkelling, while other natural lures like the Piula Cave Pool and the Papase'ea Sliding Rocks add a thrill for older kids.

### American Samoa

Make the most of the outdoors, either hiking in the national park or snorkelling in the reef-sheltered shallow waters of the eastern beaches of Tutuila. The movies are a good option on a stormy afternoon.

### Tonga

There's lots of roomy accommodation in Tonga, and plenty of things to keep kids entertained (caves, snorkels, boats, lagoons, flying foxes...).

## For Kids

### Water Activities

**Boats & kayaks** Glass-bottomed boats are always fun, peering down onto all sorts of tropical marine life. Sailing and fishing trips are stimulating for teens, but for something everyone can enjoy, most resorts and islands will have kayaks that you can hire for a lagoon paddle.

**Diving, snorkelling & swimming** Toddlers will be happy on a soft beach with a hermit crab to hassle. Anywhere with a shallow, sandy bottom is great for learning to swim, while seasoned swimmers can cruise the lagoons. Once kids are comfortable wearing a mask and snorkel, it can be hard to get them out of the water: the presence of brightly coloured tropical fish just adds to the excitement.

**Wildlife watching** Whale- and dolphin-watching is big business hereabouts; see p193 to help you make an informed decision on participation. There are also sea turtles and myriad sea birds to spy.

**Surfing** It can be hard to rent a board on many islands, but some hotels keep them for guest use. Boogie boards are often sold in local shops; if you can, buy one and make a local kid's year by leaving it with them when you leave! Hit the beach breaks with little kids; reef-breaking monsters are for experienced wave hounds only.

### On Dry Land

**Hiking & adventure** Over-eights will love tropical-island interiors, studded with waterfalls with icy pools, dark caves, lakes and even the occasional smouldering volcano!

**Archaeology** Many ancient Polynesian sites aren't cordoned off: you can climb on almost anything! Apply common sense and be respectful. The surrounding jungles often hold other discoveries, like wild passionfruit and huge banyan trees.

**Cycling** Bicycles can be rented on most islands; kid-sized bikes are harder to find (check gears and brakes are working, too).

### Eating Out

Kids are welcome at all restaurants here. Most visiting kids will happily munch on local fish, fruit, chicken and coconut. Many urban eateries offer kid pleasers (hamburgers, fried rice), while unfamiliar local foods are generally soft, unspicy and inoffensive – taro, *kumara* (sweet potato), breadfruit. Prepackaged baby food is available in most places…and when all else fails, there's always ice cream!

### Teens after Dark

It's normal for whole families to party together here: teens are welcome at any sort of local dance or show, though taking them drinking in the local bars is a no-no.

## Children's Highlights

### Beach Yourself

**Cook Islands** Snorkel in the marine-reserve waters off Rarotonga's south coast.

**Samoa** Bigger kids will adore staying in traditional open-air *fale* right on the beach.

**American Samoa** Far-flung Ofu Beach (p157): getting there is half the fun.

**Tonga** Snorkel in the shallows and watch the surfers at Ha'atafu Beach (p177).

### Natural Encounters

**Cook Islands** Aitutaki Lagoon (p72) offers myriad snorkelling, boat and island encounters.

**Samoa** Ogle the amazing saltwater sprays at the Alofaaga Blowholes (p132) and explore the eerie lava fields of northern Savai'i.

**American Samoa** Strap the kids into a kayak and explore Pago Pago Harbor.

**Tonga** Birdwatching and butterfly spotting on jungle walks at 'Ene'io Botanical Garden (p193).

### Get Cultured

**Cook Islands** 'Island nights' at resorts here are authentic and great fun, with audience participation the norm (cute kids, beware).

**Samoa** Samoa Cultural Village (p100) in Apia delivers an interactive cultural infusion.

**American Samoa** Experience White Sunday in October, when children dress completely in white and get creative with dance performances.

**Tonga** Catch the excellent cultural show at Oholei Beach & Hina Cave Feast & Show (p176).

## Planning

Lonely Planet's *Travel with Children* contains plenty of useful information. One essential is sunscreen (expensive on many islands), plus insect repellent and rain gear. BYO kid-size snorkelling gear, too.

### Babies & Toddlers

A folding pushchair is handy, despite scrappy (or nonexistent) footpaths. Strap-on baby carriers are a better idea for hiking or exploring archaeological sites. At your accommodation, having a kitchen in your room will be a big bonus.

Public baby-change facilities are rare: bring a portable change mat and disinfectant handwash gel. Disposable nappies (diapers) and powdered milk (formula) are available from pharmacies and supermarkets in many large towns, but they can be expensive. Don't expect high chairs anywhere beyond the resorts. A lightweight mosquito net to drape over your toddler's cot is also a good idea.

### Six- to 12-Year-Olds

Pack binoculars to zoom in on wildlife, surfers etc; a camera to inject some fun into 'boring' grown-up sights and walks; and field guides to island flora and fauna ('Is that a red shining parrot or a kingfisher?'). Try to stay somewhere with a pool.

### Teenagers

Getting teenagers to attempt some local language is a sure-fire way to shake off sullenness: pick up Lonely Planet's *South Pacific Phrasebook*. A dog-eared copy of *Mutiny on the Bounty* or the funny *The Sex Lives of Cannibals* will keep them in the here and now.

# Regions at a Glance

Nimble travellers will be able to visit more than one of these countries on the same trip, but you'll need to do some careful planning and some flying (or buy a yacht). Where you go depends on your interests: Rarotonga is ideal for families and those looking for a relaxing resort stay; the Samoas offer mountains and beaches for nature lovers to propel themselves up and onto; and Tonga is geared for activities like sea kayaking, diving, sailing and kitesurfing. But wherever you go, island culture will work its magic on you – even if you do only get to one of these countries, you're sure to return to the South Pacific.

## Rarotonga & the Cook Islands

Scenery
Food
History

### Mountains to Sea

Explore Rarotonga's mountainous interior before discovering your own slice of Pacific perfection sea kayaking to tiny *motu* (islands) around amazing Muri Lagoon. On isolated 'Atiu, Ma'uke and Mangaia, rugged sea cliffs conceal impossibly compact beaches.

### Culinary Sophistication

Be surprised by Rarotonga's dining scene. There's a growing emphasis on things organic and traditionally grown here: a highlight is trawling the easy-going food stalls at Saturday morning's Punanga Nui Market.

### Ancient Polynesia

Discover the spiritual and historical significance of Avana Harbour – departure point for the 14th-century 'great migration' to New Zealand. The burial caves on Mangaia and 'Atiu are equally fascinating.

p44

## Samoa

**Beaches**
**Hiking**
**Culture**

### Beaches at Every Turn

Beaches here come in a spectacular number of shapes and sizes. Choose from wide white beauties that tumble into aqua lagoons or pockets of heaven wedged between black-lava formations.

### Journey to the Centre of the Earth

Hike to spectacular waterfalls and along lava-sculpted coasts, and explore the lush grounds of Robert Louis Stevenson's villa. Or head underground via extensive lava tubes that gush with subterranean rivers.

### The Heart of Polynesia

Independent, and proud of their Polynesian culture, Samoans have Facebook and mobile phones but adhere to old values, living in villages with meeting houses, chiefs and strict customs. And they'll welcome you with genuine warmth.

p98

## American Samoa

**Hiking**
**Scenery**
**Culture**

### National Park & Beyond

National parks are rare in the South Pacific, but the National Park of American Samoa covers a huge swathe of the country. There are well-maintained trails here, from short jaunts to all-day adventures from mountain to sea.

### Dreamy Silhouettes

The sky-piercing peaks here look more like a Disney paradise than reality. Surrounded by lava-formed coves, blue water and ribbons of sparkling cream-coloured beach, they're hard to beat!

### Village Life

Travel beyond Pago Pago and the airport to where small-town American Samoa is all about church bells and traditional village customs…all in sublime natural surrounds.

p144

## Tonga

**Islands**
**Activities**
**Drinking**

### Islands Galore

Postcard-perfect tropical islands abound in Tonga. Book yourself into a luxurious beach resort (they're few but fabulous) or beach-bum it in a breezy waterside *fale* (house).

### Water Sports

Tonga is close to heaven for those who love playing in/on warm, crystal-clear water. Take your pick from sublime sailing, sea-kayaking, swimming, snorkelling and diving opportunities.

### Local Bars

Nothing happens in a hurry in Tonga! Slow down to island time with a few cold local lagers at the waterfront bars in Neiafu, or along Nuku'alofa's main drag.

p164

# On the Road

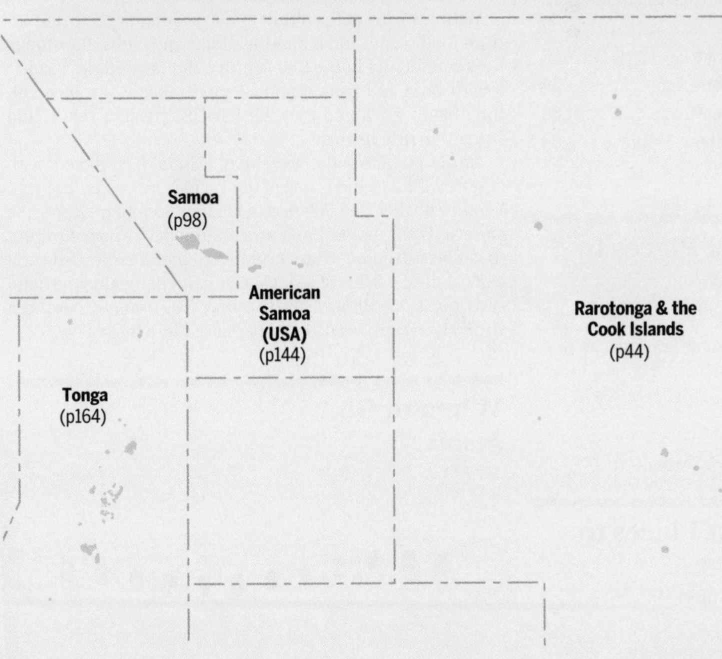

Samoa
(p98)
American
Samoa
(USA)
(p144)
Rarotonga & the
Cook Islands
(p44)
Tonga
(p164)

# Rarotonga & the Cook Islands

☎682 / POP 19,500

**Includes ➡**



## Best Places to Stay

- ➡ Sea Change (p65)
- ➡ Ikurangi Eco Retreat (p65)
- ➡ Beach Place (p65)
- ➡ Etu Moana (p75)
- ➡ Tiare Cottages (p83)

## Best Places to Eat

- ➡ Vaima Restaurant & Bar (p67)
- ➡ Tamarind House (p54)
- ➡ Punanga Nui Market (p51)
- ➡ Mooring (p66)
- ➡ Trader Jacks (p53)

## Why Go?

Fifteen droplets of land cast across 2 million sq km of wild Pacific blue, the Cook Islands are simultaneously remote and accessible, modern and traditional.

With a strong cafe culture, a burgeoning organic and artisan food scene, and a handful of bar and clubs, Rarotonga lives confidently in the 21st century. But beyond the island's tourist buzz and contemporary appearance is a robust culture, firmly anchored by traditional Polynesian values and steeped in oral history.

North of 'Raro', the lagoon of Aitutaki is ringed with deserted islands and is one of the Pacific's most scenic jewels. Venture further and Polynesian traditions emerge nearer the surface. Drink home brew at a traditional 'Atiuan *tumunu* (bush-beer drinking club), explore the *makatea* (raised coral cliffs) and taro fields of Mangaia, or swim in the underground cave pools of Mitiaro and Ma'uke. The remote Northern Group is a South Seas idyll experienced by a lucky few.

## When to Go

### Avarua

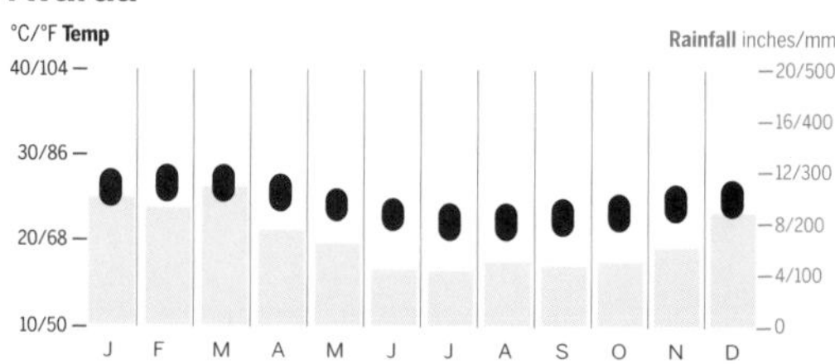


**Mar–Apr** The end of cyclone season usually brings clear, sunny days.

**Aug** Celebrate the nation's 1965 declaration of independence at the annual Te Maeva Nui Festival.

**Sep–Oct** Look forward to warmer temperatures and reduced humidity.

# RAROTONGA

POP 10,572 / AREA 67.2 SQ KM

The most populous of the Cook Islands is stunning in its natural beauty and physical drama. A halo of flame-orange coral reef encircles the island, and Rarotonga's sapphire-blue lagoon is trimmed by sparkling white beaches. Beyond the reef, breakers foam and crash like distant thunder.

Rarotonga's settlements are nestled on the coastal flatlands, with the island rising spectacularly through lush fields and rural farmland to the mountainous and thickly forested interior. These silent, brooding peaks dominate the landscape from every angle.

Rarotonga has plenty of history, too, with ancient *marae* (traditional meeting places) and monuments to explore, and some of the best-preserved coral churches in the South Pacific.

## History

Legend tells that Rarotonga was discovered by Io Tangaroa, who arrived about 1400 years ago from Nuku Hiva in the Marquesas (French Polynesia). In the early 13th century two great warrior chiefs, Tangi'ia from Tahiti and Karika from Samoa, arrived in *vaka* (ocean-going canoes) to conquer the island and rule Rarotonga as joint kings. The land was divided among six tribes, each headed by an *ariki*. The first recorded European visitor was Philip Goodenough, captain of the *Cumberland,* who came in 1814 and spent three months looking for sandalwood. In 1823 missionaries John Williams and Papeiha set out to convert the Rarotongans, and in little more than a year Christianity had taken a firm hold.

## Getting There & Away

Air New Zealand links Rarotonga to Auckland, Sydney and Los Angeles, and Virgin Australia has flights between Auckland and Rarotonga. Air Rarotonga and Air Tahiti operate code-share flights linking Rarotonga with Tahiti.

## Getting Around

### TO/FROM THE AIRPORT

Most hotels and hostels provide transfers from Rarotonga Airport. Raro Tours operates an airport-shuttle service (NZ$20 per person one way to anywhere on the island).

### BUS

Circle-island buses run around the coast road in both directions, departing from the Circle Island Bus Stop at Cook's Corner in Avarua. Buses running clockwise depart hourly from 7am to 11pm Monday to Saturday, and from 8am to noon and 2pm to 4pm Sunday.

Buses running anticlockwise depart at 30 minutes past the hour, from 8.30am to 4.30pm Monday to Friday, and from 8.30am to 12.30pm on Saturday. There are no anti-clockwise buses on Sundays.

A night bus service runs clockwise on Friday at midnight and at 2am on Saturday. Note there is no 11pm bus on Friday.

Adult/child fares are NZ$4/3 for one ride, NZ$8/5 for a return trip (two rides) or NZ$30/19 for a 10-ride ticket. A family pass, valid for two adults and two children, costs NZ$26. There's also a day pass (NZ$16). The bus can be flagged down anywhere along its route. Tickets can be purchased on board.

Pick up bus timetables from the tourist office or the bus driver, or see the website for **Cook's Passenger Transport** (☎55215, 25512; www.busaboutraro.com). Several free publications, including the *Cook Islands Sun Rarotonga Map,* also contain timetables, and they are often posted in restaurants and shops.

### CAR, MOTORCYCLE & BICYCLE

The speed limit is 50km/h outside town and 30km/h around Avarua. It's illegal for motorcyclists to ride two abreast (though many do), and if you exceed 40km/h on a motorcycle without a helmet you'll be fined. Driving is on the left-hand side of the road

To rent a car, your drivers licence from your home country is valid, but if you're planning on zipping around the island on a scooter, you'll need to get a Cook Islands drivers licence (NZ$20). If you're not licensed to drive a motorcycle at home, you'll also have to take a short practical test (NZ$5) including negotiating a simple slalom course of road cones. You can get your licence any day from 8am to 3pm, but turn up early as the police station issues many motorcycle licences daily and queues can be long.

The quintessential mode of transport in the Cook Islands is the scooter. Good rates for rental bikes are around NZ$50 for three days or NZ$100 per week. Cars and jeeps are available for around NZ$50 to NZ$70 per day. Mountain bikes are around NZ$7 per day or NZ$50 per week.

**Avis Cook Islands** Airport (☎21039; www.avis.co.ck); Avarua (Map p52; ☎22833; CITC Shopping Centre) Also has a branch at the Pacific Resort at Muri Beach (p66).

**BT Rentals** (Map p48; ☎23586; www.btrentacar.co.ck; 'Arorangi) Scooter and motorcycle hire.

**Island Car & Bike Hire** (Map p52; www.islandcarhire.co.ck) Arorangi (Map p48; ☎22632; Ara Tapu); Avarua (Map p52; ☎24632); Muri (Map p48; ☎21632).

**Polynesian Rental Cars** (www.polynesianhire.co.ck) Airport (☎21039; ⏲open only for international flights); Avarua (☎20895; 2 St Joseph's Rd); Downtown Avarua (☎26895); Edgewater Resort (☎21026; Edgewater Resort); Rarotongan Beach Resort (☎20838; Rarotongan Beach Resort); Pacific Resort (☎21838; Pacific Resort).

**Rarotonga Rentals** (Map p48; ☎22326; www.rarotongarentals.co.ck) Opposite the airport.

**Tipani Rentals** (Map p48; ☎22382; 'Arorangi) Near the Edgewater Resort in 'Arorangi.

#### TAXI

A number of operators around the island have amalgamated into the Cook Islands Taxi Association. Look for the bright green cars and vans. Rates are about NZ$3 per kilometre. From Muri to the airport will cost around NZ$40, and there is also the option of fixed-price airport transfers of NZ$15 to NZ$20 per person to destinations around the island.

**Atupa Taxi** (☎58252, 25517; Atupa) Contact Panala & Ngaoa Katuke.

**Executive Taxi** (☎52355, 21400; ivorndot@oyster.net.ck; Muri) Contact Ivor and Dorothy.

**H-K Taxi** (☎73549; teuiraka@oyster.net.ck; Muri) Contact Teuira and Shirley.

**JP Taxi** (☎55107, 26572; 'Aorangi) Contact Kim Pirangi.

**Muri Height Taxi** (☎58175, 25405; Muri) Contact Junior Wichman.

**Price Taxi** (☎57303, 50908; larryprice38@gmail.com; 'Aorangi) Contact Larry and Ina Price.

**Rainbow Taxi** (☎72318; Takuvaine) Contact Tere Poaru.

**Seeplus Taxi** (☎55297; Avatiu) Contact Rei Enoka.

## Avarua & Around

Fronting a pretty bay on Rarotonga's north coast, Avarua is the Cook Islands' only proper town. Hardly an urban jungle, Avarua's largest buildings are barely the height of a coconut tree, and the atmosphere of shops and cafes is extremely laid-back. Avarua showcases the island's twin harbours, the main market and some intriguing sights, including the National Museum and the Para O Tane Palace.

There's one main road, the Ara Maire, running through town, and past the shops at the western end of Avarua is the Punanga Nui Market and Avatiu Harbour. This is where interisland passenger freighter ships depart from, and where the Port Authority is based. The airport is 1km further west.

### Sights

**★Cook Islands Christian Church** CHURCH
(CICC; Map p52; Makea Tinirau Rd) Avarua's white-washed church was built in 1853. The graveyard contains the graves of author Robert Dean Frisbie, and Albert Henry, the first prime minister of the Cook Islands. The main church service is at 10am on Sunday, and visitors are invited to stay for morning tea.

**★BCA Art Gallery** HISTORIC BUILDING
(Map p52; ☎21939; Ara Tapu) This historical building was once an LMS missionary school. These days it houses an excellent art gallery, gift shop and courtyard cafe.

**Para O Tane Palace** HISTORIC BUILDING
(Map p52) On the inland side of the main road is this palace and its surrounding Taputapuatea *marae*. The palace is where Makea Takau, the paramount *ariki* (chief) of the area, signed the treaty accepting the Cook Islands' status as a British protectorate

### THE COOK ISLANDS IN...

#### One Week

Ease into **Rarotonga**'s holiday spirit with a relaxed combination of snorkelling, hiking and casual dining, before hopping north to **Aitutaki** and exploring one of the South Pacific's finest lagoons. Definitely find time to attend a wildly entertaining Island Night.

#### Two Weeks

From Aitutaki, fly to rocky and remote **'Atiu**. Sample the local coffee and *tumunu* (bush beer), swim in shimmering underground pools, and discover 'Atiu's rare and idiosyncratic birdlife. If your budget permits, return to Rarotonga and fly south to sleepy **Mangaia** for reef fishing and to explore the island's fascinating burial caves.

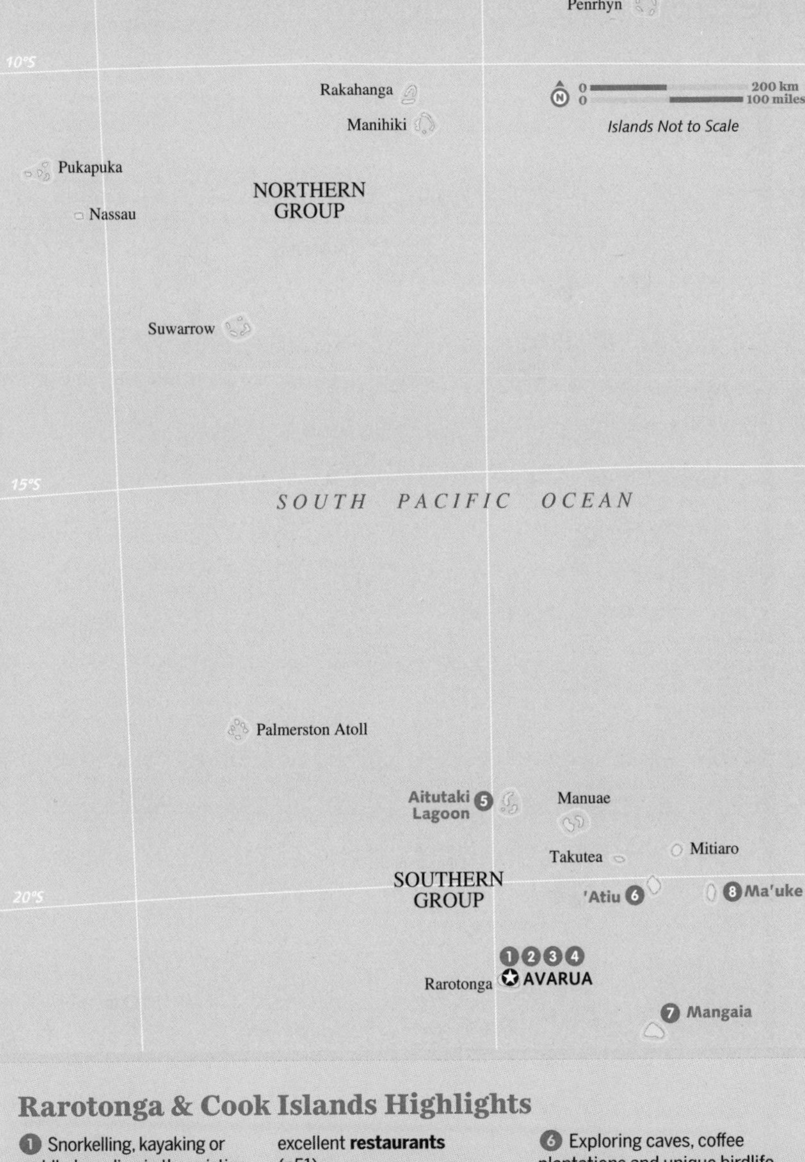


## Rarotonga & Cook Islands Highlights

1. Snorkelling, kayaking or paddle-boarding in the pristine azure waters of Rarotonga's **Muri Lagoon** (p59).
2. Trekking Rarotonga's **cross-island track** (p61), inland trails and valley walks.
3. Feasting on the freshest of seafood and organic local produce in Rarotonga's excellent **restaurants** (p51).
4. Having fun and exploring Rarotonga's heritage and history on a two- or four-wheeled **tour** (p59).
5. Exploring **Aitutaki's stunning lagoon** (p72) by kayak, and finding your own deserted *motu* (island).
6. Exploring caves, coffee plantations and unique birdlife on **'Atiu** (p77).
7. Learning about **Mangaia's** (p86) ancient ways and exploring its mysterious limestone burial caves.
8. Discovering the story of the **Divided Church** (p84) on Ma'uke.

# Rarotonga

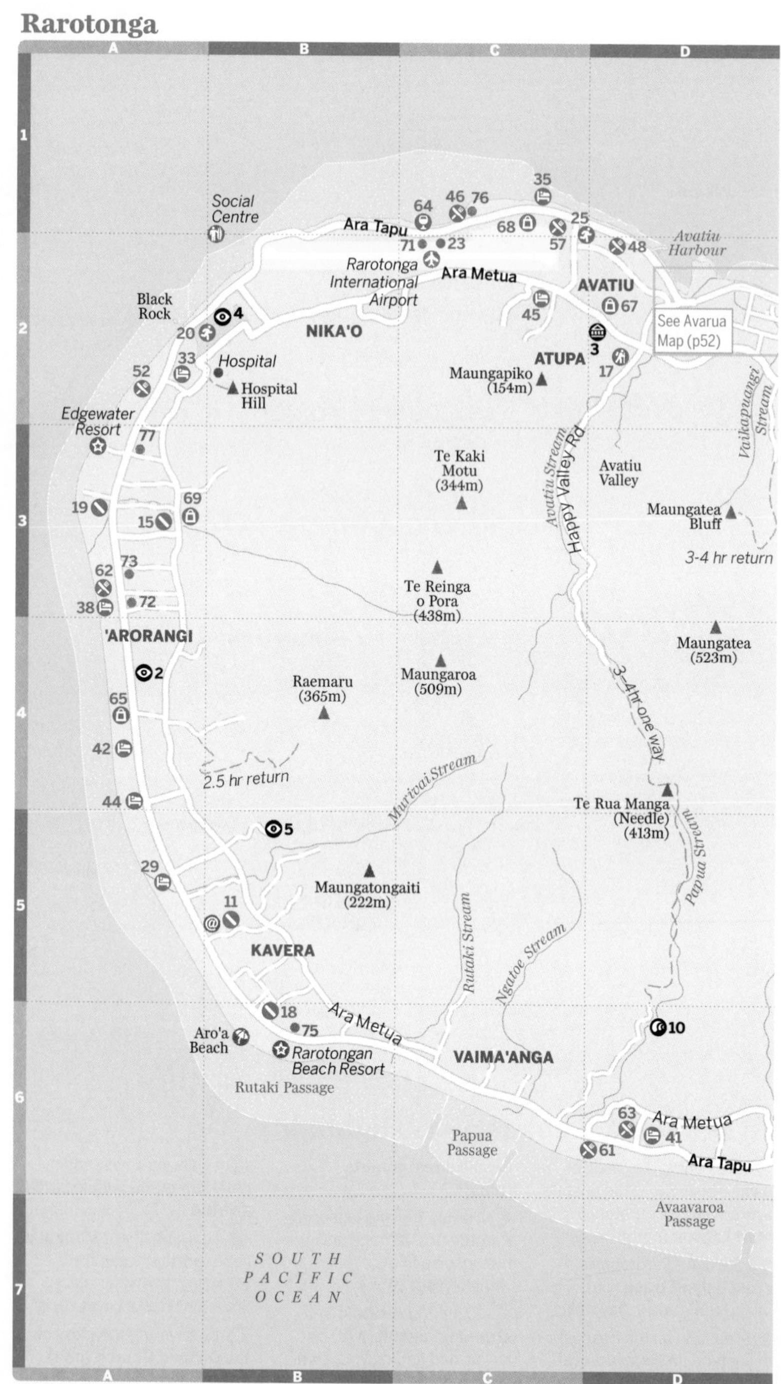

Social Centre
Ara Tapu
Rarotonga International Airport
Ara Metua
Avatiu Harbour
AVATIU
Black Rock
NIKA'O
See Avarua Map (p52)
Hospital
Hospital Hill
ATUPA
Maungapiko (154m)
Edgewater Resort
Te Kaki Motu (344m)
Avatiu Stream
Happy Valley Rd
Avatiu Valley
Vaikapuangi Stream
Maungatea Bluff
3-4 hr return
Te Reinga o Pora (438m)
'ARORANGI
Maungatea (523m)
Raemaru (365m)
Maungaroa (509m)
3-4hr one way
2.5 hr return
Muriwai Stream
Te Rua Manga (Needle) (413m)
Papua Stream
Maungatongaiti (222m)
KAVERA
Rutaki Stream
Ngatoe Stream
Ara Metua
Aro'a Beach
Rarotongan Beach Resort
VAIMA'ANGA
Rutaki Passage
Ara Metua
Papua Passage
Ara Tapu
Avaavaroa Passage
SOUTH PACIFIC OCEAN

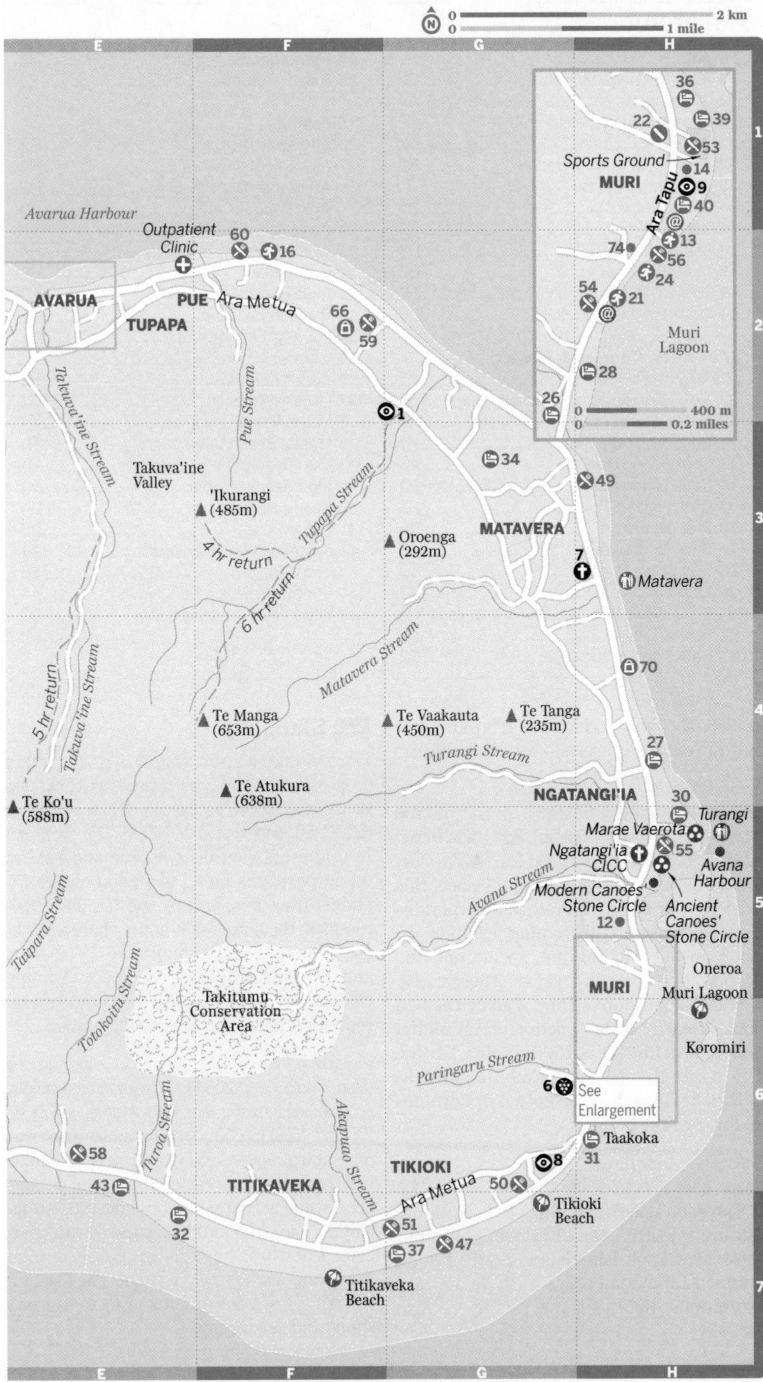

0 2 km
0 1 mile
Avarua Harbour
Outpatient Clinic
AVARUA
PUE
TUPAPA
Ara Metua
Takuva'ine Stream
Pue Stream
Takuva'ine Valley
'Ikurangi (485m)
Tupapa Stream
4 hr return
6 hr return
Oroenga (292m)
MATAVERA
Matavera
Matavera Stream
5 hr return
Takuva'ine Stream
Te Manga (653m)
Te Vaakauta (450m)
Te Tanga (235m)
Turangi Stream
Te Atukura (638m)
Te Ko'u (588m)
NGATANGI'IA
Turangi
Marae Vaerota
Ngatangi'ia CICC
Avana Harbour
Avana Stream
Modern Canoes' Stone Circle
Ancient Canoes' Stone Circle
Taipara Stream
Totokoitu Stream
Takitumu Conservation Area
MURI
Oneroa
Muri Lagoon
Koromiri
Paringaru Stream
See Enlargement
Taakoka
Turoa Stream
Akapuao Stream
TIKIOKI
TITIKAVEKA
Ara Metua
Tikioki Beach
Titikaveka Beach
Sports Ground
MURI
Ara Tapu
Muri Lagoon
0 400 m
0 0.2 miles

## Rarotonga

**Sights**

1 Arai-Te-Tonga Marae ........ G2
2 'Arorangi ........ A4
3 Cook Islands Whale & Wildlife Centre ........ D2
4 Esther Honey Foundation ........ B2
5 Highland Paradise Cultural Centre ........ B5
6 Koteka Winery ........ G6
7 Matavera CICC ........ H3
8 Matutu Brewery ........ G6
9 Te Vara Nui Cultural Village ........ H1
10 Wigmore's Waterfall ........ D6

**Activities, Courses & Tours**

11 Adventure Cook Islands ........ B5
12 Ariki Holidays ........ H5
13 Captain Tama's Lagoon Cruizes ........ H2
14 Coconut Tours ........ H1
15 Cook Island Divers ........ A3
16 Cook Islands Game Fishing Club ........ F2
17 Cross-Island Track ........ D2
18 Dive Centre ........ B6
19 Dive Rarotonga ........ A3
20 Golf Course ........ B2
21 Kitesup ........ H2
Koka Lagoon Cruises ........ (see 24)
22 Pacific Divers ........ H1
23 Raro Tours ........ C2
24 Rarotonga Sailing Club ........ H2
25 Ride Rarotonga ........ C1

**Sleeping**

26 Aito Apartments ........ G2
27 Apartments Kakera ........ H4
28 Aremango Guesthouse ........ H2
Ariki Bungalows ........ (see 12)
29 Aro'a Beachside Inn ........ A5
30 Avana Waterfront Apartments ........ H5
31 Beach Place ........ H6
32 Bella Beach Bungalows ........ E7
33 Black Rock Villas ........ A2
34 Ikurangi Eco Retreat ........ G3
35 Islander ........ C1
36 Kura's Kabanas ........ H1
37 Little Polynesian ........ G7
38 Magic Reef Bungalows ........ A3
39 Manea Beach Villas ........ H1
40 Muri Beach Shell Bungalows ........ H1
Muri Beachcomber ........ (see 24)
Pacific Resort ........ (see 13)
41 Palm Grove ........ D6
42 Rarotonga Backpackers ........ A4
43 Sea Change ........ E6
44 Sunhaven Beach Bungalows ........ A4
45 Tiare Village Airport Motel ........ C2

in 1888. The building has been renovated, but only the outside is accessible to the public.

**Cook Islands Library & Museum Society** MUSEUM
(Map p52; Makea Tinirau Rd; adult/child NZ$5/2.50; 9am-1pm Mon-Sat, 4-7pm Tue) Inland behind the Para O Tane Palace, this collection of Pacific literature incorporates a small museum. Intriguing exhibits include an old whaling pot, spears and the island's first printing press. There's also a small bookshop selling Pacific-themed books. Nearby at the junction of Ara Metua and Takuva'ine Rd is the **Papeiha Stone**. This marks the spot where Tahitian preacher Papeiha preached the gospel in Rarotonga for the first time.

**National Museum** MUSEUM
(Map p52; Victoria Rd; admission NZ$3; 9am-4pm Mon-Fri) Inside the National Culture Centre, the National Museum showcases Cook Islands and South Pacific artefacts, and sometimes hosts temporary exhibitions. Books on the Pacific are also for sale.

## Sleeping

**Tiare Village Airport Motel** MOTEL $
(Map p48; 23466; www.tiarevillage.co.ck; Ara Metua; main house per person NZ$25, chalet s/d NZ$30/50, pool unit d/tr NZ$85/115; ) In a forested glen near Avarua and behind the airport, this motel is a good choice for budget travellers, groups and families. Bedrooms in the large main house share a kitchen, bathroom and comfortable TV lounge, and outside are three compact A-frame chalets with shared bathrooms, and several roomier self-contained poolside units.

**Paradise Inn** GUESTHOUSE $
(Map p52; 20544; www.rarotongamotelaccommodation.com; Are Tapu, Avarua; s NZ$85-105, d/f NZ$135/200; ) Paradise Inn was once Rarotonga's largest and liveliest dance hall, but has been refitted to provide simple, good-value accommodation with kitchen facilities. The old building is packed with character, featuring a huge lounge, polished-wood floors and a sea-view verandah. The location is terrific, just a few minutes' walk to Avarua's shops and restaurants.

**Islander** MOTEL **$$**

(Map p48; ☎21003; www.islanderhotel.co.ck; Ara Tapu; d NZ$265; ) On the beachfront opposite the airport, the Islander offers ocean-view self-contained doubles that have been recently redecorated. There's a poolside barbecue restaurant, perfect for a cold beer and a final Cook Islands meal if you're leaving on an evening flight. Sun loungers and the attached Hula Bar – with an all-day happy hour – make for a social atmosphere.

Day use of the rooms is NZ$200.

**Jetsave Travel** ACCOMMODATION SERVICES

(☎27707; www.jetsave.co.ck; Ara Maire, Avarua) Everything from rental houses through to luxury apartments.

**Shekinah Homes** ACCOMMODATION SERVICES

(Map p52; ☎26004; www.shekinahhomes.com; Ara Tapu, Avarua) Holiday-house rental options from simple beachfront studios to larger family villas.

## Eating

**★Punanga Nui Market** MARKET **$**

(Map p52; www.punanganuiculturalmarket.co.ck; Ara Tapu, Avarua; 6am-noon Sat) Head here for fresh fruit and vegetables, fish and seafood, barbecued snacks, and stalls selling fresh bread and traditional Polynesian food. Foodie treats to discover include delicious fruit smoothies, local coffee, and the stand selling roast pork rolls with apple sauce, and delicious lemon meringue. Don't miss trying the homemade ginger lemonade either.

Hunt down local delicacies including *ika mata* (raw fish marinated in lime and coconut), *rukau* (steamed taro leaves), *poke* (banana with arrowroot and coconut) and *mitiore* (fermented coconut with onion and seafood). Also good are *firi firi,* Tahitian -style doughnuts with chocolate filling, and 100% organic artisan bread is available from 'Varaua mata, e te Miti, Vai'. There's also sourdough, croissants and wholegrain bread, and locally made dips, sauces and chutneys.

**Body Fuel** CAFE **$**

(Map p52; ☎23575; Punanga Nui Market, Avarua; salads, juices & smoothies NZ$7-13; 7.30am-3pm Mon-Sat) Some of the healthiest food on the island is at this simple market food caravan that's open throughout the week. Smoothies and tropical juices go well with gourmet

## Avarua

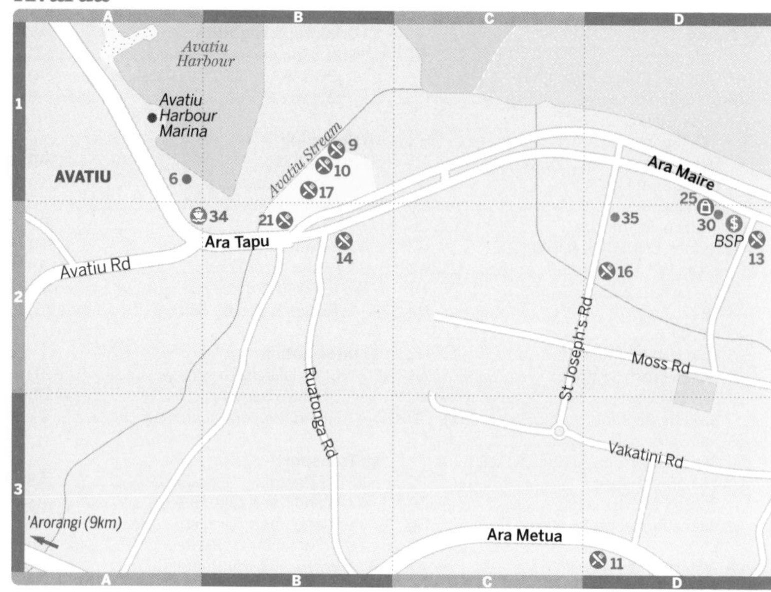


salads – try the smoked marlin one – and there's also sushi available from just NZ$1.

**Bite Time** SEAFOOD $
(Map p52; ☎23577; Punanga Nui Market, Avarua; mains NZ$10-18; ⏰8am-4pm Mon-Thu & Sat, to 8pm Fri) Specialising in fresh fish, this Monday-to-Saturday market stall has great *ika mata*, brilliant tuna carpaccio, and a stonking seafood platter (NZ$18) combining all sorts of tasty marine goodies. There's also sashimi, and fish or chicken wraps for on-the-go dining. Phone orders are welcome.

**LBV** CAFE $
(Map p52; Ara Tapu, Avarua; snacks NZ$7-10; ⏰7.30am-4pm Mon-Fri) Pop in for a fruit smoothie or coffee and croissant, and stock up on artisan breads, deli produce and other picnic-friendly goodies. Brunch and lunch is also available.

**Waffle Shack** CAFE $
(Map p52; www.facebook.com/TheWaffleShack; Punanga Nui Market, Avarua; waffles NZ$6-9; ⏰7.30am-2.30pm Tue-Fri, 7am-noon Sat) Life's pretty simple really. Some days all you need is really good coffee and a freshly made waffle crammed with tropical fruit.

**Rob's Charcoal Chicken** BARBECUE $
(Map p52; Cook's Corner Arcade, Avarua; mains NZ$10-15; ⏰9am-3pm Mon-Fri) Located in a quiet courtyard, Rob's offers expertly barbecued chickens, either served with a plate full of salad and taro chips, or doused with spicy *peri peri* flavours in a wrap. Whole chickens (NZ$20) are available for takeaway – a handy option if you're self-catering – and Rob's coconut curried fish is also very tasty.

**BCA Café** CAFE $
(Map p52; Ara Tapu, Avarua; snacks NZ$5-12; ⏰9am-3pm Mon-Fri, to 1pm Sat) This courtyard cafe in the restored BCA Art Gallery building serves up excellent juices, bagels, toasted sandwiches, and coffee and cake. There's usually a selection of New Zealand magazines to browse.

**Café Jireh** CAFE $
(Map p48; Ara Tapu, opposite the airport; snacks & mains NZ$7-18; ⏰8am-4pm Mon-Fri, from 1pm Sat) Near the airport, Café Jireh does excellent coffee and homestyle baking including creamy custard squares. It's also a popular spot for a lazy brunch.

**Kai Pizza** PIZZA $
(Map p52; ☎53330; Ara Tapu, Avarua; pizza NZ$12-19; ⏰11am-2pm Tue-Fri, plus 4-9pm Mon-

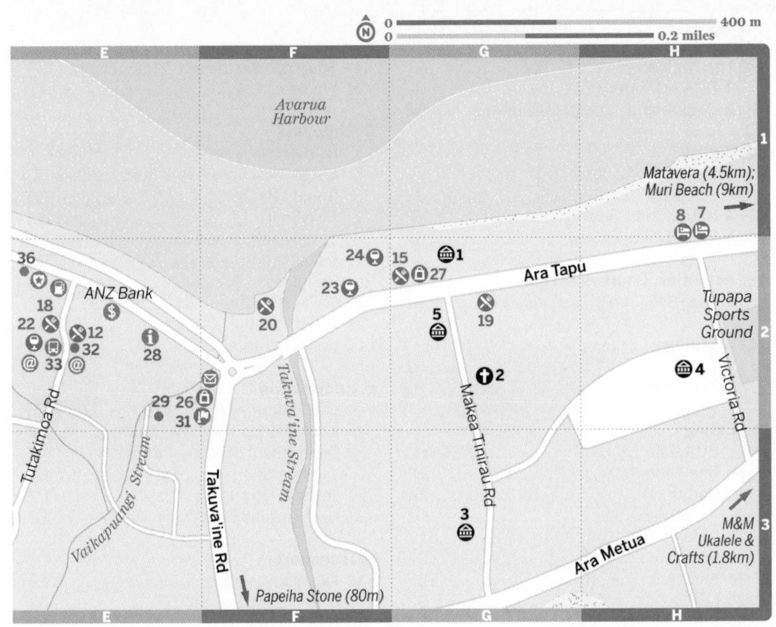




Sat) Wood-fired pizza is served from a colourful shipping container. Order the Hawaiian one with ham and pineapple, and celebrate all things Polynesian and Italian. There's outdoor seating, or oceanfront beach dining is a short drive away. Service can be slow so consider ordering by phone.

**Ocean Fresh Seafood** SEAFOOD **$**
(Map p48; Ara Tapu, Panama; 7am-4pm Mon-Sat) The best place to buy fresh fish if you're looking to barbecue up a storm or prepare your own sashimi. Fish could include wahoo, *mahimahi*, tuna, swordfish and broadbill, but it all depends on what's been caught that morning. Special export packs are also available if you're keen to take some fresh fish back on the plane.

**Prime Foods** SUPERMARKET **$**
(Map p52; 22259; www.primefoods.co.ck; St Joseph's Rd, Avarua; 8am-5.30pm Mon-Thu, to 6pm Fri, to 2pm Sat) Dining out on Raro can be expensive, so head to Prime Foods for barbecue-ready treats like gourmet sausages, and the island's best array of salami and ham for lazy afternoon snacking sessions.

**CITC Supermarket** SUPERMARKET **$**
(Map p48; Ara Tapu, Avatiu; 8am-6pm Mon-Fri, to 4pm Sat) Halfway to the airport from Avarua, the huge CITC Supermarket is great for tinned and packaged produce. There's also a liquor store attached.

**Foodland** SUPERMARKET **$**
(Map p52; Ara Tapu, Avarua; 8am-6pm Mon-Fri, to 4pm Sat) The best all-round supermarket is in the middle of Avarua's main shopping strip, with fresh bread, fruit and vegetables, packaged goods and a deli counter.

★**Trader Jacks** PUB FOOD, SEAFOOD **$$**
(Map p52; www.traderjackscookislands.com; Ara Tapu, Avarua; mains NZ$18-36; bar 11am-midnight, restaurant 11.30am-2.30pm & 6-9pm Mon-Sat) Trader Jacks is one of Rarotonga's iconic watering holes, and panoramic sea views and good food also make it a great place to eat. The front bar has top-notch pizzas, while the restaurant is more stylish and classy with meals including excellent sashimi and smoked marlin fish cakes. There's usually a live band on Friday and Saturday nights.

**Tahiti Café** SEAFOOD **$$**
(Map p52; Ara Tapu, Avarua; mains from NZ$18, seafood platters NZ$40; 11.30am-2.30pm Mon-Fri) Secure a table on the breezy deck and tuck into tasty Tahitian- and Asian-style spins on sashimi and *ika mata*. The concise

## Avarua

**Top Sights**

1 BCA Art Gallery .......... G2
2 Cook Islands Christian Church .......... G2

**Sights**

3 Cook Islands Library & Museum Society .......... G3
4 National Museum .......... H2
5 Para O Tane Palace .......... G2

**Activities, Courses & Tours**

6 Raro Reef Sub .......... A1

**Sleeping**

7 Paradise Inn .......... H1
8 Shekinah Homes .......... H1

**Eating**

BCA Café .......... (see 1)
9 Bite Time .......... B1
10 Body Fuel .......... B1
11 Cafe Ariki .......... D3
12 Café Salsa .......... E2
13 Foodland .......... D2
14 Kai Pizza .......... B2
15 LBV .......... G2
16 Prime Foods .......... D2
17 Punanga Nui Market .......... B1
18 Rob's Charcoal Chicken .......... E2
19 Tahiti Café .......... G2
20 Trader Jacks .......... F2
21 Waffle Shack .......... B2

**Drinking & Nightlife**

22 Hidie's Bar .......... E2
23 Rehab .......... F2
Staircase Restaurant & Bar .......... (see 27)
24 Whatever Bar & Grill .......... F2

**Shopping**

BCA Art Gallery .......... (see 1)
Bergman & Sons Pearl Store .......... (see 18)
Bounty Bookshop .......... (see 26)
Dive Shop .......... (see 25)
Island Craft .......... (see 25)
25 Mareko .......... D2
Perfumes of Rarotonga .......... (see 18)
26 Philatelic Bureau .......... F2
27 Tuki's Pareu .......... G2
Vonnia's Store .......... (see 25)

**Information**

CITC Pharmacy .......... (see 12)
28 Cook Islands Tourist Authority .......... E2
29 Department of Foreign Affairs & Immigration .......... E2
30 Jetsave Travel .......... D2
31 New Zealand High Commission .......... F2

**Transport**

32 Avis Cook Islands .......... E2
33 Circle Island Bus Stop .......... E2
34 Harbour Master .......... A2
Island Car & Bike Hire .......... (see 14)
Island Car & Bike Hire .......... (see 14)
35 Polynesian Car Rentals .......... D2
36 Polynesian Car Rentals .......... E2
Ports Authority .......... (see 34)

seafood-only menu also extends to fried fish and fish platters, and it's all good, and all very fresh.

**Café Salsa** CAFE **$$**

(Map p52; ☎22215; www.salsa.co.ck; Ara Tapu, Avarua; mains NZ$14-27, pizza NZ$12-20; ⏲7.30am-3pm Mon-Sat) In downtown Avarua, Café Salsa is more Auckland-chic than Polynesian-rustic. The diverse menu combines Mediterranean and Asian flavours with local produce, and standout dishes include the Thai-style *eke* (octopus) curry, and the wood-roasted *mahi-mahi* fillet with slow-roasted tomatoes, feta and pine nuts. Gourmet pizzas are also good, and there's a decent NZ-centric winelist.

**Cafe Ariki** CAFE **$$**

(Map p52; ☎22772; Ara Metua, Avarua; mains NZ$18-26; ⏲10.30am-2pm Mon-Fri, plus 6-9pm Mon-Sat) Tucked away inland behind Avarua township, this good-value cafe and bar is a big favourite with locals. Sashimi, *ika mata* and huge burgers and salads for lunch give way to barbecues for dinner. Combine grilled tuna with a few beers, and definitely leave room for dessert of peach and yogurt cake.

**Tamarind House** INTERNATIONAL **$$$**

(Map p48; ☎26487; www.tamarind.co.ck; Ara Tapu, Tupapa; mains NZ$25-37; ⏲11.30am-2pm Mon-Fri, plus 5.30-10pm Mon-Sat, 9am-2pm Sun May-Oct only) The most elegant place to dine on Rarotonga is this colonial building on the island's north shore. Book a table on the grand verandah and enjoy the cool evening breeze with an inspired fusion of European, Asian and Pacific flavours. Try the island fish curry or the excellent blackened fish (usually tuna) with breadfruit chips and steamed *rukau* (local spinach).

From May to October Tamarind House is also open for Sunday brunch.

## Drinking & Nightlife

The main after-dark action on Rarotonga is centred around Avarua. Raro's big night out is Friday, but Saturday is catching up in popularity. On Friday most places stay open to around 2am, but doors are bolted shut at midnight on Saturday out of respect for the Sabbath. Most restaurants double as bars, and resort bars are open to nonguests. Check out the *Cook Islands Sun* tourists' newspaper for what's on around the island.

For an organised Friday night out exploring Rarotonga's bars and clubs, join a Going Troppo tour (NZ$38 per person) with Raro Tours. After-dark tours on Friday nights are also arranged by Rarotonga's bigger resorts and hostels.

Trader Jacks (p53) in Avarua, and the Waterline Bar & Grill (p67) in 'Arorangi, are also good spots for a few quiet ones.

**21.3 Vaiana Bistro & Bar** BAR

(Map p48; Ara Tapu, Avatiu; 11am-10pm Tue-Fri, 4-10pm Sat) Fast track into an island state of mind with loping Pacific reggae, shimmering sunsets and cold beer at this relaxed beachside bar that's a favourite of locals and nearby accommodation owners. Weekend bands and DJs, and a pre-sunset happy hour from 4pm to 6pm, make it worth the short hop from downtown Avarua. Enjoying island life is really pretty simple.

**Whatever Bar & Grill** BAR

(Map p52; 22299; Ara Tapu, Avarua; 11am-midnight Mon-Thu & Sat, to 2am Fri) Who'd have thought – an open-air bar on a disused rooftop? Just out of Avarua, this place attracts trendy young things and gets very lively on Friday and Saturday nights. There are DJs and regular bands; check out the signboard out the front. Night-time views across town and the harbour are brilliant and there's well-priced bar food for lunch or dinner, including gargantuan burgers and fish sandwiches.

**Staircase Restaurant & Bar** CLUB

(Map p52; 22254; www.facebook.com/staircaseraro; Ara Tapu, Avarua; 6pm-midnight Thu-Sat) Upstairs behind the Topshape Health & Fitness Centre building, the Staircase is always popular. The bar is decked out with atmospheric island decor and has regular live bands, as well as good-value Island Nights on Thursday and Friday before DJs kick in from 10pm.

**Hidie's Bar** BAR

(Map p52; Cook's Corner Arcade; 9pm-midnight Wed, Thu & Sun, 4pm-2am Fri, 4pm-midnight Sat) On busy weekend nights everyone crams into Hidie's to check out the live bands, and there are usually DJs a couple of nights a week. The courtyard garden bar is a great place to be on a warm tropical night.

### KEEP YOUR COOL, RARO STYLE

Exploring Rarotonga can be thirsty work, so here's our top-five picks to cool down, island-style.

- Dive into nature's very own electrolyte, a nu (young green coconut), chilled and ready to drink from the **Punanga Nui Market** (p51). Don't be surprised if it's also the drink of choice when you're served lunch on an island tour.
- Lots of tropical fruit equals lots of tropical smoothies. Recharge after snorkelling with huge servings of creamy, liquid goodness from **Saltwater Cafe** (p68) or **Charlie's Cafe & Beach Hire** (p66).
- Pull up a bar stool at **Trader Jacks** (p53), and toast Raro's dedicated crews of outrigger paddlers with a cocktail or a cold beer.
- Yes, the craft-beer movement has even washed up on Rarotongan shores. Take a tour and sample the beers at **Matutu Brewery** (p59), or cool down a west-coast sunset with a refreshing Mai Lager at the **Shipwreck Hut** (p69)
- Discover the unique flavours of banana wine at Muri's **Koteka Winery** (Map p48; Ara Tapu, Muri; 9am-4pm Mon-Sat) or visit the winery's stall at Avarua's weekly market. The wine is mixed with whatever fruit is in season – anything from passionfruit to mango or orange. There's also vodka and fresh vanilla pods for sale. Look for the roadside signs just past Muri Beach as you're heading clockwise around the island.

**Rehab** CLUB
(Map p52; ☎25717; Ara Tapu, Avarua; ⌚9pm-midnight Wed & Sat, 10pm-2am Fri) House and electro grooves thump 'n' bump under ultraviolet and stroboscopic lights. Rehab offers occasional drink specials if you arrive before 10pm.

## Shopping

Shops around Avarua sell local basketwork, shell jewellery, necklaces, carvings and musical instruments. Many islands have their own speciality handicrafts, including *rito* (coconut-fibre) fans and hats from the Northern Group and *pupu ei* (shell necklaces) from Mangaia. Beware of cheap Asian imports. Most shops are closed on Sunday.

Printed *pareu* (sarongs) cost around NZ$20 to NZ$30, while handmade ones cost NZ$40 to NZ$50. There's always a good selection at Saturday morning's Punanga Nui Market. Great local T-shirts are also sold at the Punanga Nui market and at surfwear shops.

Only the Cooks and French Polynesia produce rarer black pearls. A single pearl costs from NZ$10 to over NZ$2000.

**BCA Art Gallery** ARTS & CRAFTS
(Map p52; www.gallerybca.com; Ara Tapu, Avarua; ⌚10am-3pm Mon-Sat, to noon Sun) BCA houses a gallery specialising in contemporary Pacific art, an excellent gift shop selling pearls, clothing and designer homeware, and a relaxed courtyard cafe.

**Island Craft** SOUVENIRS
(Map p52; Ara Tapu, Avarua; ⌚8am-5pm Mon-Fri, to 1pm Sat) The best-stocked souvenir shop is in Avarua.

**Bergman & Sons Pearl Store** JEWELLERY
(Map p52; www.bergmanandsons.com; Tutakimoa Rd, Avarua; ⌚10am-4pm Mon-Fri, to noon Sat) Unique and modern settings including necklaces, rings and bracelets. Hillary Clinton was gifted some Bergman black pearls when she visited the Cook Islands in 2012 for the Pacific Islands Forum.

**Dive Shop** CLOTHING, SPORTS
(Map p52; ☎26675; www.palm.co.ck; Ara Tapu, Avarua; ⌚9am-4pm Mon-Fri, to noon Sat) Sells good-quality fins, masks and snorkels and surfwear. See the website for an interactive map of Raro's best snorkelling sites.

**Vonnia's Store** CLOTHING
(Map p52; Ara Maire, Avarua; ⌚8am-5pm Mon-Fri, to 1pm Sat) Centrally located.

**Tuki's Pareu** CLOTHING
(Map p52; Ara Tapu, Avarua; ⌚8am-5pm Mon-Fri, to 1pm Sat) The locals' choice.

**Mareko** CLOTHING
(Map p52; Ara Tapu, Avarua; ⌚8am-5pm Mon-Fri, to 1pm Sat) Good for T-shirts.

**Bounty Bookshop** BOOKS
(Map p52; Ara Tapu, Avarua; ⌚8am-4pm Mon-Fri, to noon Sat) Historical and pictorial books

### RAROTONGA IN...

#### Two Days

Take a **circle-island tour** or hire a scooter and buzz around the back roads to get acquainted with the island. Factor in kayaking or paddleboarding around **Muri Lagoon**, before settling in for sunset drinks at the **Shipwreck Hut** and dinner at **Vaima Restaurant & Bar**. Start your second day on an active note by conquering the **cross-island track** or bicycling with **Storytellers**. After the South Pacific's best fish sandwiches at the **Mooring**, relax with swimming and snorkelling near **Charlies Cafe & Beach Hire**, before heading out for an exciting **Island Night** combining local food, singing and dancing. Look forward to a high level of audience interaction.

#### Four Days

If you're on the island on a Saturday morning, a visit to the **Punanga Nui Market** is almost mandatory. Then head to **Highland Paradise Cultural Centre** for insights into traditional Cook Islands culture. Spend the evening exploring more contemporary local culture amid the nightlife of Avarua. Walk between the **Whatever Bar** and **Trader Jacks**, or head west through town to the beachside location of **21.3 Vaiana Bistro & Bar**. If you're in the mood for dancing, break out your best island moves at **Rehab**. After a well-earned lie in, have a lazy brunch at **Café Salsa** in Avarua, or at **LBV** in Muri, before a fun and exciting island tour with **Raro Safari Tours** or **Raro Buggy Tours**. If you're in town on a Monday or Thursday night, meet the locals on a **progressive dinner** around the island.

## RAROTONGA FOR CHILDREN

Always check with the place you're staying about their policy on children, as some don't cater for kids under 12. For really little ones, you can hire strollers, car seats and portacots from **Coco Tots** (☎56986; www.cocotots.com). Ask at your accommodation or the tourist information office about babysitting services.

The top draw for kids is the island's colourful lagoon and the spectacular beach that stretches around the island. Good spots for snorkelling are Muri, Tikioki and Aro'a Beach, and smoothies and ice creams are never far away at Fruits of Rarotonga or the Saltwater Cafe.

For an in-depth look at the island's underwater inhabitants, kids will adore a glass-bottom boat tour around Muri Lagoon with either Captain Tama's Lagoon Cruizes or Koka Lagoon Cruises. An option to explore the underwater world beyond the reef is on the Raro Reef Sub. From July to October you might be lucky enough to see humpback whales cruising past the island. If they're really keen on all things cetacean, visit the excellent Cook Islands Whale & Wildlife Centre.

Active kids will love exploring the island's jungle-covered interior on the Cross-Island Track, or Raro's quieter back roads on a bicycle ride with Storytellers. Alternatively, drop by Ride Rarotonga and rent a funky, go-anywhere beach cruiser with massive, knobbly wheels.

An entertaining jeep ride around the island with Raro Safari Tours will be sure to please, or you can take them for a quad-bike spin with Coconut Tours if they're eight years or older. Another exciting offroad option is with Raro Buggy Tours, but mum or dad will definitely need to be behind the wheel.

about the Cook Islands, and international and NZ magazines.

**Philatelic Bureau** STAMPS & COINS
(Map p52; Ara Tapu, Avarua; ⏰8am-4pm Mon-Fri) Cook Islands coins and bank notes are sold here, plus Cook Islands stamps (highly prized by philatelists). The unique \$3 Cook Islands note is available in two designs. Several new coins were minted for the country's 50th anniversary of independence in 2015.

## Information

Internet access is widely available on Rarotonga. There are Bluesky wi-fi hot spots all around the island, including at most of the major resorts. Telepost shops and other stores sell pre-paid wi-fi access in denominations of NZ\$10 (150MB), NZ\$25 (500MB), and NZ\$50 (1.25GB). Another option is to buy a local Kokanet 3G sim card (NZ\$25) for your smartphone, and purchase additional data for 20 cents per MB up to 1GB for NZ\$50. At the time of writing 3G service was limited to Rarotonga, but Bluesky hot spots were available on other islands including Aitutaki and 'Atiu.

**ANZ** (www.anz.com/cookislands; ⏰9am-3pm Mon-Fri) ATMs at the main branch in Avarua, at Cook's Corner in Avarua, at Wigmore's Superstore at Vaimaanga, at Muri Beach, and at the Rarotongan Beach Resort at 'Arorangi.

**Bluesky Teleshop** (Map p52; www.telecom.co.ck; CITC Shopping Centre, Ara Maire; ⏰8am-4pm Mon-Fri, 8.30am-1pm Sat) Wi-fi access, internet terminals and mobile phone services.

**BSP** (Bank South Pacific; www.bsp.co.ck; ⏰9am-3pm Mon-Fri) The main branch is beside the Foodland supermarket in Avarua, and another airport branch opens for international flights – both have ATMs. ATMs are also at Oasis Service Centre (Nikao), JMC Store (Muri) and the Edgewater Resort ('Arorangi).

**CITC Pharmacy** (Map p52; ☎22000; CITC Shopping Centre, Ara Maire; ⏰8.30am-4.30pm Mon-Fri, 9am-1pm Sat) Part of the CITC Shopping Centre.

**Click Internet Lounge** (Map p52; Cook's Corner Arcade; ⏰8.30am-5pm Mon-Fri) Internet access via PCs.

**Cook Islands Tourist Authority** (Map p52; ☎29435; www.cookislands.travel; Avarua; ⏰8am-4pm Mon-Fri, 10am-1pm Sat) The main tourist office can help with everything from accommodation and nightspots to interisland flights and shipping services. Ask here about Island Nights around Rarotonga, and attractions and accommodation on the outer islands.

**Jetsave Travel** (Map p52; ☎27707; www.jetsave.co.ck; Ara Maire, Avarua) Has good air-fare-and-accommodation packages and deals to the outer islands.

**Post Office** (Map p52; ⏰8am-4pm Mon-Fri) Centrally located.

### SADDLE SORE?

We're not sure how many registered motorscooters there are in the Cooks, but this egalitarian form of transport is everywhere you look. To see a smartly dressed minister aboard his trusty Honda on the way to Sunday-morning church is a visionary sight indeed. People smoke and chat riding two-abreast, talk or text on the phone and maybe chew a sandwich at the same time. Robust Polynesian mamas perch on the side while tiny children cling on behind.

Locals prefer the manual 110cc 'postie bike' but the scooters hired to tourists are usually the automatic type. They're easy to ride with push-button ignitions, brakes and throttle. Even if you've never ridden a motorcycle before, after 10 minutes you'll be riding like a pro, and after a few days you'll be walking like a cowhand. Be careful with the proximity of your suntanned legs to the hot exhaust pipe. Get too close and you'll be in danger of getting a 'Rarotongan Tattoo'. Watch out also for the occasional stray dog, and avoid riding at night as there's minimal street lighting on most parts of the island.

Remember also if you don't have a motorcycle licence in your home country, you need to head along to the police station in Avarua and get local accreditation when you first arrive.

# Around the Island

Though Rarotonga is the largest of the Cook Islands, it's still compact and accessible, and is circumnavigated by a 32km coastal road known as the Ara Tapu (Sacred Rd). Inland is a second road, the Ara Metua (Ancient Rd), built in the 11th century. The Ara Metua passes through farmland, taro plantations, and rambling homesteads in the foothills of Rarotonga's mountainous centre. The island's rugged interior can be crossed only on foot. There are no private beaches on Rarotonga, but take care not to cross private land in order to access the shoreline.

## Sights

**Cook Islands Whale & Wildlife Centre** MUSEUM

(Map p48; ☎21666; www.whaleresearch.org; Ara Metua, Atupa; adult/child NZ$12/6; ⊙10am-4pm Sun-Fri) Visit this centre to learn about whales and other wildlife frequenting the Cook Islands. It's an essential stop if you're planning on going whale watching, and the centre's cosy Whale Tail Café has good coffee, snacks and wi-fi. Live critters include a giant centipede and coconut crabs, and there are also exhibits on sharks, turtles and shipwrecks.

**Black Rock** VIEWPOINT

On the northwest coast is Black Rock (Turou), traditionally believed to be where the spirits of the dead commenced their voyage to 'Avaiki (the afterworld). It's also one of the island's best snorkelling spots. Look out for the sign to the Rarotonga Hospital from where there are commanding views of the island's west coast.

**'Arorangi** HISTORIC SITE

(Map p48) On Rarotonga's west coast, 'Arorangi was the first missionary-built village, conceived as a model for other villages on the island. The missionary Papeiha is buried at the 1849 **CICC**.

**Highland Paradise Cultural Centre** CULTURAL CENTRE

(Map p48; ☎21924; www.highlandparadise.co.ck; self-guided admission adult/child NZ$30/15, guided tours adult/child $75/37.50, island nights adult/child NZ$99/55; ⊙self-guided admission 9am-3pm Mon-Fri, village tours 9.30am-1pm Tue & Thu, island nights 5.30-9.30pm Mon, Wed, Fri) High above 'Arorangi, Highland Paradise stands on the site of the old Tinomana village with panoramic views over the west and south coasts. Members of the Pirangi family, descendants of Tinomana Ariki, take visitors on guided tours including weaving, dancing and drumming exhibits. It's also possible to explore the sacred site on a self-guided basis from Monday to Friday. On Monday, Wednesday and Friday, fabulous sunset Island Nights are held. Bookings are essential and transport is included.

**Wigmore's Waterfall** WATERFALL

(Map p48) On the eastern edge of the abandoned Sheraton resort site, a road leads inland to Wigmore's Waterfall, a lovely cascade dropping into a fresh, cool swimming pool. Note that in the dry season, the cascade can be more of a trickle. The south coast also has the island's best beaches, with the best snorkelling to be found at **Aro'a**, **Titikaveka** and **Tikioki**.

**★Muri** BEACH

With its four *motu* (islets), Muri is the most beautiful section of Rarotonga's encircling lagoon. The blue water is packed with tropical fish, especially around the *motu* (Taakoka, Koromiri, Oneroa and Motutapu), and out towards the reef. Taakoka is volcanic while the others are sand cays. The swimming is wonderful over sparkling white sand. Water-sports equipment and lagoon cruises are available from Muri through Captain Tama's and Koka's Lagoon Cruises. Other attractions include kitesurfing, paddle-boarding and good restaurants.

**Matutu Brewery** BREWERY

(Map p48; ☎26288; www.matutubeer.com; Ara Tapu, Takitimu; ⏰10am-3pm Mon-Sat, tours noon & 1pm) Pop in to meet the guys behind Raro's very own craft brewery. Regular beers – also sold around the island – are Mai Lager and Kiva Pale Ale. Seasonal limited-run brews are also sometimes conjured up, and often available at the tiny brewery. Join a tour and tasting session, and don't leave the island without buying a Matutu T-shirt.

**Te Vara Nui Cultural Village** BUILDING

(Map p48; ☎24006; www.tevaranui.co.ck; Muri; village tour adult/child NZ$39/19, dinner & show adult/child NZ$89/45; ⏰village tour 5pm, dinner & show 7.30pm Tue, Thu & Sat) Te Vara Nui combines a purpose-built village showcasing local culture including traditional medicine, carving, tapa making and legends, with one of Rarotonga's most spectacular Island Nights. After-dark shows take place on pavilions and stages set above a manmade lagoon, and dinner is a sprawling *umu* (earth oven) buffet. A combination deal (adult/child NZ$109/59) for both the two-hour village tour and the dinner and show is also available.

**Matavera CICC** CHURCH

(Map p48) The old CICC is lovely at night when the outside is lit up.

**Arai-Te-Tonga Marae** HISTORIC SITE

(Map p48) A small sign points off the road to the island's most important *marae* site, Arai-Te-Tonga. Situated just off the Ara Metua, there's a stone-marked *koutu* (ancient open-air royal courtyard) site in front of you. This whole area was a gathering place, and the remains of the *marae*, the *koutu* and other meeting grounds are still visible.

## Activities

### Cycling

**Ride Rarotonga** BICYCLE RENTAL

(Map p48; ☎27433; www.riderarotonga.com; Ara Tapu; ⏰9am-5pm Mon-Fri, to 1pm Sat) Rarotonga's only bike shop has an excellent range of hire bikes, from cool beach cruisers (NZ$15/70 per day/week) to mountain bikes and road bikes (NZ$30/140 per day/week). Electric bikes are NZ$45/210 per day/week. At the time of writing, a project encompassing 28km of specialist bike paths was beginning on the island, including an exciting network of mountain-bike trails.

Drop in at the shop for the latest information on these initiatives, which will make Rarotonga one of the best mountain-biking destinations in the Pacific.

**Storytellers Eco Cycle Tours** BICYCLE TOUR

(☎53450, 23450; www.storytellers.co.ck; per person NZ$69-109) These exceptionally well-run bicycle tours exploring the byways and backroads of the island come packed with information on the history, environment and culture of Rarotonga. Three different tours range from the easygoing Discover option – around 8km to 12km on easy roads – to the Excite tour which traverses streams and

### HELPING RAROTONGA'S ANIMALS

You'll probably spy the cute animals from the **Esther Honey Foundation** (Map p48) at its stall at Saturday morning's Punanga Nui Market, but it's also worth visiting the main location to check out the excellent animal welfare work being undertaken.

Rarotonga has a much lower stray canine population compared to other Pacific islands, and significant credit is due to the Esther Honey Foundation. Dog numbers on the island have decreased from 6000 to around 2000, a reduction managed only by spaying and neutering animals, and the dog population of the Cook Islands is now noticeably healthier and more easygoing than in other Pacific destinations.

Drop by to have a chat with the international crew of vets and assistants, and there's also the chance to interact with a diverse menagerie of dogs, cats and other animals. Feeding times are in the morning.

switchbacks in a 20km adventure for more experienced and fitter riders.

All three tours end with a well-earned lagoonside lunch and the opportunity for a swim.

### Deep-Sea Fishing

Deep-sea fishing is popular in the Cook Islands, with catches of *mahimahi* and tuna (from October to May), wahoo and barracuda (April to October), and sailfish and marlin (November to March). The following operators have safety gear; contact them by telephone or down at the Avatiu wharf where most boats tie up. A half-day tour – usually around five hours from 6am – costs around NZ$150 to NZ$170 per person.

**Blue Water Rarotonga** BOATING
(☎53544, 23545; www.bluewaterrarotonga.com) Wide range of boat-based activities including fishing, whale watching, reef tours, and sunset cruises. Four- and seven-night outer-island tours are also available.

**Cook Islands Game Fishing Club** FISHING
(Map p48) Just east of Avarua, anglers swap yarns at this friendly club. Non-fishing types are also welcome at the island's most affordable bar, and adjacent is the excellent Flying Boat Fish & Chips.

**Akura Fishing Charters** FISHING
(☎54355; www.akurafishingcharters.com) Big-game fishing from NZ$170 per person.

**Captain Moko's** FISHING
(☎73083, 20385; www.fishingrarotonga.com) Expect lots of Raro humour and the opportunity to eat your catch afterwards. Half-day trips from NZ$150 per person.

**Marlin Queen** FISHING
(☎55202; www.marlinqueen.co.ck) Half- and full-day tours available.

**Seafari Charters** FISHING
(☎55096; www.seafari.co.ck) On board the MV *Seafari*, a 1934 Canadian fishing trawler.

**Wahoo Fishing Charters** FISHING
(☎73731, 25130; www.wahoofishingcharters.net) Morning and afternoon 4½-hour trips available.

### Diving & Snorkelling

Diving is fantastic outside the reef, especially around the passages along the island's southern side. There are canyons, caves and tunnels to explore, and outside the lagoon the island drops off to around 4000m, although most diving is between 3m and 30m.

Rarotonga has several well-preserved shipwrecks, including SS *Maitai* off the northern shore. Other well-known diving

## EXPLORING MURI

Start at the northern end of Muri Beach at Avana Harbour, one of the only deep-water passages into Rarotonga's lagoon. Maybe grab a fruit smoothie or fish sandwich from the **Mooring** (p66) to set you up for the walk ahead.

The great ocean-going *vaka* (canoes) set off from here in the 14th century to settle New Zealand – the so-called 'Great Migration'. There's often a replica – but still ocean-going – *vaka* anchored in the lagoon. Walk north onto the small promontory to see **Marae Vaerota**, the traditional *marae* of the Kainuku Ariki, where canoes were blessed and human sacrifices were made to the gods.

Head south to the picturesque **Ngatangi'ia CICC**, where you'll find some interesting headstones. Opposite in the park is the **ancient canoes' stone circle** and a plaque commemorating the seven canoes that completed the journey to New Zealand: *Takitumu, Tokomaru, Kurahaupo, Aotea, Tainui, Te Arawa* and *Mataatua*. There's a **modern stone circle** further south that commemorates the arrival of traditional Polynesian canoes during the sixth Festival of Pacific Arts in 1992.

To the south, glorious **Muri Beach** is one of the island's best snorkelling areas. It's a lovely walk along the shoreline with views over the four palm-covered *motu* (islets) in the lagoon. The remains of one of Rarotonga's oldest *marae* are on **Motutapu**, but you'll need to kayak out there. Pick up coffee and cake at **LBV** (p68) or a leisurely lunch at **Sails Restaurant** (p68).

If you're feeling active, sign up for kitesurfing, windsurfing or paddle-boardng with **Kitesup** (p62), or linger over a cocktail at **iSOBAR** (p69) before the **Muri Night Market** (p67) kicks off at 5pm four nights a week.

spots include **Black Rock** in the north; **Sandriver** and **Matavera Wall** on the island's east side; and the **Avaavaroa**, **Papua** and **Rutaki** passages in the south.

Rarotonga has five accredited diving operators, all offering twice-daily boat trips. Single-tank dives cost around NZ$95 and two-tank dives are about NZ$140 including gear. Introductory dives are available and three-day open-water courses cost around NZ$480.

Rarotonga's spectacular lagoon is fantastic for snorkelling and swimming. The water is crystal clear, warm and packed with technicolour fish and coral. The beaches along the island's southern and western sides are all good for swimming, but the northern and upper-eastern sides are not as good. The best snorkelling is around **Muri Lagoon**, **Aro'a Beach**, **Titikaveka** and **Tikioki** (Fruits of Rarotonga) in the south of the island, and Black Rock in the northwest. Many of these areas are protected by *ra'ui* (traditional conservation areas).

Snorkelling gear is available from the island's diving operators, and most accommodation also provides free gear for guests' use.

**Cook Island Divers** DIVING
(Map p48; ☎22483; www.cookislandsdivers.com; 'Arorangi) Offers introductory dives in the Tikioki Marine Sanctuary.

**Adventure Cook Islands** DIVING, SNORKELLING
(Map p48; ☎22212; www.adventurecookislands.com; Kavera Rd, 'Arorangi) Excellent company that offers everything from mountain treks and mountain biking through to diving, snorkelling and spearfishing. Gear rental includes sea kayaks, mountain bikes, snorkelling gear and bodyboards.

**Dive Centre** DIVING
(Map p48; ☎20238; www.thedivecentre-rarotonga.com; Aro'a Beach) Also offers special 'Bubblemaker' scuba experiences for kids.

**Dive Rarotonga** DIVING
(Map p48; ☎21873; www.diverarotonga.com; 'Arorangi) See the website for a map of Rarotonga's dive sites.

**Pacific Divers** DIVING, SNORKELLING
(Map p48; ☎22450; www.pacificdivers.co.ck; Muri Beach) Also offers night snorkelling around Muri Lagoon.

### Hiking

The island's mountainous centre is criss-crossed by walking tracks and trails. The top walk is the Cross-Island Track, but there are lots of others to discover. The best guide is *Rarotonga's Mountain Tracks and Plants* by Gerald McCormack and Judith Künzlé, also authors of *Rarotonga's Cross-Island Walk*. Guided hiking trips are offered by Pa's Mountain Walk (p62) and Adventure Cook Islands.

Wear light, breathable clothing and sturdy boots, and check the weather forecast before you go. Tell someone where you're headed and when you expect to return.

**Cross-Island Track** HIKING
(Map p48) Passing through impressive natural scenery, the three- to four-hour hike from the north to south coasts via the 413m **Te Rua Manga** (Needle) is Rarotonga's most popular walk. Don't do the walk in a south–north direction, as the chances of taking a wrong turn are much greater. Wear adequate shoes, take plenty of drinking water, and use mosquito repellent.

Parts of the walk get extremely slippery in wet weather and the upper section is quite rugged and overgrown.

The tourist office recommends walkers join a guided tour, but it's possible to do the walk on your own. Follow the orange track markers carefully, and leave your name and details in the intentions book at the start of the hike. The road to the starting point is south of Avatiu Harbour. Continue on the road up the valley by Avatiu Stream until you reach a sign announcing the beginning of the walk. A private vehicle road continues for about 1km.

From the end of the vehicle road a footpath leads off and after 10 minutes drops down and crosses a small stream. Don't follow the white plastic power-cable track up the valley, but instead pick up the track beside the massive boulder on the ridge to your left, after the stream crossing.

From here, the track climbs steeply up to the Needle (about 45 minutes). At the first sight of the Needle there's a boulder in the middle of the path – a nice place for a rest. A little further on is a T-junction; the Needle is a 10-minute walk to the right. Don't try to climb up to the Needle itself, as there have been several rockfalls and landslides, and there's a long and probably fatal drop on either side of the trail. Follow the track round to the left instead and you'll begin the long, slippery descent towards the south coast.

After 30 minutes the track meets the Papua Stream and follows it downhill, zigzagging back and forth across the stream. After about 45 minutes the track emerges into fernland. Be sure to stick to the main track, as there are several places where minor tracks seem to take off towards the stream but these end at dangerous spots upstream from the waterfall. Another 15 minutes further on, the main track turns back towards the stream, bringing you to the bottom of Wigmore's Waterfall. A dirt road leads from the south coast up to the waterfall. It's about a 15-minute walk to the coast road, where you can flag down the circle-island bus or cool off in the nearby lagoon. You're likely to get muddy and sweaty, so don't make plans for a flash lunch immediately afterwards.

**Pa's Mountain Walk** HIKING

(☎21079; www.pastreks.com; per person NZ$70) A guided trek over the cross-island track is run by the dreadlocked Pa Teuraa. He's also a herbalist, botanist and traditional healer. Pa's cross-island walk runs on Monday to Friday (weather permitting), and he conducts nature walks on Tuesdays and Thursdays. A light lunch is included on both excursions and you'll need moderate fitness for the cross-island walk.

See the website for more information. Note that on some treks, Pa's nephew leads the activity in place of Pa.

### Sailing & Water Sports

Muri Lagoon and the island's south coast are the best places for swimming, windsurfing, sailing and kayaking. Sailing races start at Muri Beach every Saturday and Sunday afternoon from around 1.30pm. Kayaks are readily available to explore the lagoon's deserted *motu* and many hotels provide them for guests' use. Kitesurfing and paddle-boarding are also very popular, and the lagoon's usually benign waters are a great place to learn these sports.

Surfing is in its infancy on Rarotonga. Bodyboarding is popular but local board riders are few and it's not the place to learn as the reef-breaks are steep and fast, and the water is shallow. Adventure Cook Islands (p61) offers bodyboard rentals.

Raro surfing is dangerous – for intermediates and experts only – and too fast for longboarders. The island's north gets swells in the November-to-March cyclone season while the south works best during the May-to-August 'winter'. There are breaks at **Social Centre** in the northwest, off the **Rarotongan Beach Resort**, **Avaavaroa** and **Papua** on the south coast, and **Koromiri**, **Turangi** and **Matavera** on the east side. Since the waves break outside the lagoon it's a long paddle to the action.

**Ariki Holidays** WATER SPORTS

(Map p48; ☎27955; www.arikiholidays.com; Ara Tapu, Muri; kiteboarding lessons NZ$90-350, night paddleboarding per person with/without barbecue dinner NZ$64/49) Kiteboarding and paddle-boarding is the focus at the family-run Ariki Holidays. Kiteboarding lessons take place on nearby Muri Lagoon, and Ariki also offers unique night paddle-boarding tours where waterproof lights suspended under the paddle-boards create a luminous halo in the lagoon's moonlit waters. Tours run Monday to Saturday by appointment for a minimum of two people.

Once you've had your fill of waterborne exercise, Ariki co-owner Julie offers sports, deep tissue and relaxation massage (NZ$80 per hour). She once helped New Zealand's All Blacks win the Rugby World Cup, so you're in safe hands.

**Kitesup** WATER SPORTS

(Map p48; ☎27877; www.kitesup.co; Ara Tapu, Muri Beach; ⏲9am-4pm Mon-Sat) Lessons and gear rental to get you out kitesurfing, windsurfing or paddle-boarding on Muri lagoon. Kitesup also acts as a booking agent for many other activities around the island.

**Learn to Sail** SAILING

(☎73653, 26668; upwind@oyster.co.ck) Learn the ropes with Kiwi Ken Kingsbury on the super-sheltered waters of Muri Lagoon. Kick off with a two-hour lesson (NZ$120), a further one hour sail with Ken (NZ$60), and you can then hire his cute and compact sailboat for NZ$70 per hour. He can also hook you up with a treddlecat, a surprisingly speedy pedal-powered catamaran which he invented.

**Captain Tama's Lagoon Cruizes** WATER SPORTS

(Map p48; ☎27350; www.captaintamas.com; Muri Beach) Beside the Rarotonga Sailing Club, Captain Tama's offers windsurfers for hire (NZ$30), and also offers windsurfing lessons (NZ$50) and paddle-boarding guidance and hire.

**Rarotonga Sailing Club** SAILING

(Map p48; ☎27349; www.sailsrestaurant.co.ck/sailingclub.htm; Muri Beach) Rents out kayaks and small sailing boats.

### Other Sports

**Volleyball** is often played on Muri Beach. **Tennis** courts are available at Edgewater Resort and Rarotongan Beach Resort.

**Golf Course** GOLF
(Map p48; ☎20621; www.rarotonga.nzgolf.net; ⊙8am-2pm Mon-Fri, members only Sat) Rarotonga's nine-hole course is near the airport.

## Tours

### Underwater Viewing

**Captain Tama's Lagoon Cruizes** BOAT TOUR
(☎55002, 27350; www.captaintamas.com; Muri Beach; adult/child NZ$79/40; ⊙11am-3.30pm) The entertaining crew from Captain Tama's runs glass-bottom boat tours, including snorkelling and a barbecue lunch on the tiny *motu* of Koromiri.

**Koka Lagoon Cruises** BOAT TOUR
(Map p48; ☎55769, 27769; www.kokalagooncruises.com; Muri Beach; adult/child NZ$79/40; ⊙10am Sun-Fri) Koka operates cruises around Muri including a barbecue fish lunch and snorkelling with friendly local guides. A percentage of all bookings is donated to support marine conservation.

**Raro Reef Sub** BOAT TOUR
(Map p52; ☎55901; www.raroreefsub.com; Avatiu Harbour; adult/child NZ$65/35; ⊙9am, 11am & 2pm daily) Explore the outer reef on Raro's very own yellow submarine. Descend into the semi-submersible's underwater-viewing area to spy on shape-shifting shoals of giant trevally and the rusting hulk of the 1916 shipwreck of the SS *Maitai*. If you're lucky you might see turtles and eagle rays, and humpback whales are sometimes sighted from July to October.

### Scenic Flights

**Air Rarotonga** SCENIC FLIGHTS
(☎22888; www.airraro.com; min 2, max 3, per person NZ$129; ⊙9am-3pm Mon-Sat) Climb aboard for 20-minute scenic flights, complete with onboard commentary.

### Walking Tours

**Takitumu Conservation Area** BIRDWATCHING
(TCA; ☎55228, 29906; kakerori@tca.co.ck; Ara Tapu, Avarua; guided tour adult/child NZ$50/30) This private forest reserve in Rarotonga's southeast corner runs guided tours where you might see the endangered *kakerori* (Rarotongan flycatcher).

### Whale Watching

Humpback whales visit the Cook Islands from July to October. Most diving, sailing and fishing charters offer whale-watching trips in season. Visit the Cook Islands Whale & Wildlife Centre (p58) to learn more about whales.

### Vehicle Tours

A round-the-island tour is a great way to see Rarotonga, especially if you're only here for a few days.

**Coconut Tours** ADVENTURE TOUR
(Map p48; ☎24004; www.coconuttours.co.ck; per person NZ$150; ⊙Mon-Sat) Lead a convoy of excited wannabe rally drivers on quad bikes through the backroads and streams of the island's rugged interior. Tours run rain or shine and kids from eight to 17 years can ride pillion on the quad bikes with an adult (NZ$190 for adult and child). Sorry, two adults on one bike isn't allowed.

**Raro Buggy Tours** DRIVING TOUR
(☎75730, 74480; 1/2 persons NZ$125/150) Take a tour of Rarotonga – on and off road – in these cool self-drive vehicles that are a cross between a go-kart and a beach buggy. Three-hour tours are conducted as a convoy with the tour leader at the front, and the bright yellow machines are very easy to drive. Tours depart from the Muri Beach Club Hotel.

Drivers need to be at least 18 years of age and have a driver's licence from their home country, and passengers must be at least six years old.

**Raro Safari Tours** TOUR
(☎23629; www.rarosafaritours.co.ck; morning tours adult/child NZ$80/40, afternoon tours adult/child NZ$70/35; ⊙9am & 1.15pm Sun-Fri) Raro's most entertaining excursions are these three-hour expeditions around the island's rugged mountains, inland valleys and historical points of interest in safari-style jeeps. A fresh-fish beach barbecue lunch is included on the morning departures, and costs include pick-up from your accommodation. Say hi to Mr Hopeless for us.

**Raro Tours** TOUR
(Map p48; ☎25325; www.rarotours.co.ck; adult/child NZ$60/30; ⊙10am-1pm Mon-Fri) Join an Island Discovery Tour and explore ancient *marae* and the island's best snorkelling spots.

**Tik-etours** TOUR
(☎53686, 28687; www.tik-etours.com; adult/child from NZ$55/35) Take a Lap of the Island Tour (90 minutes) in a colourful electric tuk-tuk

to get your bearings when you first arrive, or take the longer Highlights of Rarotonga tour (adult/child NZ$79/35) with lots of interesting stops. A fun sunset option is an island bar-hop (per person NZ$45, minimum four people) sampling the best cocktails on Rarotonga.

Airport, restaurant and market transfers are also available.

## Sleeping

Rarotonga has accommodation options to suit all budgets, although postcard-perfect views can come at a premium. High-season prices are quoted.

Renting a house is often the best-value way to visit the island, especially for families. Fully furnished two-bedroom houses cost around NZ$1000 to NZ$1500 per week. Studio units – suitable for two people – begin at around NZ$500 per week. Check out **Bookabach** (www.bookabach.co.nz), **Holiday Houses** (www.holidayhouses.co.nz) and **Rent Raro** (☎55519; www.rentraro.com).

**Muri Beach Shell Bungalows** BUNGALOW $
(Map p48; ☎22275; www.shellbungalows.co.ck; Ara Tapu; d/q NZ$100/110) In a great location 100m from Muri Beach, these two large self-contained bungalows with full kitchens are great value. One has a mezzanine level that sleeps an extra two, and there's a flat that sleeps four.

**Aremango Guesthouse** GUESTHOUSE $
(Map p48; ☎24362; www.aremango.co.ck; Ara Tapu; s/d from NZ$55/69, cottages NZ$140; @ 📶) Aremango has single and double fan-cooled rooms arrayed along a central hallway. The common lounge, bathroom and kitchens are clean and comfortable, and there's a pleasant garden area to relax in. Muri Beach and good restaurants are a short walk away. Check the website for details of Aremango's adjacent private self-contained studio. Bikes and kayaks are also available for use.

**Rarotonga Backpackers** HOSTEL $
(Map p48; ☎21590; www.rarotongabackpackers.com; Ara Tapu; dm NZ$25, s NZ$40, d NZ$50-130, bungalows NZ$85, beach house NZ$120-185; @ 📶 🏊) A west-coast beachfront site offers everything from dorms to fully self-contained suites. There's a pretty central pool, and self-contained units with private verandahs and fabulous views. Around 600m away there are new and good-value garden bungalows, and for families or groups there's the option of another new beach house and absolute beachfront units along Raro's northern coast.

**Aito Apartments** APARTMENT $$
(Map p48; ☎20029; www.aitoapartments.com; Ara Tapu, Muri; d NZ$160) These two modern apartments represent excellent value just a short walk from the cafes, restaurants and water sports of Muri Lagoon. The Cook Island-Tahitian owners are a real delight, and the spotless apartments feature spacious verandahs, designer bedrooms punctuated with Pacific textiles, and lovely bathrooms trimmed with natural river stones.

Fire up the barbecue, prepare loads of tropical fruit in the self-contained kitchen, and you'll quickly ease into island time.

**Avana Waterfront Apartments** APARTMENT $$
(Map p48; ☎20836; www.avanawaterfront.co.ck; Ara Tapu, Avana; apt NZ$192-370; ❄ 📶 🏊) Tucked away down a quiet side road, this complex consists of 10 stylish self-contained apartments, some with front-row views of the spectacular sprawl of Avana Lagoon. There's a swimming pool if the ocean waters don't appeal – unlikely on most days – and a private jetty for island kayaking trips or fishing expeditions. There's a five-night minimum stay.

**Ariki Bungalows** BUNGALOW $$
(Map p48; ☎27955; www.arikiholidays.com; Ara Tapu, Muri; d NZ$130; 📶 🏊) These three modern units share a breezy location a short uphill walk from Muri Lagoon. Each of the three units is decorated in natural wood and bright colours, and are self-contained with a small kitchenette. There's an exceedingly laid-back bar and a plunge pool, and Ariki also offers a Polynesian dinner for guests most weekends (NZ$15).

The good-value accommodation is worthy of its own recommendation, but Ariki Bungalows is also a great option if you're planning to kiteboard or paddle-board (p62) while on Rarotonga.

**Kura's Kabanas** BUNGALOW $$
(Map p48; ☎27010; www.kkabanas.co.ck; Ara Tapu; units & cabanas NZ$150; ❄ @ 📶) Shady palms, Muri Lagoon views and a glorious china-white beach are just steps from the doors of Kura's airy timber-framed cabanas. Two larger 1st-floor family studios can sleep four (children under 12 free). Fully equipped kitchens, queen beds, TVs and a great location make this hard to beat for the price.

Check the website for details of Kura's two self-contained villas at the nearby Paku's Retreat (NZ$120 to NZ$200).

**Palm Grove** BUNGALOW $$
(Map p48; 20002; www.palmgrove.net; Ara Tapu, Vaimaanga; d NZ$225-345; ) Set among lawns and coconut palms on one of the south coast's best beaches, Palm Grove has a reputation for being somewhere that regular guests return to year after year. They're lured by the spacious bungalows – and equally expansive decks with lagoon views – and a welcoming vibe that's enhanced by features like shared barbecue facilities and a compact pool.

Across the road, Palm Grove's Yellow Hibiscus is a handy restaurant and bar with live music on a Friday night. Rates include a daily breakfast buffet.

**Aro'a Beachside Inn** BUNGALOW $$
(Map p48; 22166; www.aroabeach.com; Ara Tapu, 'Arorangi; d NZ$205-290; ) Choose from beachside units or ocean-view units at this super-friendly spot on Rarotonga's sunset-friendly west coast. Rates include a tropical breakfast and free use of everything you need to explore the nearby reef. After you've invested holiday energy in kayaking, paddleboarding or snorkelling, kick back in the Shipwreck Hut bar.

**Manea Beach Villas** BUNGALOW $$
(Map p48; 25336; www.maneabeachrarotonga.com; Muri Beach; bungalows NZ$210-230, house NZ$400-590; ) Down a quiet Muri road, Manea Beach combines spotless one-bedroom bungalows – some with lagoon views – and three larger three-bedroom houses that are perfect for families or groups of friends. The decor is a winning combination of modern and tropical, and there's a pleasant shared pool overlooking nearby Muri Lagoon.

**Sunhaven Beach Bungalows** BUNGALOW $$
(Map p48; 28465; www.mysunhaven.com; Ara Tapu; studios & bungalows NZ$240-330; ) Sunhaven offers good value in some of the largest self-contained rooms on the island, set around a beachfront swimming pool on a quiet stretch of west-coast beach. The bungalows are sparkling clean and simply finished, with white-tile floors, cane furniture and functional fixtures. There's also an on-site licensed cafe, and lagoon kayaking and snorkelling on tap.

Children must be 15 years and older.

**Bella Beach Bungalows** BUNGALOW $$
(Map p48; 26004; www.shekinahhomes.com; Ara Tapu; bungalows NZ$180) With the waves all but licking the stilts of these four functional units at Titikaveka on the island's south side, they're about as close to the beach as you can get. Inside are tiled floors, kitchens, small bathrooms and comfortable king-sized beds, while outside are large sundecks overlooking the beach and lagoon.

★ **Sea Change** BOUTIQUE HOTEL $$$
(Map p48; 22532; www.sea-change-rarotonga.com; Ara Tapu; villas NZ$450-950; ) Many of Rarotonga's boutique hotels look to this place as a benchmark. The impeccably appointed free-standing thatched villas have fabulously appointed interiors with luxury king-size four-poster beds, entertainment systems, flat-screen TVs and private outdoor pools. The open-plan villas are finished in earthy tones and traditional materials, offsetting the contemporary design elements.

★ **Ikurangi Eco Retreat** BUNGALOW $$$
(Map p48; 25288; www.ikurangi.com; Titama Rd, Matavera; villas NZ$249, luxury tents NZ$359-449; ) Glamping style comes to Rarotonga at Ikurangi Eco Retreat. Accommodation is either in luxury safari-style tents – each with their own spacious deck and private bathroom – or in well-equipped villas. Luxe highlights include top of the range bed linen, and there's a focus on sustainability – including solar electricity – with the design, construction and management of the property.

The inland location has excellent views of dramatic Mt Ikurangi, and is handily placed midway between Avarua and Muri. Free use of bicycles for guests, and breakfast is included.

★ **Beach Place** RENTAL HOUSE $$$
(Map p48; www.airbnb.com/rooms/870875; Ara Tapu, Tikioki Beach; d NZ$280) With an absolute beachfront location, this spacious heritage villa has wooden floors, wraparound decks, and a winning combination of a well-equipped kitchen with lagoon views and a chic bathroom with a clawfoot bath. One double room and a pair of bunks make it good for families, but it's also a quietly romantic spot for holidaying couples.

It's just a 10-minute stroll to Muri Beach to the north, and there's good snorkelling at Tikioki to the south. Out front is good for swimming and for lazy days paddling in the property's colourful kayaks.

**Black Rock Villas** VILLA $$$
(Map p48; ☎21233; www.blackrockvillas.com; d NZ$350; ❄📶🏊) With an infinity pool and views towards Rarotonga's rugged northwest coast, the two self-contained apartments at Black Rock Villas are spacious, breezy and decked out with colourful local art. Tropical blooms frame the property's lovely gardens, and each villa has two bedrooms and two bathrooms, making them ideal for families or couples travelling together. Nearby is the excellent Tuoro Cafe.

**Pacific Resort** RESORT $$$
(Map p48; ☎20427; www.pacificresort.com; units NZ$430-1180; ❄@📶🏊) Right on Muri Beach and shaded by palm trees, the Pacific Resort's 64 self-contained units are smart and elegant, harnessing local elements of design and decor – the best have sitting rooms and private verandahs. Amenities include the beachfront Barefoot Bar and the open-air Sandals Restaurant. Spa and beauty services are on tap so you can look your best in paradise.

**Apartments Kakera** APARTMENT $$$
(Map p48; ☎20532; www.apartmentskakera.com; Ara Tapu; apt NZ$245-360; ❄@📶🏊) With three huge modern apartments blending sleek modern decor with lovely Polynesian touches, Kakera also boasts a long list of eco-credentials. The split-level apartments have high ceilings, private courtyard gardens with plunge pools, full kitchens and flat-screen TVs and entertainment systems. An excellent choice for travelling families.

### WE DO

Many couples come to the Cook Islands to get married as it's a very romantic destination. Most hotels and resorts offer wedding packages and there are also several specialist wedding companies. Cook Islands marriages are legally binding worldwide. You'll need a copy of your birth certificate and passport. If you've been married before, you'll also need your divorce papers or a death certificate. The Marriage Registrar requires a minimum of three working days before the wedding day to issue a marriage licence, so you need to be resident in the country for that long before the nuptials. If you and your loved one simply can't wait, an additional NZ$50 fee can be paid to speed up the process.

**Muri Beachcomber** RESORT $$$
(Map p48; ☎21022; www.beachcomber.co.ck; Ara Tapu; d units NZ$305-460; ❄@📶🏊) With a choice of garden and sea-view units and luxury villas overlooking lovely grounds and a tropical lily pond, the Muri Beachcomber has a relaxed family-friendly village feel. The accommodation is modern – clean lines and tasteful appointments – and on-site facilities include guest lounge, laundry, pétanque court, free kayak use and snorkelling gear.

**Little Polynesian** BOUTIQUE HOTEL $$$
(Map p48; ☎24280; www.littlepolynesian.com; Ara Tapu; villas NZ$680-1140; ❄@📶🏊) The 10 beachfront and four garden villas at Little Polynesian are a superb blend of traditional Polynesian design (with traditional Mangaian coconut-fibre sennit binding) and modern architecture, and the uninterrupted lagoon view from the foyer, pool and villas is sublime. Check online for substantial discounts.

**Magic Reef Bungalows** BUNGALOW $$$
(Map p48; ☎27404; www.magicreef.co.nz; Ara Tapu; d NZ$325-430; ❄@📶🏊) On a golden stretch of sand on the sunset side of the island, Magic Reef features tastefully decorated bungalows with four-poster beds, fans and air-con, galley kitchens, private outdoor showers and separate bathrooms with bathtubs.

## Eating

★ **Mooring** SANDWICHES $
(Map p48; Avana Lagoon; sandwiches NZ$13, salads $19; ⏰9.30am-3.30pm Mon-Fri, noon-4pm Sun) Tuck into tuna and *mahimahi* sandwiches on grilled Turkish bread at this funky blue shipping container on the edge of Avana Lagoon. Variations include Tijuana Tuna or Cajun Spiced, and other goodies include Rustys – marinated chicken pieces with pawpaw salsa. Refresh with a fruit smoothie or a *nu* (fresh coconut), and park yourself with views of Avana's sparkling waters.

**Charlie's Cafe & Beach Hire** CAFE $
(Map p48; ☎28055; chosking@oyster.net.ck; Ara Tapu, Titikaveka; snacks NZ$10-12; ⏰10am-4pm Mon-Sat, from noon Sun) The biggest fish sandwiches on the island, fruit smoothies, and freshly baked muffins are all available at this family-run beachside shipping container that also doubles as a rental centre for gear to explore the nearby reef. Kayaks, paddleboards, and snorkelling gear are all available. Stay out there for long enough, and you might even be hungry enough to finish your sandwich.

**Cook Islands Coffee Company** CAFE $
(Map p48; Ara Tapu, Matavera; coffee from NZ$3; from 7.30am Sun-Fri) Kiwi expat Neil Dearlove blends and roasts gourmet coffee at his home in Matavera. Many locals stop in for their fix on the way into work or pick up a few fresh croissants. If the orange road cone is outside the shop, Neil is open and dispensing perfect espressos and flat whites. Ground coffee is also available for takeaway.

**Deli-licious** CAFE $
(Map p48; www.delilicious.net; Ara Tapu, Muri Beach; lunch NZ$10-19; 8am-3.30pm Mon-Sat; ) Right in the heart of the Muri, Deli-licious serves up cooked breakfasts, and salads and sandwiches for lunch. Excellent coffee is served along with shakes and smoothies. This place is always buzzing and has an alfresco deck. Try the smoked marlin pie, with local fish caught from just beyond the lagoon.

**Muri Night Market** MARKET $
(Map p48; Ara Tapu, Muri Beach; mains NZ$7-12; 5-8pm Tue-Thu & Sun) Welcome to the biggest game in Muri for four nights a week. There's occasional live music to partner seafood curries, garlic prawns, and tuna with papaya salad, and dessert of a slab of coconut and chocolate pie is mandatory. It's OK to bring your own wine or beer, and the meals are so big you'll probably need a lie-down afterwards,.

**Vili's** FAST FOOD $
(Map p48; Ara Tapu, Muri; burgers NZ$7-12; 8am-8pm) Colourful outdoor tables, winning smiles from the kitchen team, and rocking Pacific ukulele beats combine at this humble spot on Muri's main drag. The fish burger is massive, so consider taking one of the beach cruiser bicycles for a spin (NZ$10 per day), and balancing the holiday ledger between virtue and vice. Of course the fish and chips (NZ$10) are briny-fresh.

**Flying Boat Fish & Chips** FISH & CHIPS $
(Map p48; 22230; Ara Tapu, Game Fishing Club, Tupapa; snacks & mains NZ$7-20; 11am-9pm Mon-Sat) Tuck into Raro's best fish and chips at this funky reconfigured fishing boat. The lagoon's waters are just metres away, and cheap-as-chips drinks are available from the bar at the adjacent Game Fishing Club. The club's a good place to drop by if you're looking to watch live rugby featuring New Zealand's mighty All Blacks. Phone orders are also welcome.

**Fruits of Rarotonga** CAFE $
(Map p48; 21509; Ara Tapu, Tikioki; snacks & smoothies NZ$5-9; 10am-4pm Mon-Sat) Homemade jams and tropical chutneys are divine at this shop opposite Tikioki beach, but it's good for cakes and fruit juices too. Kayaks are available for hire (NZ$5 per hour), and you can leave gear here when you go snorkelling in the lagoon. Don't leave Rarotonga without recharging on a creamy pawpaw-and-banana smoothie. Opening hours can be somewhat flexible.

**Wigmore's Superstore** SUPERMARKET $
(Map p48; Ara Tapu, Vaima'anga; 6am-10pm) The south coast's only proper grocery store is more expensive than Avarua's supermarkets. It's the only large supermarket that trades on Sunday though, and it has a small liquor store. Drop in on a Sunday afternoon for lots of still-warm freshly baked local produce.

**Super Brown** SUPERMARKET $
(Map p48; Ara Tapu, Tupapa; 24hr) Super Brown is Raro's only all-night convenience store and petrol station, with a fair selection of beer, wine, groceries and takeaway food.

★**Vaima Restaurant & Bar** POLYNESIAN $$
(Map p48; 26123; www.vaimarestaurant.com; Ara Tapu, Vaima'anga; mains NZ$28-34; 4-9pm Mon-Sat, dining from 6pm) Perched near a sandy beach on the island's south coast, Vaima is one of Rarotonga's best eateries and bookings are essential. The stylish dining room features local artworks, and there's a beachfront patio and breezy outside terrace. Combine Pacific cuisine with the sand between your toes for a quintessential Raro experience. Partner the seafood curry with a Matutu Mai lager.

Pizza is also available for takeaway from 4pm to 7pm, and there are happy-hour drinks deals from 4pm to 6pm.

**Waterline Bar & Grill** INTERNATIONAL $$
(Map p48; 22161; www.waterline-restaurant.com; Ara Tapu, 'Arorangi; mains NZ$20-36; 11.30am-2.30pm Tue-Fri, from 6pm Tue-Sat) Welcome to the South Pacific restaurant of your dreams with a rustic beachfront pavilion and absolute waterfront tables and chairs. Book in for around 30 minutes before sunset to enjoy a cocktail before graduating to a restaurant table for calamari, prawns and steak. Lunchtime is a more informal offering, with BLT sandwiches and kebabs.

**LBV** CAFE $$

(Map p48; 28619; Ara Tapu, Muri Beach; lunch mains $21-27, dinner mains NZ$28-32; 7.30am-late Tue-Fri, 7.30am-5pm Sat-Mon) Come for a morning combo of an espresso and a cinnamon doughnut or chocolate brioche – LBV is the best bakery for many miles – and then return for a more leisurely lunch of Caprese salad, or dinner of seafood paella. Cooked breakfasts are also available, and there's a good drinks list with local beers and wines from New Zealand.

The setting, in a restored colonial house nestled in gardens and lawns, is very peaceful, and local art is regularly displayed for sale. Get the kids burning off some holiday energy by running around on the grass or getting active in the small playground. Bookings are recommended for dinner.

**Sails Restaurant** FUSION $$

(Map p48; 27349; www.sailsrestaurant.co.ck; Muri Beach; breakfast & lunch mains NZ$16-25, dinner mains NZ$25-34; 8am-late) Overlooking the sands and sea of Muri Lagoon, breezy Sails is an open-air bistro-bar serving light breakfast and lunchtime fare, and heartier evening meals daily. Try the island-style fries with the yellowfin tuna *ika mata*. Bookings are recommended for dinner, and brunch is available from 9.30am on the weekend. The attached iSOBAR is a fun place for a few drinks.

**Tuoro Cafe** CAFE $$

(Map p48; 21233; www.blackrockvillas.com; Black Rock Villas, Nika'o; tapas NZ$10-18, mains NZ$22; 11am-3pm Tue-Fri & Sun) Asian-inspired tapas – try the steamed pork dumplings – combine with fish, chicken and steak lunch dishes at this welcoming elevated spot on Raro's northwestern coast. There's a good selection of beer, gin and tonics are served with a generous addition of the good stuff, and there are top views from the sunny deck to the landmark of Black Rock.

**Kikau Hut** INTERNATIONAL $$

(Map p48; 26860; Ara Tapu, 'Arorangi; mains NZ$21-35; 6-11pm) Candles and dim lighting make this circular restaurant in 'Arorangi a great place for an evening meal. The international cuisine is well prepared and the welcome is friendly and convivial. There's regular live music and a breezy relaxed atmosphere. Just come as you are and fast forward to an easygoing holiday state of mind.

**Saltwater Cafe** CAFE $$

(Map p48; Ara Tapu, Titikaveka; mains NZ$19-28; 10am-6pm Sun-Thu) This roadside eatery on the south coast at Titikaveka is a great place for lunch or a cold drink. The menu includes pad Thai and garlic prawns, and there's also cold beer and punchy tropical cocktails. The homemade cheesecake ($10) is excellent, and it's a handy spot on Sundays when not much else is open.

The kitchen normally closes around 2.30pm, but coffee, cocktails and cakes are served until 6pm. If you're traversing the island by scooter, you've just reached the halfway point from Avarua.

**Hidden Spirit Café & Grill** CAFE $$

(Map p48; 22796; www.hiddenspirit.net; Ara Tapu, Titikaveka; mains NZ$18-26; 10am-4pm Mon-Sat) Set in the verdant surroundings of the Maire Nui Gardens, this cafe offers delicious cakes and desserts – try the lemon meringue pie (NZ$16) – and healthy salads. Lunches are also available, and afterwards you can take a relaxing stroll around the gardens (NZ$5).

**Rickshaw** ASIAN $$

(Map p48; www.facebook.com/TheRickshawRarotonga; Are Tapu, Muri; mains NZ$20-24; 5.30-10pm Mon-Sat) Variations on dishes you enjoyed in Bangkok and Hanoi feature at this pan-Asian eatery. Reserve a spot on the breezy deck and feast on beef rendang, Vietnamese squid or Singapore chilli prawns. Covering lots of culinary bases, the flavours aren't always totally authentic, but considering you're dining on a far-flung Pacific island, the Rickshaw's still worth a visit. Bookings recommended.

**La Casita** TEX-MEX $$

(Map p48; 20693; www.facebook.com/LaCasitaRarotonga; Are Tapu, Muri; mains NZ$14-21; 5.30pm-11pm Mon-Sat, 11.30am-2pm Sat) Combining Tex-Mex (burritos, quesadillas and enchiladas) with Italian (pizza and pasta), La Casita is a bustling and colourful spot that's a reliable standby after a busy day snorkelling, paddle-boarding, or just taking it easy on nearby Muri Lagoon. The pescado tacos come crammed with chunks of local fish. Bookings recommended.

**Progressive Dining** POLYNESIAN $$$

(20639; per person NZ$90; dinner Mon & Thu) Eat your way around the island during this progressive dinner held in locals' homes. The relaxed, easygoing occasions run to three courses across four to five hours and include live music and visits to gardens and plantations. It's a great way to meet the locals and tuck into dishes including *ika mata* and pawpaw salad.

Booking ahead is essential, and note that dinners only take place when there are sufficient numbers.

## Drinking & Entertainment

**Shipwreck Hut** BAR
(Map p48; Ara Tapu, 'Arorangi; ⏲4-9pm) The Shipwreck Hut is a wonderfully rustic spot with an absolute waterfront location. There's regular live music, great pub meals and barbecue dinners, and it's a top west-coast location to watch Rarotonga's incredible sunsets. Come along on a Saturday night for the dulcet tones of Jake Numanga. He's the ukulele whiz who welcomed you when you flew in.

**iSOBAR** BAR
(Map p48; Muri Beach; ⏲3-10pm Mon-Sat) Twelve-buck happy-hour cocktails and regular 3pm to 6pm DJ sets from Wednesday to Saturday make this a top lagoon-side spot to ease into another Raro evening. Live bands often raise the tropical tempo on Friday nights. There's also good dining in the associated Sails Restaurant.

## Shopping

**Mike Tavioni** ARTS, CRAFTS
(Map p48; ☎24003; Ara Metua, Atupa; ⏲Mon-Sat) Visit the workshop of Rarotonga's most renowned sculptor and carver on the back road near Avarua. See his stone carvings at the Punanga Nui Market and the National Culture Centre.

**M&M Ukalele & Crafts** MUSIC
(Map p48; ☎20662; www.facebook.com/mmukalele682; Ara Metua; ⏲9.30am-4pm Mon-Fri) M&M sells handmade ukuleles and has a great selection of local music on CD. Phone ahead to make sure it's open.

**Prison Craft Shop** ARTS, CRAFTS
(Map p48; 'Arorangi; ⏲8.30am-3pm Mon-Fri) A good spot for unique gifts including handmade ukuleles.

**Tivaevae Collectables** ARTS, CRAFTS
(www.tivaevaecollectables.com; Nikao; ⏲9am-4pm) Visit for beautiful Cook Islands *tivaevae* (hand-sewn quilted fabrics) harnessing traditional designs such as bedspreads and bed linen, but also reworked as cushion covers, tablecloths and women's clothing. Shopping online and worldwide shipping are both possible if you're concerned about excess baggage.

**Art Studio** ARTS, CRAFTS
(Map p48; www.theartstudiocookislands.com; 'Arorangi; ⏲10am-5pm Mon-Fri) Contemporary art from owners Ian and Kay George combines with works from other Pacific artists. Handpainted or printed textiles are available, as are spectacular wall-covering screen-printed photographs.

**Tokerau Jim** JEWELLERY
(Map p48; ☎24305; www.tokeraujim.com; ⏲9am-3.30pm Mon-Fri) Located in Matavera, Tokerau Jim does beautiful and incredibly fine carvings on pearls and pearl shell. On



### ISLAND NIGHTS

Rarotonga's traditional form of evening entertainment is the Island Night – a spectacular showcase combining traditional dance and music *(karioi)* with a lavish buffet of local food *(kai)*. Dancing, drumming and singing are always on show, and fire juggling, acrobatics and storytelling are often thrown into the mix.

Island Nights are held regularly at the large resorts, and every night except Sunday you can catch a show somewhere on the island. Extravagant affairs are featured at the **Pacific Resort** (p66), **Edgewater Resort** (☎25435), **Crown Beach Resort** (☎23953) and the **Rarotongan Beach Resort** (☎25800). You'll pay between NZ$15 and NZ$35 for the show only, or NZ$55 to NZ$99 for the show and buffet.

On Monday, Wednesday and Friday nights, **Highland Paradise** (p58) offers a NZ$99 show that includes transport, a cocktail and an *umukai* (underground oven) feast. Another *umukai* is provided at **Te Vara Nui Village** (p59) on Tuesday, Thursday and Saturday nights. On Thursday and Friday nights the **Staircase Restaurant & Bar** (p55) features a show costing just NZ$35 including food (NZ$5 for show only).

Ask the tourist information office in Avarua for its handout listing the many Island Nights on offer around the island from Monday to Saturday.

Saturday mornings you'll find him at the Punanga Nui market.

**Turtles & Ocean/Earth** CLOTHING
(Map p48; Avatiu; ⏲8am-4pm Mon-Fri) Interesting designs spoofing global brands and also that Cook Islands rugby shirt you've always wanted.

**Perfumes of Rarotonga** GIFTS
(Map p48; www.perfumes.co.ck; ⏲9am-4.30pm Mon-Sat) Near the airport, this place makes its own perfumes, soaps, liqueurs and scented oils. There's another **outlet** (Map p52; Cooks Corner Arcade, Avarua; ⏲9am-4.30pm Mon-Sat) in Cook's Corner Arcade in central Avarua that also sells excellent fudge full of tropical fruit and coconut flavours.

**Croc Tatau** TATTOOS
(Map p48; ☎76384; www.facebook.com/croctatau; Muri) Englishman 'Croc' is the only man on Rarotonga crafting *tata'u* (tattoos) the traditional way, using pigment and hand tools. Check out his blog (www.croctatau.wordpress.com) for information and photos. He's sometimes off the island working in Europe, so email him before you travel. You'll find other local tattooists offering traditional designs but modern techniques at Avarua's weekly Punanga Nui Market.

## ℹ Information

**Bluesky Teleshop** (Map p48; www.bluesky.co.ck; Ara Tapu, Muri, opposite Pacific Resort; ⏲10am-6pm Mon-Fri, noon-4pm Sun; 📶) Internet and wi-fi hotspot and data sales.

**Cook Islands Pharmacy** (Map p48; Ara Tapu, Muri Beach; ⏲10am-5pm Mon-Fri, 10am-2pm Sun) Convenient location in Muri.

**Deli-licious** (Map p48; Ara Tapu, Muri Beach; ⏲8am-3.30pm Mon-Fr; 📶) Wi-fi internet access.

**Dr Uka's Surgery** (Map p48; ☎23680; Ara Tapu, Muri, opposite Pacific Resort; ⏲9.30am-1.30pm Mon-Thu, 9.30am-noon Fri) Handy for minor accidents and ailments if you're staying around Muri Beach.

**Hospital** (Map p48; ☎22664; ⏲emergency 24hr) On a steep hill behind the golf course.

**Island Hopper Vacations** (Map p48; ☎22576; www.islandhoppervacations.com; Turama House, Nika'o) Has good airfare-and-accommodation packages and deals to the outer islands.

**Kavera Central** (Map p48; Kavera; ⏲8am-4pm Mon-Sat) Internet access.

**Outpatient Clinic** (Map p48; ☎20065; ⏲8am-4pm Mon-Fri) About 1km east of Avarua. Also has emergency dental services.

# AITUTAKI

POP 2035 / AREA 18.3 SQ KM

Aitutaki, the Cooks' second-most-visited island, curls gently around one of the South Pacific's most stunning lagoons. The aqua water, foaming breakers around the perimeter reef and broad sandy beaches of its many small deserted islets make for a glorious scene. From the air or on the water, Aitutaki will take your breath away.

It's just 45 minutes by air from Rarotonga but it feels like another world. Although there are some impressive, plush resorts, this island is slower and much less commercialised. Many visitors come on Air Rarotonga's day tour or opt to stay at upmarket resorts, but there are still good-value accommodation options, and it's worth spending a few days to slow down to island time.

Sunday is solemnly observed as the day of prayer and rest. Take the opportunity to see a local church service, as the singing is spine-tingling. Sunday flights from Rarotonga continue to inspire protest from elements of the island's religious community, and you may see a few banners and placards when you arrive.

Aitutaki is shaped like a curved fishhook, and you'll fly into the north of the island near O'otu Beach and the private Aitutaki Lagoon Resort. On the west side are most of the hotels and Arutanga, the island's main town. On the east coast are the small villages of Tautu, Vaipae and Vaipeka. The *motu* around the edge of Aitutaki's lagoon are uninhabited.

## History

Legend tells that Ru from 'Avaiki (Ra'iatea in French Polynesia) arrived at Aitutaki by *vaka* (canoe). He came with four wives, four brothers and their wives, and 20 royal maidens at the Akitua *motu* (now the Aitutaki Lagoon Resort).

Aitutaki's first European visitor was Captain William Bligh, who arrived on the *Bounty* on 11 April 1789 (17 days before the famous mutiny). In 1821 John Williams left Tahitian preachers Papeiha and Vahapata here to convert the islanders to Christianity. Charles Darwin passed by on the 1835 *Beagle* voyage, and in the 1850s Aitutaki become a favourite port of call for

## Aitutaki

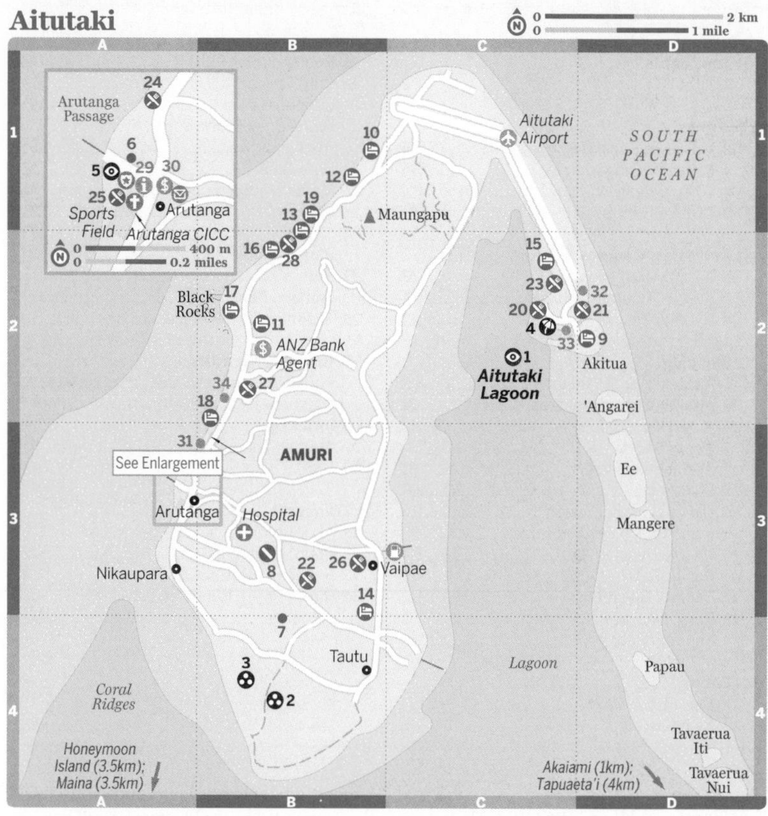


whaling ships. During WWII American soldiers arrived to build two long runways, and in the 1950s the lagoon was used as a refuelling stopover for the Tasman Empire Air Line's (TEAL; Air New Zealand's predecessor) luxurious 'coral route' across the Pacific, flown by Solent flying boats. Hollywood acting legends John Wayne and Cary Grant were just two of the celebrities who spent time on Akaiami *motu* while their Solent was refuelled. Most lagoon cruises stop at Akaiami where the crumbling foundations of TEAL's absolute waterfront terminal are still visible.

## Sights

The lagoon may be what draws the tourists here, but Aitutaki's ancient *marae* are also notable for their large stones and cultural significance. **Marae Orongo** (Map p71) is today in the main village of Arutanga. The main road runs through another large *marae*, and on the inland road between Nikaupara and Tautu are the islands' most magnificent *marae* – including **Tokangarangi** (Map p71) and **Te Poaki O Rae** (Map p71) – mostly reclaimed by the jungle.

**Arutanga** TOWN

Compared to Rarotonga, Arutanga, Aitutaki's only town, seems astonishingly quiet, with few signs of life even on weekdays when the shops are open. The island's main harbour is by the Orongo Centre. The lovely weather-beaten **CICC** church near the Administration Centre was built in 1828, making it the oldest in the Cooks. Beautifully restored in 2010, the church has lovely stained-glass windows, fine carved-wood panelling and an old anchor precariously suspended from the ceiling.

Try to attend a service on the first Sunday of every month, when Aitutaki's female parishioners wear pristine white dresses.

## Aitutaki



**Maungapu** VIEWPOINT

The 30-minute hike to the top of Maungapu (124m), Aitutaki's highest peak, provides splendid views over the entire atoll and the sapphire-blue lagoon. The track starts off pretty gently opposite the bungalows of Paradise Cove, but gets more challenging towards the summit.

★ **Aitutaki Lagoon** LAGOON

(Map p71) Aitutaki's stunning lagoon, brimming with marine life and ringed by 15 palm-covered *motu* (islets), is a South Pacific treasure. **Maina** (Little Girl) offers superb snorkelling and is home to the red-tailed tropicbird, once prized for its crimson feathers. Nearby is the wreck of cargo freighter *Alexander,* which ran aground in the 1930s. **Tapuaeta'i** (One Foot Island) is the best-known *motu,* fringed by white beaches and divided from its neighbour, **Tekopua**, by a deepwater channel that's teeming with tropical fish.

Akaiami *motu* is where the old TEAL flying boats landed to refuel on the trans-Pacific 'Coral Route' between Fiji, Samoa and Tahiti – the remnants of the old jetty can still be seen.

## Activities

The best swimming, snorkelling and beaches are around the *motu,* especially near Maina, accessible by boat. Just south of Black Rocks, on the main island's northwest coast, you can walk out to the outer reef on a coral causeway that starts 50m from the shore. The nicest swimming beaches on the main island are **O'otu Beach** (Map p71) and the wharves at **Vaipae** and **Tautu**. The island's east coast is mainly shallow mud and mangrove swamp.

Scuba diving is fantastic in Aitutaki. The visibility is great, and features include drop-offs, multilevels, wall dives and cave systems. Many divers ask to dive on the wreck of the *Alexander,* but it sits in a mere metre of water and is just as suitable for snorkellers.

In recent years the popularity of kitesurfing has really soared, and the skies and beaches around Honeymoon Island are often dotted with kitesurfers zipping along in robust tropical breezes.

Check out www.aitutaki.net, www.cookislands.travel/aitutaki/ and www.aitutaki.com for more activities listings.

**Bubbles Below** DIVING
(Map p71; ☎31537; www.diveaitutaki.com; 1/2 dives NZ$105/170, PADI discover/open-water course NZ$170/550) Offers dive trips and courses. The entertaining manager Onu (Turtle) Hewett really knows the waters surrounding Aitutaki.

**Wet & Wild** KITESURFING
(☎75980, 56558; www.wetnwild-aitutaki.com) This versatile outfit runs its own kitesurfing centre on Honeymoon Island – including gear hire and lessons for beginners – and also offers marine adventures as diverse as snorkelling, fishing, whale watching and spearfishing.

## Tours

Most tour operators on Aitutaki don't have offices. Arrange a cruise by calling the operator or ask the people you're staying with to arrange it. The operator will collect you from your hotel.

### Fishing

**Aitutaki Game Fishing Club** FISHING
(Map p71; ☎31379; 5pm-midnight Wed-Sat) Find out about the fishing scene at Aitutaki Game Fishing Club, by the wharf in Arutanga. It's also a good place for a cold beer from 5pm from Wednesday to Saturday. Bonefish are among the fastest and most exciting fighting fish in the world, and Aitutaki's lagoon has some of the biggest on the planet.

**Black Pearl Charters** FISHING
(☎31125; www.blackpearlaitutaki.com) Hooking wahoo, giant trevally and *mahimahi* from NZ$180 per person. Spearfishing trips in the lagoon (half-/full day NZ$250/500) are also available.

**Bonefish E2** FISHING
(☎52077, 31686; www.e2sway.com) Local guide Itu Davey has been hooking Aitutaki's bonefish since he was a boy. Half-/full-day charters per two people are NZ$350/450.

**Slice of Heaven Charters** BOATING
(☎71847, 31747; www.sliceofheavencharters.com; half-day deep-sea fishing per person from NZ$180, lagoon tours for 2 people from NZ$350) Marine adventures ranging from deep-sea fishing excursions catching wahoo, *mahimahi*, barracuda and tuna, to lagoon trips incorporating island visits, snorkelling and lunch. Full-day combinations of deep-sea fishing and exploring the lagoon are also available.

### Lagoon Cruises

For many travellers an Aitutaki lagoon cruise is a Cook Islands highlight. There are several operators that cruise around the *motu* and snorkelling spots. All provide snorkelling gear, a barbecue fish lunch and a stop at Tapuaeta'i (One Foot Island) – remember to take your passport to get it stamped at the One Foot Island 'post office' for NZ$2. You can also send Aitutaki postcards to the folks back home.

**Aitutaki Adventures** CRUISE
(☎31171; captpuna@aitutaki.net.ck; adult/child NZ$99/45; ⊙10am-4pm Sun-Fri) Lagoon cruises with a family-owned company including snorkelling, fish-feeding and a terrific lunch on One Foot Island. Most trips also stop at Honeymoon Island to see the kiteboarders soar like frigatebirds.

**Bishop's Cruises** BOAT TOUR
(☎31009; www.bishopscruises.com; per person NZ$95; ⊙ Mon-Sat) Lagoon tours visit Maina, Moturakau and Tapuaeta'i, and there are also honeymoon cruises and *motu* drop-offs.

**Kia-Orana Cruises** CRUISE
(☎73750; www.kiaoranacruise.com; per person NZ$125; ⊙Sun-Fri) The main Seven Wonders of Paradise Cruise from 9.30am to 3.30pm visits Maina, Moturakau, Honeymoon Island and Tapuaeta'i. Sunset snorkelling excursions from noon to 6pm are also available.

**Vaka Cruise** CRUISE
(☎31398; www.aitutaki.net; per person NZ$125; ⊙10am-4pm daily) Cruises are on a Polynesian-style catamaran, the *Titi Ai Tonga* (Wind from the South), which has a roof and onboard bar. Look forward to lots of onboard entertainment and the company of daytrippers from Rarotonga.

**Teking** CRUISE
(☎31582; www.tekingtours.com) Offers a 'Snorkeling Safari' lagoon cruise (per person NZ$119) and a romantic sunset cruise for two with champagne (NZ$269). Expect tasty lunches and a healthy dose of Aitutaki humour.

### Other Tours

**Aitutaki Punarei Cultural Tours** CULTURAL TOUR
(Map p71; ☎50877, 31757; www.facebook.com/Punarei; adult/child NZ$80/40; ⊙9am-1pm Mon, Wed & Fri) Local guide Ngaa Pureariki is a

keen archaeology buff, and this island experience visits the Punarei Cultural Village he has established to showcase traditional structures before the arrival of Christianity. Tours also incorporate a visit to an ancient *marae*, an *umukai* lunch, and Ngaa is a passionate advocate and learned source of information about earlier centuries on Aitutaki.

## Sleeping

**Matriki Beach Huts** BUNGALOW **$**
(Map p71; ☎31564; www.matrikibeachhuts.com; s/d NZ$79/99) These knocked-up beachfront fibro shacks with mural-painted walls and one self-contained garden unit comprise this most delightfully ramshackle place to stay. The split-level huts share toilet facilities but are otherwise self-contained with kitchenettes and showers and the most brilliant location. Matriki runs snorkelling trips outside the lagoon reef and can arrange fishing charters and activities.

**Gina's Garden Lodges** LODGE **$**
(Map p71; ☎31058; www.ginasaitutakidesire.com; s/d NZ$75/120; ) Set amid a peaceful garden of fruit trees and flowers in Tautu, these four large family-friendly lodges are the best value on Aitutaki. Queen Manarangi Tutai, one of Aitutaki's three *ariki* (high chiefs), is the proprietor and one of the island's most gracious and charming hosts. The self-contained lodges have high ceilings and large verandahs overlooking the gardens and swimming pool.

Each lodge has beds in a small loft that are perfect for kids. Gina's is a few kilometres from town, so you'll need transport.

**Amuri Guesthouse** GUESTHOUSE **$**
(Map p71; ☎31231; s/d NZ$50/80) Amuri has six double bedrooms and two shared bathrooms with a large dining and kitchen area in the owner's house. Accommodation is very clean, friendly and excellent value, and fresh fruit is often supplied *gratis* for breakfast. You'll be around 100m from the beach, but handily placed for food shopping.

**Aitutaki Seaside Lodges** BUNGALOW **$$**
(Map p71; ☎70458, 31056; www.seaside-aitutaki.com; Amuri Beach; d NZ$250; ) These three comfortable self-contained bungalows enjoy an absolute beachfront location at the quieter northern end of Amuri Beach. Complimentary use of kayaks and sun-loungers makes it a tough decision how to spend most mornings.

**Paradise Cove** BUNGALOW **$$**
(Map p71; ☎31218; www.paradisecove-aitutaki.com; garden/beachview bungalow NZ$150/180) Paradise Cove features beachfront bungalows on a glorious beach shaded by coconut palms. The thatched pole-house bungalows offer uninterrupted views across the lagoon from private verandahs. Inside are king-sized beds, kitchenettes with fridges, bathrooms and ceiling fans. They're not huge, but the larger garden suites can sleep up to four – a good option for families.

Its rustic beachside restaurant and bar is perfect for a sand-between-the-toes beer at the end of another Aitutaki day.

**Amuri Sands** BUNGALOW **$$**
(Map p71; ☎50613, 31130; www.aitutaki-vacation.com; Amuri; s/d NZ$155/175) These beach bungalows offer all you need for an island sojourn: a lagoon-facing location, trade-wind-friendly decks and a grassy lawn studded with coconut palms and a few soaring pine trees. Decor is simple but trendy, and the bathrooms and self-contained kitchens are spotless and modern. Look forward to a central location near good restaurants and cafes.

**Inano Beach Bungalows** BUNGALOW **$$**
(Map p71; ☎31758; www.inanobeach.com; lagoon-view/beachfront bungalows NZ$130/160, family bungalows NZ$170) Offering excellent value for money, Inano Beach Bungalows have been built using largely local materials and traditional methods. There are woven pandanus walls, ironwood balconies and mahogany tabletops. Near the end of the airport, fronting a nice stretch of beach, Inano's self-contained bungalows are large with good kitchen facilities.

**Paparei Bungalows** BUNGALOW **$$**
(Map p71; ☎73275; www.papareibungalows.com; d NZ$225) Paparei offers two modern self-contained beachfront bungalows near the centre of town. They're large, clean, well equipped and nicely decorated in an unfussy way. Operators Trina and Steve are lovely hosts, and guests also receive a discount on food and beverages at the Koru Cafe near the airport.

**Gina's Beach Lodge** BUNGALOW **$$**
(s/d incl transfers NZ$210/380) Queen Tutai from Gina's Garden Lodges also runs Gina's Beach Lodge on Akaiami island, and guests can choose to spend a while at each.

**★Etu Moana** BOUTIQUE HOTEL **$$$**
(Map p71; ☎31458; www.etumoana.com; villas NZ$505-750; ❄@🛜🏊) These boutique beach villas have thatched roofs and luxurious furnishings showcasing gleaming Tasmanian oak floors, loft ceilings, king-sized beds, private outdoor showers and teak sundecks. The design and decor are very classy, and there's a tear-drop pool complete with rock garden, sun-shaded tables and a deluxe honesty bar. If you prefer your luxe resorts understated, then this is the place. No kids under 12.

**Pacific Resort** RESORT **$$$**
(Map p71; ☎31720; www.pacificresortcom; beachfront bungalows/ste/villas NZ$600/1190/1890; ❄@🛜🏊) Pacific Resort Aitutaki is a benchmark in luxury Polynesian. From the Oriental lily ponds and enormous carved-timber reception desk of its sumptuous foyer to the rough-rendered walls and timber floors, decor and views of the split-level restaurant, the Pacific Resort is breathtaking. The rooms are superb, with commanding views, huge private beach decks and private garden bathrooms with outdoor showers.

Even if you can't afford to stay, come and enjoy the resort's restaurants. Our favourite is the more informal Black Rock Cafe.

**Aretai Beach Villas** APARTMENT **$$$**
(Map p71; ☎31645; www.aretaibeachvillas.com; villas NZ$300; ❄@) The lovely two-bedroom villas at Aretai are among the largest on the island, and definitely the best presented and best value for money in this price range. Halfway between Arutanga and the airport, with wonderful sea views and outstanding facilities – including full kitchens, dining areas, gorgeous furniture and huge patios – these stylish villas are ideal for travelling families or groups.

**Aitutaki Lagoon Resort** RESORT **$$$**
(Map p71; ☎31201; www.aitutakilagoonresort.com; beachfront/over-water bungalows NZ$750/1135; ❄@🛜🏊) Aitutaki Lagoon Resort, ensconced on its own Akitua island, has everything glam jet-set patrons would expect. It's truly beautiful, with great expanses of glistening white beach and a private ferryman to shunt you to and from the mainland. There are bars and restaurants, and a pool and day spa. The thatched garden and beachfront villas are large, light and comfortable

Over-water bungalows – the only ones in the Cook Islands – and premium beachfront bungalows are also special. Nonguests are welcome, so drop in for a visit and dine at its excellent restaurant with astounding lagoon views. The resort offers packages and discounts for extended stays – see the website.

**Tamanu Beach** RESORT **$$$**
(Map p71; ☎31810; www.aretamanu.com; bungalows NZ$340-550; ❄@🛜🏊) The elegant Tamanu Beach has chic bungalows ranging in size from studio to one-bedroom, all arrayed around a lush garden, or with excellent lagoon views. 'Casual luxury' is the resort's slogan and we reckon that's very accurate. There's also a breezy open-sided restaurant that does a good Island Night on Thursdays.

## Eating

**Maina Traders Superstore** SUPERMARKET **$**
(Map p71; ☎31055; ⏲7am-8pm Mon-Sat) Centrally located in Arutanga.

**Rerei's** SUPERMARKET **$**
(Map p71; ⏲7am-9pm Mon-Sat) Stock up on groceries at this Amuri store with a Heineken sign out the front. Unfortunately it's not a bar, but it does have a pretty good selection of beer and wine.

**Neibaa** SUPERMARKET **$**
(Map p71; ⏲7am-8pm) On the island's east side in Vaipae, Neibaa is the only shop that opens Sundays.

**Market** MARKET **$**
(Map p71; Orongo Centre; ⏲6am-2pm Mon-Fri, to noon Sat) Self-caterers can stock up on fruit, vegetables and fruit at Aitutaki's market.

**Black Rock Cafe** FUSION **$$**
(Map p71; Pacific Resort; mains NZ$20-35; ⏲11am-5pm) The Pacific Resort's more casual daytime restaurant is a stunner. The lagoon is just a cocktail shake away, towering palms shade the swimming pool, and the easygoing staff serve up lighter lunch dishes and fruit-laden cocktails. Standouts are the tuna sashimi and the hearty grilled chicken wraps.

**Flying Boat Beach Bar & Grill** CAFE **$$**
(Map p71; Aitutaki Lagoon Resort; mains NZ$23-30, pizza NZ$25-25; ⏲11am-6pm) Open to outside diners, the daytime restaurant at the Aitutaki Lagoon Resort has quite possibly the most stunning location in all of the Cooks. Lagoon views stretch for 180°, a few tiny *motu* feature on the near horizon, and the above-water deck is perfect for an afternoon

beer, cocktail or grilled seafood. Just maybe the Cooks' best pizzas too.

You'll need to make the short hop across the lagoon to the resort's private island. Just ask the boatman on the resort's nifty barge.

**Blue Lagoon** CAFE **$$**
(Map p71; O'otu Beach, Aitutaki Village; lunch NZ$12-25, dinner NZ$25-37; 11.30am-10pm) With a sandy floor and a thatched roof, this easygoing eatery at the Aitutaki Village resort is a cool and rustic place for a beer, lunch by the lagoon, or an evening meal at sunset. The food is simple – fish, burgers, steaks and salads – but the view is serene and the ambience relaxed. Try the excellent Thai-style red fish curry.

Blue Lagoon has regular Island Nights and a good Sunday afternoon barbecue from around noon. Live music often kicks off at 6pm on Sunday.

**Koru Café** CAFE **$$**
(Map p71; 31110; www.korucafe.biz; O'otu Beach; breakfast NZ$10-19, lunch NZ$10-30; 7am-3pm; ) Koru is a spacious and breezy Aitutaki spin on a trendy New Zealand cafe. All-day cooked breakfasts and lunches – including Caesar salad, steak sandwiches, BLT, pasta and salt-and-pepper calamari – all complement the island's best coffee. Wi-fi is available, and you can call to arrange ready-to-eat meals, picnic lunches and barbecue packs.

Locally made arts and crafts, including weaving, jewellery and ukuleles, are also available.

**Café Tupuna** POLYNESIAN **$$**
(Map p71; 31678; Tautu; mains NZ$20-27; 11am-3pm) In a lovely rural setting in the hills behind Arutanga, Café Tupuna is Aitutaki's only independent restaurant offering fine dining. The menu features fresh local fish and seafood cooked with island flavours and exotic spices. On our last visit we enjoyed baked *mahimahi* stuffed with shrimps. The lush garden setting is very relaxed and there's a good wine list.

Bringing insect repellent is often a wise move.

**Tamanu Beachfront** POLYNESIAN **$$**
(Map p71; Tamanu Beach; lunch NZ$15-25, dinner NZ$30-35; noon-3pm & 6.30-9.30pm) The breezy, thatched-roof, open-sided restaurant of the Tamanu Beach hotel is also open to outside guests. Here's your chance to dine at sunset on Pacific-style fresh fish, top-notch salads and other local dishes. Tamanu's Island Night on Thursday is renowned as one of Aitutaki's best, and bookings are recommended. Robust cocktails and a good winelist are other fine attractions.

**Coconut Shack** CAFE, BAR **$$**
(Map p71; Paradise Cove; mains NZ$24-30; 6-10pm Sun-Tue, Thu & Fri) With a circular bar built around a coconut tree, and plenty of absolute beachfront tables and chairs, the Coconut Shack at Paradise Cove fulfills every expectation of a rustic South Pacific watering hole. Cocktails come packed with booze and tropical fruit, hearty mains include fish curry and chicken stuffed with prawn salsa, and whole parrotfish for NZ$28 is good value.

**Boatshed Bar & Grill** SEAFOOD, BAR **$$**
(Map p71; 31739; Popaara Beach; mains NZ$21-37; 11am-11pm; ) A sprawling array of maritime memorabilia and classic country music makes the Boatshed a very laid-back spot. Try to secure a space on the deck for reef views, and feast on seafood classics like fish and chips, *ika mata* and sashimi. The beer's cold, the wine's reasonably priced, and booking for dinner is recommended.

Don't be surprised to see the guys that were there at 2pm still downing cold ones a few hours later.

**Tauono's Garden Cafe** CAFE **$$**
(Map p71; 31562; www.tauonos.com; cake & dessert NZ$10-22, lunch NZ$19-28; market 10am-5pm Mon, Wed & Fri, lunch noon-2pm, afternoon tea 3-5pm Mon, Wed, Fri only; ) Tauono's is a delight, a tiny garden cafe run by one-time Canadian-Austrian Sonja and her occasional team of travellers and WWOOFers (Willing Workers on Organic Farms). Renowned for its coconut cake, fruit smoothies, and afternoon teas, Tauono's also offers home-cooked cuisine served alfresco for lunch. The food is prepared according to what's been freshly picked from the on-site organic garden.

Stop by for homemade cake and fresh fruit and veg from Sonja's market shop, and ask about joining a plantation tour (per person NZ$35). Fresh and frozen meals are also available to take away. Sonja's tasty breadfruit lasagne is deservedly world famous in Aitutaki.

**Rapae Bay Restaurant** FUSION **$$$**
(Map p71; 31720; Pacific Resort; mains NZ$27-55; 5.30-10pm) The island's standout resort restaurant is in Pacific Resort. It offers superb Pacific fusion cuisine in a brilliant split-level patio setting. Look forward to interesting combinations of Pacific and South-

east Asian flavours including tuna sashimi and fresh Vietnamese-style spring rolls.

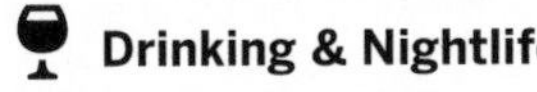

## Drinking & Nightlife

**Puffy's Beach Bar & Grill** BAR

(Map p71; ⏲noon-2pm & 6-8.30pm Mon-Sat) Puffy's is a tiny bar popular with both locals and visitors from nearby Paradise Cove. Simple meals – mainly burgers and fish and chips – and cheap booze are served, and there's also a really good weekly Island Night, usually on a Friday at 7.30pm. Keep an eye on the noticeboard out the front for details of funky local bands too.

## Information

Ask at your hotel if you should boil the water before drinking it. Many places get their drinking water from separate rain tanks.

There are no dogs on Aitutaki (the island's canine population was blamed for a leprosy outbreak) but there are plenty of roosters – bring earplugs if you're planning on sleeping in.

The main police station is behind the Orongo Centre near the wharf in Arutanga.

**Aitutaki Tourism** (Map p71; ☎31767; www.cookislands.travel/aitutaki; ⏲8am-4pm Mon-Fri) Helpful office in Arutanga.

**ANZ Bank Agent** (Map p71; ⏲8am-3pm Mon-Fri) With an ATM outside.

**BSP** (Bank South Pacific; Map p71; ⏲9am-3pm Mon-Fri) Also has an ATM.

**Hospital** (Map p71; ☎31002; ⏲24hr) On the hill behind Arutanga.

**Post Office & Bluesky** (Map p71; ⏲8am-4pm Mon-Fri; 📶) In the Administration Centre in Arutanga. Also offers phone, internet and has a wi-fi hotspot.

## Getting There & Away

### AIR

**Air Rarotonga** (Map p71; ☎in Arutanga 31888, in Rarotonga 22888; www.airraro.com) Several flights to Aitutaki from Rarotonga Monday to Saturday, and one flight on Sunday. Regular one-way fares from NZ$181 to NZ$270. There's also a direct flight from Aitutaki to 'Atiu on Monday, Wednesday and Friday. One-way fares are priced from NZ$250. Also available is an Aitutaki/'Atiu combo fare combining travel from Rarotonga to Aitutaki to 'Atiu and back to Rarotonga.

Air Rarotonga also runs Aitutaki Day Tours from Monday to Saturday, leaving Rarotonga at 8am and returning at 5.30pm. The cost is NZ$493 per person, including hotel transfers, flights, and a lagoon cruise on Vaka Cruise (p73) with snorkelling gear and lunch.

### BOAT

Cargo ships travelling to the Northern Group occasionally stop at Aitutaki.

## Getting Around

### TO/FROM THE AIRPORT

**Island Tours** (☎31379) Island Tours offers a minibus transfer service that costs NZ$20 to and from the airport. The larger resorts provide transfers for their guests.

### CAR, MOTORCYCLE & BICYCLE

Various places rent out bicycles (NZ$5 per day), scooters (NZ$25), cars and jeeps (NZ$70 to NZ$100). Try **Popoara Rentals** (Map p71; ☎31739; O'otu Beach), **Ranginui's Retreat** (Map p71; ☎31657; O'otu Beach) or, for the best range, **Rino's Beach Bungalows & Rentals** (Map p71; ☎31197; Arutanga).

# PALMERSTON

POP 60 / AREA 2.1 SQ KM

Palmerston, 500km northwest of Rarotonga, is the Southern Group's only true atoll, halfway towards the Cooks' Northern Group. The lineage of all Palmerston Islanders can be traced to just one man – prolific Englishman William Masters, a ship's carpenter, who arrived from Manuae with two Polynesian wives in 1863. Having quickly added a third wife, over the next 36 years Masters created his own island dynasty. He came from Gloucester and his progeny spoke excellent English with a thick Gloucester accent. Today, there are three main families on Palmerston (who spell their name Marsters), and you'll find Marsterses scattered throughout the Cooks and the rest of Australasia – the total number of William's descendants is now well into the thousands.

There's no organised accommodation on Palmerston, but if you're planning to travel there, contact the island secretary **Tere Marsters** (☎37615, 37620; palmerstonisland@hotmail.com). The only way to reach the island is by interisland freighter or private yacht.

# 'ATIU

POP 470 / AREA 27 SQ KM

In pre-European times 'Atiu was an important seat of regional power and its warriors were renowned for ferocious fighting and ruthlessness. By contrast, the rocky, reef-fringed island is now known for gentler

# 'Atiu

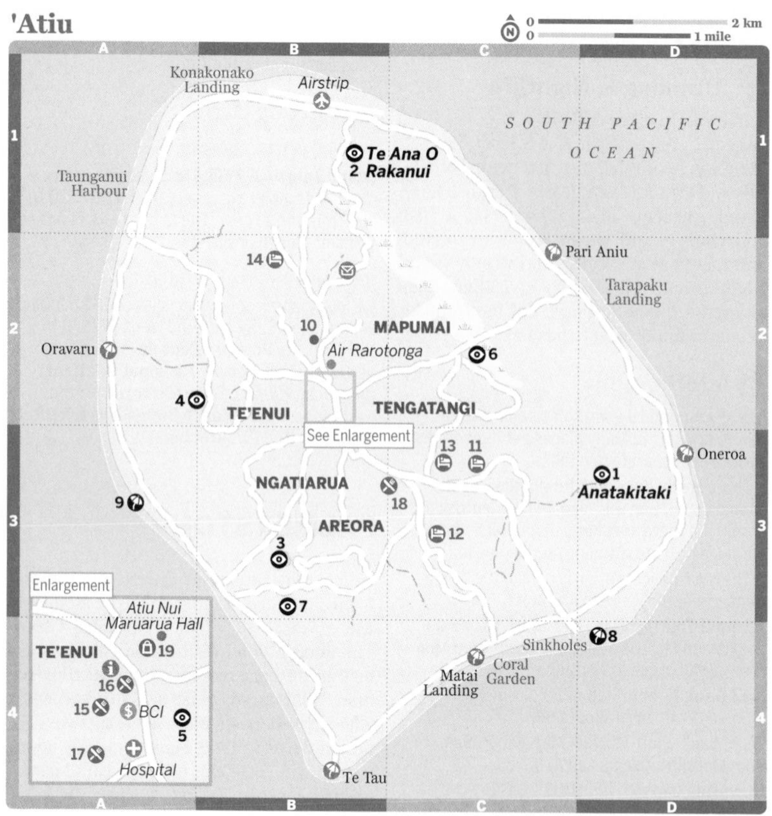


## 'Atiu

**Top Sights**

1 Anatakitaki........D3
2 Te Ana O Rakanui........B1

**Sights**

3 Lake Te Roto........B3
4 Marae Orongo........A2
5 Marae Te Apiripiri........A4
6 Marae Vairakai........C2
7 Rima Rau........B3
8 Takauroa Beach........D4
9 Taungaroro & Tumai........A3

**Activities, Courses & Tours**

10 Atiu Island Coffee........B2
Paiere Mokoroa........(see 14)

**Sleeping**

11 Atiu Bed & Breakfast........C3
12 Atiu Villas........C3
13 Kopeka Lodge........C3
14 Taparere Lodge........B2

**Eating**

15 Akai Bakery........A4
16 Jumbo Bakery........A4
Kura's Kitchen........(see 12)
17 Super Brown........A4
18 Terangi-Nui Café........C3

**Shopping**

Parua Tavioni........(see 18)
19 Vainetini Te Akapuanga........A4

pursuits. It's the Cooks' eco-capital and a haven for naturalists and bird lovers. It also attracts adventurous travellers in search of an island with a more traditional edge.

'Atiu's five main villages (Areora, Tengatangi, Mapumai, Te'enui and Ngatiarua) are clustered together on the island's central plateau, surrounded by a band of fertile swampland

and lush taro plantations. The *makatea* – the dramatic ring of upthrust rock that's rich in marine fossils and was once the island's exterior reef – is just one of 'Atiu's natural features. The island is also covered with forest and honeycombed with limestone caves. 'Atiu's most famous cave is Anatakitaki, the only known home of the *kopeka* ('Atiuan swiftlet).

## History

'Land of Birds' or 'Land of Insects' is the translation of 'Atiu's traditional name 'Enua Manu. Along with its neighbours Ma'uke and Mitiaro, 'Atiu makes up the Nga Pu Toru (Three Roots). In the recent pre-European times, 'Atiuan *ariki* overlorded smaller Ma'uke and Mitiaro. 'Atiuan warriors also made incursions on Rarotonga and Aitutaki, but without success. James Cook was the first European to land on 'Atiu on 3 April 1777. Reverend John Williams landed on 19 July 1823. Rongomatane, the leading 'Atiuan chief, was converted to Christianity after Williams' missionaries boldly ate sugarcane from Rongomatane's sacred grove – he subsequently ordered all the idols on the island to be burnt. The arrival of missionaries Williams and Tahitian Papeiha is celebrated on Gospel Day (19 July).

## Sights & Activities

Deep limestone caves, hidden away deep in the bush-covered *makatea,* are the most famous feature of 'Atiu. A torch and sturdy walking shoes are essential, and the coral is razor sharp. The main caves are on private land and you'll need a guide to visit them. Many caves were used for burials – it's *tapu* (taboo) to disturb the bones, so unless you fancy taking home a curse...

**★Anatakitaki** CAVE

(Map p78) Eerie Anatakitaki is 'Atiu's most spectacular cave, a multichambered cavern surrounded by banyan roots and thick jungle. It's also home to the rare *kopeka,* or 'Atiuan swiftlet – listen for its distinctive echo-locating clicks.

**★Te Ana O Rakanui** CAVE

(Map p78) Te Ana O Rakanui is a burial cave packed with musty old skulls and skeletal remains. It's a tight squeeze inside – claustrophobics be warned.

**Rima Rau** CAVE

(Map p78) Another of 'Atiu's burial caves, Rima Rau is reached by a vertical pothole and still contains skeletal remains. Many will find it claustrophobic.

**Lake Te Roto** LAKE

(Map p78) Lake Te Roto is noted for its *itiki* (eels), a popular island delicacy. On the western side of the lake, a cave leads right through the *makatea* to the sea.

**Taunganui Harbour & Oravaru Beach** BEACH

'Atiu's barrier reef is close to shore. The surrounding lagoon is rarely more than 50m wide and its waters quite shallow. Taunganui Harbour, on the west coast where the water is clear and deep, is the best spot for swimming. About 1km south is Oravaru Beach, where Captain Cook's party made its landing.

**Taungaroro & Tumai** BEACHES

(Map p78) South of Oravaru Beach, Taungaroro and Tumai are two of the most popular swimming beaches.

**Takauroa Beach** BEACH

(Map p78) You can swim in the three lovely **sinkholes** west of Takauroa Beach only at low tide. Between Takauroa Beach and Matai Landing, the falling tide empties through the sinkholes and fish become trapped in a fascinating natural aquarium known as the Coral Garden.

**Marae Orongo** HISTORIC SITE

(Map p78) Near Oravaru Beach, this was once 'Atiu's most sacred *marae,* and it's still a powerfully atmospheric place – many locals are reluctant to go near it. You'll need a guide as it's on private land.

**Marae Vairakai** HISTORIC SITE

(Map p78) Along a walking track north of Kopeka Lodge, Marae Vairakai is surrounded by 47 large limestone slabs, six of which have curious projections cut into their top edges.

**Marae Te Apiripiri** HISTORIC SITE

(Map p78) This *marae* is where the Tahitian preacher Papeiha first spoke the words

### EATING PRICE RANGES

The following price ranges refer to the cost of a main meal.

**$** less than NZ$15

**$$** NZ$15–30

**$$$** more than NZ$30

of the Gospel in 1823. There's not much left to see, but a stone commemorates the site.

## Tours

**Atiu Tours** TOUR
(☎33041; www.atiutoursaccommodation.com) Run by Englishman Marshall Humphreys, Atiu Tours offers an informative 3½-hour circle-island tour (NZ$50 per person) visiting *marae*, beaches and historical points of interest. Lunch includes probably the best banana muffins in the Pacific, and there's often the opportunity for bodysurfing. There's also an excellent 2½-hour tour to Anatakitaki (NZ$35 per person) and Rima Rau burial cave ($30 per person).

Don't miss having a candlelit swim in the beautiful underground pool in the Anatakitaki cave.

**George Mateariki** BIRDWATCHING
(☎33047; per person NZ$50) Also known as Birdman George, George Mateariki is 'Atiu's resident ornithologist and a local celebrity thanks to his highly entertaining ecotour. George oversaw the release of the endangered *kakerori* (Rarotongan flycatcher) here from Rarotonga, and also the more recent introduction of the *kura* (lorikeet) from the French Polynesian island of Rimatara. George also offers a specialist tour for birdwatchers.

Ask about having a tropical feast at his 'Restaurant at the Beach' at 4pm on Sundays.

**Paiere Mokoroa** TOUR
(Map p78; ☎33034; macmokoroa@gmail.com) Historical tours taking in *marae* and battle sites around the island cost NZ$30 per person. Paiere Mokoroa is based at Taparere Lodge.

**Andrew Matapakia** FISHING
(☎33825) Offers reef and lagoon fishing tours (NZ$30), and also deep-sea excursions (around NZ$100 per person) trolling for tuna, wahoo and *mahimahi*, or catching flying fish at night. Give him a call or see him during his sideline as barman at Kura's Kabana at Atiu Villas.

**Atiu Island Coffee** TOUR
(Map p78; ☎33088) Mata Arai, whose family had grown coffee in the 1950s, returned to 'Atiu in the 1990s and resumed production. Her coffee is hand picked, hand dried and hand roasted, using coconut cream to give the coffee its flavour. Tours are NZ$30 per person and include delicious pikelets and coconut cream.

## Sleeping

**Kopeka Lodge** LODGE $
(Map p78; ☎33283; kopeka1@kopekalodges.co.ck; s/d NZ$85/120) Three rustic plywood chalets sit in rural grounds southeast of Areora village, with one single and two double units complete with self-contained kitchen. The stained-wood and pale-green colour scheme is simple, but the units are quite comfortable. On Rarotonga contact **Eddie Drollet** (☎52884).

**Taparere Lodge** LODGE $
(Map p78; ☎33034; macmokoroa@gmail.com; s/d NZ$50/100) With two large breeze-block units, Taparere is bright, airy and cheerfully decorated. Accommodation is self-contained with kitchen facilities and (sometimes) hot-water showers. Shady verandahs overlook a pleasant valley.

**Atiu Villas** VILLA $$
(Map p78; ☎33777; www.atiuvillas.com; bungalows NZ$210-250, extra person NZ$20; @ 🛜 🏊) The extra money goes a long way at Atiu Villas, which was built from local materials around 35 years ago by Kiwi expat Roger Malcolm and his 'Atiuan wife Kura. Six delightful villas are arrayed around a shady garden and have decks from where you can take in the valley views. There's a pool, tennis courts and a large bar-restaurant.

Complimentary wi-fi is provided, as is internet access on resident computers. Prepaid bookings made 12 weeks in advance earn a 15% discount, and last-minute bookings (seven days in advance) attract a 40% discount.

**Atiu Bed & Breakfast** B&B $$
(Map p78; ☎33041; www.atiutoursaccommodation.com; r per person NZ$60; @) Tour provider Marshall Humphreys rents out rooms in his very comfortable family home near Areora. A double and a twin comprise the accommodation (with shared bathrooms), and guests have the run of the house. A tropical breakfast is complimentary, and evening meals and packed lunches can be arranged.

Marshall's wife Jéanne is a celebrated local artist, and her colourful and tropical work is for sale (from NZ$30).

## Eating & Drinking

Self-catering from the slim pickings at the grocery stores – largely tinned and frozen food – is the most reliable eating option. Ask George Mateariki about his regular Sunday afternoon 'Restaurant at the Beach'.

LOCAL KNOWLEDGE

### TUMUNU

Christian missionaries took to eradicating kava drinking among Cook Islanders, so 'Atiuans developed home-brewed alcohol, and the *tumunu* (bush-beer drinking clubs) were born. Men would retreat into the bush and imbibe 'orange beer', made from fermented oranges and malt extract. *Tumunu* are still held regularly on 'Atiu; the *tumunu* is the hollowed-out stump of a coconut palm traditionally used for brewing beer. *Tumunu* retain some of the old kava-drinking ceremonies, but these days the vessel is likely to be plastic.

Most tours of 'Atiu can also include a visit to a *tumunu*, or ask at your accommodation. It's customary to donate $5 per person to help pay for ingredients for the next brew. Traditionally, it's for men only, but the rules are relaxed for tourists, and males and females are both welcome. Be warned – 'orange beer' can be pretty potent stuff, but it's actually pretty tasty with a subtle effervescence.

The 'Atiu Tumunu Tutaka, when there is a hard-fought competition and taste-off to find the best *tumunu* of 'Atiu, is held occasionally.

**Akai Bakery** BAKERY **$**
(Map p78; Mapumai; ⏲10.30am Sun-Fri, 11pm Sat) Fresh-baked bread is ready for the milling crowd by about 10.30am each day. Saturday is the Seventh-Day Adventist Sabbath and the baking doesn't begin until dusk – at 11pm there's that milling crowd again. Stocks usually last just a few minutes.

**Super Brown** FAST FOOD **$**
(Map p78; Areora; burgers NZ$7-10; ⏲6.30am-9pm Mon-Sat; 📶) Drop in for burgers, toasted sandwiches and fish and chips at this friendly spot in Areora village. You can even have a cold beer while you wait. There's a handy BlueSky wi-fi hotspot and data vouchers are sold. Super Brown is also a good bet for takeaway groceries, beer and wine.

**Jumbo Bakery** BAKERY
(Map p78; Teenui; ⏲5.30-7am Mon-Sat) Early risers and fans of freshly baked doughnuts and buns should head to Jumbo when the doors open to eager locals at 5.30am.

**Kura's Kitchen** POLYNESIAN **$$**
(Map p78; ☎33777; Atiu Villas; dinner NZ$30; ⏲7pm Mon-Sat) Kura at Atiu Villas cooks up evening vittles whenever there's a quorum, and sometimes there's an informal Island Night that kicks off in the thatched restaurant-bar area (NZ$30 with food, or NZ$40 including the show). Kura's Kitchen is open to outside guests, but booking before 3pm is essential. Bring along your favourite flag to add to the Pavilion Bar's collection.

**Terangi-Nui Café** CAFE **$$**
(Map p78; ☎33101; Areora; dinner NZ$25; ⏲craft shop 9am-2pm, dinner from 6pm) The lovely Parua Tavioni offers a two-course dinner every night, but you'll need to book by noon, either by popping in to her small shop selling local crafts, gifts and *pareu*, or by phone.

## Shopping

Around the villages, you'll occasionally hear the rhythmic percussion of local women beating tapa cloth, and most are happy to explain what they are doing.

**Parua Tavioni** HOMEWARES
(Map p78; ☎33101; Arerora; ⏲9am-2pm) Working from her village house – a corner residence that doubles as the Terangi-Nui Cafe for dinners – Parua Tavioni crafts intricate *tivaevae* (appliqué work) that makes beautiful bedspreads and other homewares. Some of the hand-sewn work can sell for around NZ$5000.

**Vainetini Te Akapuanga** CRAFTS
(Map p78; ☎33134, 33269; beside Atiu Town Hall) Local crafts are for sale at this centre next to the Atiu Town Hall. Opening hours are flexible.

## Information

**BCI** (Bank of the Cook Islands; Map p78; Areora; ⏲9am-noon Mon-Fri) Can provide cash advances on credit cards, but note there is no ATM on the island.

**Post & Telecom** (Map p78; ⏲8am-4pm Mon-Fri) North of Mapumai village.

**Tourist Information Office** (Map p78; www.atiutourism.com; Areora; ⏲9am-1pm Mon-Fri) Very helpful local tourism office.

## Getting There & Around

### TO/FROM THE AIRPORT

Return airport transfers by accommodation owners are NZ$24 per person.

### AIR

**Air Rarotonga** (Map p78; ☎33888; www.airraro.com) Air Rarotonga flies between Rarotonga and 'Atiu on Monday, Thursday and Saturday. One-way fares cost from NZ$213. On Monday, and from Wednesday to Saturday, you can fly direct from Aitutaki to 'Atiu from NZ$213. Also available is an Aitutaki/'Atiu combo fare for travel from Rarotonga to Aitutaki to 'Atiu and back to Rarotonga. Check the website for the latest fares.

### CAR, MOTORCYCLE & BICYCLE

You'll need transport to get around 'Atiu. The circle-island road is fun for exploring by motorbike, and walking tracks lead down to the dramatic beach. Accommodation places and **Super Brown** (p81) can provide motorbikes (NZ$25 per day), and most also have mountain bikes(NZ$10 to NZ$12). Atiu Villas rents a soft-top Jeep for NZ$55 a day.

# MA'UKE

POP 310 / AREA 18.4 SQ KM

Although much flatter than 'Atiu and only slightly larger than Mitiaro, Ma'uke is also characterised by its *makatea* and thick coastal forest. Ma'uke is a sleepy and quietly charming island, traditional in its ways, and circled by a rough coastal track. It's pockmarked with many underground caverns, including Motuanga, a network of limestone chambers said to stretch right out underneath the reef. Known as the Garden Island, Ma'uke is one of the Cooks' main exporters of tropical flowers, which means your goodbye '*ei* is likely to be particularly impressive.

## Sights

Like its sister islands, 'Atiu and Mitiaro, Ma'uke's raised-coral *makatea* is riddled with caves, many filled with cool freshwater pools. Interesting caves around the island include **Vai Ou** (Map p83), **Vai Tukume** (Map p83), **Vai Moraro** (Map p83), **Vai Ma'u** (Map p83) and **Vai Moti** (Map p83), reached by old coral pathways across the *makatea*.

**★Vai Tango** CAVE

(Map p83) Vai Tango is the best cave for swimming, a short walk from Ngatiarua village. Schoolkids often head there at weekends and after school, and they can show you where to find it.

**★Motuanga** CAVE

(Map p83) Motuanga (the Cave of 100 Rooms) is a complex of tunnels and caverns in the island's southeast that's said to extend all the way under the reef and out to sea. The cave was used as a hiding place from 'Atiuan war parties. Access is via a small crawlspace into a surprisingly compact subterranean atrium complete with an underground pool.

**Circle-Island Road** BEACHES

An 18km-long circular road negotiates Ma'uke's secluded coves and beaches, which are among the island's main attractions. One of the nicest is **One'unga** (Map p83), on the east side, and **Teoneroa** (Map p83) and **Tukume** (Map p83) on the island's southwestern side are also delightful. **Anaraura** (Map p83) and Teoneroa have sheltered picnic areas that are popular with the island's pigs. **Kea's Grave** (Map p83) is on the cliffs above Anaiti, where the wife of Paikea (the Whale Rider) is said to have perished while waiting for her husband's return.

Just south of Tiare Cottages is **Kopupooki (Stomach Rock) Beach** (Map p83), with a beautiful fish-filled cave that becomes accessible at low tide. Around 3km south from Tiare Cottages, the fractured rusting hulk of the Te Kou Maru sits groaning on the edge of the reef. The cargo ship floundered in October 2010, but quick work from Ma'uke locals ensured most cargo was ferried by hand across the rugged *makatea* to safety. Walk towards the coast around 50m south of Ma'uke's rubbish tip to find the wreck.

**Marae Rangimanuka** HISTORIC SITE

(Map p83) Marae Rangimanuka, the *marae* of Uke, is one of Ma'uke's many *marae* that are now overgrown, but you can still find it with a guide.

**Marae Puarakura** HISTORIC SITE

(Map p83) Marae Puarakura is a modern *marae,* still used for ceremonial functions, complete with stone seats for the *ariki, mataiapo* and *rangatira* (subchief).

## Tours

**Tangata Ateriano** TOUR

(Map p83; ☎73009, 35270) Based at Tiare Cottages, 'Ta' Ateriano takes visitors around the island (NZ$15 per person per hour), either in his 4WD or on a scooter tour. Highlights include the island's caves, beaches,

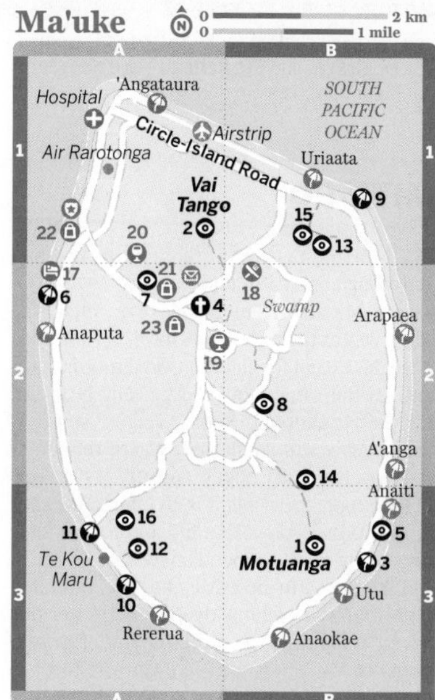


## Ma'uke

**Top Sights**



**Sights**



**Activities, Courses & Tours**



**Sleeping**



**Eating**



**Drinking & Nightlife**



**Shopping**



Kea's Grave, the Divided Church, and one of the world's largest banyan trees. Customised tours are also available.

## Sleeping

**Tiare Cottages** GUESTHOUSE **$$**
(Map p83; ☎35270, 73009; www.maukeholiday.com; bungalows & lodges NZ$75-85, house NZ$150) The garden units are basic, with a main sleeping area and a simple kitchen, toilet and shower tacked on the end. The newer self-contained lodge is more comfortable, with a better-equipped kitchen and an airy and cheerily furnished bedroom. There's also a brilliant house – O'Kiva – with panoramic sea views from its cliff-top perch.

It's self-contained and excellent value, and one of the nicest places to stay on the Cooks' outer islands. Dinner costs NZ$20 per person, and you'll need to provide for your own breakfast and lunch.

**Ri's Retreat** BUNGALOW **$$**
(☎35181; keta-ttn@oyster.net.ck; bungalows NZ$125) Ri's Retreat has bungalows located near Anaraura Beach, and a few near the airport. The airport bungalows are all sparkling clean and brightly decorated, with large beds, modern bathrooms and verandahs. The seaside bungalows have the nicer location, built on stilts beside the gorgeous and remote Anaraura Beach, and are often enlivened by robust trade winds.

## Eating & Drinking

The best of Ma'uke's grocery stores is **Virginia's** (Map p83) near the Divided Church, and a less-well-stocked back-up option is the **Ariki Store** (Map p83). **Kato's Store** (Map p83) is well stocked and is also the island's only bakery. Kato's also hosts a **takeaway bar** (Map p83; ⏲11am-1pm & 5-9pm Mon-Sat), turning out good burgers, fish and chips and milkshakes. Pull up a chair in the adjacent gazebo and get chatting to the locals.

From 8.30am on Friday morning you can buy fresh produce at **Ma'uke market** (Map p83; ⏲8.30-11am Fri), near the wharf.

**Tura's Bar** BAR

(Map p83) Liquid refreshment is available at this humble spot opposite Ma'uke College. Opening nights vary, so ask Ma'uke locals for the latest. Tuesday night is usually darts night and Ma'uke players are renowned across the Cooks.

**Tua's Bar** BAR

(Map p83) Another option for a relaxed beer with the locals, Tua's is near the island's rugby field and normally open on a Friday and Saturday night.

## Information

**Hospital** (Map p83; 35664; 8am-noon & 1-4pm Mon-Fri) Ma'uke hospital.

**Police Station** (Map p83; 35086) Between the Administration Centre and the wharf.

**Post Office & Telecom Office** (Map p83; 8am-noon & 1-4pm Mon-Fri; ) There's a 24-hour Kiaorana cardphone outside and pricey internet access.

## Getting There & Around

### TO/FROM THE AIRPORT

Transfers to/from the airport cost NZ$25.

### AIR

**Air Rarotonga** (Map p83; Kimiangatau 35888, airport 35120; www.airraro.com) Air Rarotonga operates flights between Rarotonga and Ma'uke on Monday and Friday (one way NZ$318).

DON'T MISS

### THE DIVIDED CHURCH

Ma'uke's **Cook Islands Christian Church (CICC)** (Map p83) was built by two villages, Areora and Ngatiarua, in 1882. When the outside was completed, there was disagreement between the villages about how the inside should be decorated so they built a wall down the middle. The wall has since been removed, though the interior is decorated in markedly different styles. Each village has its own entrance, sits at its own side and takes turns singing the hymns. The minister stands astride the dividing line down the middle of the pulpit. Look for the Chilean coins that are set into the wooden altar. Chilean currency was frequently traded throughout the South Pacific in the 19th century.

### MOTORCYCLE & BICYCLE

You can hire scooters for NZ$30 per day from Tiare Cottages and Ri's Retreat. Tiare also rents out mountain bikes.

# MITIARO

POP 180 / AREA 22.3 SQ KM

The tourism juggernaut that churns through Rarotonga and Aitutaki is a world away from sleepy Mitiaro. Here people live much the same way as their ancestors have for hundreds of years (except for electricity and motorscooters). Mitiaro may not be classically beautiful in the traditional South Pacific sense – the beaches are small and, where the land's not covered with boggy swamp, it's mainly black craggy rock – yet it is an interesting slice of traditional Polynesian life and makes for a rewarding place to spend a few days.

Like on 'Atiu and Ma'uke, the *maketea* of Mitiaro has many deep and mysterious caves, including the brilliant underground pools of Vai Nauri and Vai Marere. Mitiaro also has the remains of the Cook Islands' only fort. The islanders on Mitiaro are great craftspeople and you'll discover that the weaving, woodcarving and traditional outrigger canoes are all beautifully made. Another highlight is staying a few days in a homestay, either in a local's private home or in one of three *kikau* cottages dotted around the tiny island's only settlement.

## Sights & Activities

**Vai Marere** LANDMARK

(Map p85) The Cook Islands' only sulphur pool is Vai Marere, a 10-minute walk from Mangarei village on the Takaue road. From the main road it's barely visible and easy to miss, but as you duck into the cave it broadens out into a gloomy cavern covered with stalactites. According to locals, the water here has healing properties.

★**Vai Nauri** LANDMARK

(Map p85) A real highlight in this region is the deep sparkling-blue Vai Nauri, Mitiaro's natural swimming pool. Local women used to hold gatherings known as *terevai* at Vai Nauri and at nearby Vai Tamaroa, where they met to swim and sing the bawdy songs of their ancestors. With Mitiaro's declining population, the *terevai* tradition is now largely limited to holiday periods like Christmas and New Year when islanders return to Mitiaro from their homes in Australia and New Zealand.

## Mitiaro

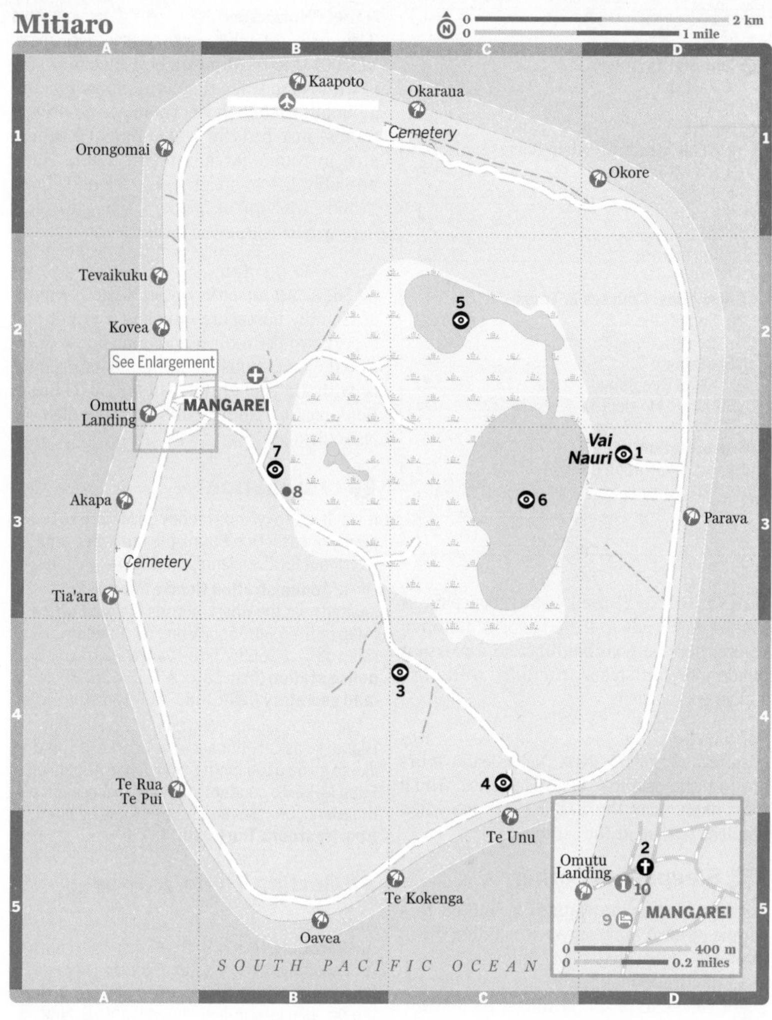




**Marae Takero** HISTORIC SITE
(Map p85) The *marae* of Mitiaro are largely consumed by jungle, but you are still able to see the stone seat of the *ariki* and several graves at Marae Takero, located near the abandoned Takaue village.

**Te Pare Fort** HISTORIC SITE
(Map p85) The remains of Te Pare Fort, set deep in the *makatea,* are Mitiaro's most impressive ancient ruins. The fort was built as a defence against 'Atiuan raiders. In times of danger, people would assemble in the underground shelter, while above stood a lookout tower from which approaching canoes could be seen. The only tour guide to Te Pare Fort is **Julian Aupuni** (☎70131, 36180), who has permission to visit from the site's owner, Po Tetava Ariki.

**Cook Islands Christian Church** CHURCH
(Map p85) The white-painted CICC is a fine sight, with its blue trim, stained-glass windows and parquet ceiling decorated with black-and-white stars. The Sunday church singing is inspirational.

**Te Rotonui & Te Rotoiti** LAKES
Mitiaro is unique in the Cooks for its twin lakes, **Te Rotonui (Big Lake)** (Map p85)

and **Te Rotoiti (Small Lake)** (Map p85). A rough track leads to the edge of Te Rotonui, where there's a boat landing and a pleasant picnic spot. Both lakes are stuffed with *itiki*, a local eel delicacy.

**Papa Neke** TOUR
(Map p85; ☎36347) Papa Neke leads tours around the island's historical sites. You'll most likely meet the affable patriarch when he picks you up at the airport.

## Sleeping & Eating

Accommodation on Mitiaro is limited to a couple of local homestays, or bedding down in one of the island's *kikau* bungalows.

Limited food supplies are sold at the small village food shops and at **Pa's Store**, but all accommodation includes meals.

**Kikau Bungalows** BUNGALOW $
(Map p85; ☎20639; office@cookislandsconnect.co.ck; per person incl meals NZ$100) Made from woven panels of *kikau* leaves, this village accommodation is light and airy and features en suite bathrooms and spacious verandahs. The bungalows are arrayed around the main village of Mangarei, and meals are provided by host Vivian and local families. For reservations and more information, contact Cook Islands Tours (office@cookislandsconnect.co.ck).

**Nane's Homestay** HOMESTAY $
(Map p85; ☎36106; per person incl meals NZ$100) One of Mitiaro's best places to stay is with Nane Pokoati, a local *mataiapo* and a bubbly, friendly host. There are no private rooms, just beds in a communal sleeping area in Nane's large, modern house. You'll probably get to meet a few friendly Cook Island government workers who also stay here when visiting the island.

**Aunty Mii O'Brian** HOMESTAY $
(☎36106; per person incl meals NZ$100) Another friendly homestay, either in a bright and breezy two-bedroom standalone house or inside the main house with shared bathrooms, is with the delightful Aunty Mii O'Brian. Bookings at Aunty Mii's are handled by Nane Pokoati.

## Information

It's difficult to change money on Mitiaro so bring plenty of cash. Don't drink the tap water, and watch out for the island's vicious mosquitoes.

The **Administration Centre** (Map p85), located near the wharf, houses the **post office** (Map p85; ⏰9am-4pm Mon-Fri), **Telecom** (Map p85; ☎36680; ⏰8-10am & 1-3pm), **police station** (Map p85; ☎36124, 36110), **island secretary** (☎36108, 36157) and the mayor.

Everybody knows everyone else on the tiny island, so ask at your accommodation if you'd like to go on a tour with either Julian Aupuni or Papa Neke. To conduct your own exploration of the island, bicycles and scooters can be hired from **Ngarouru Tou** (☎36148).

## Getting There & Away

### AIR

**Air Rarotonga** (☎22888; www.airraro.com) Air Rarotonga flies to Mitiaro on Monday and Friday. The return cost is around NZ$580.There are occasionally unscheduled flights linking Ma'uke and Mitiaro, and flights from 'Atiu to Rarotonga also occasionally stop on Mitiaro to pick up passengers.

# MANGAIA

POP 573 / AREA 51.8 SQ KM

Next to Rarotonga, Mangaia (pronounced mung-EYE-ah) is the Cooks' most geographically dramatic island. It is the second largest of the islands – it's only slightly smaller than Rarotonga – with a towering circlet of black two-tiered raised-coral *makatea* (three-tiered in the island's north) concealing a huge sunken volcanic caldera that falls away on each side of the 169m Rangimotia ridge, the island's central spine. This sunken interior is swampland planted with taro fields and vegetables.

Mangaia is the Pacific's oldest island – at once craggy and lushly vegetated – and riddled with limestone caves that once served as sacred burial grounds and havens during tribal fighting. There are lakes in the island's centre, dramatic cliffs and many spectacular lookout points. Mangaians have a reputation for haughtiness and superiority, and they're perhaps a little less voluble on first meetings, but they are friendly, gracious and impeccably well mannered.

Mangaia's three main villages are on the coast: Oneroa in the west, Ivirua in the east and Tamarua in the south. Oneroa, the main village, has three parts: Tava'enga to the north and Kaumata to the south on the coast, and Temakatea high above the second *makatea* tier overlooking the ocean. The island's interior is cross-hatched by tracks and dirt roads, which are great for walking, but they can get very muddy after heavy rain. The airstrip is in the north of the island.

## History

Mangaian legend tells that the island was not settled by voyagers on canoes, but that the three sons of the Polynesian god Rongo – Rangi, Mokoaro and Akatauira – lifted the island up from the deep, and became the first settlers and ancestors of the Nga Ariki tribe.

James Cook landed in 1777 but found the Mangaians were hostile and quickly moved on. Cannibalism had already been outlawed by Mangaian chief Mautara 100 years before the first missionaries arrived. John Williams was the first missionary to land in 1823 but, like James Cook, he was not welcome. Subsequent Polynesian missionaries had more success – the Mangaians were eventually converted to Christianity by the Rarotongan preacher Maretu.

## Sights

Mangaia has many spectacular caves, including **Te Rua Rere** (Map p88), a huge burial cave that has crystalline stalagmites and stalactites, and some ancient human skeletons. Other caverns worth exploring include the multilevel **Tuatini Cave** (Map p88) and the long, maze-like **Toru a Puru Cave** (Map p88).

Some of the finest old CICCs in the Cooks are on Mangaia. **Tamarua CICC** (Map p88) is especially beautiful, and still has its original roof beams, woodcarved interiors and sennit-rope binding. The interiors of the **Oneroa** (Map p88) and **Ivirua** (Map p88) CICCs were once even more impressive, but were sadly mostly removed in the 1980s.

The island also has 24 pre-missionary *marae,* but you'll need a guide to find them since they have been mostly overtaken by bush.

**Avarua Landing** HARBOUR
(Map p88) Fishermen return from their morning's exploits around 8am or 9am in tiny outrigger canoes with several huge wahoo and tuna. Hang around for the cleaning and gutting because there are three giant green turtles that come to feed on the entrails and off-cuts that are cast into the water. Whales pass just beyond the reef in the July-to-October season.

**★Rangimotia** VIEWPOINT
At 169m, Rangimotia is the highest point on the island, with stunning coastal views. From the Oneroa side, a dirt road leads to the top.

**Te-Toa-A-Morenga Lookout** VIEWPOINT
(Map p88) This stunning viewpoint is just inland from Ivirua.

**Maumaukura Lookout** HISTORIC SITE
(Map p88) Has a glorious view inland from the top of the *makatea* cliff.

**Te Pa'ata Lookout** VIEWPOINT
(Map p88) Above Oneroa.

## Tours

**Doreen Tangatakino & Ura Herrmann** TOUR
(☎34092; Babe's Place) Takes visitors on a full-day island tour for NZ$50, which includes the inland taro plantations and Lake Tiriara. Tours to Tuatini Cave cost NZ$30. Doreen's husband Moekapiti Tangatakino is the school history teacher and runs an informative three-hour tour that takes in the lookouts over the taro farms, lakes, the 1909 wreck site of the coal freighter *Saragossa* (only the anchor remains), the human *umu* (underground pit-oven used to cook human flesh), villages and *marae* for NZ$50.

**Maui Peraua** FISHING
(☎34388) Maui Peraua leads tours to his family cave of Toru a Puru (NZ$35) and runs

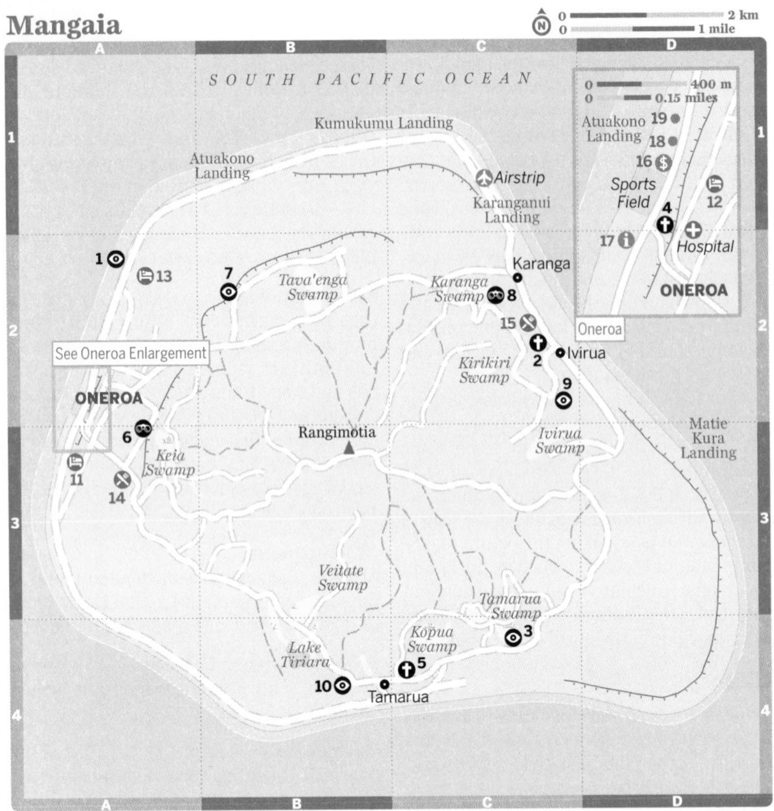


## Mangaia

**Sights**

1 Avarua Landing .......... A2
2 Ivirua CICC .......... C2
3 Maumaukura Lookout .......... C4
4 Oneroa CICC .......... D1
5 Tamarua CICC .......... C4
6 Te Pa'ata Lookout .......... A3
7 Te Rua Rere Cave .......... B2
8 Te-Toa-A-Morenga Lookout .......... C2
9 Toru a Puru Cave .......... C2
10 Tuatini Cave .......... B4

**Sleeping**

11 Babe's Place .......... A3
12 Mangaia Lodge .......... D1
13 Mangaia Villas .......... A2

**Eating**

14 Akeke Trading .......... A3
Babe's Store .......... (see 16)
15 Kirikiri Store .......... C2

**Drinking & Nightlife**

Babe's Bar .......... (see 11)

**Information**

16 Babe's Store .......... D1
17 Visitor Information Centre .......... D2

**Transport**

18 Air Rarotonga .......... D1
19 Moana Rentals .......... D1

popular traditional pole-fishing tours on the reef (NZ$25) – you can have your catch cooked on the beach.

## Sleeping

**Babe's Place** MOTEL $

(Map p88; ☎34092; mangaia@babesplace.co.ck; Oneroa; s/d incl meals NZ$75/120) With all meals included, a terrific location, and four large comfortable motel-style rooms, Babe's Place is good value for money. Babe is the island's entrepreneur, owning the island's main store, liveliest bar and this motel. The units have mosquito nets, colourful bedspreads and small patio areas.

Guests have 24-hour use of the main kitchen – with a fridge, tea and coffee – and the lounge area with a TV. Lively Babe's Bar, next door, parties on well into the night on Friday and Saturday.

**Mangaia Lodge** LODGE **$**
(Map p88; ☎34324; Oneroa; s/d NZ$40/70) This tumbledown colonial-style lodge has three plain bedrooms and a sunny, enclosed terrace overlooking the gardens. The accommodation is basic but the old building has a rustic charm and million-dollar views over the ocean. The separate shared toilet and shower block is pretty rustic. Meals are included.

★**Mangaia Villas** VILLA **$$$**
(Map p88; ☎29882; www.mangaiavillas.com; Oneroa; villas NZ$300) These six one-bedroom villas are hands-down the Cook Islands' finest accommodation beyond Rarotonga and Aitutaki. Spacious verandahs showcase ocean views, whale watching and tropical sunsets, and the villas are constructed of local Mangaia limestone with thatched roofs and shimmering hardwood floors. Modern touches include designer kitchens and bathrooms, and rates include a tropical breakfast. Dinner can be also be arranged.

## Eating & Drinking

There's no eating out on Mangaia, but meals are usually provided with accommodation. A weekly Friday-morning **market** kicks off at 8am beside the Oneroa post office.

**Babe's Store** SUPERMARKET **$**
(Map p88; Tava'enga; ⏰7am-9pm Mon-Sat) The best-stocked shop.

**Kirikiri Store** SUPERMARKET **$**
(Map p88; ⏰7am-9pm Mon-Sat) North of Ivirua.

**Akeke Trading** SUPERMARKET **$**
(Map p88; ⏰7am-9pm Mon-Sat) Inland from Oneroa.

**Babe's Bar** BAR
(Map p88; Oneroa; ⏰5pm-midnight Fri-Sat) Opens Friday and Saturday nights.

**SLEEPING PRICE RANGES**

The following price ranges refer to the cost of a double room in high season.

**$** less than NZ$125

**$$** NZ$125–250

**$$$** more than NZ$250

## Shopping

Basketwork, tie-dyed *pareu,* stone pounders and *pupu ei* are Mangaia's most famous handicrafts.

**Mangaia Airport Shop** ARTS, CRAFTS
(⏰open when flights arrive and depart) This tiny shop opens for incoming flights. It also doubles as a booking office for tours and activities.

## Information

**Babe's Store** (Map p88; Oneroa; ⏰8am-7pm) The island's ANZ agent.

**Post & Telecom** (internet access per 30min NZ$5; ⏰8am-4pm Mon-Fri) On the hill above Oneroa.

**Visitor Information Centre** (Map p88; ☎34289; ⏰8am-4pm) In the Administration Centre at the bottom of the Temakatea road cutting.

## Getting There & Around

### AIR

**Air Rarotonga** (Map p88; ☎34888; www.airraro.com) Air Rarotonga flies between Rarotonga and Mangaia two to three times a week for around NZ$550 return.

### MOTORCYCLE

**Moana Rentals** (Map p88; ☎34307) You'll need a motorbike to get around Mangaia. There are some very rough sections of road in the island's south, and the cross-island roads are muddy and perilous after rains. Moana Rentals hires out motorcycles for NZ$25 per day.

# NORTHERN GROUP

These sparsely populated tropical idylls are breathtaking in their beauty and remoteness. This sublime isolation inspired writers Tom Neale and Robert Dean Frisbie, who both lived as castaways on these far-flung coral atolls. Only the hardiest and most intrepid travellers ever make it to the Northern Group. Flights are few and mind-bogglingly expensive but, if you can surmount the financial and logistical challenges, the rewards are sublime.

## Getting There & Away

### AIR

**Air Rarotonga** (☎22888; www.airraro.com) Flights from Rarotonga to Manihiki once every two weeks, and to Pukapuka occasionally. Flights take about 3½ hours, and the return fare is a staggering NZ$3100. Penrhyn is very occasionally serviced for a return fare of around NZ$4000. Bad weather, limited fuel supplies and too few bookings can cause the flights to be cancelled at short notice.

### BOAT

The only other regular transport to the Northern Group islands is on the Taio Shipping cargo ship. To reach Rakahanga, you must fly to Manihiki and then take a boat.

### YACHT

Suwarrow is accessible only by private yacht.

# Manihiki

POP 243 / AREA 5.4 SQ KM

Manihiki, 1046km from Rarotonga, is where most of the Cooks' black pearls are farmed. It has a magnificent lagoon – one of the South Pacific's finest – and is a highlight of the Northern Group. Nearly 40 tiny *motu* encircle the enclosed lagoon, which is 4km wide at its broadest point. The island is the summit of a 4000m underwater mountain. The US ship *Good Hope* made the first European discovery in 1822, and Manihiki was a US territory until it was ceded in 1980.

Tauhunu is the main village, and the airstrip is at Tukao on this island's northern point. Black pearls are the island's economic mainstay and they're harvested from September to December. The lung-busting abilities of the island's pearl divers are legendary – they can dive to great depths and stay submerged for minutes at a time.

Beachside retreat **Manihiki Lagoon Villas** (☎43123; www.manihikilagoonvillas.co.ck; bungalow s/d incl meals NZ$110/200, guesthouse incl meals NZ$80) offers bungalows and a guesthouse built on the water's edge of the lagoon. The accommodation is simple but the location is deluxe.

# Rakahanga

POP 77 / AREA 4.1 SQ KM

With two major islands and many smaller *motu* dotted in a turquoise lagoon, Rakahanga is another idyllic island. The lagoon here is unsuitable for pearl farming and the few families who live here are concentrated in Nivano village in the southwestern corner. The only export is copra, although the island is still renowned for its fine *rito* (coconut-fibre) hats, which are mostly sold on Rarotonga.

# Penrhyn

POP 203 / AREA 9.8 SQ KM

Penrhyn is the northernmost of the Cook Islands and boasts one of the largest lagoons in the country – so huge that the twin islands on opposite sides of the lagoon are barely visible from each other. Penrhyn has three deepwater passages that make excellent harbours, a fact that attracted whalers and traders in the 19th century. Peruvian blackbirders (slave traders) also visited the island in the 1860s. Penrhyn is another centre for black-pearl production and some interesting shell jewellery is produced on the island. The remains of a crashed B17 bomber are reminders of the WWII US servicemen who were stationed here and built the airstrip.

**Soa's Guesthouse** (☎42181; Omoka village; r NZ$100) is run by Soa Tini, a local fisherman and pearl farmer, who has a three-bedroom family house in the centre of Omoka village.

# Pukapuka

POP 453 / AREA 5.1 SQ KM

Well known for both its sensuous dancers and beautiful girls, remote Pukapuka is in many ways closer to Samoa than to the rest of the Cook Islands. Pukapuka's most famous resident was the American travel writer Robert Dean Frisbie, who lived here in the 1920s and wrote several evocative accounts of his life on the islands. Pukapuka sustained severe damage during the 2005 cyclones. In 2015 Pukapuka achieved 100% electricty sustainabilty through a solar energy network, and it is hoped this initiative will encourage emigre Pukapukans to resettle on their home island.

Contact the **island secretary** (☎41712) or the **island council** (☎41034) to arrange homestay accommodation.

## Suwarrow

POP 0 / AREA 0.4 SQ KM

The Cook Islands' only national park is a nature-lover's paradise, home to colonies of seabirds and some of the country's richest marine life. Two atoll managers live here six months of the year to oversee the park. During cyclone season they head back to Rarotonga. Suwarrow is best known as the home of Tom Neale, who lived here for three long stints between 1952 and his death in 1977. You can relive his adventures in his classic book *An Island to Oneself,* and visit his old house on Anchorage Island – one room is still furnished just as it was when he lived here. The only way you're likely to be able to visit Suwarrow is by private yacht, or on the annual expedition on the SRV *Discovery.*

# UNDERSTAND RAROTONGA & THE COOK ISLANDS

## Rarotonga & the Cook Islands Today

Imbued with the cosmopolitan influence of Auckland, Rarotonga has developed as one of the Pacific's most versatile travel destinations. To the north, Aitutaki is morphing into a more upmarket option, while the nation's other outer islands are increasing the emphasis on authentic and eco-aware traveller experiences. Stay in a traditional *kikau* homestay on Mitiaro, discover 'Atiu's fascinating birdlife, or go underground in the storied burial caves on Mangaia. All around the Cook Islands, the welcome for visitors continues to be friendly and gregarious, so remember to pack a good sense of humour.

## History

Cook Islanders are Maori people closely related to indigenous New Zealanders and French Polynesians. The Maori had no written history, but historians believe that Polynesian migrations from the Society Islands in French Polynesia to the Cooks began around the 5th century AD. Oral histories speak of around 1400 years of Polynesian activity on Rarotonga. A *marae* (religious meeting ground) on tiny Motutapu in Rarotonga's Muri Lagoon is estimated to be around 1500 years old. In the 14th century great ocean-going *vaka* (canoes) departed from Rarotonga for Aotearoa (New Zealand), and the settlers were ancestors of present-day New Zealand Maori.

During his disastrous second voyage from Spanish-occupied Peru, Don Alvaro de Mendaña y Neyra came upon Pukapuka on 20 August 1595 – he would die just months later in the Solomon Islands. Eleven years later, Mendaña's chief pilot Pedro Fernández de Quirós led another Pacific expedition, stopping at Rakahanga. James Cook explored the Cooks in 1773 and 1779. Only ever setting foot on Palmerston and never finding Rarotonga, Cook named the group the Hervey Islands in honour of a British Lord of the Admiralty. In his 1835 *Atlas de l'Océan Pacifique,* Russian explorer and cartographer Admiral Adam Johann von Krusenstern renamed them in honour of Captain Cook.

Reverend John Williams of the London Missionary Society (LMS) arrived on Aitutaki in 1821. In 1823 Papeiha, a convert from Ra'iatea in the Societies, moved to Rarotonga and set about converting the islands to Christianity. Though many *marae* were destroyed and sacred artefacts were carted off to British museums, much of the island's culture survived, including the traditional titles of *ariki* (chief) and *mataiapo* (subchief), the land-inheritance system and the indigenous language. The missionaries imposed a catalogue of strict rules and doctrines (known as the Blue Laws) and brought deadly diseases such as whooping cough, measles, smallpox and influenza, leading to a long-term decline in population numbers.

The Cook Islands became a British protectorate in 1888, in response to fears of French colonisation. In 1901 the islands were annexed to New Zealand, and the Southern and Northern Groups together became known as the Cook Islands.

During WWII the US built airstrips on Penrhyn and Aitutaki, but the Cooks escaped the war largely unscathed, unlike many of their South Pacific neighbours. In 1965 the Cook Islands became internally self-governing in free association with New Zealand.

Since self-governance was achieved, successive Cook Islands governments have struggled to maintain fiscal balance. In the early 1990s a series of bad investments – including the failed Sheraton resort on Rarotonga's south coast – left the country almost

NZ$250 million in debt, representing 113% of national GDP. An economic stabilisation plan in 1996 slashed public spending and the public sector workforce. Many Cook Islanders voted with their feet and left for greater opportunities in New Zealand and Australia.

Population decline and the country's national debt remain major issues. Growth in tourism is an ongoing opportunity, especially from New Zealand and Australia, and the country experienced strong visitor numbers in 2015 for the Cook Islands' celebrations for 50 years of independence.

# The Culture

## The National Psyche

Cook Islanders carry New Zealand passports, which allows them to live and work in New Zealand and, by extension (courtesy of the Special Category Visa), to live and work in Australia. This means many Cook Islanders are well travelled, worldly people. Rarotonga is a cosmopolitan place, yet beneath this Westernised veneer many Maori traditions remain, including traditional titles, family structure and the system of land inheritance. All native islanders are part of a family clan connected to the ancient system of *ariki*. Many still refer to themselves as from their 'home island' – Mangaian or Aitutakian.

But there is still a continuing exodus from the outer islands to Rarotonga, New Zealand and Australia, and some claim that Cook Islands' nationhood is undermined by that Kiwi passport – when the going gets tough the islanders move away to Auckland or Melbourne. Tourism is the Cooks' only major industry, but few tourists go beyond Rarotonga and Aitutaki. The outer islands have a fraction of the populations they had a few decades ago.

Politics, sport, dance, music, land and inheritance remain important, as do community, family and traditional values. Christianity is taken very seriously.

## Lifestyle

Islanders from Rarotonga are thoroughly First World in their lifestyles, with modern houses, regular jobs and reasonable salaries. Elsewhere in the Cooks, people live a more traditional lifestyle by fishing, growing crops and practising traditional arts and crafts. Family and the church are the two most influential elements in most islanders' lives, but people remain relaxed and informal about most aspects of day-to-day living. Like elsewhere in the Pacific, Cook Islanders are especially relaxed about timekeeping – things will happen when they do.

## Population

The resident population of the Cook Islands is around 19,500, but around 80% of Cook Islanders live overseas. More than 50,000 Cook Islanders live in New Zealand, half that number in Australia, and several thousand more in French Polynesia, the Americas, Europe and Asia. Of those who do live in their country of origin, more than 90% live in the Southern Group, with 60% living on Rarotonga.

Like many Pacific islands, the Cooks are struggling with a long-term population drain, as islanders move overseas in search of higher wages. More than 90% of the population is Polynesian, though the people of some of the Northern Group islands are more closely related to Samoans than to other Cook Islanders.

# Arts

## Dance & Music

Cook Islanders love to dance and they're reputed to be the best dancers in Polynesia. Don't be surprised if you're invited to join them at an Island Night. Traditional dance forms include the *karakia* (prayer dance), *pe'e ura pa'u* (drum-beat dance), *ate* (choral song) and *kaparima* (action song). Men stamp, gesture and knock their knees together, while women shake and gyrate their hips in an unmistakeably suggestive manner.

The islanders are also great singers and musicians. The multi-part harmony singing at a Cook Islands' church service is truly beautiful, but pop music is popular too. Polynesian string bands, featuring guitars and ukuleles, often perform at local restaurants and hotels.

## Arts & Crafts

Traditional woodcarving and woven handicrafts (pandanus mats, baskets, purses and fans) are still popular in the Cooks. You'll see women going to church wearing finely woven *rito* (coconut-fibre) hats, mainly made on the Northern Group islands.

Ceremonial adzes, stone taro pounders and *pupu ei* (snail-shell necklaces) are produced on Mangaia, and the best place to see traditional *tivaevae* (appliqué work, used for bedspreads, cushion covers and home decoration) is at the Atiu Fibre Arts Studio on 'Atiu. Black pearls are grown in the Northern Group and are an important export. *'Ei* (floral necklaces) and *'ei katu* (tiaras) are customarily given to friends and honoured guests. You're bound to receive a few, especially on the outer islands.

Traditional *tata'u* (tattooing) is also making a resurgence, with intricate designs often showcasing an individual's genealogy. Ask at Avarua's bookshops for *Patterns of the Past: Tattoo Revival in the Cook Islands* by Therese Mangos and John Utanga.

## Literature

Purchase these in Avarua's bookshops.

*An Island to Oneself* by Tom Neale is the classic desert-island read, written by a New Zealander who lived as a virtual hermit on Suwarrow during the 1950s and 1960s.

Robert Dean Frisbie ran a trading outpost on Pukapuka in the 1920s and wrote two evocative memoirs, *The Book of Pukapuka* and *The Island of Desire*.

Sir Tom Davis (Pa Tuterangi Ariki) was – among many things, including medical doctor and NASA scientist – the Cook Islands' prime minister for most of the 1980s (he died in 2007). His autobiography is called *Island Boy*.

If you're after local legends, pick up *Cook Islands Legends* and *The Ghost at Tokatarava and Other Stories from the Cook Islands*, both by notable Cook Islands' author Jon Tikivanotau Jonassen. Pukapukan poet Kauraka Kauraka published several books of poems including *Ta 'Akatauira: My Morning Star*.

*Akono'anga Maori: Cooks Islands Culture*, edited by Ron and Marjorie Tua'inekore Crocombe, is an excellent book that looks at culture manifested in traditional Polynesian tattooing, poetry, art, sport and governance. *Patterns of the Past: Tattoo Revival in the Cook Islands* by Therese Mangos and John Utanga is a beautifully illustrated title on *tata'u* in the Cook Islands.

*Guide to Cook Islands Birds* by DT Holyoak is a useful guide to the islands' native birds, with colour photos and tips for identification.

# Environment

The Cook Islands' small land mass (just 241 sq km) is scattered over 2 million sq km of ocean, midway between American Samoa and Tahiti.

The 15 islands are divided into Northern and Southern Groups. Most of the Southern Group are younger volcanic islands, although Mangaia is the Pacific's oldest island. The Northern Group are 'low islands', coral atolls with outer reefs encircling lagoons, that have formed on top of ancient sunken volcanoes. 'Atiu, Ma'uke, Mitiaro and Mangaia are 'raised islands' characterised by *makatea* – rocky coastal areas formed by uplifted coral reefs.

Waste management is a major issue in the Cook Islands. Glass, plastic and aluminium are collected for recycling, but there's still a huge surplus of rubbish. Water supply is also a major concern.

Rising sea levels associated with global warming are a huge threat to the Cooks. Many of the islands of the Northern Group are low lying and could be uninhabitable within the next 100 years. Climate scientists predict that severe cyclones are likely to become much more common.

In 2011, the Cook Islands' government announced plans to become the Pacific's 'greenest' destination, and was targeting 100% reliance on solar and wind-generated energy by 2020. In 2015 a new solar electricity farm funded by the New Zealand government was installed on Rarotonga for the Cooks' 50th anniversary of independence, and less-populated islands in the Northern Group achieved 100% energy sustainability.

## Wildlife

Rarotonga's mountainous centre is covered with a dense jungle of ferns, creepers and towering trees, providing habitat for the island's rich birdlife. Coconut palms and spectacular tropical flowers grow almost everywhere in the Cook Islands, though the once-common pandanus trees are now rare on Rarotonga and 'Atiu.

The only native mammal is the Pacific fruit bat (flying fox), found on Mangaia and Rarotonga. Pigs, chickens and goats were introduced by the first Polynesian settlers, along with rats, which devastated the islands' endemic wildlife, especially native birds. The *kakerori* (Rarotongan flycatcher) was almost wiped out, but is now recovering thanks to the establishment of the Takitumu

Conservation Area on Rarotonga. Other native birds include the cave-dwelling *kopeka* ('Atiu swiftlet) on 'Atiu, the *tanga'eo* (Mangaian kingfisher) and the *kukupa* (Cook Islands fruit dove).

# SURVIVAL GUIDE

## Directory A–Z

### ACCOMMODATION

Officially, visitors are required to have booked accommodation before arriving in the Cook Islands, although you can usually arrange a hotel when you arrive at the airport. However, many places to stay on Rarotonga are booked up in advance, so it pays to plan ahead.

Rarotonga's accommodation includes hostels, motel-style units, self-contained bungalows and expensive top-end resorts. All the major Southern Group islands have organised accommodation. Even for couples, renting a house can be a good way to cut costs.

Manihiki and Penrhyn are the only Northern Group islands with simple accommodation.

For a dorm bed, budget travellers can expect to pay around NZ$30.

### ACTIVITIES

The Cook Islands are perfect for relaxation, but there's plenty of activities to keep energetic travellers busy. Rarotonga is an excellent place for hiking, and Aitutaki's backcountry roads and deserted beaches are good for exploring. 'Atiu, Ma'uke, Mitiaro and Mangaia have many trails winding through the *makatea*. History enthusiasts will enjoy visiting the historic *marae* on most of the islands. Many of these traditional religious meeting grounds are still used today for formal ceremonies, such as the investiture of a new *ariki* or *mataiapo*.

#### Water Sports

The sheltered lagoons and beaches on Rarotonga and Aitutaki are great for swimming and snorkelling. Diving is also excellent, with good visibility and lots of marine life, from sea turtles and tropical fish to reef sharks and eagle rays. You can hire snorkelling gear on Aitutaki and Rarotonga, as well as kayaks, sailboards and other water-sports equipment.

Raro has just a handful of resident surfers, but there are serious waves outside Rarotonga's perimeter reef and a budding community of bodyboard riders.

Kite surfing, paddle-boarding and small-boat sailing are popular in Rarotonga's Muri Lagoon. Glass-bottomed boats also operate from Muri Beach, and there are several lagoon-cruise operators in Aitutaki. Deep-sea fishing boats can be chartered on Rarotonga and Aitutaki, and bonefishing on Aitutaki lagoon is growing in popularity. From July to October, whale-watching trips are available on Rarotonga.

#### Caving

The Cook Islands has some extraordinary caves to explore including Anatakitaki and Rima Rau on 'Atiu, Motuanga on Ma'uke, Vai Nauri on Mitiaro, and Te Rua Rere on Mangaia.

### CHILDREN

Travelling with kids presents no special problems in the Cook Islands, although many smaller hotels and bungalows don't accept children aged under 12 – ask about the policy before booking.

### CUSTOMS

The following restrictions apply: 2L of spirits or wine or 4.5L of beer, plus 200 cigarettes or 50 cigars or 250g of tobacco. Quarantine laws are strictly enforced, and plants, animals or any related products are prohibited. Firearms, weapons and drugs are also prohibited.

### DANGERS & ANNOYANCES

Swimming is very safe in the sheltered lagoons but be wary around reef passages, where currents are especially strong. Rarotonga's main passages are at Avana Harbour, Avaavaroa, Papua and Rutaki. They exist on other islands as well, often opposite streams.

Mosquitoes can be a real nuisance in the Cooks, particularly during the rainy season (around mid-December to mid-April). Use repellent; mosquito coils are available everywhere.

### ELECTRICITY

240V AC, 50Hz, using Australian-style three-blade plugs. Power is available 24 hours throughout the Southern Group.

### EMBASSIES & CONSULATES

**Department of Foreign Affairs & Immigration** (Map p52; ✆29347; www.mfai.gov.ck) Citizens from countries other than New Zealand seeking consular advice should talk to the Secretary of the Department of Foreign Affairs & Immigration on the 3rd floor of the Trustnet building in Avarua.

**New Zealand High Commission** (Map p52; ✆55201, 22201; nzhcraro@oyster.net.ck; PO Box 21, Avarua) New Zealand High Commission is located above the Philatelic Bureau in Avarua. New Zealand the only country with diplomatic representation in the Cook Islands.

### EMERGENCY

**Police** ✆999

**Ambulance** ✆998

## FESTIVALS & EVENTS

**Dancer of the Year** (April) Dance displays are held throughout April, culminating in the Dancer of the Year competition.

**Gospel Day** (July) The arrival of the gospel to the Cook Islands is celebrated with *nuku* (religious plays), held on 20 July on 'Atiu, 21 July on Mitiaro, 25 July on Rarotonga, and elsewhere on 26 October.

**Constitution Celebration** (Te Maeva Nui; August) Celebrating the 1965 declaration of independence, this is the Cook Islands' major annual festival.

**Tiare (Floral) Festival Week** (August) Celebrated with floral-float parades and the Miss Tiare beauty pageant.

**Vaka Eiva** (November) This week-long canoe festival celebrates the great Maori migration from Rarotonga to New Zealand. There are many race events and celebrations of Cooks culture.

## INTERNET ACCESS

BlueSky Teleshops in Avarua, Muri Beach and on Aitutaki offer internet access and sell prepaid wi-fi access which can be used at hotspots around the main islands and also on 'Atiu. Convenience stores also sell this pre-paid wi-fi access in denominations of NZ$10 (150MB), NZ$25 (500MB), and NZ$50 (1.25GB). Another option is to buy a local Kokanet 3G SIM card (NZ$25) for your smartphone or tablet, and purchase data for 20 cents per MB up to 1GB for NZ$50. Note that at the time of writing, 3G service was limited to Rarotonga. Most Telecom offices on the outer islands have small cyberbooths, though the connections are slow and expensive.

## MONEY

New Zealand dollars are used in the Cook Islands. You'll probably get a few Cook Islands coins in change (in denominations of 5c, 10c, 20c, 50c, $1, $2 and $5). The Cook Islands prints a $3 note that's quite collectable and available at the Philatelic Bureau in Avarua. Note that Cook Islands currency cannot be exchanged anywhere in the world.

There are limited ATMs and banks on Rarotonga and Aitutaki, and credit cards are widely accepted on the nation's main two islands. Credit cards are accepted at the larger hotels on Aitutaki and at some places on 'Atiu, but for other islands cash is essential.

A 15% VAT (value-added tax) is included in the price of most goods and services. All prices quoted include VAT. A departure tax when leaving the Cook Islands is already incorporated into international air tickets.

Tipping is not customary in the Cook Islands, but it's not frowned upon for exceptional service. Haggling over prices is considered rude.

## OPENING HOURS

Sunday is largely reserved for churchgoing and rest, although a few cafes and restaurants around Rarotonga and Aitutaki open in the afternoon.

**Banks** 9am to 3pm on weekdays. Only Avarua's Westpac is open on Saturday morning.

**Businesses and shops** 9am to 4pm Monday to Friday, most shops open until noon on Saturday.

**Small grocery stores** 6am or 7am until 8pm or 9pm.

## PRACTICALITIES

**Newspapers** Rarotonga's *Cook Islands News* is published daily except Sunday, and the *Cook Islands Herald* comes out on Wednesday. Both feature local and international news.

**Radio** Radio Cook Islands (630 kHz AM; www.radio.co.ck) reaches most islands and broadcasts local programs, Radio New Zealand news and Radio Australia's world news. The smaller KC-FM (103.8 MHz FM) station can be received only on Rarotonga.

**TV** Cook Islands Television (CITV) screens across Rarotonga; international cable channels are available at some hotels. On outer islands, Sky Fiji is available and programming is usually controlled by each island's mayor. If you're engrossed in CNN or a wildlife documentary, there's every chance it will be switched mid-program to the rugby. Only in the Pacific! Aitutaki has a small station that broadcasts intermittently on local issues.

**DVDs** Can be hired all over Rarotonga and many accommodation places can provide DVD players.

**Weights & Measures** Metric system.

**Language** Cook Islands Maori – closely related to the Maori language of New Zealand – is the local language, but virtually everyone also speaks English.

### POST

Poste-restante mail is held for 30 days at post offices on most islands. To collect mail at the post office in Avarua it should be addressed to you c/o Poste Restante, Avarua, Rarotonga, Cook Islands.

### PUBLIC HOLIDAYS

**New Year's Day** 1 January

**Good Friday & Easter Monday** March/April

**Anzac Day** 25 April

**Queen's Birthday** First Monday in June

**Gospel Day** (Rarotonga only) 25 July

**Constitution/Flag-Raising Day** 4 August

**Gospel Day** (Cook Islands) 26 October

**Christmas Day** 25 December

**Boxing Day** 26 December

### TELEPHONE

All the islands are connected to the country's modern telephone system. Each island has a BlueSky Telecom office, usually incorporating a payphone and an internet booth. Most of these offices also offer a pre-paid wi-fi service.

The country code for the Cook Islands is ☎682, and there are no local area codes. Dial ☎00 for direct international calls and ☎017 for international directory service. The local directory operator is ☎010. You can make collect calls from any phone by dialling ☎015.

For mobile phones, a GSM network is available through BlueSky, and international roaming and local SIM cards available. 3G data services are available on Rarotonga only.

### TIME

The Cook Islands are east of the International Date Line, 10 hours behind Greenwich Mean Time (GMT). The country has no daylight-saving time. When it's noon in the Cooks it's 10pm in London, noon in Tahiti and Hawai'i, 2pm in LA, 10am the next day in Fiji and New Zealand, and 8am the next day in Sydney.

### TOURIST INFORMATION

**Aitutaki Tourism** (www.cookislands.travel/aitutaki) Excellent for accommodation and activities on Aitutaki.

**Bluesky Cook Islands** (www.telecom.co.ck) Searchable telephone directories.

**Cook Islands Government Online** (www.cook-islands.gov.ck) Government news and press releases.

**Cook Islands Herald** (www.ciherald.co.ck) Online edition of the popular weekly newspaper.

**Cook Islands News** (www.cookislandsnews.com) Online edition of the daily Cook Islands newspaper.

**Cook Islands Website** (www.ck) Local business details including tourist operations.

**Enjoy Cook Islands** (www.enjoycookislands.com) Website for the *Cook Islands Sun* newspaper, including lots of traveller-friendly information.

**Escape** (www.escapemagazine.travel) Website for *Escape*, an excellent travel and lifestyle magazine covering the Cook Islands.

**Lonely Planet** (www.lonelyplanet.com/rarotonga-and-the-cook-islands) Author recommendations, traveller reviews and insider tips.

**Tourism Cook Islands** (www.cookislands.travel) Central information site for the main tourist office.

**www.cookislands.org.uk** Hosted out of the UK, this is the only noncommercial website covering the Cooks.

**www.jasons.com** New Zealand-based portal for Pacific travel including accommodation bookings.

##  Getting There & Away

### AIR

Rarotonga has international flights to Auckland, Sydney, Los Angeles and Tahiti. Low-season travel to the Cooks is from mid-April to late August, and the high season runs from December to February. There's heavy demand from New Zealand to the Cooks in December, and in the other direction in January. Demand for flights from New Zealand and Australia is also strong during those countries' respective school holiday periods.

**Air New Zealand** (www.airnewzealand.com) Regular flights between Auckland and Rarotonga (return fares around NZ$850). Weekly direct flights between Sydney and Rarotonga on a Saturday (return fares from around A$800). Weekly direct flights between Rarotonga and Los Angeles (return fares from around US$1300).

**Virgin Australia** (www.virginaustralia.com) Regular flights between Auckland and Rarotonga (return fares around NZ$850).

**Air Tahiti** (www.airtahiti.aero) Direct codeshare flights on Thursday with Air Rarotonga linking Tahiti with Rarotonga (return fares from around NZ$950).

### SEA

Rarotonga is a favourite port of call for South Pacific cruise ships but they don't take on passengers, typically arriving in the morning and departing in the afternoon after quick island tours and souvenir shopping.

The Cooks are popular with yachties except during the cyclone season (November to March). Once you arrive at Rarotonga, fly your Q flag and visit the **Harbour Master** (Map p52; ☎28814; Avatiu Harbour, Rarotonga). There are other official ports of entry at Aitutaki, Penrhyn and Pukapuka, which have good anchorages.

Virtually uninhabited, Suwarrow Atoll is a trophy destination for cruising yachties, but isn't an official entry.

There's a slim chance of catching a crewing berth on a yacht from the Cook Islands to Tonga, Samoa, Fiji, French Polynesia or New Zealand. You can ask at Rarotonga's **Ports Authority** (Map p52; Avatiu Harbour), where yachties leave messages if they are looking for crew.

## Getting Around

Unless you're sailing your own yacht, travel between the Cook Islands is limited to slow cargo ships and Air Rarotonga flights. Flights to the Northern Group islands are expensive, and only Manihiki, Penrhyn and Pukapuka have airstrips.

### AIR

**Air Rarotonga** (☎22888; www.airraro.com), the only domestic airline in the Cook Islands, has several daily flights to Aitutaki, and several weekly flights between Rarotonga and the rest of the Southern Group. Other than the high-traffic Rarotonga–Aitutaki route, Air Rarotonga sometimes cancels or moves flights to consolidate passengers if there are too many empty seats.

Flights to the Northern Group are more erratic – there's a scheduled flight to Manihiki every second Tuesday, and flights to Penrhyn operate only when there's sufficient demand.

The baggage allowance for the Southern Group is 16kg, for the Northern Group it's 10kg. Passengers are allowed one piece of hand luggage not exceeding 3kg.

### BOAT

Shipping schedules are notoriously unpredictable – weather, breakdowns and unexpected route changes can all put a kink in your travel plans. Ships stop off at each island for just a few hours, and only Rarotonga and Penrhyn have decent harbours. At all the other islands you go ashore by lighter or barge.

**Taio Shipping** (☎24905; taio@oyster.net.ck; Avatiu Wharf) is the only interisland shipping company and its vessels are far from luxury cruise liners: there's limited cabin space and some ships have no cabins at all. Showers and toilets are available to all passengers. Return trips to the islands of the Southern Group cost NZ$250. To the Northern Group, return fares are NZ$1200 in a cabin and NZ$450 for deck space. Ships only run one or two times per month.

### LOCAL TRANSPORT

All the islands are good for cycling. Rarotonga has a regular circle-island bus service, taxis, and bicycles, motorcycles and cars for hire. Aitutaki has a taxi service, and bicycles, motorcycles and cars for hire. 'Atiu has a taxi service, rental motorcycles and a couple of Jeeps. You can rent scooters and bicycles on Ma'uke, Mitiaro and Mangaia.

Hitchhiking is legal, though of course never entirely safe, and if you're walking along an empty stretch of road someone will stop and offer you a lift before too long.

### TOURS

Circle-island tours on Rarotonga offer a good introduction to the island's history, geography and traditional culture. Guided tours are also offered on Aitutaki, 'Atiu, Ma'uke and Mangaia.

Rarotongan travel agencies can organise single-island or multi-island package tours. Day trips from Rarotonga to Aitutaki are available.

# Samoa

685 / POP 190,372

**Includes ➡**



## Best Places to Stay

- ➡ Seabreeze Resort (p119)
- ➡ Namu'a Island Beach Fale (p118)
- ➡ Lupe Sina Treesort (p120)
- ➡ Dave Parker's Eco Lodge (p115)
- ➡ Joelan Beach Fales (p127)

## Best Places to Eat

- ➡ Bistro Tatau (p112)
- ➡ Palusami (p111)
- ➡ Amoa Restaurant (p127)
- ➡ Sunday lunch (p129)
- ➡ Taefu T Matafeo Store (p127)

## Why Go?

Serene but spirited, wild yet well-manicured, hushed but birthed by volcanic explosions; stunning Samoa is a paradisaical paradox. Despite its intense natural beauty – all iridescent seas, jade jungles and crystal waterfalls – this is a humble place, devoid of mega-resorts and flashy attractions, but with welcomes as warm as the island sun.

Geographically and culturally, this small nation is considered the heart of Polynesia. Though the missionaries of the 1800s were enormously influential, the country has nevertheless clung to *Fa'a Samoa* (the Samoan Way), making it one of the most authentic and traditional of all Pacific societies: in some parts of the islands you're more likely to see someone juggling fire than a house with walls.

Despite its isolation, Samoa offers accessible adventures. From the relative ruckus of Apia to the soul-stirring silence of Savai'i, you'll find a paradise that is safe, sweet and easy to get around.

## When to Go

### Apia

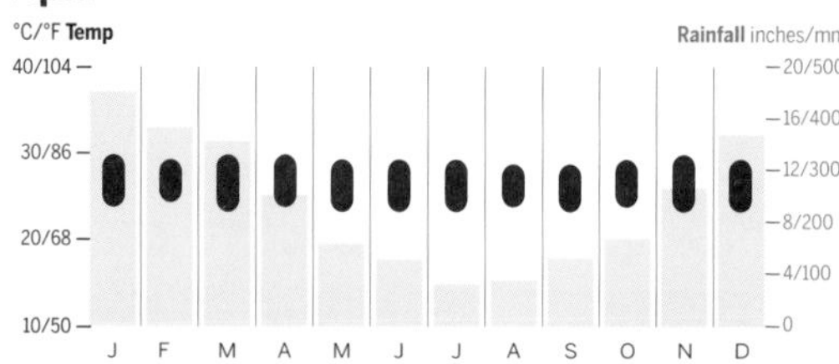


**Dec–Jan** Peak holiday period when Samoans living abroad visit home.

**May–Oct** Dry season and festival time.

**Nov–Apr** Steamy weather and cyclone season.

# UPOLU

POP 143,418 / AREA 1125 SQ KM

Enchanting Upolu may be small in size, but it's huge on options. Beach-bumming or bushwalking? Resort cocktails or billiard-hall beers? Diving or do-nothing? Whatever floats your holiday boat, odds are you'll find it here.

Home to the international airport, the capital city and the bulk of the country's population, Upolu is where nearly all travellers begin their Samoan sojourn. The majority get their first glimpse of local life on the 35km drive from the airport to Apia, where a procession of tidy villages, incongruously large churches and rickety fruit stalls line perhaps the slowest highway in the world (the speed limit is 40km/h).

Most visitors devote themselves to the dazzling strips of sand skirting Upolu's southern shoreline, with forays into pristine offshore lagoons that shelter colourful coral groves and schools of fish; the ethereal To Sua Ocean Trench attracts those keen on the surreal swim of a lifetime. But Upolu also has its fair share of terra firma treasures: the tangled rainforest of the interior, rough coastal cliffs formed by the cooling of lava rivers and fascinating craters and caves. The urban delights of Apia shouldn't be neglected either – not if you fancy the odd boogie, movie, or the country's best eating and drinking establishments.

## Getting Around

### TO/FROM THE AIRPORT

Faleolo Airport is on the coast, 35km west of Apia. Many resorts and hotels offer transfers; otherwise there's always an armada of taxis ready to ferry arrivals to the city or other Upolu destinations. The fare to Apia is around ST60.

If you're travelling alone, it's cheaper to catch an airport shuttle. It pays to prebook, but you'll usually spot them waiting across from the terminal for all of the major international flights. **Samoa Scenic Tours** (p103) has shuttles that stop at any of Apia's hotels (about ST47, 45 minutes); it also offers transfers to other Upolu resorts.

Many of the international flights arrive and depart at ungodly hours, but if you're lucky enough to have one at a reasonable time, buses are an option. Walk out to the main road and hail any bus approaching from your right to get to Apia. To get to Faleolo Airport from Apia (ST4), take any bus marked 'Pasi o le Va'a', 'Manono-uta', 'Falelatai' or 'Faleolo'.

### BUS

Buses connecting Apia with almost every other part of Upolu leave from both Maketi Fou (the main market) and from behind the Flea Market. Drivers circle between the two until the bus is full (this can take up to an hour) and are liable to veer off route to deposit locals at their front doors. There are set bus stops on the coastal road, but if you hail the driver they'll stop almost anywhere. Pay as you leave the bus. Fares within Apia range from ST1 to ST1.80. The most you'll pay for a trip anywhere in Upolu is ST8.50. Buses begin running early in the morning and stop in the early afternoon, though services are limited on Sundays.

A bus schedule for Upolu that includes fare information is available by emailing the **Samoa Tourism Authority** (Map p106; ☎63500; www.samoa.travel; Beach Rd; ⏰9am-5pm Mon-Fri, 8am-noon Sat).

To reach the Aleipata district at the eastern end of the island, catch the Lalomanu bus. To head east along the north coast, take the Falefa, Fagaloa or Lotofaga bus. For any point along the Cross Island Rd, take either the Si'umu or Salani bus. For Togitogiga and O Le Pupu-Pu'e National Park, take the Falealili or Salani bus.

### CAR

The main roads in Upolu range from pristine to potholed. The national speed limit maxes out at 56km/h and drops to 40km/h through villages (omnipresent speed humps ensure you never forget to slow down); as there are very few stretches of road that don't pass through villages, expect to be driving at a snail's pace most of the time. The sealed Main Coast Rd winds its way around Upolu, while three roads cross over the island's east–west central ridge and divide it roughly into quarters.

Be aware: though there are very few main roads, there is an even greater dearth of street signs. Those that exist mostly point the way to obscure villages (rather than, say, the airport). Roads often veer off in the opposite direction of the one you might wish to take, with no notice at all. Don't be shy about asking for directions.

A high-clearance 2WD vehicle should be adequate for all but the roads to Uafato and to Aganoa Black Sand Beach (4WD only). Outside of Apia and the stretch between the city and the airport, petrol stations are in short supply.

# Apia

POP 36,735

Few people come to a Pacific paradise to hang around in a small city with not much in the way of beaches. But it's worth taking some time to explore the (relative) sprawl

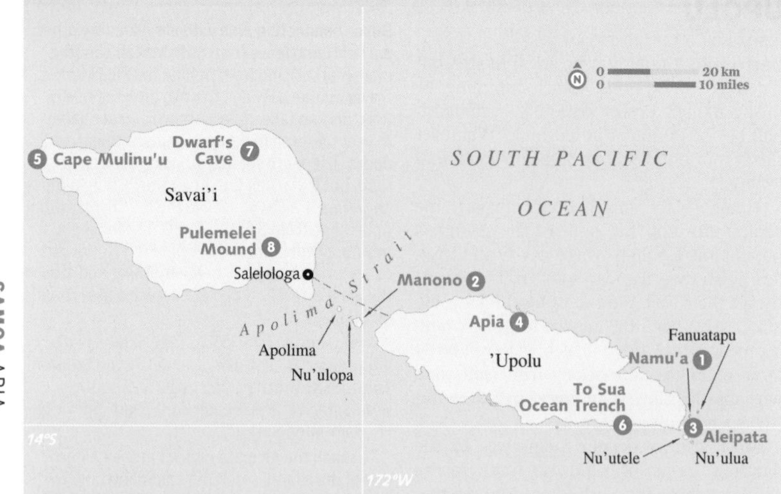


## Samoa Highlights

1. Sleeping in a traditional Samoan *fale* such as those on **Namu'a island** (p118).
2. Soaking up the village vibe while strolling around the white-sand-encircled island of **Manono** (p123).
3. Stepping off the perfect flax-coloured sands into the turquoise waters of **Aleipata's beaches** (p115).
4. Partying with the locals in the bars and nightclubs in **Apia** (p112).
5. Admiring the sunset from the sacred sites of **Cape Mulinu'u** (p131).
6. Bathing in the idyllic sunken waters of the **To Sua Ocean Trench** (p115).
7. Exploring an old lava tunnel, swimming and getting covered in mud at Savai'i's **Dwarf's Cave** (p130).
8. Having a lost-world moment battling overgrown weeds and lost trails before standing atop the mysterious **Pulemelei Mound** (p132).

of Apia: with an excellent cultural centre, three buzzy markets and an eclectic collection of local eateries and nightspots, the capital offers an immersive introduction to island life. Plentiful accommodation, facilities galore and proximity to some fascinating natural and historic attractions – and, given the island's small size, pretty much everything else on Upolu – makes Apia a handy base for visitors with their own wheels.

## Sights & Activities

**Vaiala Beach** BEACH

(Map p106; Vaiala) The closest beach to Apia town, immediately east of the harbour. The currents can be strong, so take care and avoid the area marked by buoys where there's a dangerous whirlpool.

★ **Samoa Cultural Village** CULTURAL CENTRE

(Map p106; www.samoa.travel; Beach Rd; 9am-5pm Mon-Fri, interactive sessions 10.30am-12.30pm Tue-Thu) FREE Though this 'village' is open every weekday, it's the interactive sessions that are an absolute must. Knowledgeable and extremely affable hosts take visitors through all aspects of Samoan cultural and traditional life, with workshops on weaving, woodworking, *siapo* cloth making, traditional *tatau*, dance and music. Guests are also treated to an *'ava* (kava) ceremony and lunch from the *umu* (hot-stone oven).

The village is tucked away behind the Samoa Tourism Authority's information *fale*.

**Maketi Fou** MARKET

(Food Market; Map p106; Fugalei St; 24hr) Abuzz with local merchants, shoppers, loiterers and men slamming it down over games of *mu* (Samoan checkers), this 24-hour market is a must-see shopping and social experience. Though primarily a produce market, pretty much everything is sold here. Souvenir hunters will find *siapo* (decorated bark cloth), woodcarvings, coconut-shell jewellery, *lava-lava* (wraparound sarongs) and T-shirts. A cold *niu* (drinking coconut) will give you strength to shop on, despite the oppressive humidity of the place.

The ambience is somewhat enlivened by the fume-ridden chaos of the adjacent bus station.

**Flea Market** MARKET

(Map p106; cnr Fugalei St & Beach Rd; ⌚8am-4pm Mon-Fri, to noon Sat) Down on the waterfront, this steamy labyrinth is packed with small stalls selling craftwork, clothing and souvenirs. Don't bother to test your bargaining skills here, as haggling is not an element of Samoan commerce.

**Fish Market** MARKET

(Map p106; off Beach Rd) A scramble takes place here at the crack of dawn every Sunday to snag the freshest catches for the post-church *to'ona'i* (Sunday lunch). Unsurprisingly, Apia's best fish and chips are also found here.

**Falemata'aga** MUSEUM

(Museum of Samoa; Map p106; ☎26036; www.museumofsamoa.ws; cnr Ififi & Vaitele Sts; ⌚9.30am-4pm Mon-Fri) FREE The German-era school building houses an enchanting collection of artefacts and displays focusing on four themes: history, culture, Pacific and environment. Donations are appreciated.

**Government House** BUILDING

(Map p106; Beach Rd) While Government House isn't a thrilling landmark in itself (though the giant, modern rendition of a *fale* roof atop it is cause for a snapshot), it's worth a visit to see the Samoa Police Brass Band – in full regalia – toot out the national anthem as it raises the flag each weekday morning between 7.30am and 8am.

**Immaculate Conception Cathedral** CHURCH

(Map p106; Beach Rd) Looming over the harbour, this lofty cathedral is breathtakingly beautiful. Originally constructed in 1884, the building was recently rebuilt at an estimated cost of ST13 million: it's a hefty price tag for a country that isn't exactly rolling in it, but the devout believe its ornate timber-crafted ceilings, dazzling stained-glass windows and gaspingly huge interior (2000-person capacity; it previously held 400) make it priceless.

**Vanya Taule'alo Gallery** GALLERY

(Map p116; ☎20011; Mulivai Lane, Taumeasina; ⌚8am-4pm Mon-Sat) This small but special gallery showcases the works of Samoan and other Pacific Island artists: prints, paintings, woodcarvings, jewellery, and other handicrafts are all top quality, and are all for sale. The gallery is attached to the equally worthy **Legends Cafe**. It's about a five-minute drive from the centre of Apia.

## SAMOA IN...

### Five Days

Spend a day or two exploring **Apia**, making sure to visit the Samoa Cultural Village, Palolo Deep Marine Reserve, the Robert Louis Stevenson Museum and catching a *fiafia* (dance performance) or *fa'afafine* show. The following day begin the loop around Upolu, heading east and soaking up the sights and village calm. Spend your first night at **Namu'a Island Beach Fale** then continue on around the island, stopping two more nights at the resort or *fale* of your choice. Don't miss splashing around the **To Sua Ocean Trench** and stopping at the stunning **beaches** of the south coast.

### Ten Days

Follow the five-day itinerary, then continue north up the coast of Upolu, stopping for a night on the island of **Manono**. The following day take the ferry to **Savai'i** and spend the next four days leisurely driving around the island counter-clockwise: get covered in mud at **Dwarf's Cave**, take the eerie, scenic drive to **Fafa O Sauai'i**, and get blown away by the **Alofaaga Blowholes**. If you're keen on archaeology and adventure, search for the mysterious **Pulemelei Mound**.

## Upolu

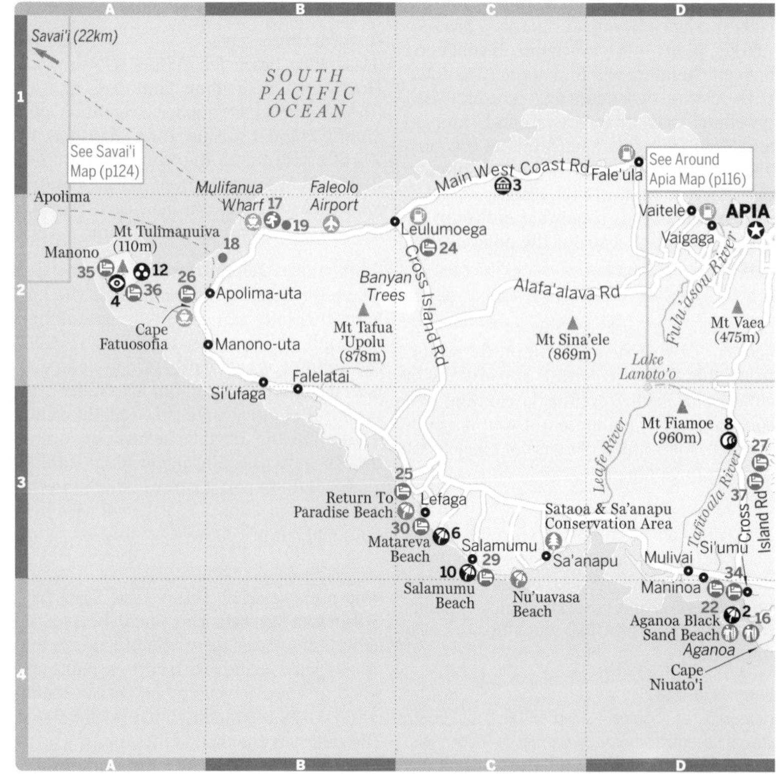


**Mormon Temple** CHURCH

(Map p106; Vaitele St) One of the most impressive buildings in Samoa is this massive temple taking up 1736 sq metres on the western approach to town. Completed in 2005 after a fire destroyed the previous building, the white granite edifice has an elegant art-deco sensibility and is capped by a golden angel.

**Palolo Deep Marine Reserve** SNORKELLING

(Map p106; Vaiala Beach Rd; adult/child ST4/1, hire of mask & flippers/snorkel ST5/2; 8am-6pm) Between Vaiala Beach and Apia's harbour, this reserve is a magnificent stretch of shallow reef (best visited at high tide) that features a deep, coral-encrusted hole thronging with marine life. To reach the drop-off, swim out from the beach to the dark patch of water to the left of the marker stick. It's around 100m from the shore, and you'll need flippers and a snorkel to get you out there without damaging the coral (or your feet).

**A Touch of Samoa** SPA

(Map p116; 843 0034; Falealili St (Cross Island Rd), Tanugamanono; 60min massage ST50; 9am-7pm Mon-Sat, 11am-7pm Sun) Take a load off at this popular spa, where they use massage techniques based on both Samoan and European traditions. Waxing, pedicures, manicures, eyebrow and eyelash tinting and more also available.

**Misiluki Day Spa** SPA

(Map p106; 20759; www.misilukispa.com; Falealili St; massage per 30min from ST50; 9am-7pm Mon-Fri, to 3pm Sat, 2pm-7pm Sun) For massage, as well as mani-pedis, waxing, facials and body treatment, this serene yet simple spa gets top marks from locals.

### Tours

**Polynesian Xplorer** TOUR

(Map p116; 26940; www.samoaaccommodation.co; Falealili St) Full-service boutique

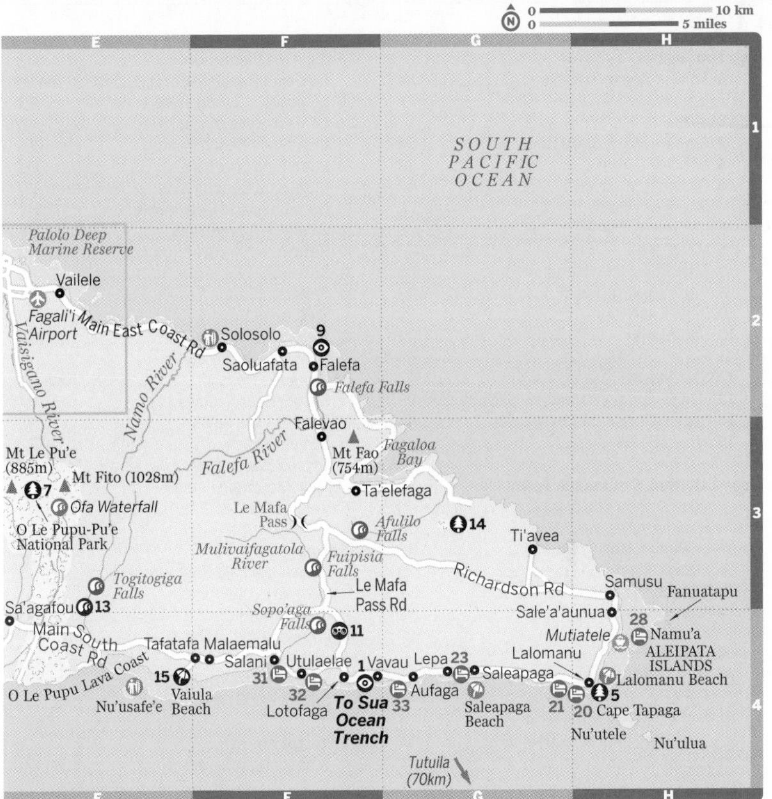




travel agency that runs recommended tours in Upolu (half-day ST120, full-day from ST220) and day tours to Manono (ST230) and Savai'i (ST397). Groups are small and you can design your own custom itinerary including lodging and transfers. Also has an airport office.

**Samoa Scenic Tours** TOUR
(Map p106; ☎26981; www.samoascenictours.com) Runs a huge variety of tours around Upolu, Savai'i and to Manono: see the website for full listing and prices. It can also tailor tours for groups and special interests.

## Sleeping

Most places in Apia include breakfast in their rates; many also offer airport transfers.

Just out of town, on Taumeasina Island, the upmarket **Taumeasina Resort** was nearing completion at research time: check www.taumeasinasamoa.com for details.

**Aniva's Place** GUESTHOUSE $
(Map p116; ☎20501; www.anivasaccommodationsamoa.com; off Falealili St (Cross Island Rd), Moto'otua; s/d ST120/140, without bathroom ST100/120; P ❄ 📶 🏊) Run by the exceptionally charming Aniva, this two-storey suburban dwelling offers a homey, welcoming atmosphere with clean, comfortable rooms, an honesty bar, a library and a small pool. Excellent home-cooked meals are available on request for a small fee.

**Annabelle Inn** INN $
(Map p106; ☎20505; inbound@samoascenic.com; Beach Rd; r with/without bathroom from ST60/50; 📶) Set in a quaint, early-20th-century home, this sweet place offers comfortable, homey rooms and a sunny, sociable verandah restaurant that looks over to the marina. It's a quick stroll to the Palolo Deep Marine Reserve; those interested in a different kind of wildlife will rejoice in Annabelle's

## Upolu

**Top Sights**

1 To Sua Ocean Trench ........ F4

**Sights**

2 Aganoa Black Sand Beach ........ D4
3 EFKS Museum ........ C1
4 Grave of 99 Stones ........ A2
Grave of Afutiti ........ (see 12)
5 Lalomanu Crater ........ H4
6 Matareva ........ C3
7 O Le Pupu-Pu'e National Park ........ E3
8 Papapapai-tai Falls ........ D3
9 Piula Cave Pool ........ F2
10 Salamumu ........ C3
11 Sopo'aga Falls ........ F4
12 Star Mound ........ A2
13 Togitogiga Waterfalls ........ E3
14 Uafato Conservation Area ........ G3
15 Vaiula Beach ........ E4

**Activities, Courses & Tours**

AquaSamoa Watersports ........ (see 17)
16 Boulders ........ D4
17 Le Penina Golf Course ........ B2
Manoa Tours ........ (see 22)
18 Outdoor Samoa ........ B2
19 Samoa Adventure ........ B2

**Sleeping**

20 Aga Reef Resort ........ H4
Airport Lodge ........ (see 18)
21 Anita's Beach Bungalows ........ G4
22 Coconuts Beach Club Resort ........ D4
23 Faofao Beach Fales ........ G4
24 Ifiele'ele Plantation ........ C2
Le Uaina Beach Resort ........ (see 9)
25 Le Valasi's Beach Fales ........ C3
26 Le Vasa Resort ........ A2
Litia Sini's Beach Resort ........ (see 20)
27 Lupe Sina Treesort ........ D3
Manusina Beach Fales ........ (see 23)
28 Namu'a Island Beach Fale ........ H4
29 Offshore Adventures ........ C3
30 Return to Paradise Resort ........ C3
31 Salani Surf Resort ........ F4
32 Saletoga Sands Resort & Spa ........ F4
Sa'moana Resort ........ (see 29)
33 Seabreeze Resort ........ G4
Sheraton Aggie Grey's Lagoon Resort ........ (see 17)
34 Sinalei Reef Resort ........ D4
35 Sunset View Fales ........ A2
36 Sweet Escape ........ A2
Taufua Beach Fales ........ (see 20)
37 Tiavi Mountain Escape ........ D3
Vaiula Fales ........ (see 15)

**Eating**

Laumo'osi Fale Restaurant & Ava i Toga Pier Restaurant ........ (see 34)
Lupe's Cocktail Bar & Restaurant ........ (see 22)
Mika's Restaurant ........ (see 22)
Seabreeze Restaurant ........ (see 33)

**Entertainment**

Whitesands Casino ........ (see 17)

proximity to Apia's best bars and clubs. Non-night owls, be warned: it can get noisy.

**Taumesina Hideaway** BUNGALOW **$**
(Map p116; ☎774 7905, 758 9255; taumesina.hideaway@gmail.com; Taumesina Reserve, Moata'a; bungalow from ST95; P Wi-Fi) This quiet place, crouched by a lovely lagoon, offers the only beach *fales* in Apia. All are enclosed; three have shared bathrooms, while the rest come with ensuites and small fridges. Though the ocean views were somewhat spoiled by a nearby construction project at time of research, this is a good – if basic - getaway for those seeking proximity to Apia without the city buzz.

**Su Accommodation** APARTMENT **$$**
(Map p106; ☎27001; www.su-accommodation.com; Fugalei St; r/ste ST190/290; P A/C Wi-Fi) This friendly, family-run spot is an excellent choice for self-caterers and families. While there are clean motel-like rooms on-site, the spacious, fully appointed suites are the best option, with serviceable kitchens ideal for cooking up your finds from Maketi Fou (directly across the road) or either of the two large supermarkets bookending the property.

The family also offers private units (ST160) in the less urban surrounds of Vaitele, about 7km out of Apia.

**Lynn's Getaway Hotel** B&B **$$**
(Map p116; ☎20272; www.lynnsgetaway.com; Salenesa Rd, Moto'otua; s/d ST150/170, without bathroom ST130/150; P A/C Wi-Fi Pool) This eccentric, social little spot attracts return visitors and long-term guests by the boatload. The two comfy common rooms, shared kitchen, poolside barbecue area and library lend Lynn's a true home-away-from-home feel, as do the hearty, host-prepared dinners (ST20, available on request). Discounted rental car rates are available for guests; if driving isn't your thing, island tours and hiking expeditions can be booked here.

## GET ACTIVE ON UPOLU

### Diving

Diving is undeveloped in Samoa. On Upolu this means that experienced divers can partake in exploration trips with AquaSamoa Watersports and potentially get sites named after them! Top dives include the Manono Wall (just off of Manono island) and Magic Mushrooms, where you'll find the namesake unique mushroom-shaped coral formations that are frequented by schools of sharks.

**AquaSamoa Watersports** (Map p102; ☎45662; www.aquasamoa.com; Sheraton Aggie Grey's Lagoon Resort, Mulifanua) Upolu's only dive centre offers dives for beginner and skilled divers (two-tank dive ST340), plus PADI courses (open-water course ST1250), waterskiing, wakeboarding, and snorkelling tours (ST80); it's also got an on-site tattooist on hand!

### Hiking

Shorter tracks that don't require a guide include the short but steep walk to Robert Louis Stevenson's grave near the summit of Mt Vaea and the Mt Matavanu crater walk. Even on short walks, the sun and hot, humid conditions can take their toll. Good walking shoes are essential. For longer hikes, a guide is imperative.

Based in Apia, Eti at **SamoaOnFoot** (p115) offers expert guided hikes to Lake Lanoto'o, Uafato Conservation Area and O Le Pupu-Pu'e National Park. On Savai'i, Mt Silisili offers a challenging multiday trek.

### Surfing

Upolu has great surf but most of it is reef-breaking, far offshore and within limits of a village's water rights, so you'll need permission. It's best to go with an operator. **Salani Surf Resort** (p122), **Samoa Surf Secrets** (at Vaiula Fales; p122), **Offshore Adventures** (p122), **Sa'moana Resort** (p120) and **Manoa Tours** (Map p102; ☎777 0007; www.manoatours.com; Coconuts Beach Club resort) all offer surf packages; some offer shuttle services to the breaks for nonguests.

### Other Activities

For information on fishing charters and tournaments, visit the Samoa International Game Fishing Association website (www.sigfa.ws).

**Outdoor Samoa** (Map p102; ☎45991; www.outdoorsamoa.com; Airport Lodge, Mulifanua) Based near Faleolo Airport and Mulifanua Wharf, this outfit offers a huge range of biking and kayaking adventures ranging from day trips to multi-day/week expeditions. It also hires kayaks (ST75 per day) and bikes (ST45/65 half-/full day) for solo jaunts.

**Samoa Adventure** (Map p102; ☎777 0272; www.samoa-adventure.com; Sheraton Aggie Grey's Lagoon Resort, Mulifanua) This lovely 35ft catamaran makes sunset tours (from ST110), and a slew of other excursions including cruises to Savai'i (10 hours, from ST320) and Manono (from ST250 per person including fishing, food and drinks) and personalised fishing trips.

**Le Penina Golf Course** (Map p102; ☎45611; www.sheratonsamoaaggiegreysresort.com/golf; Main West Coast Rd; 9/18 holes ST30/50, club hire ST15; ⏲8am-5pm Mon-Sat, noon-5pm Sun) This par-72 course winds around the Sheraton Aggie Grey's Lagoon Resort.

**Oceanic Sportfishing Adventures** (☎775 9606; www.grandermarlin.com) Go with Captain Chris to catch the big ones – from tuna to marlin – on the new, 37ft Merritt *Leilani*. Best from April to October.

**Insel Fehmarn Hotel** HOTEL **$$**
(Map p116; ☎23301; www.inselfehmarnsamoa.com; Falealili St (Cross Island Rd), Moto'otua; d from ST280; P ❄ ✉ 🏊) Blocky and nondescript from the outside, this large hotel is surprisingly welcoming and well equipped. All rooms have plenty of space (families should request a Garden Room on the ground floor) and excellent kitchens; ours had a full gas stove. Genuinely friendly staff are quick to

# Apia

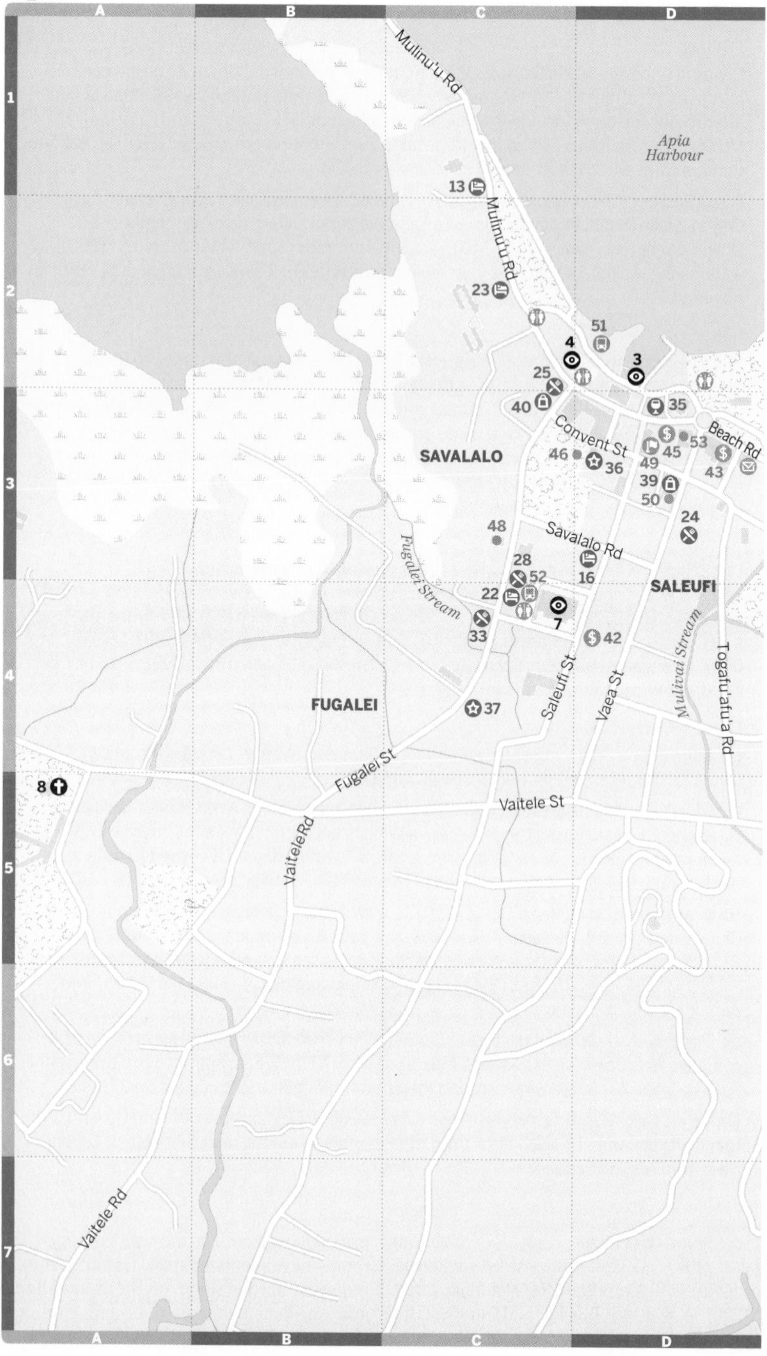

A B C D

1 2 3 4 5 6 7

Apia Harbour

Mulinu'u Rd

13

Mulinu'u Rd

23

51

4

3

25

40

35

Convent St

Beach Rd

46

36

45

53

49

43

39

50

SAVALALO

48

Savalalo Rd

24

28

52

16

SALEUFI

22

7

33

42

Fugalei Stream

Mulivai Stream

Togafu'afu'a Rd

Saleufi St

Vaea St

FUGALEI

37

Fugalei St

8

Vaitele St

Vaitele Rd

Vaitele Rd

A B C D

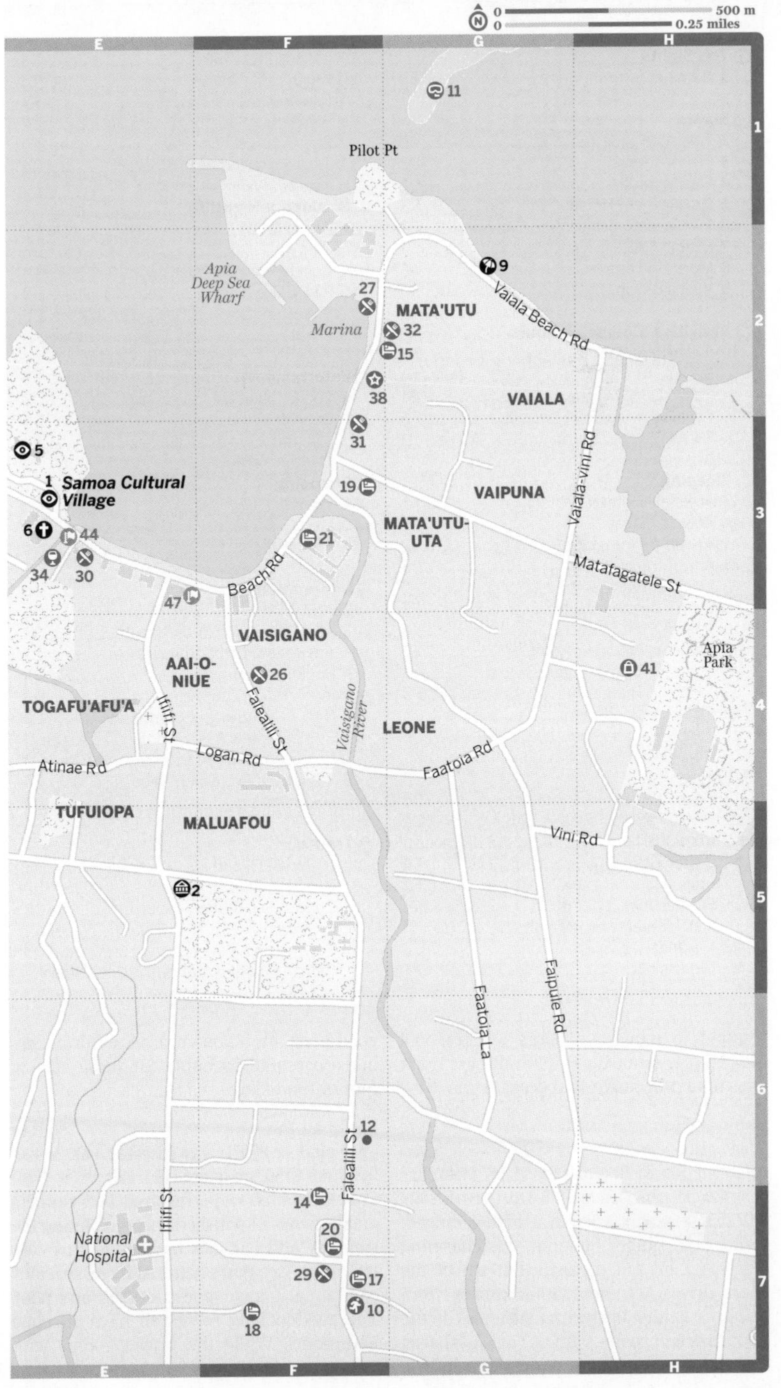
0
500 m
0
0.25 miles
E
F
G
H
1
2
3
4
5
6
7
11
Pilot Pt
Apia Deep Sea Wharf
27
MATA'UTU
Marina
32
15
38
9
Vaiala Beach Rd
VAIALA
31
5
1 Samoa Cultural Village
19
VAIPUNA
Vaiala-Vini Rd
6
44
21
MATA'UTU-UTA
34
30
Beach Rd
Matafagatele St
47
VAISIGANO
AAI-O-NIUE
26
41
Apia Park
TOGAFU'AFU'A
Ififi St
Fealalili St
Vaisigano River
LEONE
Logan Rd
Faatoia Rd
Atinae Rd
TUFUIOPA
MALUAFOU
Vini Rd
2
Faipule Rd
Faatoia La
12
Falealili St
14
Ififi St
20
National Hospital
29
17
10
18

## Apia



respond to requests. There's a large pool area and a fantastic restaurant-bar; don't miss the Friday night barbecues.

**Samoan Outrigger Hotel** HOTEL $$
(Map p116; ☎20042; www.samoanoutrigger-hotel.com; Falealili St (Cross Island Rd), Moto'otua; bungalow per person from ST75, s/d/f from ST140/170/255; P❄☜≋) Set in a high-ceilinged, century-old timber building, this charming place is a bit out of town, but worth the short drive. Accommodation ranges from *fale*-style garden huts with mattresses on the floor to bright rooms with a choice of shared bathroom or ensuites. Bonuses include a good pool, afternoon cultural performances and car-rental discounts for those staying four or more days.

**Pasefika Inn** HOTEL $$
(Map p106; ☎20971; www.pasefikainn.ws; Matautu St; dm ST50, s/d from ST190/220; P❄☜≋) Carved beams, *siapo*-inspired bed runners and bunches of polished coconuts lining the stairway add Samoan touches to this central, airy place that's bettered by its spacious communal lounge, guest kitchen and pool. The good-looking rooms all have attached bathrooms. While the pricier rooms with

terraces are bigger, they also pick up more noise from the busy road out front.

**Apia Central Hotel** HOTEL $$
(Map p106; ☎20782; www.apiacentralhotel.com; Savalalo Rd; s/d from ST140/170; P❄📶) As the name suggests, this is one for those who want to be in the thick of it; everything from Maketi Fou, supermarkets, restaurants and nightlife are but a short walk away. The hotel doesn't rest on its good-location laurels, however, with big, impeccably clean rooms, bend-over-backwards staff and a lovely outdoor courtyard for escaping the humid din of Apia.

★ **Samoa Tradition Resort** RESORT $$$
(Map p116; ☎25699; www.traditionresort.com; Papaseea Rd, Ululoloa Heights; r/apt/ste/villa ST320/410/450/490; P❄📶🏊) Gorgeous grounds, divine digs and five-star service make this resort an absolute stand-out. Accommodation ranges from spanking new hotel rooms all the way up to massive luxury villas. The restaurant gets rave reviews; the Thursday night *fiafias* are superbly theatrical and shouldn't be missed. It's not cheap, but you'd be hard-pressed to find a more 'resorty' resort in Apia.

**Sheraton Samoa Aggie Grey's Hotel & Bungalows** HISTORIC HOTEL $$$
(Map p106; ☎22880; www.aggiegreys.com; Beach Rd; s/d/ste from US$138/160/350; ❄@🏊) If you ever wanted to step into a 1940s-era tale of the South Seas, this iconic hotel gives you the chance. Though completely refurbished in 2016, Aggie Grey's has retained its breezy, near-colonial atmosphere, while giving its spacious rooms a much-needed overhaul. In addition to the old-school ambience, the hotel boasts three on-site eateries, a bar, a spa, a gym and three pools, one with a swim-up bar.

**Tanoa Tusitala** HOTEL $$$
(Map p106; ☎21122; www.tanoatusitala.com; Mulinu'u Rd; r/ste from ST470/640; P❄📶🏊) One of the swankiest and most professionally run places in town, this hotel – instantly recognisable by its huge, traditional-roofed lobby – is nestled in lush gardens across from the sea wall. Rooms are big and elegant. Facilities include a pool with plenty of lounge chairs (there's also a kids' pool and playground, a rarity in Samoa), tennis court and gym, plus an excellent bar-restaurant.

**Amanaki Hotel & Restaurant** HOTEL $$$
(Map p106; ☎27889; www.amanakihotel.com; Mulinu'u Rd; d ST285-360; ❄📶🏊) This popular, two-storey hotel enjoys an excellent location – and equally excellent ocean breezes – across from the sea wall. The huge, comfortable rooms face a nicely landscaped pool. Guests and locals flock to the on-site restaurant for its breezy atmosphere and



## THERE'S SOMETHING ABOUT BLOODY MARY

Agnes Swann was the daughter of a Lincolnshire chemist who had migrated to Samoa in 1889, and a Samoan girl from Toamua village. In 1917 she married and had four children; after her first husband died, she married Charlie Grey, a compulsive gambler who lost everything they had. Aggie had to look for some means of supporting the family.

In 1942 said means arrived in the form of American soldiers in Apia carrying 'unimaginable wealth'. Aggie borrowed US$180, bought the site of a former hotel and began selling hamburgers and coffee to the servicemen. Response was overwhelming and, although supplies were difficult to come by during WWII, Aggie built up an institution that became famous Pacific-wide as a social gathering place for war-weary soldiers. She even succeeded in getting through the New Zealand–imposed prohibition of alcoholic beverages.

When James Michener published his enormously successful *Tales of the South Pacific*, Aggie was so well-known that it was widely assumed she was the prototype for the character of Michener's Tonkinese madam, Bloody Mary. Michener has said that he did visit Aggie's place whenever he could from Pago Pago, where he was frequently stationed, though he denied that anything but the good bits of Bloody Mary were inspired by Aggie Grey.

Over the next few decades, the snack bar expanded into a hotel where numerous celebrities stayed while filming or travelling in the area. If you'd like to read more about Aggie Grey, who died in June 1988 at the age of 91, track down *Aggie Grey of Samoa*, by Nelson Eustis.

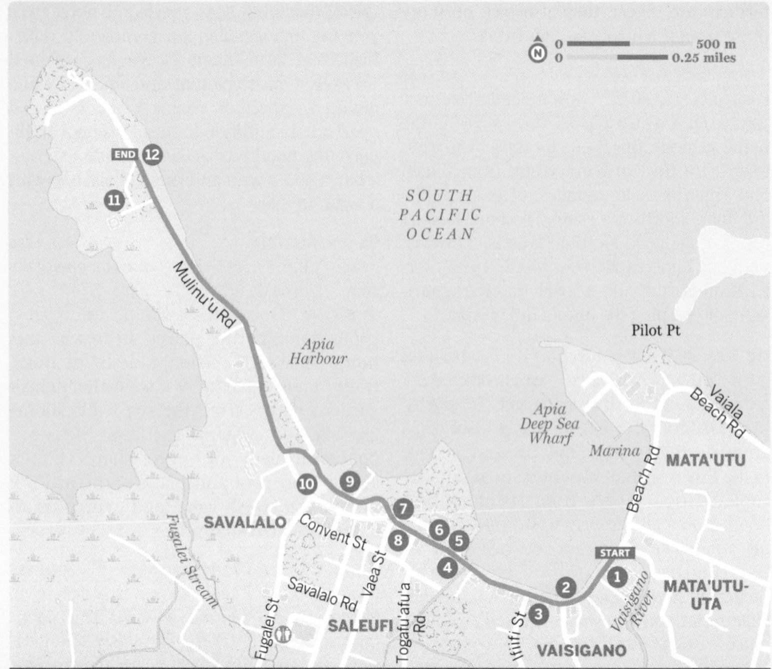


# City Walk
# Historical Apia

**START** SHERATON SAMOA AGGIE GREY'S HOTEL & BUNGALOWS
**END** INDEPENDENCE MEMORIAL
**LENGTH** 3.5KM; 1½ HOURS

Start from 1 **Sheraton Samoa Aggie Grey's Hotel & Bungalows** (p109), Samoa's most famous address. Founded in 1933, it became a popular haunt of American servicemen during WWII. The late Aggie Grey is said to have been the inspiration for the Bloody Mary character in James Michener's *Tales of the South Pacific*.

Cross the road and walk west along the sea wall to the 2 **John Williams monument**. It celebrates an early missionary who was killed and eaten in 1839 while evangelising in Vanuatu. His bones were recovered and buried under the church across the road. A little further along you'll pass the genteel wooden colonial-style building that once housed the 3 **Supreme Court**.

As you continue along Beach Rd, gaze up at the grand and glorious 4 **Immaculate Conception Cathedral** (p101) on your left and then the *fale*-style 5 **Samoa Tourism Authority office** (p114) on your right; if you time your visit right, stop at the 6 **Samoa Cultural Village** (p100) behind the *fale* for an immersive and entertaining experience. Further along you'll see the 7 **clock tower** (now in the middle of a busy roundabout), constructed in memory of those who fought and were killed in WWI. Across the road are the elegant arches of the Spanish Mission–style 8 **Chan Mow's building**.

From the clock tower, take the smaller road heading behind the library to check out the 9 **Fish Market** (p101) and then the 10 **Flea Market** (p101).

Amble north through the park beside the sea wall that buttresses the eastern shore of the Mulinu'u Peninsula until you reach Samoa's parliament house, the 11 **Fale Fono**. In case you had any doubts about Samoa's Christian leanings, cross the road to read the 12 **Independence Memorial**. It was built to celebrate the independence of Western Samoa on 1 January 1962 and bears the inscription 'Samoa is founded on God', with thanks to each member of the Holy Trinity.

high-quality, reasonably priced seafood meals (supplied by the hotel's own fishing boats); the bar gets buzzy after dark too.

## Eating

Apia is the one of the few places in Samoa where you won't be held hostage to the culinary abilities (or lack thereof) of your accommodation provider. There's a decent selection of eateries scattered around town, with most of the upmarket ones lining the waterfront.

For self-caterers, Apia's best-stocked supermarkets are **Frankies** (Map p106; Fugalei St; 6am-9pm) and **Farmer Joe** (Map p106; www.farmerjoe.ws; Fugalei St; 6am-9pm); both are open seven days a week.

**Krush** VEGAN $
(Map p116; 27874; Falealili St (Cross Island Rd), Tanugamanono; mains ST10-15; 9am-5pm Mon-Fri, to 3pm Sat; ) Apia's only vegan restaurant has a small menu, but it's a tasty one that's sure to make visiting herbivores happy. Inventive salads and risottos are served by the scoop; other items include 'beefless burgers' and meat-free takes on Samoan cuisine. It also whizzes up a massive range of fresh juices and smoothies.

**Burger Bill's** FAST FOOD $
(BB's; Map p106; 26388; Fugalei St; meals from ST9; 9am-10pm Mon-Thu, to 1am Fri & Sat, 10am-10pm Sun) This much-beloved, locally owned fast-food chain serves up exceptional fish and chips that – despite hefty portion sizes – are ridiculously moreish. As per the name, it also creates great burgers; fried chicken is another speciality.

**Fish Market** SEAFOOD $
(Map p106; off Beach Rd; fish & chips ST8; 7am-3pm Mon-Fri, to noon Sat & Sun) Battle local crowds for the best and freshest fish and chips in town in an endearingly gritty, local-style setting.

**Coffee Bean** CAFE $
(Map p106; www.thebeansamoa.com; Falealili St (Cross Island Rd); mains ST10-25; 8am-4.30pm Mon-Fri, to 1pm Sat, to noon Sun; ) Along with excellent, strong coffees, the Bean serves big breakfasts like eggs Benedict (ST25) as well as lighter choices; at lunch choose from sandwiches, savoury pies and casseroles. It also operates **Bean Central** (Map p106; www.thebeansamoa.com; Vaea St; mains ST10-25; 7am-3.30pm Mon-Fri, to noon Sat), about 1km west; it's just as good.

★ **Palusami** FUSION $$
(Map p106; 771 3177; www.palusami.biz; Beach Rd; mains ST13-50; 5.30pm-midnight Tue-Sat) This wonderful place uses organic, locally sourced produce to create incredible meals that combine Samoan flavours with international favourites (coconut beef stroganoff, anyone?). Other inventive fare includes eggs Benedict with spicy taro cakes, grilled pork on a *palusami* gratin and a to-die-for *Koko Samoa* chocolate tart. *Niu* (coconut) cocktails – including a very, very good mojito – served in the shell are a must.

**Edge** INTERNATIONAL $$
(Map p106; 775 5174; Apia Marina; mains ST10-30; 8am-late Mon-Sat) An excellent addition to Apia's up-and-coming dining-entertainment precinct at the marina, this laid-back spot is a top choice for a lazy lunch or dinner. A diverse menu offers Samoan classics, international favourites and a long list of sinful all-day breakfast options; it also does excellent espressos. Stick around for cocktails (happy hour 4pm to 7pm) and DJ sets (7pm to midnight Thursday to Saturday).

**Sips Tapas & Wine Bar** TAPAS $$
(Map p106; 770 1888; Apia Marina; tapas/mains from ST18/25; 11am-10pm Tue-Thu, to midnight Fri & Sat, 5.30-10.30pm Sun) What this hip and happening spot lacks by way of an extensive menu (the pickin's are tasty, but slim), it more than makes up for with good vibes and top views. An extensive wine list makes this an excellent spot for sunset drinks; if you're in town on a Sunday afternoon, drop in for its lively pizza-and-barbecue parties.

**Giordano's** ITALIAN $$
(Map p116; 25985; off Falealili St (Cross Island Rd), Moto'otua; small pizzas ST20-26; 3-11pm Tue-Sat, 5-10pm Sun) Sit in the tropical back courtyard and tuck into exceptional pizzas featuring such exotic (for Samoa) toppings as olives, blue cheese, parmesan, pepperoni and anchovies. It was the first pizza place to open in Samoa and many think it's still the friendliest and the best. Gluttons take note: the XL pizzas are *really* XL!

**Tifaimoana Indian Restaurant** INDIAN $$
(Map p106; 29604; Fugalei St; dishes from ST15; 7am-9am, 11am-3pm & 5-10pm Mon-Sat; ) The chef here (from the Punjab region of India) orders ingredients from his homeland and you can taste it. The *thali* set meals

(many vegetarian; prices from ST25) are Samoan-sized and include a lassi; if you're ordering à la carte, the chicken korma is memorable.

**Italiano Pizza Bar** ITALIAN $$
(Map p106; ☎24330; Beach Rd; small pizzas ST16-25; ⏰9am-10pm Mon-Fri, to midnight Sat, 4-10pm Sun) Locals and travellers converge on this humble waterfront pizzeria to talk, drink jugs of lurid alcoholic mixtures and add their scrawl to the graffiti on the walls. On top of all that, the pizzas are great.



★**Bistro Tatau** FUSION $$$
(Map p106; ☎22727; www.bistrotatau.ws; Beach Rd; mains ST40-70; ⏰noon-2pm Mon-Fri, from 6.30pm Mon-Sat; ❄✍) This upmarket spot ranks as one of Samoa's best and most innovative restaurants, fusing local favourites such as *palusami* into soufflé and ravioli. Polished floorboards, white tablecloths, vibrant local art, tropical floral arrangements and efficient barefoot waiters in *lava-lava* complete the experience.

**Paddles** ITALIAN $$$
(Map p106; ☎21819; Beach Rd; mains ST25-60; ⏰5-11pm Mon-Sat) A delightful Italian-Samoan family serves superb home cooking and ready conviviality at this attractive and rightfully popular terrace restaurant across from the seafront. It has that perfect balance of laid-back and chic. Try the smoked fish lasagne or the divine mushroom risotto.

## Drinking & Nightlife

Apia's waterfront is well supplied with drinking options, though few places open their doors on a Sunday. Some of the dodgier pool halls aren't pleasant places to be at closing time.

**Ace of Clubs** CLUB
(Map p106; ☎20430; off Beach Rd; ⏰club 5pm-midnight, bar from 10.30am Mon-Sat) Hitch your fancy threads on for Apia's newest and classiest nightclub. Laser-lit and loud, it attracts an enthusiastic crowd with pumping dance hits, good drinks menu and brilliant security staff that ensures everyone – especially women – have a great, safe night. There's a dress code, and cover charges apply most nights (ST5 to ST25). There's a more low-key bar and bistro on the ground floor.

**Y-Not** BAR
(Map p106; Beach Rd; cover charge ST10; ⏰4-10pm Mon & Tue, to midnight Wed-Sat) Ask anyone of any age where to go for a drink in Apia and this is always the enthusiastic answer. It's no wonder. Looking over the Apia Harbour with deck seating, a pool table, live or DJ music on Friday and Saturday nights and a reliable mix of expats, locals and visitors, Y-Not is bucketloads of fun.

**Club X** CLUB
(Map p106; Beach Rd; admission ST15-20; ⏰7pm-midnight Wed-Sat) This waterside club is a local institution for all the right reasons: blaring pop hits, cheap drinks, good bartenders and a sociable – if young – crowd. The small dancefloor gets packed and sweaty most nights.

**Sheesha's Cocktail Bar** COCKTAIL BAR
(Map p106; ☎775 1500; Apia Marina; ⏰5-10.30pm Tue-Thu, to 12.30am Fri & Sat) One of the classiest bars in Apia – all chandeliers and fancy wallpaper – Sheesha's has a fantastic cocktail menu that attracts a slightly older (25 and up) clientele. It's a tiny place, but its size just adds to the intimate ambience (though there's more room outside overlooking the water).

**Apia Yacht Club** BAR
(Map p106; ☎28584; Mulinu'u Rd; ⏰5-10pm Tue-Sun) Its private-club status makes it one of the few sure-fire places for a drink on a Sunday evening. Its location on the sea wall – and resultant breezes – merely reinforces the relaxing effects of a cold Vailima beer. Meals are also available.

**Cocktails on the Rocks** BAR
(Map p106; Beach Rd; ⏰3-10pm Mon-Thu, to midnight Fri & Sat) Also known as 'Cocks on the Rocks' and 'The Hole in the Wall', this small bar is much loved by tourists, expats and locals for its mellow vibe, sea breezes, 5L 'towers' of Vailima beer and live music most nights (bar Mondays).

**RSA Club** BAR
(Returned Services Association; Map p106; ☎20 171; Beach Rd; ⏰9am-10pm Mon-Thu, to midnight Fri & Sat) This down'n'dirty – but characterful – place is a top spot for meeting locals and checking out some live music (Thursday to Saturday). If you're after posh cocktails and a well-heeled crowd, best go elsewhere: you

don't want to be here if a fight breaks out (avoid the pool tables at closing time).

## ☆ Entertainment

Many hotels and resorts in Apia host weekly *fiafia* nights, celebrations of Samoan culture through vibrant song, dance and storytelling performances. Ask at your accommodation, or pop into the Samoa Tourism Authority's information *fale* on Beach Rd for a full list of weekly shows.

**Divas of Samoa** CABARET
(Map p106; Maliu Mar Bar & Restaurant, Fugalei St; adult/child ST10/5; ⌚from 9pm Wed) The only *fa'afafine* show in Samoa is outrageous fun, full of glitter, glamour and cheesy music. It's a drag show, but maybe not as you know it: children are enthusiastically welcomed at the performances.

**Siva Afi** DANCE
(Map p106; ☎26029; Beach Rd; dinner & show ST75) Named after the Samoan fire dance that is its hallmark, this place has a commitment to training young performers and keeping the traditional arts alive. Check out its dramatic fire- and knife-dancing shows every Tuesday night (Samoan-style dinner 7.30pm, show starts at 8.30pm). Bookings are recommended.

**Apollo Cinemas** CINEMA
(Map p106; ☎28127; Convent St; adult/child ST15/10; ⌚screenings from 9.30am Mon-Sat) Big Hollywood blockbusters often hit the screens here before they reach Australia or NZ and for a fraction of the price. Its two cinemas are blissfully air-conditioned, and there's a new cafe attached if popcorn isn't doing it for you.

## Shopping

Memorable souvenirs can be bought at various shops around Apia, including *siapo, ie toga* (fine mats) and finely made, multi-legged *'ava* (kava) bowls. Such crafts, plus jewellery and clothes, are available from Maketi Fou (p100) and the Flea Market (p101).

**Plantation House** HANDICRAFTS, GIFTS
(Map p116; ☎22839; Lotopa Rd, Alafua; ⌚9am-5pm Mon-Fri, to 1pm Sat) Stop in for high-quality, locally made art, craft and gifts, including hand-blocked fabric, *lava-lava,* prints, tailored shirts, bedding and jewellery.

**Mailelani** BEAUTY
(Map p116; ☎22111; www.mailelani-samoa.com; Mailelani Rd (just off Cross Island Rd), Papauta; ⌚9am-5pm Mon-Fri, to noon Sat) The handmade soaps, creams and goodies here are made with organic coconut oil; everything smells and feels divine. Stop by and you'll



### PIMP MY RIDE

Samoa is a quiet and polite place, but a wallflower it ain't: from its blazingly blue waters to its ludicrously large and looming village churches, there's much about this country that screams 'Look at me!' And there's nothing that seizes the eye with more insistence than Samoa's wonderfully over-the-top buses (*pasi*).

More than just a means of transportation, *pasi* are a form of self-expression by their independent owners. While a few are content to merely splash their bus sides in solid blocks of lurid colours, the majority have gone down the airbrush route, creating rolling kitschmobiles as glorious as they are garish. There are buses plastered with knock-off odes to Bon Jovi and Guns-n-Roses, starburst-heavy declarations of support for Manu Samoa (the national rugby union team), a startling number of Jesus-and-Mary glamour portraits hovering above the muffler, and way too many featuring depictions of what appears to be a psychotic, perhaps vampiric, Mickey Mouse.

The fun continues inside, with carpeted ceilings, flags, family photos, plastic garlands, religious trinkets (often neon) and a few thousand dangling air fresheners prettily obscuring parts of the windscreen. Extremely loud music is a must on buses, and visitors will soon develop either a taste for Samoan pop or earplugs. Such distractions cleverly divert passengers' attentions from the fact that there is no air-conditioning and seats are made of bum-busting hardwood. If the bus is crowded, a Samoan will probably sit on your lap. Roll with it!

probably get a tour showing how the products are made.

**Mena** CLOTHING
(Map p106; ☎31293; www.menashop.com; MacDonald Bldg, Fugalei St; ⏲8.30am-5pm Mon-Fri, to 2pm Sat) High Samoan fashion in the form of well-cut dresses in traditional fabrics or painted with floral patterns. It's a bit pricey but there's something for all shapes and sizes.

**Pacific Jewell** HANDICRAFTS, GIFTS
(Map p106; ☎32888; Levili Blvd, Levili; ⏲8am-5pm Mon-Fri, to 2pm Sat) This little nook has an on-site gallery and beautiful outdoor cafe. Locally made jewellery, carvings, art and more are all of exceptional quality.

**Janet's** HANDICRAFTS, GIFTS
(Map p106; ☎23371; www.janetssamoa.com; 2nd fl, Lotemau Mall, Vaea St; ⏲9am-5.30pm Mon-Fri, 8.30am-1.30pm Sat) Janet's stocks a large range of woodcarvings, *siapo* and gifts.



## Information

**ANZ Bank** (Map p106; Beach Rd; ⏲9am-4.30pm Mon-Fri, 8am-1pm Sat) The ANZ also has ATMs on Salenesa Rd (just off Cross Island Rd) and on Saleufi St opposite Maketi Fou.

**Bank South Pacific** (BSP; Map p106; ☎66100; Beach Rd; ⏲9am-4pm Mon-Wed, to 4.30 Thu & Fri, 8.30am-12.30pm Sat) Has an ATM out the front that accepts overseas cards.

**Main Post Office** (Map p106; ☎27640; www.samoapost.ws; Beach Rd; ⏲8.30am-4.30pm Mon-Fri, 8am-noon Sat) For poste restante, go to the separate office next to the main post office. Have mail addressed to you care of: Poste Restante, Chief Post Office, Apia, Samoa.

**National Hospital** (Map p116; ☎66600; Ilifi St, Moto'otua) Apia's main hospital.

**Samoa Tourism Authority** (Map p106; ☎63500; www.samoa.travel; Beach Rd; ⏲9am-5pm Mon-Fri, 8am-noon Sat) For information, assistance, bus schedules and maps. You'll find them in a prominently positioned *fale* across from the Catholic cathedral on the main drag.

## Getting Around

As visitors will soon discover (after hearing 'Taxi?' for the millionth time), Apia has an extraordinary number of cabs prowling its streets. Meters are optional, but fares are low; you shouldn't be charged more than ST5 for a ride within town. Be sure to agree upon a price before you hop in.

Buses are equally plentiful (though not so much on Sundays) and cheap; fares within town run at about ST1.

# Around Apia

## Sights & Activities

**★Robert Louis Stevenson Museum & Mt Vaea National Reserve** MUSEUM
(Map p116; ☎20798; www.rlsmuseum.org; Cross Island Rd, Vailima; adult/child ST20/5; ⏲9am-4.30pm Mon-Fri, to noon Sat) The Scottish author's former residence is an enchanting estate, with a centrepiece lawn and perfectly manicured gardens. Stevenson's mansion, substantially destroyed in the cyclones in the early 1990s, was lovingly rebuilt and opened as a museum in 1994 on the centenary of Stevenson's death. Access is by a half-hour tour that leads through rooms filled with antiques and sepia family photographs.

Stevenson is buried in the adjacent **Mt Vaea National Reserve** (Map p116; Cross Island Rd, Vailima; ⏲6am-6pm Mon-Sat) FREE. Follow the signs for the path – known as the 'Road of Loving Hearts' – to the tomb. At the first unmarked fork, turn left. The path soon forks again: the right-hand trail (30 minutes) is steeper but shorter; the left-hand trail (50 minutes) is gentler but still involves a final slippery section. At the top you'll be greeted by wonderful views of Apia, Stevenson's stately Victorian tomb, and clouds of vicious mosquitoes. Cool off after after your hike with a dip in the natural swimming hole that was once the author's pool; it's right near the museum carpark.

A taxi from Apia to the museum costs ST10 one way, or take the Vaoala bus (ST2) from Maketi Fou.

**★Papase'ea Sliding Rocks** WATERFALL
(Map p116; off Maugafolau Rd; adult/child ST5/2; ⏲8.30am-5.30pm Mon-Sat, 11am-6pm Sun) Kids and adults have a brilliant time skimming down these natural slides – actually small waterfalls – into blessedly cool waterholes; you'll hear happy hoots even before you make your way down the long, precarious stairway to the pools. The longest slide is 5m long; there are a couple of smaller ones at the bottom of the stairs. During the dry season, check that the water is deep enough for sliding; if not, it's still a top spot for a dip.

The site is 6km from central Apia, well-signposted from the road past the Mormon Temple. Take the Se'ese'e bus (ST2.80) from Maketi Fou and ask to be dropped at the turn-off for Papase'ea. A return taxi trip is about ST25.

**Papapapai-tai Falls** WATERFALL
(Map p102; Cross Island Rd) About 14km south of Apia is the lookout for Papapapai-tai Falls, a 100m waterfall that plunges into a forested gorge; they're one of the longest falls in Samoa. Roughly 100m before the lookout, an unmarked track leads to the **Tiavi waterhole**, a delightful place to cool off on a hot day.

**Lake Lanoto'o National Park** LAKE
The pea-green crater of Lake Lanoto'o is about as removed from human habitation as you can get on Upolu. Its remote central-highlands location and alternating warm and cold currents lend it an eerie nature. Keep your eyes peeled for wild goldfish.

The steep trail leading to the lake from the car park (3km along a very rough side road) is overgrown and forks repeatedly. Many hikers (including locals) have gotten lost; a guide is a must. A dependable outfit is **SamoaOnFoot** (☎759 4199, 31252; www.bestsamoatours.com).

**Bahá'í House of Worship** RELIGIOUS SITE
(Map p116; ☎20385; www.bahaisamoa.ws; Cross Island Rd, Tiapapata; ⊙6am-6pm) FREE The architecturally interesting Bahá'í House of Worship is one of only eight such structures in the world; all are different except for being domed – this one is 28m high – and having nine sides and entrances, reflecting the faith's tenet of a basic unity of religions and peoples.

A taxi from Apia costs around ST30, or catch the Siumu bus (ST6) from Maketi Fou. Contact the temple if you wish to attend a Sunday session (10am); it may be able to offer you a free lift.

### Sleeping

**★Dave Parker's Eco Lodge** LODGE $
(Map p116; ☎842 8899; www.daveparkerecolodge.ws; Tapatapao Rd, Aleisa East; s/d bungalow ST45/65, lodge ST78/98, ste ST125/155; P ✦ ✦) Surrounded by rainforest and boasting jaw-dropping views of the coast, this delightful hilltop spot is an excellent escape from the heat of the big smoke. The main lodge houses eight tidy rooms and a suite; those wishing to get even further away from it all should opt for one of four bungalows set beside the very swimmable river.

Birdwatchers and hikers will find their bliss here; if the isolation gets too much, Dave offers free city transfers Monday to Saturday. There's also an excellent restaurant and bar on-site.

## Eastern Upolu

The pointy end of Upolu is blessed with some of Samoa's best beaches, offering the winning combination of white sand, clear waters and excellent snorkelling. Heading east from Apia there's a succession of beautiful, sleepy villages along the surf-battered shoreline. The road turns sharply inland not far past Piula Cave Pool and skirts rainforest and plantations before hitting the glorious glowing sands of the Aleipata coast.

### Sights & Activities

**Aleipata Beaches & Reefs** BEACH
At the southeastern end of Upolu, Aleipata district has a reef system that's making a good comeback after being pummelled by the 2009 tsunami. It already has surprisingly good snorkelling, and the beaches here are among the most spellbindingly beautiful in the world. Check out the undersea magic by walking in off the spectacular white beach at **Lalomanu**. If you're lucky you might spot a turtle, but beware of strong currents.

The bus from Apia to Lalomanu (ST7.70) takes around two hours. If you're driving, don't be surprised if you get hit up for a fee for simply parking your car at a beach. Villages earn income from this, but some 'toll collectors' do push it a bit (one man tried to charge us ST50 for the pleasure); feel free to negotiate or move along elsewhere.

**★To Sua Ocean Trench** LANDMARK
(Map p102; Main South Coast Rd; adult/child ST20/10; ⊙8.30am-6pm) This outrageously photogenic spot is a Samoan icon; skip it to your everlasting regret. Though the first thing you'll see upon entering the grounds is To Le Sua (a smaller, drier depression), it's To Sua that is the star of the show: more akin to a giant sinkhole than a trench, its sheer, green-draped rock walls plummet 20-odd metres to the almost hallucinatory-blue waters of the magnificent pool below. Swimming access is via a precipitous but sturdy

## Around Apia

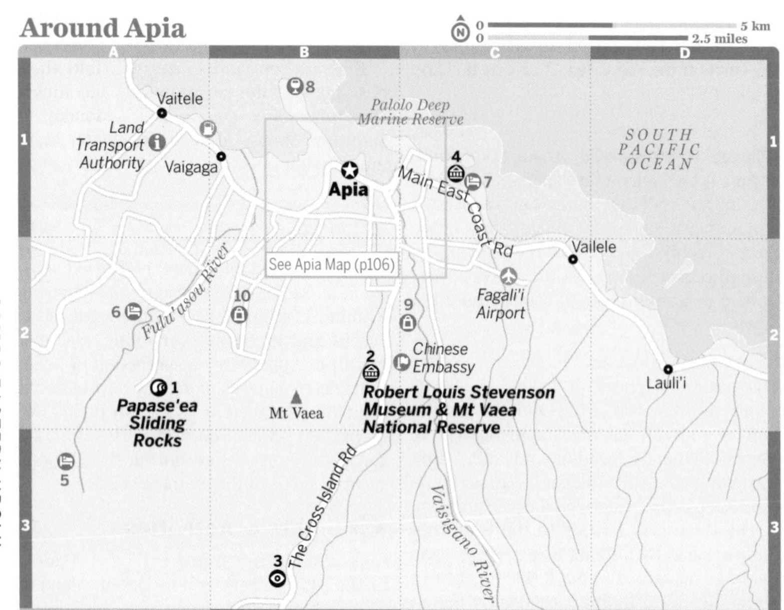




wooden ladder; believe us, it's worth the clamber.

When you've had your fill of this enchanted waterhole, take the short track to the wave-battered cliffs. The well-groomed garden is a great spot for a picnic.

Gorgeous though it is here, visitors still need to exercise caution: swimming through the underwater passage that feeds the waterhole from the sea is a big no-no, and if you're with kids, beware the child-sized gaps between the ground and the fence that circles the top of the trench.

**Piula Cave Pool** LANDMARK
(Map p102; Main East Coast Rd; adult/child ST5/3; ⊙8am-4pm Mon-Sat) Secreted beneath the campus of Piula Methodist Theological College, Piula Cave Pool consists of two blue-green, fish-filled freshwater grottoes, only metres from the sea. The brave can swim between them via a creepy 3m underwater passage that's difficult to find in the darkness. The pools are concreted in so it's not a completely *au naturel* experience but it is refreshing and the college grounds are beautiful.

From Apia, take the Falefa or Lalomanu bus (ST4).

**Lalomanu Crater** NATURE RESERVE
(Map p102; Lalomanu) A short but steep walk (10 to 15 minutes) leads to this extinct crater, blanketed in jungle overgrowth. Home to a huge colony of flying foxes, and with magnificent ocean and island views, it's worth the trek. If you go with a guide (about ST10; ask at your lodgings), they'll usually throw in a tour of the nearby taro plantation.

**Uafato Conservation Area** FOREST
(Map p102) The 14 sq km of wild and rugged terrain that comprise the Uafato Conservation Area boast untouched rainforest that marches down from Upolu's northeastern hills to dip its toes in the ocean. Flora lovers can track down a rare stand of *ifilele* (the tree used for '*ava* bowls), while fauna fans can observe numerous bird and bat species going about their aerial business. Uafato village is known for its traditional carvers, who are usually willing to demonstrate their art to visitors.

Uafato can be reached via a rough road that winds around Fagaloa Bay from the turn-off at Falefa Falls. This route offers beautiful views, but don't go past Saletele without a high-clearance vehicle. Another option is the road (4WD only; 10km) signposted off Le Mafa Pass Rd to the village of Ta'elefaga.

## Around Apia

**Top Sights**
1 Papase'ea Sliding Rocks........A2
2 Robert Louis Stevenson Museum & Mt Vaea National Reserve........B2

**Sights**
3 Bahá'í House of Worship........B3
4 Vanya Taule'alo Gallery........C1

**Sleeping**
5 Dave Parker's Eco Lodge........A3
6 Samoa Tradition Resort........A2
7 Taumesina Hideaway........C1

**Drinking & Nightlife**
8 Apia Yacht Club........B1

**Shopping**
9 Mailelani........C2
10 Plantation House........B2

Contact SamoaOnFoot (p115) for tours and transport.

**Sopo'aga Falls** VIEWPOINT
(Map p102; Le Mafa Pass Rd; adult/child ST5/free; 8am-4pm) The 54m-high Sopo'aga Falls empty themselves into an enormous gorge close to where the Main South Coast Rd meets Le Mafa Pass Rd. The well-signposted lookout is quite a distance from the falls, but the owners make an effort to give value for the entrance fee by touring visitors around their well-labelled kitchen garden. Traditional artefacts are also displayed, including drums and an *umukuka* (cooking house).

## Sleeping & Eating

### Around Falefa

**Le Uaina Beach Resort** RESORT $$
(Map p102; 40270; www.leuaina.com; Main East Coast Rd, Faleapuna; villas ST155-290; P) Located on a sweet stretch of coast just before the turn off leading to Aleipata (it's right next door to the Piula Cave Pool), friendly Le Uaina makes for an excellent base for exploring Upolu. Villas are clean with great beds; the best are on the beachfront. Steps lead from the white sand into calm, blue waters that are great for snorkelling or kayaking.

The restaurant dishes up big portions of Western standards (the burgers are excellent) and a few Samoan favourites; dining is indoors or outside on a big deck that surrounds a magnificent old tree.



### HERE HE LIES WHERE HE LONGED TO BE

In December 1889 the already-famous Scottish author and poet Robert Louis Stevenson and his wife Fanny Osborne arrived in Apia. Stevenson had left Europe in search of relief from worsening tuberculosis and the general sickliness that had plagued him all his life. He was enchanted by Samoa, and in 1890 he paid £200 for 126 hectares of land in the hills above Apia; it was here he constructed Vailima, the grandest home ever seen on the island. They imported furniture from Scotland and dressed their Samoan employees in *lava-lava* patterned with the Stuart tartan.

In the 1890s, during the period of strife in Samoa between Britain, the USA and Germany, Stevenson became an activist for Samoan rights, maintaining that the people should be left to determine their own destiny in accordance with their customs. He came to be loved by the Samoans for his friendliness and his ability to entertain with stories; they affectionately referred to him as Tusitala (Teller of Tales).

On 3 December 1894 Stevenson died of a stroke at Vailima. When the Samoan chief Tu'imaleali'ifano spoke of Stevenson's death, he echoed the sentiments of many Samoans, saying 'Our beloved Tusitala. The stones and the earth weep.' Two months before his death, in gratitude for his kindness, a delegation of Samoan chiefs had arranged for a hand-dug road to be made between Apia and Vailima, which they called O Le Ala O Le Alofa, the Road of the Loving Heart.

Stevenson had stipulated that he wished to be buried at the top of Mt Vaea, part of the Vailima estate. After a Christian burial service, the coffin was laid on a base of coral and volcanic pebbles and the grave lined with black stones, a practice normally reserved for Samoan royalty.

## Namu'a & Lalomanu

Lalomanu Beach stretches long and white in front of a lagoon so blue it looks radioactive. Beach *fale* on this strip are all right next to each other, making this the most 'built up' (take this term lightly) strip outside of Apia. The accommodation is all simple and local style; while it's not tops for privacy, it feels more social and fun than touristy or spoiled. There are a number of very basic places here, so you can easily shop around.

**★Namu'a Island Beach Fale** BUNGALOW **$**
(Map p102; ☎751 0231; Namu'a Island; bungalow incl 2 meals & return boat transfers per person ST120) Namu'a is only a short boat ride from Mutiatele, but once you're on this tiny private island, Upolu seems light years away (though it's clearly visible across the strait). *Fale* are open, basic and right on the beach – there's no electricity so everything is lit by oil lamps at night. Meals are mostly local style: simple yet delicious.

It's a perfect place for lounging and languid swims; the more active can do a circumnavigation of the shoreline (low tide only), clamber up the steep central peak and snorkel the surrounding reef.

If you're driving, park (ST10 per day) at the shop with the Namu'a sign in Mutiatele; they'll call the resort to come pick you up.

**Anita's Beach Bungalows** BUNGALOW **$$**
(Map p102; ☎777 9673; anitasbeachbungalows@hotmail.com; Main South Coast Rd, Lalomanu; open/enclosed/ensuite bungalow, all incl breakfast & dinner ST155/215/360; P 📶) Unmissable in pink and green, Anita's is a longtime Lalomanu favourite: it's fun, friendly and its location can't be beaten. The open *fale* offer the usual mattress on the floor and pull-down plastic sheets, the enclosed ones have a modicum more privacy, while the ensuite *fale* have fans, lockable doors and their own bathroom. There's a sociable restaurant (mains ST13 to ST25) and bar.

**Taufua Beach Fales** BUNGALOW **$$**
(Map p102; ☎844 1051; www.taufuabeachfales.com; Main South Coast Rd, Lalomanu; s/d bungalow from ST120/180, unit from ST120/240, all incl buffet breakfast & dinner; P 📶) Yellow and mint-green *fale* are as bright as the smiles of the owner and staff, and the spectacular Lalomanu beach is steps away. Basic open *fale* have mattresses on the floor; closed ones have walls, fans and proper beds. If *fale* aren't your thing, choose one of the simple units about 900m up the hill.

A *fiafia* (open to nonguests) is held on Wednesday and Saturday nights in the sociable dining *fale*; guests are treated to a full traditional lunch on Sunday afternoons.

**Litia Sini's Beach Resort** BUNGALOW **$$**
(Map p102; ☎41050; www.litiasinibeach.ws; Main South Coast Rd, Lalomanu; s/d bungalow garden ST265/300, beachfront ST295/365, all incl breakfast & dinner; 3-night minimum stay; P 📶) It's well worth shelling out for the enclosed beachfront *fale*, which have terraces right over the outrageous Lalomanu beach and are decorated in bright whites and blues; the garden *fale* are decent but drab. All have shared bathrooms and there's a big restaurant area overlooking the water. The prices are steep for *fale*, but you do get a ceiling fan, electric light and lockable door.

**Aga Reef Resort** RESORT **$$$**
(Map p102; ☎47800; www.agareefresort.com; Main South Coast Rd, Lalomanu; r ST550, villa ST790-1040; P ❄ 📶 🏊) This posh boutique resort, perched over a stunning stretch of water, is one for the luxury lovers: it's stylish, spotless and the staff is exceptional. There are beautiful rooms available in the large wooden main building, but for a real splurge, nab an Island Villa with an overwater deck (the VIP Villas take indulgence up yet another notch, with private plunge pools).

The picture-perfect lagoon is ideal for snorkelling and kayaking (both are free to guests), or lap up the views from the two wonderful pools.

## Saleapaga to Aufaga

There are several beach *fale* places along **Saleapaga Beach** – a stretch almost as gorgeous as Lalomanu (nitpickers may notice a few pebbles blemishing otherwise perfect white sand).

**Faofao Beach Fales** BUNGALOW **$**
(Map p102; ☎844 1067; www.beachfalesamoa.com; Main South Coast Rd, Saleapaga; bungalow ST70, s/d r ST150/250, all incl breakfast & dinner ; P ❄ 📶) Faofao treats guests like family, and their charming, all-natural thatched *fale* make for a wonderful home away from home (the air-conditioned rooms are pretty pleasant too). The beach is a stunner, and great for swims or snorkelling (gear ST5 per

day). Mealtimes often feel like social events; nonguests are welcome to join the Saturday night *fiafia* and Sunday *umu* feasts.

**Manusina Beach Fales** BUNGALOW **$$**
(Map p102; ☎846 5398; www.manusinabeachfales.ws; Main South Coast Road, Saleapaga; s/d bungalow open ST80/150, enclosed ST100/180, all incl breakfast & dinner; P 📶) This place may be simple, but if you're after a warm welcome, gorgeous views, fresh food and cleanliness (even the shared toilets are spotless, a *fale* rarity), it's a tough one to beat, especially at these prices. There are six beachfront *fale* (two of which are enclosed); all have glorious views and working power points. The family that runs it is exceptionally friendly and helpful.

★**Seabreeze Resort** RESORT **$$$**
(Map p102; ☎41391; www.seabreezesamoa.com; off Main South Coast Rd, Aufaga; d/tr/q incl breakfast from ST587/806/1006; ❄📶🏊) Set in a black-lava-rock bay lined with palm trees and dotted with tiny islands, this exclusive resort has beautifully built bungalows decorated in minimal, tropical style. Kayaks are available or you can snorkel in front and swim to isolated patches of beach. There's an excellent restaurant and bar; optional full meal plan ST130 per day. No kids under 13.

**Seabreeze Restaurant** INTERNATIONAL **$$$**
(Map p102; ☎41391; www.seabreezesamoa.com; off Main South Coast Rd, Aufaga; mains ST35-75; ⏰8am-9pm) Beautifully appointed and idyllically situated on the edge of the bay, this restaurant offers the best food by far at this end of the island. The slow-cooked smoky barbecue ribs melt in your mouth, as do the real Indian curries; for the ultimate experience, let the chef choose for you. Fridays are *fiafia* night; try the gourmet woodfired pizzas on weekends (noon to 4pm).

## South Coast

The fact that Samoa's swankiest resorts are clumped on this stretch of coastline says much about its beauty. It's a delight to drive through the villages, with their brightly painted houses echoing the vibrant colours of the native flora. While the lowlands are impeccably manicured, those seeking untamed nature can explore the rugged the O Le Pupu-Pu'e National Park.

Many of the beaches are a bumpy drive from the main road, and give a welcome sense of seclusion after the road-hugging bays of Aleipata.

### Sights & Activities

The south coast of Upolu is dotted with secluded, surf-lapped beaches that you're likely to have all to yourself; if you've ever wanted to play castaway, this is the place to do it. You'll likely be asked to pay admission to most beaches; prices depend on the size of your vehicle (and who's doing the asking), but expect to shell out anywhere from ST15 to ST30.

**Vaiula Beach** BEACH
(Map p102; South Coast) There's decent surfing to be had at this pretty beach, accessed from Tafatafa village.

**Aganoa Black Sand Beach** BEACH
(Map p102; admission per car ST15, surf fee ST15) This gorgeous beach is a beautiful spot for a paddle or a picnic. The water is deep enough for swimming but there's no reef to protect you – the snorkelling, however, is some of the best on the island. There's a popular surf-break (for experienced boarders only) called **Boulders** (Map p102; Main South Coast Rd) here, just off Cape Niuato'i. The rough 3km track to Aganoa is 150m east of the stone bridge in Sa'agafou – don't attempt it without a 4WD. The beach is a 10-minute walk to the east.

**Salamumu** BEACH
(Map p102) This village is home to a beautiful set of beaches reached by a potholed 5.5km track.

**Matareva** BEACH
(Map p102) You'll find a series of delightful coves with shallow snorkelling areas and lots of rock pools.

**O Le Pupu-Pu'e National Park** NATIONAL PARK
(Map p102; Main South Coast Rd; ⏰7am-6pm) FREE The name of this 29-sq-km national park means 'from the coast to the mountaintop'. There are some superb (if rough) hikes to be had here. A trail (six hours return) winds through thick jungle to **Pe'ape'a Cave**, a large lava tube inhabited by *pe'ape'a* (swiftlets); bring a torch. From here, the hardcore can continue along a heavily overgrown trail to **Ofa Waterfall** (three days return). For a less intense tramp, the 700m **Ma**

**Tree Walk** ends at a gigantic rainforest tree with huge buttress roots.

For the longer walks, a guide, such as Eti from SamoaOnFoot (p115), is essential.

At the park's western boundary, a bumpy 3km unsealed access road (open 7am to 4pm) leads to the magnificently rugged **O Le Pupu Lava Coast**, where a rocky coastal trail leads along lava cliffs, the bases of which are constantly harassed by enormous waves.

**Togitogiga Waterfalls** WATERFALL
(Map p102; Off Main South Coast Rd) FREE A glorious spot for a splash, this series of gentle waterfalls are separated by blessedly cool waterholes. It's best to visit in the wet season. To get here, take the access road for O Le Pupu-Pu'e National Park and stop at the parking area. There are changing rooms and toilets on-site.

## Sleeping

**Le Valasi's Beach Fales** BUNGALOW $
(Map p102; 35221; www.valasisfales.com; Main South Coast Rd, Savaia-Lefaga; per person incl breakfast & dinner ST120; P) This sweet spot is a winner, with spotless, traditional *fale*, extremely welcoming owners, family-style fresh food and a wonderful location beside a giant clam reserve (snorkel it for ST5). It feels more like a homestay here than a hotel. Bikes, kayaks and snorkelling gear are available.

**Tiavi Mountain Escape** CABIN $
(Map p102; 774 7810; off Cross Island Rd, Tiavi; cabin ST95; P) This is a great little place: away from the swelter of the coast but with a million-dollar view of it. Cabins have small decks that catch the mountain breeze; there's also a guest kitchen, a friendly posse of dogs and a playground. Bring your own supplies, mossie coils and a deck of cards: there's a whole lot of wonderful nothing to do up here.

★**Coconuts Beach Club Resort** RESORT $$$
(Map p102; 24849; www.cbcsamoa.com; Main South Coast Rd, Maninoa; ste/beach bungalow/villa/overwater bungalow from ST1000/1200/1400/1800; P) This the hippest resort in the country. Samoa's only overwater *fale* are found here, and what a find they are, with huge, luxuriously-appointed bedrooms, outdoor sunken tubs and two sun decks apiece. Back on land, beach *fale* have covered decks and stylish interiors; many of the villas line a river and are accessed via bridges. 'Treehouse' suites are back from the beach but have good views.

No kids under three.

★**Lupe Sina Treesort** BOUTIQUE HOTEL $$$
(Map p102; 773 5875; www.lupesinatreesort.net; off Cross Island Rd, Tiavi; treehouse ST520-730; P) If you're looking for a (literal) love-nest, grab your bags – and your beloved – and head up the hill to Lupe Sina, home to two extraordinary treehouses. The bigger one is built 12m up a gigantic banyan tree; the other is 10m up an ava tree, with a suspended bedroom and a glass ceiling for unforgettable star-gazing.

The views, obviously, are magnificent; the professional staff, free pancake breakfasts and facilities are equally remarkable. There's an excellent on-site restaurant and tour desk. No kids under seven.

**Return to Paradise Resort** RESORT $$$
(Map p102; 35055; www.returntoparadiseresort.com; Lefaga; r/ste/villa from ST600/1100/1700; P) Sitting smack on the beach that starred in the 1953 Gary Cooper film *Return to Paradise*, this sparkling, upmarket resort is a destination unto itself: with four pools, three restaurants and activities galore (including traditional spearfishing and kayaking lessons, turtle swimming and snorkelling over a giant clam reserve), there's no chance of tropical ennui setting in. Accommodation ranges from tidy hotel rooms to luxurious villas and suites.

**Sa'moana Resort** RESORT $$$
(Map p102; 842 8880; www.samoanaresort.com; Salamumu; fale ST520-890, beach house ST1200; ) Sa'moana has a divine location on a white-sand beach that tumbles past black lava formations into a stunning lagoon. Upscale bungalows sit directly on the beach; there's a two-storey house (with a private stretch of sand) for larger groups. As well as offering tons of tours and special surf packages, there are family-friendly activities galore, babysitters, fab pool and a free kids' menu for those under 11.

**Saletoga Sands Resort & Spa** RESORT $$$
(Map p102; 41212; www.saletogasands.com; Main South Coast Rd, Matatufu; villas ST610-1080; P) This new resort is more akin to one you'd find in Fiji than far-less-touristed Samoa: it's big, shiny, and draws everyone from honeymooners to families (it's one of the few resorts in Samoa that offer a kids'

club). Villas are modern and have outdoor showers. Flash facilities include a great pool (with swim-up bar), a gym, a spa and a splendid restaurant; its *fiafia* nights (Wednesdays) shouldn't be missed.

**Sinalei Reef Resort** RESORT **$$$**
(Map p102; ☎25191; www.sinalei.com; Main South Coast Rd, Maninoa; villas ST973-3000; P ❄ 📶 ≋) If you like lazing around the pool and being handed cocktails by charming waiters, Sinalei is the place to do it. This beautifully landscaped plot by the ocean offers well-appointed stand-alone units, plus two restaurants, tennis courts, a golf course, a watersports centre and good snorkelling around an ocean spring. The staff are delightful; rooms are comfy but a bit plain for the price. No kids under 12.

## Eating

**Lupe's Cocktail Bar & Restaurant** INTERNATIONAL **$**
(Map p102; ☎31223; www.lupesbeachfale.com; Main South Coast Rd, Maninoa; mains from ST12; ⏲8am-late) For a down-to-earth, filling and home-cooked meal by the sea, check this little place out. They whip up anything and everything here, from pasta to *palusami*, and their trademark burgers are outstanding. Sunday lunches aren't to be missed. You can sleep your meal off in one of the basic beach *fale* (from ST60).

Get there by taking the Coconuts Beach Club Resort entrance, then turn left.

**Laumo'osi Fale Restaurant & Ava i Toga Pier Restaurant** INTERNATIONAL **$$$**
(Map p102; ☎25191; www.sinalei.com; Sinalei Reef Resort, Main South Coast Rd, Maninoa; mains ST25-75; ⏲8am-9pm) Sinalei alternates evening meals between its two restaurants. The pier restaurant is the pick of the two, offering an eclectic menu of Samoan dishes, Japanese noodles, pastas, salad and grills in a romantic waterside setting. Themed buffet dinners are served in the *fale* restaurant. Wednesdays are *fiafia* nights (the knife-throwing show is famous); stuff yourself silly at the Saturday barbecue.

**Mika's Restaurant** INTERNATIONAL **$$$**
(Map p102; ☎24849; www.cbcsamoa.com; Coconuts Beach Club Resort, Main South Coast Rd, Maninoa; mains ST25-75; ⏲8am-9pm) Chef Mika travels the globe for inspiration, serving delicious Italian, French and Samoan dishes and a wonderful Hawaiian *ahi poke* salad (raw fish with sesame oil and chilli). Save room for a treat from the extensive tropical desserts menu.

### THE RISE OF THE BLUE WORMS

Samoa's most anticipated party has an unlikely guest of honour: the humble worm. Called Palolo Rising, festivities begin on the seventh day after the full moon in October or November (or sometimes both) when the palolo reef-worm emerges from the coral reefs to mate. The blue-green vermicelli-shaped worms – rich in calcium, iron and protein – are a prized delicacy, and are said to be a powerful aphrodisiac. Parties take place on beaches at the worm-catching spots; when the creatures finally appear at around midnight, crowds carrying nets and lanterns hurriedly wade into the sea to scoop them up.

# Northwestern Upolu

The main reason for staying here is to be near the airport, the ferries to Savai'i and the boats to the Apolima Strait islands. The coastline is quite built-up (for Samoa, that is), particularly between Apia and the airport, and the brilliantly coloured lagoon is too shallow for a truly satisfying swim.

## Sights

**EFKS Museum** MUSEUM
(Map p102; ☎42967; www.cccs.org.ws; Main West Coast Rd, Malua; adult/child ST10/5; ⏲8.30am-4.30pm Mon-Fri) About halfway between the international airport and Apia, this museum – run by the Congregational Christian Church – is Samoa's largest. While the displays aren't earth-shatteringly exciting, interesting local contemporary artworks and inspiring woodcarvings make this a worthwhile stop if you're in the area. As might be expected, there are also artefacts dating back to Samoa's early missionary days. An outdoor turtle pond will give the littlies respite from the collections within.

## DO DROP IN

Upolu's south coast is blessed with top-notch breaks that draw experienced surfers (these waves are *not* for newbies) from around the world. Though one of the biggest attractions here is the lack of crowds, there is a cluster of surf camps and package tours catering to those who crave waves. Hang ten with any of these recommended operators:

**Vaiula Fales** (Map p102; ☎729 5595; www.samoasurfsecrets.com.au; Tafatafa; bungalow incl breakfast & dinner per person from ST60; P 📶) Cheap *fale*, close to the breaks and with a sociable surf bar on the beach. **Samoa Surf Secrets** is based here.

**Salani Surf Resort** (Map p102; ☎41069; www.salanisurfresort.com; Salani; surfer package per d/share ST675/400, min 3-night stay; ❄ @ 📶) On the mouth of the Fupisia River, with excellent left- and right-hand breaks in view.

**Offshore Adventures** (Map p102; ☎750 8825; www.offshoreadventuressamoa.com; Salamumu; accommodation & surfing packages per person per day from ST320; P 📶) Runs popular 'surfaris' for a maximum of five guests.

**Sa'moana Resort** (p120) A more upmarket resort that also offers surf packages.

## Sleeping & Eating

**Airport Lodge** HOTEL **$$**
(Map p102; ☎45584; www.airportlodgesamoa.com; Main West Coast Rd, Mulifanua; s/d bungalow from ST150/180, r ST280; P ❄ 📶) As uninspiring as its name may be, Airport Lodge actually has a lot going for it. It's close to the airport and wharf, the hotel rooms are huge and clean (the cute enclosed garden *fale* are smaller but perfectly serviceable) and it's a lot cheaper than nearby resorts, though meals are expensive for what they are (the gigantic baked mac and cheese offers the best value).

There's no pool, but guests can swim off a private landing across the road. Outdoor Samoa (p105) is based here.

**★Ifiele'ele Plantation** B&B **$$$**
(Map p102; ☎42554; www.ifieleele.com; off Main West Coast Rd, Fasitoo-Uta; villa/studio ST560/460; P ❄ 📶 🏊) 🍃 Set on a six-hectare working tropical fruit plantation, this self-catering retreat is the definition of intimate, with just one villa and a studio (both are modern and clean). Active guests can play tennis, tramp the private walking track or partake in cultural activities; those giving in to the languid surrounds can paddle in the lap pool or watch resident goats at play.

Full kitchens are provided, though catered meals can be arranged.

**Sheraton Aggie Grey's Lagoon Resort** RESORT **$$$**
(Map p102; ☎45663; www.sheratonsamoaaggiegreysresort.com; Main West Coast Rd, Mulifanua; r/ste from ST650/790; P ❄ 📶 🏊) The best things about this sprawling resort are its large pool, spacious grounds, proximity to the airport and wharf, and long list of facilities, including a 160-acre golf course, free kids club (ages four to 12), two restaurants, Samoa's only **casino** (Map p102; ☎759 9909; www.whitesandscasino-samoa.com; Sheraton Aggie Grey's Resort, Mulifanua; ⏲2pm-4am) and AquaSamoa (p105), the lone dive centre on Upolu. Aggie's turns on a scintillating *fiafia* every Friday night (ST85). Rooms are comfy enough but lack pizazz.

The resort allows nonguests to use its facilities for ST25: kids will tell you that the resort pool is worth every cent.

**Le Vasa Resort** RESORT **$$$**
(Map p102; ☎46028; www.levasaresort.com; Main West Coast Rd, Cape Fatuosofia; r ST200, bungalow ST300-375, villa ST600-675, all incl breakfast; P ❄ 📶 🏊) A millennium ago the Tongans were booted out of Samoa at this grassy headland, but you can expect a warmer welcome at this personable little resort. It's set on a stunning lagoon (no beach, though there is one within strolling distance) and there's a good pool. All *fale* and villas have gorgeous sea views; cheaper rooms look over a landscaped garden.

Anyone is welcome at the open-air **restaurant** (mains from ST50) and the fun **Ugly Mermaid Bar**.

## MANONO

POP 889 / AREA 3 SQ KM

If you thought Upolu was mellow, try the tiny, tranquil island of Manono on for size. Canines and cars have been banished here, and the only things that might snap you out of a tropical reverie are occasional blasts from stereos and the tour groups that periodically clog the island's main trail.

It's obligatory for visitors to do the 1½-hour circumnavigation of the island via the path that wends its way between the ocean and people's houses. They're friendly sorts here; expect to be greeted with a cheery '*malo*' a dozen or so times.

The trail winds through Lepuia'i, where you'll see the two-tiered **Grave of 99 Stones** (Map p102; Manono). Translated from the Samoan, the name actually means 'Grave of the Missing Stone' and is dedicated to high chief Vaovasa, who was killed after an unsuccessful attempt to abduct his 100th wife from Upolu. The missing stone at the grave's centre represents the missing wife. The trail's most beautiful section is Manono's less-populated northern edge, where little bays offer terrific views of Apolima. Apai village has the island's best beach.

If you follow the path behind the women's committee building in Salua, you'll eventually end up on top of Mt Tulimanuiva (110m), where there's a large **star mound** (Map p102; Manono). Nearby is the **grave of Afutiti** (Map p102; Manono), a chief who was buried standing up to keep watch over the island. Allow 90 minutes to two hours for this side trip.

### Sleeping

**Sunset View Fales** BUNGALOW $

(Map p102; ☎759 6240; bookings@samoahotels.ws; Lepuia'i; bungalow per person with/without bathroom ST130/100) Rustic but bright beach shacks are offered here (now up on the hill since the 2009 tsunami wiped out the waterfront ones), along with a daily boat trip out to the edge of the reef for memorable snorkelling stints. Price includes all meals and boat transfers.

**Sweet Escape** BUNGALOW $

(Map p102; ☎728 0914; www.sweetescapesamoa.com; Faleu; bungalow per person incl breakfast & dinner ST120) Facing Upolu, these enclosed, bright-yellow *fale* are closely clustered together on a sandy spit looking over the lagoon. Tours and cooking classes are available.

### Getting There & Away

Both **Samoa Scenic Tours** (p103) and **Polynesian Xplorer** (p102) offer day tours of Manono. **Outdoor Samoa** (p105) runs kayaking trips (from ST140) to the island.

If you'd rather go it alone, head for the jetty just south of Le Vasa Resort at Manono-uta village. Buses marked either 'Manono-uta' or 'Falelatai' (ST6.50) will get you here from Apia (allow 90 minutes). The boats leave when there are enough people (usually when the bus arrives) and the cost is ST5 each way. If you want to charter the whole boat expect to pay about ST40 each way. Although the boats are small, Manono is inside the reef so the 20-minute trip isn't usually rough.

## APOLIMA

POP 80 / AREA 1 SQ KM

Few travellers make the trip out to the minuscule but marvellous Apolima. From a distance, its steep walls look completely inaccessible; when you get closer you can spy the narrow gap in the northern cliffs, through which small boats can enter the crater and land on a sandy beach. The small settlement consists of a handful of buildings interspersed with pigpens, jungly foliage and (naturally) a large church. To get an overview of the island, climb up to the small **lighthouse** perched high on the crater's northern rim.

Getting to Apolima isn't easy. You'll need an invitation to stay with a local family; Sunset View Fales, on nearby Manono, may be able to arrange this – plus a boat to come and collect you – but you'll have to negotiate a fee.

## SAVAI'I

POP 43,142 / AREA 1700 SQ KM

Samoa's 'Big Island' offers a spectacular scenic smorgasbord of riotous rainforest, sea-smashed cliffs, pristine waterfalls and ragged volcanic cones (around 450 of them). Though visitors will be taken by Savai'i's gentle, snoozy ambience, the island itself – the largest shield volcano in the South Pacific – has volatile tendencies, most dramatically displayed in the eerie lava fields,

## Savai'i

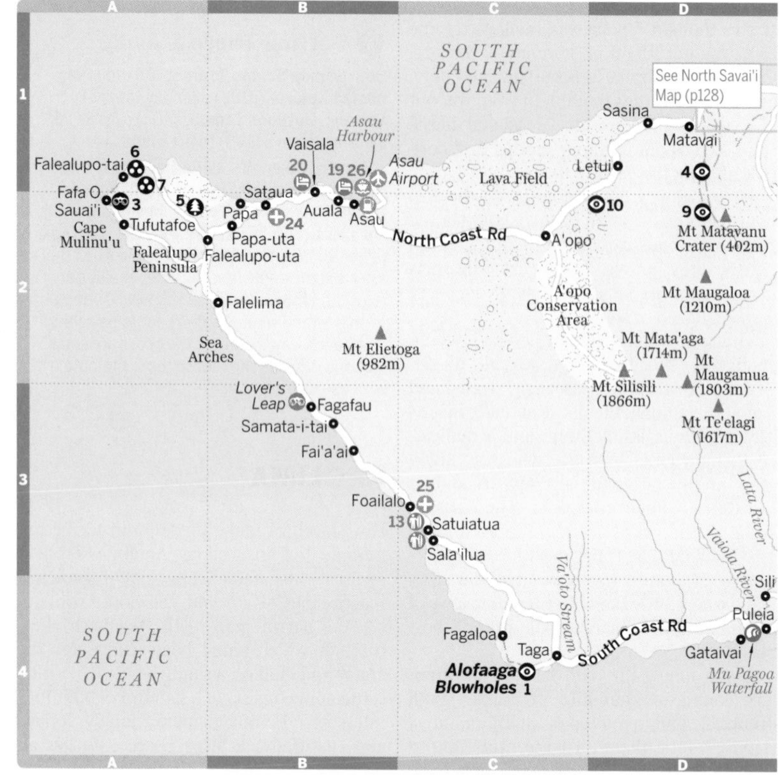


village ruins and craters of the north and the explosive blowholes of the south coast.

Though it's the largest island in Samoa (and the fourth largest in Polynesia), Savai'i is home to less than a quarter of the country's population, and has little in the way of facilities or infrastructure. *Fa'a Samoa* (the Samoan Way) remains strong in Savai'i's orderly villages, where the humid hush is broken only by the squeals of playing children, the buzz of weed-whackers and the soaring hymns of Sunday services.

## Getting There & Away

### AIR

**Samoa Air** (p142) operates charter flights between **Maota Airport** (Map p124; Maota) and **Asau Airport** (Map p124) on Savai'i and Faleolo and Fagali'i airports on Upolu. Email for bookings and fares.

### BOAT

Two car ferries tackle the 22km Apolima Strait between Upolu and Savai'i daily. The larger of the two boats, the *Lady Samoa III,* is the more comfortable. The trip across can take anywhere from 45 minutes to over an hour, depending on conditions.

Vehicles should be prebooked through the **Samoa Shipping Corporation** (p141); many hotels and car rental agencies can also do this for you. Before putting your car on the ferry at Mulifanua Wharf, you must have its underside cleaned (free) at the spraying station 100m before the boat terminal. This is done to prevent the spread of the giant African snail.

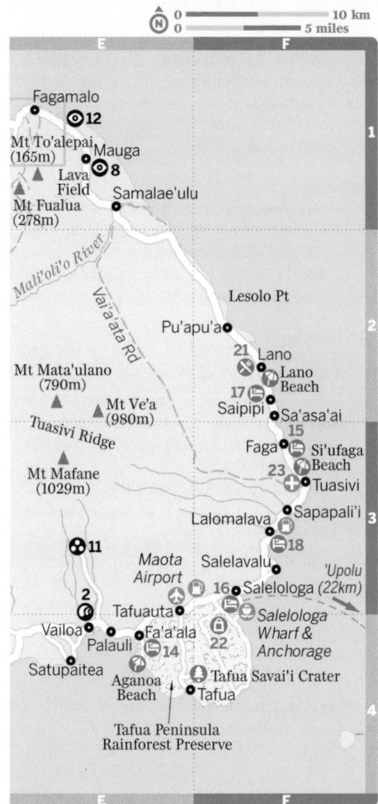


### Lady Samoa III 'Big Boat' Ferry Departures

| Departs Salelologa | Departs Mulifanua |
|---|---|
| Sun 11am & 3pm | Sun 1pm & 5pm |
| Mon 6am, 10am & 2pm | Mon 8am, noon & 4pm |
| Tue 6am & 2pm | Tue 8am & 4pm |
| Wed 6am, 10am & 2pm | Wed 8am, noon & 4pm |
| Thu 6am & 2pm | Thu 8am & 4pm |
| Fri 6am, 10am & 2pm | Fri 8am, noon & 4pm |
| Sat 6am, 10am & 2pm | Sat 8am, noon & 4pm |

## Getting Around

### BUS

Salelologa's market is the main terminal for Savai'i's colourful, crowded buses. For the east-coast beaches take the Pu'apu'a bus, or to continue on to Fagamalo, take the Lava Field Express. To carry on to Manase, take the Manase or Sasina bus. The Falealupo bus will take you around the Falealupo Peninsula, while the Salega or Fagafau buses trundle past the Alofaaga Blowholes and Satuiatua Beach. The most you'll pay for a ride is ST10 (to Asau). Buses to out-of-the-way destinations are timed with the ferries.

### DON'T MISS THE BOAT

The ferries to and from Savai'i can get very full, especially on weekends, holidays and Friday afternoons. Arrive at least an hour early on these days and get in the queue (in your car if you're driving or in the departure lounge if you're on foot) or you'll risk not getting on – the captains are (fortunately) quite strict about not overloading the boats. If you're driving, buying your ticket in advance is a must.

Boats seldom run on 'Samoa time'. A 2pm departure means a 2pm departure.

### CAR

It's a joy to drive the sealed coast road that circles the island, but keep an eye out for stray children, pigs, dogs and chickens. Off the main road you'll encounter a few bumpy tracks where at the very least you'll need a high-clearance 2WD (if not a 4WD if there's been heavy rain). This includes the steep, rocky climb up Mt Matavanu.

There are several petrol stations around Salelologa but only a few scattered around the island.

Cars can be hired on Savai'i but, as there's more competition on Upolu, if you're staying several days it works out cheaper and easier to bring a car over on the ferry. A small 2WD Hyundai costs around ST170 per day.

The spanking new **MotoSamoa** (☎764 5435; www.motosamoa.com; per day ST59, discounts for longer hire) group rents out 110cc scooters from three locations on Savai'i (see website for details); they'll also deliver to your accommodation.

### TAXI

A small army of taxis congregates around the Salelologa Market and the wharf.

## Salelologa & the East Coast

Ragtag Salelologa stretches up from the ferry terminal, offering little of interest except for a fairly languid **market** (Map p124; Salelologa; ⏱early-late Mon-Sat); if your needs run more to groceries than geegaws, the

## Savai'i

**Top Sights**
1 Alofaaga Blowholes ... C4

**Sights**
2 Afu-A-Au Falls ... E3
3 Cape Mulinu'u ... A2
4 Dwarf's Cave ... D1
5 Falealupo Canopy Walk ... A2
6 Falealupo Ruins ... A1
7 House of Rock ... A1
8 Mauga Village Crater ... E1
Moso's Footprint ... (see 7)
9 Mt Matavanu Crater ... D2
10 Pe'ape'a Cave ... D2
11 Pulemelei Mound ... E3
12 Sale'aula Lava Fields ... E1

**Activities, Courses & Tours**
13 Satuiatua ... C3

**Sleeping**
14 Aganoa Lodge ... E4
15 Amoa Resort ... F3
16 Ieu & Winnie's Islands View Motel ... F3
Jet Over Hotel ... (see 16)
17 Joelan Beach Fales ... F2
Lauiula Beach Fales ... (see 17)
Lusia's Lagoon Chalets ... (see 16)
Satuiatua Beach Fales ... (see 13)
18 Savaiian Hotel ... F3
19 Va-i-Moana Seaside Lodge ... B1
20 Vaisala Beach Hotel ... B1

**Eating**
Amoa Restaurant ... (see 15)
CC's Restaurant and Bar ... (see 16)
LeSogaimiti Restaurant & Bar ... (see 18)
21 Taefu T Matafeo Store ... F2

**Shopping**
22 Frankies ... F4
Salelologa Market ... (see 22)

**Information**
ANZ Bank ... (see 16)
Bank South Pacific ... (see 16)
23 Malietoa Tanumafili II Hospital ... F3
Post Office ... (see 16)
24 Sataua Hospital ... B2
25 Satuiatua Hospital ... C3

**Transport**
26 Anchorage ... B1
Bus Station ... (see 22)

big **Frankies** (Map p124; Salelologa; 6am-9pm) supermarket across the road has loads of fresh produce and groceries. There's nowhere better for supplies on the entire island.

Heading north you'll pass a tight series of villages fronting a shallow lagoon. It's only once you round the point at Tuasivi that things get exciting, as long white-sand beaches come into view, outlining the vivid aquamarine lagoon. The best of them, **Si'ufaga** and **Lano**, are among Savai'i's finest. The area also has numerous freshwater pools and springs for bathing.

## Sleeping

Salelologa is handy to the wharf and makes a fine base, but it's only once you head out of town that you really start to experience the restful charms of Savai'i.

### Salelologa & Around

**Ieu & Winnie's Islands View Motel** MOTEL $
(Map p124; 722 2557; islandsviewsavaii@gmail.com; Wharf Rd, Salelologa; 1-/2-bedroom units ST90/145; P) This small, hospitable family-run motel is a short stumble from the wharf. There are six simple units, a restaurant serving home-cooked meals, and – as the name promises – splendid views of nearby islands.

**Savaiian Hotel** RESORT $
(Map p124; 51296; www.savaiianhotel.com; North Coast Rd, Lalomalava; s/d without bathroom ST55/80, bungalow ST85/115, unit ST175/205; P) The large enclosed *fale* here are many steps above your average beach hut, with balconies, fans and private bathrooms. The units have amenities including air-conditioning, while new budget rooms are basic but excellent value. They're all set in a sparse garden between the village and the sea; the water's too shallow for swimming, but there is a small pool.

It also rents snorkelling gear and kayaks, and can arrange tours of Savai'i.

**Lusia's Lagoon Chalets** BUNGALOW $$
(Map p124; 51487; www.lusiaslagoon.com; South Coast Rd, Salelologa; bungalow s ST70-270, d ST120-320, s/d 145/200; ) Fall asleep to the lullaby of lapping waves at this charming, slightly ramshackle place. Accommodation varies dramatically: the cheapest *fale* teeter on stilts over the lagoon and are very basic (though their sea-gazing decks are adorably

atmospheric), while those with private facilities have air-conditioning, mod-cons and a sturdier feel. The on-site restaurant-bar is social, scenic and open to all.

Kayaks are free, and there's deep enough water for a proper swim off the pier.

**Jet Over Hotel** HOTEL **$$**
(Map p124; ☎51565; www.jetoverhotel.com; r/ste ST225/250; P ❄ 📶 ≋) Just off the main road behind a cluster of shops, this is a surprisingly stylish place: the pool and grounds are impeccable, the restaurant serves up sublime meals (pancake lovers may embarrass themselves at the free buffet breakfasts), and the sea views are glossy-mag gorgeous. While the cheapest rooms are decent enough (if plain), the two-storey, self-contained beach-facing suites get top marks.

It turns on a mean *fiafia* every Thursday night.

## Tuasivi & Lano

★**Joelan Beach Fales** BUNGALOW **$**
(Map p124; ☎722 9588; www.joelanbeachfales.ws; North Coast Rd, Lano Beach; open/enclosed bungalow incl breakfast & dinner ST120/140; P 📶) Long, languid Lano Beach easily rates as one of the best strips of sand on Savai'i, and Joelan's simple but well-kept thatched *fale* nab the best bit – some are so close to the water you could almost dangle your toes in the surf. The food here is bountiful and beautiful, as is the down-home hospitality. Ask about taking its *paopao* (traditional canoe) for a paddle.

**Lauiula Beach Fales** BUNGALOW **$**
(Map p124; ☎53897; www.lauiulabeachfales.com; North Coast Rd, Lano Beach; bungalow beach/garden per person incl breakfast & dinner from ST70/50; P 📶) Right next to Joelan's, the beach here has eroded away quite a bit but huddled-together *fale* are more 'posh' thanks to linoleum floors and a more sturdy thatch enclosure: for an extra ST10 you can have actual walls. There's a pro set-up with tours and transport on offer. Breakfast and dinner are served in a gorgeously carved seafront dining *fale*.

**Amoa Resort** RESORT **$$$**
(Map p124; ☎53518; www.amoaresort.com; North Coast Rd, Tuasivi; bungalow/villa ST520/640; P ❄ 📶 ≋) This recently revamped and rebranded boutique resort sits pretty across the road from an eye-smartingly turquoise lagoon. Large luxurious villas and beautiful bungalows hook around a lushly landscaped pool (with swim-up bar), and its magnificent restaurant – specialising in nouveau-Pacific cuisine – deserves many stars. It's easily the most upmarket choice on this stretch of coast.

## Eating & Drinking

★**Taefu T Matafeo Store** CAFE **$**
(Map p124; ☎764 5435; North Coast Rd, Asaga; snacks ST1-10; ⏱7am-8pm Mon-Sat, 7am-9am & 5-8pm Sun; 📶) If you're driving between Salelologa and the north coast, do yourself a favour and stop at this absolute gem of a place. It doesn't look like much, but there are sweet surprises in store: excellent espresso, indescribably wonderful homemade cakes (the chocolate is legendary), icy beers and light meals, including a mindblowing kimchi, all served in a delightful courtyard. There's even free wi-fi!

**CC's Restaurant and Bar** INTERNATIONAL **$$**
(Map p124; ☎51487; www.lusiaslagoon.com/dining; Lusia's Lagoon Chalets, Salelologa; mains ST19-45; ⏱7am-10pm) Overlooking a lovely lagoon with views to Upolu, this casual place serves super-fresh seafood, traditional Samoan dishes, curries and hearty grilled meats. Pop by in the morning for strong espresso and homemade cake, or watch the sun set with a cold cocktail in hand.

**LeSogaimiti Restaurant & Bar** INTERNATIONAL **$$**
(Map p124; ☎51296; www.savaiianhotel.com; Savaiian Hotel, Main North Rd, Lalomalava; mains ST15-45) At the Savaiian Hotel, this decent, dependable restaurant offers water views and some truly filling meals. A varied menu lists everything from (very good) seafood, chicken, sausages and steak to Samoan classics and spicy curries. It also has a kids' menu and vegetarian options.

★**Amoa Restaurant** INTERNATIONAL **$$$**
(Map p124; ☎53518; www.amoaresort.com; Amoa Resort, North Coast Rd, Tuasivi; mains ST25-75) This place is a true gem, and unlike anywhere else you'll find on Savai'i: it's a foodie destination unto itself. Fresh, locally sourced ingredients are used to create truly innovative takes on Samoan and Pacific classics, including *palusami* risotto balls, coconut-crusted chicken and homemade pasta infused with taro leaves.

## North Savai'i

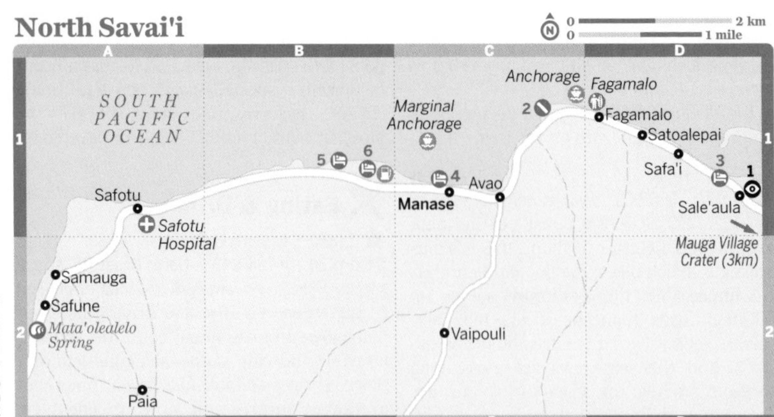




### Information

**ANZ Bank** (Map p124; Salelologa; ⏲8.30am-3pm Mon-Fri, to noon Sat) Has an outdoor ATM.

**Bank South Pacific** (Map p124; Salelologa; ⏲8.30am-3pm Mon-Wed, to 4pm Thu-Fri) The outdoor ATM accepts most cards.

**Malietoa Tanumafili II Hospital** (Map p124; ☎53511; North Coast Rd, Tuasivi) Has on-call doctors and a pharmacy. Other basic hospitals are at Safotu and Sataua.

**Post Office** (Map p124; Blue Bird Mall, Salelologa; ⏲8.30am-noon & 1-4pm Mon-Fri) Has telephones.

## Central North Coast

Sporting surreal lava fields, captivating caves and arguably the best beaches on the Big Island, it's no surprise that this is the most popular stretch on Savai'i. The coast has an abundance of accommodation options ranging from traditional *fale* to sumptuous suites; lovely little Manase offers the most choice. The high chief here had the foresight to ban dogs, making this one of the most unstressful villages to explore outside of Manono.

The bus from Salelologa to Manase costs about ST7; there's an ATM and petrol station at Manase.

### Sights

The Mt Matavanu eruptions between 1905 and 1911 created a moonscape in Savai'i's northeastern corner as a flow of lava 10m to 150m thick rolled through plantations and villages. The North Coast Rd crosses this dark, fractured lava field.

**Sale'aula Lava Fields** HISTORIC SITE

(Map p124; North Coast Rd, Sale'aula; adult/child ST5/3; ⏲8.30am-5pm) This striking spot offers a fascinating glimpse of the destruction wrought by the 1905 eruption of Mt Matavanu. Most photogenic is the ruined **LMS Church**: 2m of lava flowed through its door and was eerily imprinted by corrugated iron when the roof collapsed. Nearby, the **Virgin's Grave** purportedly marks the burial place of a girl so pure that lava flowed around her grave, leaving it untouched.

Amid all the lava, there are some nice grassy picnic spots here; littlies will enjoy chasing the squillion resident chickens.

**Mauga Village Crater** SCENIC AREA

(Map p124; North Coast Rd, Mauga) The modern, iron-roofed *fale* of Mauga village encircle a shallow, almost perfectly circular crater populated by banana palms. The access road is guarded by an enormous Catholic church. Approach a villager if you'd like to be shown around. It's 5km south of Sale'aula

**Mt Matavanu Crater** VOLCANO

(Map p124; ST20; ⏲9am-4pm Mon-Sat) If you've got a 4WD and a sturdy pair of boots, a visit to the volcano responsible for the devastation visited upon northeastern Savai'i a century ago is worth a few hours of your time. In addition to the fun of the very bumpy ride and pleasant views, you'll also get to meet 'Da Craterman', who maintains the track and collects the fee for his village (charming as he is, don't let him charge you more than ST20 per person).

## North Savai'i

**Sights**

1 Sale'aula Lava Fields ........ D1

**Activities, Courses & Tours**

2 Dive Savai'i ........ C1

**Sleeping**

3 Bayview Resort ........ D1
Le Lagoto Resort & Spa ........ (see 2)
4 Regina's Beach Fales ........ C1
Savai'i Lagoon Resort ........ (see 2)
5 Stevenson's at Manase ........ B1
Tailua Beach Fales ........ (see 4)
6 Tanu Beach Fales ........ B1

**Eating**

Leilina's Pizza ........ (see 2)

From Safotu take the turn-off to Paia village, then follow the signposted track up the mountain. After a lengthy stint of bouncing over the old lava flow, you'll reach Craterman's *fale*: if he's not around, keep heading up and you'll doubtless find him. From here there's an even bumpier 2km to the car park, where a 10-minute trail leads to the crater's edge. Keep the kids tight at hand: there's a vertiginous drop into the lush greenness below. The whole route is lined with Craterman's cheesy signs representing the visitors from 110-and-counting countries who have made the trek.

**Pe'ape'a Cave** CAVE
(Map p124; North Coast Rd; adult/child ST7/4; 8am-5pm) This cave sits beside the coast road just south of Letui. A round-trip guided exploration of this small lava tube takes only 10 minutes, but you'll see white-rumped Polynesian swiftlets and their nests up close. Bring your own torch.

## Activities

**Dive Savai'i** DIVING
(Map p128; 54172; www.divesavaii.com; North Coast Rd, Fagamalo; closed Sun) Besides diving interesting sites including a Missionary-era shipwreck (two-tank dives ST275), this family-friendly outfit offers PADI open-water courses (ST1260) and half-day snorkelling tours (ST65, snorkelling gear ST20); turtle and dolphin sightings aren't guaranteed, but they are common. It also hires snorkelling equipment on a casual basis (full set per 24 hours ST30).

## Sleeping & Eating

There are many quality *fale* places lining the North Coast Rd. Most places include breakfast in the rates; those in Manase throw in lunch and dinner as well.

### Sale'aula

★ **Bayview Resort** RESORT $$
(Map p128; 54170; www.bayviewresort.ws; North Coast Rd, Sale'aula; bungalow ST220-300; P ❄ ☎) First you'll be taken by its dramatic location on a solid river of black lava, then you'll be knocked for six by the dazzling turquoise bay it's named for, and by the time you're lounging on the massive deck attached to the best cottages, you'll be deadset on extending your stay. Swimming and white-sand sunning is superb; check out the lava pool at high tide.

The restaurant means well, but is very hit-or-miss; if you're driving, there's an excellent pizza place five minutes up the road.

### Fagamalo

**Le Lagoto Resort & Spa** RESORT $$$
(Map p128; 58189; www.lelagoto.ws; North Coast Rd, Fagamalo; d ST775-900; P ❄ ☎ ≋) The wooden bungalows at this boutique beachside resort are the plushest you'll find on the island; they're wonderfully atmospheric with intricate Samoan-style interiors and

### SUNDAY LUNCH

On Sunday mornings you'll find the islands shrouded in smoke as villagers light fires to warm stones needed for the *umu* (ground ovens) used to bake *to'ona'i* (Sunday lunch). Visitors sometimes complain that nothing happens in Samoa on Sunday, but it's hardly true – after a small breakfast (on account of the looming lunch), Samoans go to church and sing their lungs out, at noon they eat an enormous roast dinner and in the afternoon they sleep.

You may be lucky enough to be invited to a family *to'ona'i*. A typical spread includes baked fish and other seafood (freshwater prawns, crabs, octopus cooked in coconut milk), suckling pig, baked breadfruit, bananas, *palusami* (coconut cream wrapped in taro leaves), salads and curry dishes.

WORTH A TRIP

## DWARF'S CAVE

**Dwarf's Cave** (Map p124; Near Paia Village; guide per group around ST20; ⏲8.30am-5pm Mon-Sat) This intriguing subterranean lava tube leads downwards as if to the centre of the earth. The cave is named after a legendary group of dwarves, who apparently still live in its depths, and leave the occasional footprint. It's said that no one – except maybe the dwarves – has reached the end of it, and your guides (the village *matai* or local boys) will keep leading you through its prodigious depths, crossed by underground rivers, until you tell them to turn around.

Bring your own torch and reliable footwear, and be prepared to swim and get seriously muddy.

The cave is signposted off the Main North Coast Rd, just west of the Mt Matavanu turn-off. In Paia, look for the faded signpost on the right and wait outside the blue *fale* at this intersection; someone should appear to guide you to the cave.

blue-sea views. The **restaurant** (⏲7.30am-9pm, mains ST20-70) is great some nights, uninspired the next, but it has an extensive kids' menu and good *fiafia* nights (Thursdays). It's open to nonguests.

**Savai'i Lagoon Resort** RESORT **$$$**
(Map p128; ☎54168; www.savaiilagoon.co.nz; North Coast Rd, Fagamalo; studio ST350, bungalow ST315-450; P 📶) Taking the plum spot on one of Savai'i's best and most protected beaches, these large self-contained units are clean and inviting, but overpriced for their bland interiors and lack of air-conditioning. The resort owns Samoa's only glass-bottomed boat; tours run twice daily (except Sundays) and cost ST40/20 for adults/children. Free activities include bocce, volleyball, kayaking and zooming around in a dinghy.

**Leilina's Pizza** PIZZA **$$**
(Map p128; ☎54454; North Coast Rd, Fagamalo; pizzas ST24-45; ⏲10am-8pm Mon-Sat, 11am-8pm Sun) If you're hankering for pizza – especially crunchy, super-thin-crust pizza – this place is a godsend. The smell emanating forth from the kitchen is enough to work up a good drool; you'll be positively slobbering after a few bites of the wickedly spicy 'diavolo' (with pepperoni, chilli and garlic). Take it with you for a beach picnic, or dine in the small courtyard restaurant.

### Manase

**Tailua Beach Fales** BUNGALOW **$**
(Map p128; ☎54102; tailuasbeachfales@gmail.com; North Coast Rd, Manase; bungalow per person incl breakfast & dinner ST70; P 📶) This is a small, family-run collection of recently upgraded *fale* that are a step above their competition for their sea-facing decks, raised beds and spotlessness. Snorkellers report an abundance of turtles in the reef channel here. Nothing is too much trouble for the wonderful hostess Lua; you'll dream of her cooking long after you leave.

**Regina's Beach Fales** BUNGALOW **$**
(Map p128; ☎54054; reginabeachfales@gmail.com; North Coast Rd, Manase; bungalow per person incl breakfast & dinner ST60; P 📶) The *fale* here are of the traditional variety with woven blinds and mattresses on the floor, but they do have electric lights. Meals are low-key social events, with substantial local dishes such as roast breadfruit and taro served up at a communal dining table.

**Tanu Beach Fales** BUNGALOW **$**
(Map p128; ☎54050; tanubeachfales@gmail.com; North Coast Rd, Manase; bungalow per person incl breakfast & dinner ST70, s/d ST95/170; P 📶) This long-standing establishment is huge, which is only fitting as it's owned by the village's *ali'i* (high chief; the man to be thanked for the dog ban). There are dozens of simple *fale* dotting the beach; the accommodation block across the road offers basic rooms with real beds and shared bathrooms. It runs occasional – and very lively – *fiafia* nights.

**Stevenson's at Manase** RESORT **$$$**
(Map p128; ☎58219; www.stevensonsatmanase.com; North Coast Rd, Manase; bungalow/villa ST280/400, ste ST550-950; P ❄ 📶) This is the most upmarket place in Manase, with accommodation ranging from enormous, supermodern suites and posh beach villas to boutique *fale*, complete with fridges and cool stone ensuites. Its popular outdoor bar overlooks a glorious beach, while across the road, its Tusitala Restaurant (mains ST28 to ST55) does the usual mix of international classics with a sprinkling of Samoan samples.

## Northwestern Savai'i

Jutting out from the western end of Savai'i is the beautiful Falealupo Peninsula, rich with sites associated with significant Samoan legends. The peninsula's remoteness and protected tracts of rainforest lend it an almost unnerving calm.

In past years, burglars have targeted tourists in this area, so lock your car and don't leave anything of value in it or in your *fale*. Even if you don't have anything stolen, you'll likely feel robbed after having been asked for so many exaggerated 'custom fees' to tour the sites. It's definitely one of the more beautiful areas of the island, though, so weigh the pros and cons of feeling swindled.

### Sights & Activities

**Cape Mulinu'u** VIEWPOINT

(Map p124; Falealupo Rd; ⌚8.30am-5pm Mon-Sat) The country's most western point is not only gorgeously scenic (until Samoa hopped the dateline, it was the last place in the world the sun set each day), but home to many fascinating cultural and archaeological sites. The **Fafa O Sauai'i** outlook was one of Samoa's most sacred spots in pre-Christian times; there's a great swimming hole here. Nearby is a **star mound**, **Vaatausili Cave** and the **Vai Sua Toto** (the 'Blood Well' – named after the warrior Tupa'ilevaililigi, who threw his enemies' severed heads in here).

You may be hit up for an exorbitant admission fee; you can probably get away with ST10 per person.

**Falealupo Canopy Walk** NATURE RESERVE

(Map p124; Falealupo Rd; admission ST20; ⌚7am-6pm) This wobbly walk takes you across a 24m jerry-built bridge strung between two large trees almost 10m above the rainforest floor. After you cross the walkway to the second tree, climb via a slightly sturdier wooden ladder to a platform up a magical, nearly 230-year-old banyan tree. The walk is part of the **Falealupo Rainforest Preserve**, a customary-owned conservation area.

The ST20 admission also covers you for nearby attractions Moso's Footprint and the House of Rock.

**Moso's Footprint** ARCHAEOLOGICAL SITE

(Map p124; Falealupo Rd; admission incl in Canopy Walkway ticket; ⌚7am-6pm) This ancient 1m-by-3m rock depression is decidedly unremarkable apart from the legend that surrounds it: apprently, the giant Moso made the footprint when he stepped over from Fiji to Samoa. You'll find it well signposted in front of a tidy *fale*.

**House of Rock** ARCHAEOLOGICAL SITE

(Map p124; Falealupo Rd; admission incl in Canopy Walkway ticket; ⌚7am-6pm) Legend says this site – a partially collapsed lava tube – is the result of a house-building competition between Falealupo's men and women, a contest the women won; it's a symbol of motivation for Samoan women to this day. It doesn't look like much (though it does make a handy cyclone shelter), but a good guide (ST5) with stories to tell will enliven the experience.

**Falealupo Ruins** RUIN

(Map p124; Falealupo) Cyclones Ofa and Val struck the peninsula in 1990 and 1991, completely destroying the village of Falealupo. The decision was made to rebuild the village further inland and the ruined village was left in tatters, though some families have since moved back to rebuild. The ruins of the **Catholic church** (Falealupo Rd) are particularly enigmatic and eerily beautiful. You may be shaken down here, even if you just want to take a photograph.

**A'opo Conservation Area & Mt Silisili** HIKING

The two- to three-day return trip to the summit of Mt Silisili (1858m), the highest point in Samoa, traverses some wonderful rainforested sections of the A'opo Conservation Area and Savai'i's mountainous backbone. To organise a guide, speak to the *pulenu'u* (a combination of mayor and police chief) of A'opo; ask in the town's small shop for directions.

You'll pay around ST50 per person per day and will need to supply food and water and all the requisite camping and hiking equipment.

### Sleeping & Eating

**Vaisala Beach Hotel** HOTEL $

(Map p124; ☎58016; South Coast Rd, Vaisala; s/d from ST100/120, bungalow ST75; P ❄ 📶) Quirky Vaisala has a distinct retro charm, with mismatched furnishings and a dated, barracks-like main building. Rooms are slightly oddball but comfortable, and all have terraces; the *fale* have traditional thatched roofs and louvres. The hotel's restaurant has an outdoor deck and serves filling dinners, including a much-lauded lobster dish. It faces its own beautiful – and swimmable – beach.

**Va-i-Moana Seaside Lodge** BUNGALOW $$
(Map p124; ☎58140; www.vaimoanaseasidelodge.com; South Coast Rd, Asau; open bungalow per person ST95, closed bungalow s ST140-170, d ST250-300, ste ST320-400, all incl breakfast & dinner; P ❄ 📶) This friendly place sits on a sparkling cove, with a hodgepodge of lodgings that range from traditional open *fale* and enclosed bungalows perched over the surf to blissfully air-conditioned suites. There's a good restaurant and bar, free kayaks and fishing tours on offer (from ST800 for two anglers). Ask the lovely owners about the site's fascinating history.

## South Coast

With less reef to protect it, Savai'i's south coast bears witness to dramatic confrontations between land and sea, resulting in blustering blowholes and some great surfing spots. Away from Mother Nature's theatrics, this delightfully drowsy, sparsely populated stretch is a wonderful place to do very little at all.

### Sights

★**Alofaaga Blowholes** GEYSER
(Taga Blowholes; Map p124; via Taga Village; admission ST5; ⏰7am-6pm) These powerful blowholes are among the most spectacular on Earth, and well worth going out of your way for. Strong waves are pushed through a series of lava tubes, causing rip-roaring, geyser-like explosions that shoot dozens of metres into the air. If this wasn't dramatic enough, villagers throw coconuts (for a fee: don't pay more than ST10) into the blowholes, where they blast up like cannonballs: it's thrilling stuff, and photographs extremely well. DO NOT get too close to the blowholes, no matter what the locals do.

Pay admission at the first *fale* and park your car at the second *fale*, near the main blowhole. You shouldn't have to pay admission again, though you may be asked to; there are a few crafty sorts around here, so keep your doors locked, even when you're inside the car.

**Pulemelei Mound** ARCHAEOLOGICAL SITE
(Map p124; off South Coast Rd) Polynesia's largest ancient structure is the intriguing, pyramidal Pulemelei Mound (sometimes called Tia Seu Ancient Mound). Constructed sometime between AD 1100 and 1400, it measures 65m by 60m at its base and rises to a height of more than 12m. Its original purpose continues to baffle experts; for more information about its possible purpose see p151. It's a stirring place, with views from its stony summit to the ocean and into thick rainforest. The surrounding area is presumably covered in important archaeological finds but, for now, the jungle hides its secrets.

It's very difficult to visit the mound as it's located on disputed land. There's no signage or upkeep: the path to the site and the mound itself are very overgrown. Guides often refuse to take people here because they worry that someone who has an ambiguous claim to the land may hassle them into handing over an exorbitant fee, or worse, just kick them off. That said, it may be possible to pick up a guide; ask at the *fale* at nearby Afu-A-Au Falls.

If you want to try it sans-guide, head down the road flanked by iron poles that starts about 300m beyond the iron-girder bridge on the opposite side of the river from Afu-A-Au Falls (no sign). You'll soon reach a rocky ford over a stream (impassable without a good 4WD). Park here, cross the creek at the bend and enter an overgrown track between two poles. The track follows an old road bordered by stone walls, then continues up a fern-filled path to the mound. The walk takes about an hour each way: you'll need water and sturdy shoes.

This is a very secluded area – women especially should not walk alone, and don't leave any valuables in your car.

**GATEWAY TO THE UNDERWORLD**

The natural beauty of the Falealupo Peninsula befits its spiritual significance. In pre-Christian times it was believed to be the gateway for souls into the next world. According to tradition, there are two entrances to the underworld: one for chiefs and another for commoners. One entrance is through a cave near Cape Mulinu'u and the other is on the trail made by the setting sun over the sea.

**Afu-A-Au Falls** WATERFALL
(Map p124; off South Coast Rd; adult/child ST5/2; ⏲8am-6pm Mon-Sat) Gorgeous Afu-A-Au Falls, also known as Olemoe Falls, are a dream come true on a steamy Samoan day (which is, truthfully, almost every day). Cascading down to a blessedly cool 3m-deep waterhole in a secluded jungle, the falls are spring-fed, meaning swimming is possible even during the dry season. It's only signposted if you're travelling from the east; if you're coming from the west, turn left immediately after crossing the steel bridge. Pay at the *fale* by the entrance.

**Tafua Peninsula Rainforest Preserve** NATURE RESERVE
(admission ST5) This preserve contains superb stands of rainforest and rugged stretches of lava coast studded with cliffs and sea arches. A highlight is the **Tafua Savai'i crater**: its sheer, deep walls are choked with vegetation, giving it a lost-world feel. This place is a birdwatcher's delight, and you will probably catch glimpses of flying foxes napping in the trees far below.

Take the side road signposted to Tafua opposite Ma'ota Airport and pay the 'custom fee' about 50m along. The hiking track to the crater is overgrown and can be hard to follow, so it's worth taking the services of a guide (be sure to agree on a price beforehand) or at least asking directions from the village kids.

## Activities

At the western end of Fa'a'ala village, a track leads to lovely **Aganoa Beach**. There are strong currents here, so swim with care. Ask at at Aganoa Lodge before surfing.

**Satuiatua** SURFING
(Map p124; per person ST10) Surfers will find an excellent left-hand surf-break at Satuiatua; the fee is used to support the local school.

## Sleeping & Eating

**Satuiatua Beach Fales** BUNGALOW $
(Map p124; ☎846 4119; South Coast Rd, Satuiatua; bungalow per person incl breakfast & dinner ST75; P 📶) Run by a family of women, this spotless place is loaded with simple and effective touches. Open *fale* have proper beds and are well maintained, while enclosed *fale* are more like large cottages; there are also a couple of ensuite units. The marvellous treehouse (with swings!) perched in a huge banyan tree is reason alone to stay, though the idyllic snorkelling and fantastic surfing get high marks too.

The **restaurant** (lunch ST20) serves good, hearty meals. It's a good stop for lunch if you find yourself in these parts when the tummy rumbles.

**Aganoa Lodge** BUNGALOW $$$
(Map p124; ☎+1 310 990 6269; www.pegasuslodges.com; Aganoa Beach; 6-night surfer packages from ST5080; P 📶) Recently rebranded and given a high-end makeover, this all-inclusive surf resort exploits the beauty of an exquisite little beach and its proximity to some of Savai'i's best breaks. Surfers (and their nonsurfing partners and families) shack up in luxurious *fale* with real beds, ensuites, open-air showers, electricity and surf-facing decks. Set meals are top-notch, locally sourced and served communally.

Surf package prices include all meals, accommodation, guided surf trips and return airport transfers.

# UNDERSTAND SAMOA

## Samoa Today

In 2012 Samoa celebrated 50 years of independence with huge pomp and partying. Though Samoa is very much its own country, it still relies heavily on foreign aid, particularly from Australia and New Zealand, with whom ties are very close. In 2014 Samoa hosted the third international Small Island Developing States (SIDS) conference, which culminated in the adoption of the Samoa Pathway, a document which – in part – saw global leaders pledge their support to sustainable development and the battles against climate change faced by small, vulnerable island nations.

## History

### Prehistory

The oldest evidence of human occupation in Samoa is Lapita village, partially submerged in the lagoon at Mulifanua on the island of Upolu. Carbon tests date the site to 1000 BC.

Archaeologists have discovered more than a hundred star-shaped stone platforms across the islands. It's believed that these platforms, dubbed 'star mounds', were used to snare wild pigeons, a favoured pastime of *matai* (chiefs). Savai'i's Pulemelei Mound is the largest ancient structure in the Pacific.

Around AD 950 warriors from Tonga established their rule on Savai'i, and then moved on to Upolu. They were eventually repelled by Malietoa Savea, a Samoan chief whose title, *Malie toa* (Brave warrior), was derived from the shouted tributes of the retreating Tongans. There was also contact with Fiji, from where legends say two girls brought the art of tattooing. The Samoans never really trusted their neighbours – *togafiti* (tonga fiji) means 'a trick'.

## European Contact

Whalers, pirates and escaped convicts apparently introduced themselves to Samoa well before the first officially recorded European arrival in the region. This was the Dutchman Jacob Roggeveen, who approached the Manu'a Islands in American Samoa in 1722. Other visitors followed in his wake and over the next 100 years numerous Europeans settled in. The settlers established a society in Apia and a minimal code of law in order to govern their affairs, all with the consent of Upolu chiefs, who maintained sovereignty in their own villages. Along with technological expertise, the *palagi* (Europeans) also brought with them diseases to which the islanders had no immunity.

## Missionaries

In August 1830 missionaries John Williams and Charles Barff of the London Missionary Society (LMS) arrived at Sapapali'i on Savai'i's eastern coast. They were followed by Methodist and Catholic missionaries, and in 1888 Mormons added to the competition for souls. Samoans were quite willing to accept Christianity due to the similarity of Christian creation beliefs to Samoan legend, and because of a prophecy by war goddess Nafanua that a new religion would take root in the islands. Although interdistrict warfare was not abolished until the start of the 20th century, schools and education were eagerly adopted.

## Squabbling Powers

There were – and still are – four paramount titles relating to four '*aiga* (extended families equivalent to royal dynasties), in what is now Samoa: Malietoa, Tupua Tamasese, Mata'afa and Tu'imaleali'ifano. During the 1870s a civil dispute broke out between two of these families, dividing Samoa. Much land was sold to Europeans by Samoans seeking to acquire armaments to settle the matter.

The British, Americans and Germans then set about squabbling over Samoan territory, and by the late 1880s Apia Harbour was crowded with naval hardware from all three countries. Most of it subsequently sunk – not because of enemy firepower, but because of a cyclone that struck the harbour in March 1889. After several attempted compromises, the Tripartite Treaty was signed in 1899, giving control of Western Samoa to the Germans and eastern Samoa to the Americans.

## Foreign Administration

In February 1900 Dr Wilhelm Solf was appointed governor, and the German trading company DHPG began to import thousands of Melanesians and Chinese to work on its huge plantations. But although the Germans had agreed to rule 'according to Samoan custom', they didn't keep their word. In 1908 there was widespread discontent, and the organisation of the *Mau a Pule* (Mau Movement) by Namulau'ulu Lauaki Mamoe; he and his chief supporters were sent into exile soon after.

In 1914, at the outbreak of WWI, Britain persuaded NZ to seize German Samoa. Preoccupation with affairs on the home front prevented Germany from resisting. Under NZ administration Samoa suffered a devastating (and preventable) outbreak of influenza in 1919; more than 7000 people (one-fifth of the population) died, further fuelling anger with the foreign rulers. Increasing calls for independence by the Mau Movement culminated in the authorities opening fire on a demonstration at the courthouse in Apia in 1929.

Following a change of government (and policy) in NZ, Western Samoa's independence was acknowledged as inevitable and even desirable, and in 1959 Prime Minister Fiame Mata'afa was appointed. The following year a formal constitution was adopted and, on 1 January 1962, independence was finally achieved.

## Since Independence

The Human Rights Protection Party (HRPP) has been in power for most of the period since independence. Economic development has been excruciatingly slow or nonexistent, far below population growth, but at least the country has been politically stable.

Upolu and Savai'i have been battered by several huge tropical storms over the past two decades, including the severe Category Four cyclones Val (1991) and Evan (2012).

In 2009 the government switched driving from the right-hand side of the road to the left, apparently to allow access to cheap secondhand vehicle imports from NZ.

# The Culture

Many visitors correctly sense that below the surface of the outwardly friendly and casual Samoan people lies a complex code of traditional etiquette. Beneath the light-heartedness, the strict and demanding *Fa'a Samoa* (Samoan Way) is rigorously upheld.

## The National Psyche

*'Aiga,* or extended family groupings, are at the heart of the *Fa'a Samoa*. The larger an *'aiga,* the more powerful it is, and to be part of a powerful *'aiga* is the goal of all traditionally minded Samoans. Each *'aiga* is headed by a *matai,* who represents the family on the *fono* (village council). *Matai* are elected by all adult members of the *'aiga* and can be male or female, but over 90% of current *matai* are male.

The *fono* consists of the *matai* of all of the *'aiga* associated with the village. The *ali'i* (high chief of the village) sits at the head of the *fono*. In addition, each village has one *pulenu'u* (a combination of mayor and police chief) and one or more *tulafale* (orators or talking chiefs). The *pulenu'u* acts as an intermediary between the village and the national government, while the *tulafale* liaises between the *ali'i* and outside entities, carries out ceremonial duties and engages in ritual debates.

*'Ava* (kava) is a drink derived from the ground root of the pepper plant. The *'ava* ceremony is a ritual in Samoa, and every government and *matai* meeting is preceded by one.

Beneath the *matai,* members of a village are divided into four categories. The society of untitled men, the *aumaga,* is responsible for growing food. The *aualuma,* the society of unmarried, widowed or separated women, provides hospitality and produces various goods such as *siapo* (decorated bark cloth) and the *ie toga* (fine mats) that are an important part of *fa'alavelave* (lavish gift-exchange ceremonies). Married women are called *faletua ma tausi*. Their role revolves around serving their husband and his family. The final group is the *tamaiti* (children). Close social interaction is generally restricted to members of one's own group.

Individuals are subordinate to the extended family. There is no 'I', only 'we'. The incapable are looked after by their family rather than by taxpayers, and with such onerous

### EARTHQUAKE & TSUNAMI DISASTER IN THE SAMOAS

On 29 September 2009 Upolu's southern and eastern coasts and the south coast of Tutuila in American Samoa were struck by a tsunami that killed approximately 190 people and left thousands homeless. It began with an 8.1 magnitude earthquake with its epicentre 190km south of Apia, which struck at 6.48am local time. Eight minutes later, a 10m-high wave demolished Upolu's south coast where people had little to no warning. On Tutuila, four tsunami waves between 4m and 6m were reported; these waves surged up to 1.6km inland, destroying homes and wiping out the electricity infrastructure.

In the years after the tsunami, resorts were rebuilt, new all-weather access roads were constructed, and visitors to many coastal regions will notice street signs pointing to tsunami evacuation routes leading to higher ground.

family (plus village and church) obligations, it's a struggle for any individual to become wealthy. Life is not about individual advancement or achievement, but about serving and improving the status of your *'aiga*. The communal ownership of land and lack of reward for individual effort tend to stymie Western-style economic development, but have kept control of most of Samoa's resources in Samoan hands.



### Lifestyle

Parents and other relatives treat babies with great affection, but at the age of three the children are made the responsibility of an older sibling or cousin. *Fa'aaloalo* is respect for elders, the most crucial aspect of the *Fa'a Samoa*, and children are expected to obey not just their immediate relatives, but all the *matai* and adults in the village as well as older siblings. Parents rarely hug or praise their children, so the youth often suffer from low self-esteem and lack confidence and ambition. Fun family activities are few and far between; a rare exception is White Sunday in October, when children eat first, star in church services, and are bought new clothes and toys. Some teenagers resort to *musu* (refusing to speak to anybody) as a form of protest.

Overriding all else in Samoa is Christianity. Every village has at least one large church, ideally a larger one than in neighbouring villages. These operate as the village social centre, the place where almost everyone makes an appearance on Sunday, dressed up in their formal best. Sunday-morning church services are inevitably followed by *to'ona'i* (Sunday lunch), when families put on banquets fit for royalty.

*Sa*, which means 'sacred', is the nightly vespers, though it's not applied strictly throughout all villages. Sometime between 6pm and 7pm a gong sounds, signifying that the village should prepare for *sa*. When the second gong is sounded, *sa* has begun. All activity should come to a halt. If you're caught in a village during *sa*, stop what you're doing, sit down and quietly wait for the third gong, about 10 or 15 minutes later, when it's over.

A rigid approach to Christianity has led to conservative attitudes on many social issues, including homosexuality, but this is tempered by a generally tolerant attitude to *fa'afafine* – men who dress and behave like women. The name *fa'afafine* means 'like a woman' and has no obvious parallel in Western society. *Fa'afafine* fulfil an important role in the social fabric, often helping out with the children and looking after their parents in old age. A *fa'afafine* may have a relationship with a man, but this isn't seen as homosexual. Neither are they seen as women, per se.

### Population

Three-quarters of Samoans live on the island of Upolu. The urban area of Apia houses around 21% of the nation's population, with the rest sprinkled around the small villages that mainly cling to the coastline. Minorities include both expat and Samoan-born Europeans (called *palagi* in Samoan) and a small number of Chinese; both minorities are centred on Apia.

## Sport

Sport in Samoa is a community event, which might explain why this tiny nation turns out a disproportionate number of great sportspeople. Drive through any village in the late afternoon and you'll see people of all ages gathering on the *malae* (village green) to play rugby, volleyball and *kirikiti*. *Fautasi* (45-person canoe) races are held on special occasions. Samoa's main obsession is rugby union and the members of the national team, Manu Samoa, are local heroes – as are the many Samoan players who fill the ranks of rugby union, rugby league and netball teams in NZ, Australia, the UK and France.

## Arts

### Architecture

Traditional (not to mention highly practical) Samoan architecture is exemplified by the *fale*, an oval structure with wooden posts but no walls, thus allowing natural airflow. It's traditionally built on a stone or coral foundation and thatched with woven palm or sago leaves. Woven coconut-leaf blinds can be pulled down to protect against rain or prying eyes, but in truth, privacy in such a building is practically impossible.

*Palagi*-style square homes with walls, louvre windows and doors, though uncomfortably hot and requiring fans, have more status than traditional *fale* and are becoming more common in Samoa.

## Fiafia

Originally, the *fiafia* was a village play or musical presentation in which participants would dress in costume and accept money or other donations. These days the term '*fiafia* night' usually refers to a lavish presentation of Samoan fire- and slap-dancing and singing, accompanied by a buffet dinner. But traditional *fiafia* are still performed during weddings, birthdays, title-conferring ceremonies and at the opening of churches and schools.

Drummers keep the beat while dancers sing traditional songs illustrated by coordinated hand gestures. A *fiafia* traditionally ends with the *siva,* a slow and fluid dance performed by the village *taupou* (usually the daughter of a high chief), dressed in *siapo* with her body oiled.

## Literature

Towering over Samoan literature is Albert Wendt, a novelist, poet, academic and latterly visual artist, now resident in NZ. Many of his novels deal with the *Fa'a Samoa* bumping against *palagi* ideas and attitudes, and the loss of Samoa's pre-Christian spirituality; try *Leaves of the Banyan Tree* (1979), *Ola* (1995) or *The Mango's Kiss* (2003). Perhaps some of the prose is too risqué for the Methodists who run most of Samoa's bookshops, as copies are hard to track down in Samoa – you'll have better luck overseas or online.

*The Beach at Falesa* by Robert Louis Stevenson is a brilliant short story set in Samoa by a master stylist with inside knowledge of the South Pacific. Stevenson spent the last four years of his life in Samoa.

## Music

Music is a big part of everyday life in Samoa, whether it be the exuberant drumming that accompanies *fiafia* nights, the soaring harmonies of church choirs or the tinny local pop blaring out of taxis.

Traditionally, action songs and chants were accompanied by drums and body slaps, but guitars, ukuleles and Western-style melodies are now a firm part of the *fiafia* repertoire. Songs were once written to tell stories or commemorate events and this practice continues today. Love songs are the most popular, followed by patriotic songs extolling local virtues. *We are Samoa* by Jerome Grey is Samoa's unofficial national anthem.

While clubs in Apia host local hip-hop and reggae-influenced acts, it's offshore that Samoan artists have hit the big time, especially NZ-based rappers such as King Kapisi, Scribe and Savage.

## Siapo & Ie Toga

The bark cloth known as *siapo* is made from the inner bark of the *u'a* (paper mulberry tree) and provides a medium for some of the loveliest artwork in Samoa.

The fine mat called *ie toga* is woven from pandanus fibres split into widths of just a couple of millimetres and can involve years of painstaking work. *Ie toga,* along with *siapo,* make up 'the gifts of the women' that must be exchanged at formal ceremonies. Agricultural products comprise 'the gifts of the men'.

## Tattooing

Samoa is the last of the Polynesian nations where traditional tattooing (*tatau*) is still widely practised (albeit against the wishes of some religious leaders). The traditional *pe'a* (male tattoo) covers the man's body from the waist to the knees. Women can elect to receive a *malu* (female tattoo), but their designs cover only the thighs.

The skills and tools of the *tufuga pe'a* (tattoo artist) were traditionally passed down from father to son, and sharpened shark teeth or boar tusks were used to carve the intricate designs into the skin. It was believed that the man being tattooed must not be left alone in case the *aitu* (spirits) took him. In most cases the procedure takes at least a fortnight. Noncompletion would cause shame to the subject and his *'aiga*.

# Environment

Current environmental issues faced by Samoa include soil erosion, overfishing (including dynamite fishing), deforestation and invasive species. As a low-lying nation with the majority of its population living along the coast, Samoa is – like all islands in the region – vulnerable to effects

**SLEEPING PRICE RANGES**

The following price ranges refer to a double room or *fale*:

**$** less than ST150

**$$** ST150–300

**$$$** more than ST300

of climate change including rising sea levels, increase in cyclones, drought and coral damage.

## Geography

Samoa lies in the heart of the vast South Pacific, 3700km southwest of Hawai'i. Tonga lies to the south, Fiji to the southwest, Tuvalu to the northwest and Tokelau to the north, while the Cook Islands are to the southeast.

The country has a total land area of 2934 sq km and is composed primarily of high, eroded volcanic islands with narrow coastal plains. It has two large islands: Savai'i (1700 sq km) and Upolu (1115 sq km). The nation's highest peak, Mt Silisili on Savai'i, rises to 1866m. The small islands of Manono and Apolima lie in the 22km-wide Apolima Strait that separates Upolu and Savai'i. A few other tiny, uninhabited rocky islets and outcrops lie southeast of Upolu.

## Ecology

The heights of Savai'i and Upolu are covered in temperate forest vegetation: tree ferns, grasses, wild coleus and epiphytic plants. The magnificent *aoa* (banyan tree) dominates the higher landscapes, while other areas are characterised by scrublands, marshes, pandanus forests and mangrove swamps. The rainforests of Samoa are a natural apothecary, home to some 75 known medicinal plant species.

Because Samoa is relatively remote, few animal species have managed to colonise it. The Lapita brought with them domestic pigs, dogs and chickens, as well as the ubiquitous Polynesian rat. But apart from two species of fruit bat (protected throughout the islands after being hunted close to extinction) and the small, sheath-tailed bat, mammals not introduced by humans are limited to the marine varieties. Whales, dolphins and porpoises migrate north and south through the islands, depending on the season.

*Pili* (skinks) and *mo'o* (geckos) can be seen everywhere, and various types of turtles visit the islands. The only land creature to beware of (besides the unloved and unlovely dogs) is the giant centipede, which packs a nasty bite.

# SURVIVAL GUIDE

## Directory A–Z

### ACCOMMODATION

It's fair to say that accommodation options in Samoa are limited. There's little budget accommodation outside the ubiquitous *fale;* and at the other end of the scale, only a handful of resorts qualify as truly luxurious. At both ends of the scale, many properties are overpriced given the quality offered. That said, much of the country's accommodation occupies idyllic settings on the beautiful sands that fringe the islands – this meets the minimum requirements for most visitors.

An excellent source of accommodation information is the **Samoa Hotels Association** (Map p106; ☎30160; www.samoahotels.ws; Samoa Tourism Authority information fale, Beach Rd, Apia). It also acts as a booking agent, taking its fee from the provider, not the guest.

Beach *fale* are the most interesting budget option. Hotel, motel and resort accommodation ranges from rooms in slightly dilapidated buildings with cold-water showers to well-maintained rooms with all the mod cons. There's sometimes access to a shared kitchen. Resorts tend to offer bungalow-style accommodation (sometimes called *fale* to sound exotic), with the bigger ones having swim-up cocktail bars and multiple restaurants.

Traditional village homestays can be organised through **Samoa Village Stays** (☎22777; www.samoavillagestays.com; ST100 per person per night).

### ACTIVITIES

Visiting Samoa is less about seeing sights as doing things – particularly things that involve tropical beaches.

#### Diving

Samoa's dive industry is far less developed than those of some of its neighbours, meaning there are some fantastic sites to explore, with access to a multitude of tropical fish and larger marine creatures, such as turtles and dolphins. Two-tank dives start from ST275 and PADI open-water courses are around ST1250.

### Fishing

Samoan reefs and their fishing rights are owned by villagers, so you can't just drop a line anywhere; seek permission first. If you'd like to go fishing with locals, inquire at your accommodation or speak to the *pulenu'u* of the village concerned.

Game fishing is becoming increasingly popular in the islands – in fact, Samoa has been rated one of the top 10 game-fishing destinations in the world. The Samoa International Game Fishing Tournament (www.sigfa.ws) heads out from Apia Harbour in late April.

### Hiking

Samoa's rugged coastal areas, sandy beaches, thick rainforests and volcanoes all invite exploration on foot. However, trails can quickly become obscured due to tangled tropical growth and half-hearted track maintenance. Combine this with the effects of heavy rain and there's often a good chance of getting lost (or at the very least covering yourself in mud). For more remote treks, it pays to take a guide with you.

Costs vary enormously. Sometimes villagers will be happy to accompany you for nothing; at other times, they'll be seeking goods as a reward (like cigarettes), but mostly they'll be interested in cash.

### Kayaking

Kayaks are perfect for pottering around lagoons; several accommodation providers have them available. Longer kayaking excursions can be organised through **Outdoor Samoa** (p105).

### Snorkelling & Swimming

The novice snorkeller will find Samoa's waters fascinating and teeming with life. In places the reef has been damaged by cyclones, tsunamis and human contact, but will still reveal live corals and an abundance of colourful fish, often just a short paddle out from the beach. Some particularly good and accessible spots are Lalomanu, Namu'a and Palolo Deep Marine Reserve. Many places hire out snorkelling gear, but it's worth bringing your own mask and snorkel.

The majority of Samoan beaches are great for splashing about in, but too shallow for satisfying swimming. Always ask permission from local villagers before using their beach.

### Surfing

Powerful conditions, sharp reefs and offshore breaks that are difficult to access mean that surfing in Samoa is challenging, to say the very least, and probably one of the worst places in the world to learn the sport. While the surf can be magnificent at times, offering waves of a lifetime in glorious surroundings, conditions are generally difficult to assess, with some very dangerous situations awaiting the inexperienced or reckless. That said, the islands are an increasingly popular destination for experienced surfers. The wet season (November to April) brings swells from the north; the dry season (May to October) brings big swells from the south.

It's best to hook up with a surfing outfit. They know all the best spots and provide boat transport to them and, perhaps more importantly, they have established relationships with local villagers and understand the culture – they know where it is and isn't OK to surf.

## CHILDREN

The Samoan climate (discounting long periods of heavy rain or the odd cyclone), warm waters and dearth of poisonous creatures make the islands a paradise for children. You'll find that Samoans tend to lavish attention on very young children, and foreign toddlers will not be starved for attention or affection while visiting the islands.

Never leave your child unsupervised near beaches, reefs or on walking tracks, particularly those running along coastal cliffs (these

### THE BEACH FALE: SAMOA'S SIGNATURE ACCOMMODATION

The simple structures called *fale* come in a variety of styles. At their most simple and traditional, they're just a wooden platform with poles supporting a thatched roof, surrounded by woven blinds for privacy. Woven sleeping mats are laid on the floor, topped by a mattress with sheets and a mosquito net. From this basic model, various degrees of luxury can be added: electric lights, ceiling fans, proper beds, wooden walls, lockable doors and decks. Avoid those with plastic-sheeting walls; they tend to flap around in the wind without letting much air through. Bathroom facilities are usually a communal block, with cold water being the norm. The price usually includes breakfast and often a set lunch and dinner as well.

*Fale* are usually priced per person, ranging from a reasonable ST70 (including meals) to well over ST200. As a result, couples or larger groups may find themselves paying much more than they would for a midrange hotel, for what is basically one step up from camping on the beach.

are never fenced). Typically only the upmarket resorts provide cots, and only some car-rental agencies have car seats (and these can be of questionable quality), so it may pay to bring your own.

## EMBASSIES & CONSULATES

The following diplomatic missions are based in Apia.

**Australian High Commission** (Map p106; ☎23411; www.embassy.gov.au/ws.html; Beach Rd; ⏲9am-4.30pm Mon-Fri) Canadian consular services are also provided here.

**Chinese Embassy** (Map p116; ☎22474; www.ws.chineseembassy.org/eng; Cross Island Rd, Vailima; ⏲8.30am-noon & 2-4.30pm Mon-Fri)

**New Zealand High Commission** (Map p106; ☎21711; www.nzembassy.com/samoa; Beach Rd; ⏲8.30am-4.30pm Mon-Fri)

**US Embassy** (Map p106; ☎21631; www.samoa.usembassy.gov; 5th fl, ACC Bldg, Apia; ⏲9-11am Mon-Fri, phone enquiries to 5pm)

## EMERGENCY

**Ambulance** ☎996

**Police** ☎994

## FESTIVALS & EVENTS

**Independence Day celebrations** (1–3 June) Festivities commemorating Samoa's 1962 independence from New Zealand.

**Teuila Festival** (September) Apia reels in the tourists with canoe races, food and craft stalls, traditional dancing and a beauty pageant.

**White Sunday** (second Sunday in October) The day that Samoan children rule the roost.

**Palolo Rise** (October/November) Marking the annual emergence of the edible reefworm.

**Samoana Jazz and Arts Festival** (late October–early November) Hosts local and international artists, and jumps between Apia and American Samoa.

The first annual **Upolu-Savaii swim** (22km) event is due to take place in early April 2016.

### EATING PRICE RANGES

The following price ranges refer to a meal. Unless otherwise stated tax is included in the price.

**$** less than ST20

**$$** ST20–35

**$$$** more than ST35

## INTERNET ACCESS

Wi-fi in Samoa is offered by LavaSpot (www.lavaspot.ws) or Bluezone (www.bluezone.ws) hotspots on a pay-by-the-minute basis. You can buy time directly from their websites, or at your accommodation's front desk.

Hotspots are found at restaurants and hotels all around Apia and at some resorts around Upolu and Savai'i.

Note that web connections can drop out with frustrating frequency on these remote islands.

## MAPS

The free Jasons *Samoa Visitor Map* is updated annually and is widely available. It's reasonably basic but should suit most visitors' needs. They're also available to order online (free) at www.jasons.com/samoa.

## MONEY

The tala (dollar), divided into 100 sene (cents), is the unit of currency in use in Samoa.

### ATMs

Several branches of the ANZ and BSP banks are equipped with ATMs. Be aware that ATMs can be prone to running out of bills at the start of the weekend. Take plenty of cash with you (in small denominations) when you're heading outside the bigger settlements.

### Tipping

Not expected or encouraged, though it is acceptable for exceptional service at finer restaurants.

## OPENING HOURS

On Sunday almost everything is closed, although ripples of activity appear in the evening. Markets normally get underway by about 6am; Maketi Fou in Apia is active more or less 24 hours a day.

Standard opening hours:

**Banks** 9am to 3pm Monday to Friday, some open 8.30am to 12.30pm Saturday

**Bars** noon to 10pm or midnight

**Government offices** 8am to 4.30pm Monday to Friday

**Restaurants** 8am to 4pm and 6pm to 9pm

**Shops** 8am to 4.30pm Monday to Friday, 8am to noon Saturday (kiosks and convenience stores keep longer hours)

## TELEPHONE

The country code for Samoa is ☎685. The nation does not use area codes.

The mobile phone providers in Samoa are Digicel (www.digicelsamoa.com) and Bluesky (www.blueskysamoa.ws). Prepay top-ups can be purchased from dozens of shops around both islands, including at the international airport. Reception is generally very good.

### TOURIST INFORMATION

The excellent, comprehensive website of the Samoa Tourism Authority (www.samoa.travel) has easy-to-browse information on activities, attractions, accommodation and useful organisations, plus an up-to-date events calendar.

### TIME

At midnight on 29 December 2011, Samoa officially switched to the west side of the International Date Line. This means its dates are the same as those of NZ, Australia and Asia. Local time is GMT/UTC plus 13 hours. Therefore, when it's noon in Samoa, it's 11am the same day in Auckland.

Samoa adopted daylight saving time in 2010. In early October the clocks go forward (to GMT/UTC plus 14 hours), returning to normal in late March.

### VISAS

A free, 60-day visitor permit is granted to all visitors on arrival in Samoa (except for American Samoans).

Samoan visitor permits may be extended by several weeks at a time by the country's **Immigration Office** (Map p106; ☎20291; www.samoaimmigration.gov.ws; Convent St, Apia; ⊙9am-4pm Mon-Fri). Take along your passport, wallet and two passport-sized photos and don't make any other plans for the rest of the day. You may also need to have proof of hotel accommodation, onward transport and sufficient funds for your requested period of stay.

## Getting There & Away

### AIR

Aside from a few flights from American Samoa, all flights to Samoa arrive at **Faleolo Airport** (Map p102; ☎21675; www.apia.airport-authority.com; West Coast Rd, Upolu), 35km west of Apia. Many arrive and depart in the early hours of the morning, but airport transfer and accommodation providers are well used to this. **Fagali'i Airport** (Map p116; Fagali'i), on Apia's eastern outskirts, is mainly used for flights to/from American Samoa.

Direct flights head to Samoa from American Samoa, Fiji, Auckland, Brisbane and Sydney. If you're flying from the northern hemisphere, flights via Honolulu are likely to be the most straightforward.

Airlines that service Samoa include the following (phone numbers are local):

**Air New Zealand** (NZ; Map p106; ☎20825; www.airnz.com; cnr Convent & Vaea Sts, Apia; ⊙8.30am-4.30pm Mon-Fri, 9am-noon Sat)

**Fiji Airways** (Map p106; ☎22983; www.fijiairways.com; Saleufi St, Apia; ⊙8.30am-5pm Mon-Fri, 8am-noon Sat)

**Inter Island Airways** (☎42580; www.interislandair.com; Faleolo Airport)

**Polynesian Airlines** (Map p106; ☎21261; www.polynesianairlines.com; Beach Rd, Apia)

**Virgin Australia** (www.virginaustralia.com)

### SEA

#### Ship

**Samoa Shipping Corporation** (☎20935; www.samoashipping.com; one way adult/child ST12/6, vehicles from ST80) runs a car ferry/cargo ship (MV *Lady Naomi*) between Apia and Pago Pago (American Samoa) once a week. It departs from Apia every Thursday at 11pm; it departs Pago Pago the following day (also a Thursday, thanks to the bizarre dateline) at 4pm. The ferry takes foot passengers as well as vehicles. The journey takes about seven hours. Return deck fares are ST120/75 per adult/child. Note that American passport holders can only buy one-way tickets from Apia. All tickets must be purchased at least one day in advance: book online or ask your accommodation in Apia for assistance.

Cargo ships sail between Apia and remote Tokelau two to three times a month. Bookings for the 24- to 26-hour trip (return fares NZ$450) can be made in Apia at the **Tokelau Apia Liaison Office** (Map p106; ☎20822; www.tokelau.org.nz; Fugalei St, Apia; ⊙9am-5pm Mon-Fri). You must obtain a Tokelau visa before booking.

#### Yacht

Between May and October (outside the cyclone season), South Pacific harbours swarm with yachts from around the world. Apia is the official entry point for private yachts visiting Samoa. In Savai'i, there are also anchorages at Fagamalo, Salelologa Wharf and Asau Harbour.

Before entering Apia's harbour, yachts must call Apia Port Control on VHF 16. Officially, yachties must contact each clearance department – customs, immigraton and quarantine –

> **PRACTICALITIES**
>
> **Language** Samoan, English
>
> **Media** The website of the country's main newspaper, the *Samoa Observer* (www.sobserver.ws), is a good resource for news relating to Samoa and the Pacific region.

separately (see www.samoagovt.ws for directories); however, Port Control will most likely do it for you once you've made contact.

## Getting Around

### AIR

**Samoa Air** (☎27905; www.samoaair.ws) operates charter flights between Upolu and Savai'i. Email them for bookings and fares.

### BICYCLE

Touring Upolu and Savai'i by bicycle is a scenic, reasonably relaxed option – we say 'reasonably' because aggressive dogs are a prevalent problem. The roads are generally in good condition and traffic is minimal. The major roads encircling the islands are sealed and relatively flat, but you'd need a sturdy mountain bike to tackle most of the trails to beaches and other coastal attractions. You can transport a bike between Samoa's two main islands on the ferry.

A big challenge for cyclists is the heat. Even during the coolest months of the year (July, August and September), afternoon temperatures will still be high. Plan to avoid cycling long stretches in the heat of the day. Also bear in mind that buses are unlikely to be able to accommodate bicycles should you run out of leg power.

It shouldn't be hard to track down a bike repairer if you really need one, but it's best to bring your own repair kit, a decent lock and heavy-duty panniers. Some accommodation providers offer bike hire, but these are for day touring, not long-distance rides.

### BOAT

The ferry from Mulifanua Wharf regularly plies the waters between Upolu and Savai'i. Small boats leave from Cape Fatuosofia for Manono.

The **Apia Yacht Club** (p112) is a good place to share information on sailing around the islands over a cold beer.

### BUS

Travelling by public bus in Samoa is an experience in itself. The vibrantly painted, wooden-seated vehicles (more often than not blasting Samoan pop music at deafening volumes) each have their own character. Drivers are often as eccentric as the vehicles, and services operate completely at their whim: if a driver feels like knocking off at 1pm, he does, and passengers counting on the service are left stranded. Never rely on a bus after about 2pm. Buses are also scarce on Saturday afternoon and often only cater to church services on Sunday.

All buses prominently display the name of their destination in the front window. To stop a bus, wave your hand and arm, palm down. To get off, either knock on the ceiling or clap loudly. Fares are paid to the driver – try to have as near to the exact change as possible.

Although most visitors don't notice it at first, there is a seating hierarchy on Samoan buses. Unmarried women normally sit together, while foreigners and older people must have a seat and sit near the front of the bus. Don't worry about arranging this yourself – the locals will see to it that everything is sorted out. The way in which Samoans stack themselves on top of each other on crowded buses without losing any dignity is akin to a social miracle.

### CAR

Getting around by car in Samoa is quite straightforward. The coastal roads on Upolu and Savai'i are sealed; most of the other main roads are pretty good. A 4WD will make trips down rough, unsealed side roads more comfortable, but nearly all of these can be tackled in a high-clearance 2WD (unless there's been heavy rain).

Petrol stations are few and far between on both islands.

#### Driving Licence

Visitors to Samoa need to obtain a temporary driving licence. Most car-hire companies issue these, or you can call into the **Land Transport Authority** (LTA; Map p116; ☎26740; www.lta.gov.ws; Off Vaitele St (opposite Vailima Brewery), Vaitele; licence per month ST21; ⏲9am-5pm Mon-Fri) in Apia. You'll need to present a valid overseas driving licence.

#### Hire

There are dozens of car-hire agencies in Samoa and, on top of this, some of the larger accommodation providers also hire vehicles. Most of the agencies are in or around Apia and the airport, and prices can be quite competitive. Note that you can usually take hire cars from Upolu over to Savai'i and back, but cars hired on Savai'i cannot be taken to Upolu. It's sometimes cheaper to hire in Upolu even given the ferry fee, especially if you obtain a discount for a longer booking.

When hiring a vehicle, check for any damage or scratches and note everything on the rental agreement, lest you be held liable for damage when the car is returned. Furthermore, fend off requests to leave your passport or a cash deposit against possible damages. Many places will require a credit card pre-authorisation by way of a deposit and it's usual to pay in advance.

Prices start at around ST110 per day, with discounts offered for longer-term rentals.

### Insurance

It's essential to have your hire car covered by insurance as repair costs are extremely high in Samoa. Insurance costs aren't always included in the price of a quote, so always double-check this.

### Road Rules

In 2009 the Samoan government decided to change the law from driving on the right-hand side of the road to the left-hand side. Still, don't be surprised to see a mixture of left-hand-drive and right-hand-drive vehicles on the road. When renting a car, insist on a right-hand drive vehicle. The speed limit within central Apia and through adjacent villages is 40km/h; outside populated areas it's 56km/h.

## LOCAL TRANSPORT

On Upolu, taxis can be a useful transport option for day tripping; however, the same can't be said for taxis on Savai'i, which are only convenient for short trips. It always pays to have the correct change as drivers can be (perhaps too conveniently) relied upon not to have any.

If you find a driver you hit it off well with early on, it can be worth getting their telephone number and using their service during your stay. You may be able to negotiate a decent day rate that compares favourably with a hire car.

Local buses are cheap and run all over the islands frequently (apart from on Sundays).

# American Samoa

☎1-684 / POP 55, 519

**Includes ➡**



## Best Places to Stay

➡ Moana O Sina (p152)

➡ Vaoto Lodge (p158)

➡ Tisa's Barefoot Bar (p153)

➡ Le Falepule (p152)

➡ Homestays organised by the National Park Visitor Information Center (p156)

## Best Beaches

➡ Ofu Beach (p157)

➡ Fagatele Bay National Marine Sanctuary (p150)

➡ Alega Beach (p151)

➡ Two Dollar Beach (p151)

## Why Go?

There but for a more exotic name goes American Samoa. Mention of this distant archipelago more often than not elicits a blank stare, but despite its mundane moniker and confusing status (it belongs to, but isn't a part of, the US), American Samoa is one of the most breathtakingly beautiful pockets of Polynesia.

A photogenic feast of green jagged peaks, electric blue depths and idyllic beaches, American Samoa's islands are the stuff South Pacific daydreams are made of. Tutuila is home to Pago Pago, a blue-collar fishing town nestled beside one of the world's most stunning natural harbours; outside city limits, flower-scented villages cling to deep-rooted traditions. For more extreme escapism, head to the remote Manu'a Islands, believed to be the birthplace of Polynesia, or hike the trails of the National Park of American Samoa. Whichever adventure you choose, this is one Pacific paradise you're likely to have all to yourself.

## When to Go

### Pago Pago

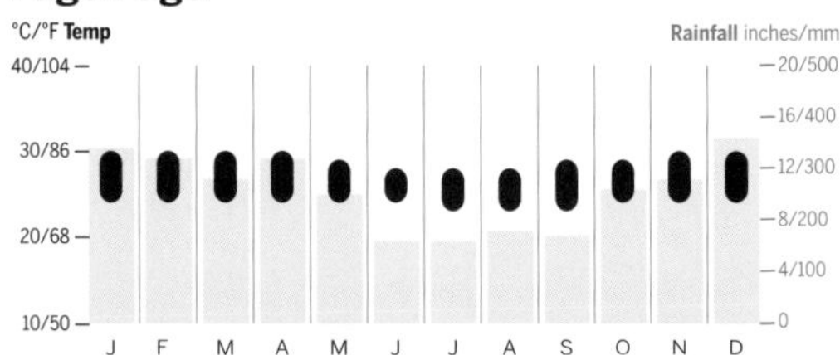


**Dec–Jan** Peak holiday period when Samoans living abroad visit home.

**May–Oct** Dry, cool season with minimal to no risk of cyclones.

**Oct** Festival month and whale season.

# TUTUILA

POP 54,145 / AREA 140 SQ KM

Tutuila is a dramatic mass of sharp edges and pointy peaks, softened by a heavy padding of rainforest. Its craggy green silhouettes loom over the island's blindingly white sands, turquoise shallows, inviting islets and the stunning Pago Pago Harbor, one of the best-protected natural harbours in the world.

While the airport road offers a disappointing first impression, rest assured that there's more to Tutuila than fast-food joints and shabby shacks: between the urban delights of Pago Pago, ancient sacred sites, secret swimming spots and scenic hiking trails, this is one of Polynesia's most eclectic – if little-known – destinations. The island's claims to fame don't stop there: the tiny village of Poloa, on Tutuila's west coast, is the last place on earth to see the sun set each day.

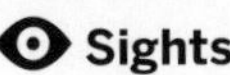

## Sights

### Pago Pago

While the urban environs of Pago Pago are as gritty as they come (two tuna canneries, a huge working seaport and potholed streets lined with ramshackle buildings), its evocative natural harbour, white-sand beaches and backdrop of magnificent geometric peaks give the city a dreamy, paradisaical feel. It's an incongruous combination, but somehow it works, lending Pago Pago a unique and explore-worthy charm.

Though pretty well stuck together, Pago Pago is technically a string of villages. Confusingly, 'Pago Pago' (pronounced pung-o pung-o) is used to describe the small village at the far end of the harbour, the harbour itself, the 'town', the whole island of Tutuila or even the whole of American Samoa.



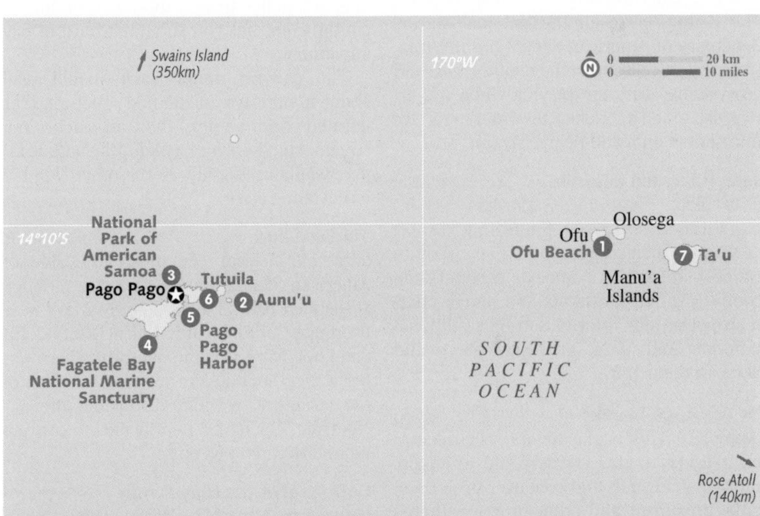


## American Samoa Highlights

1. Ogling rainforest-clad mountains and white sands while floating in the crystalline waters off **Ofu Beach** (p157).
2. Strolling the plantations and crater lakes on the diminutive island of **Aunu'u** (p157).
3. Hiking the jungle trails of the **National Park of American Samoa** (p149).
4. Snorkelling and whale watching in **Fagatele Bay National Marine Sanctuary** (p150).
5. Paddling about calm **Pago Pago Harbor**, fringed by magnificently jagged peaks.
6. Enjoying a traditional Samoan meal with a modern twist, beachside at Tutuila's **Tisa's Barefoot Bar** (p155).
7. Exploring the mysteries of ancient Polynesia on the isolated island of **Ta'u** (p159).

**Utulei** is edged by a **beach** dotted with day *fale* (houses), offering shelter from the sun between swims. **Fagatogo** is the administrative centre and contains the **Fono** (Map p150; Fagatogo), a large, *fale*-shaped building that houses American Samoa's Senate and House of Representatives.

**★Fatu ma Futi** ISLAND
(Flowerpot Rock; Map p148; Fatumafuti) Get your camera ready: you'll spot these iconic offshore rock formations on your drive into Pago Pago from the airport. Legend has it that a couple named Fatu and Futi had sailed from Savai'i (Samoa), looking for Tutuila; their canoe sank, and the pair were transformed into these beautiful tree-topped mini-islands. You can swim here and cross between the two at low tide.

**Tauese PF Sunia Ocean Center** MUSEUM
(Map p150; ☎633 6500; www.americansamoa.noaa.gov; Pago Pago Harbor; ⏲9am-4pm Mon-Fri) The visitor centre for the National Marine Sanctuary of American Samoa has informative exhibits relating to the region's reefs and ecosystems; if it's not playing when you arrive, ask to see its 'globe show', an interactive film shown on a 360-degree screen.

**Jean P Hayden Museum** MUSEUM
(Map p150; Fagatogo; ⏲8am-4pm Mon-Fri) FREE Has a small but interesting display of Samoan artefacts, including *va'a* (bonito canoes), *alia* (war canoes), coconut-shell combs, pigs' tusk armlets and native pharmacopoeia, plus information on traditional tattooing and native medicinal plants and Samoan medicine.

**★Fagatogo Market** MARKET
(Map p150) This is the town's social centre on a Friday night. Locals come to gossip, ransack food stalls and pick over fresh coconuts, breadfruit and other produce; there's often live music and entertainment, too. When a cruise ship is in town (as they frequently are), stalls selling souvenirs, locally made crafts and clothes pop up in their dozens. There are a few 'fast-food'-style places at the back selling Samoan-sized meals (US$2 to US$5) for lunch.

The main bus station is behind the market.

## Western Tutuila

Most of the western end of Tutuila is taken up by the rainforest-wreathed mountains that line the northern coast. The bulk of the population inhabits the flat plains to the south, particularly the strip-mall suburbs of Tafuna and Nu'uuli. Once you pass Leone, there's a succession of cute villages lining pretty beaches.

**Nu'uuli Falls** WATERFALL
(Map p148; Nu'uuli) Standing in stark relief to Nu'uuli's scruffy strip of restaurants and convenience stores, this secluded waterfall with a deliciously cool swimming hole at its base is a magical place. The surrounding rainforest muffles the sound of the water cascading down 20m of jagged black lava rocks.

It's a little hard to find. Coming along the main road from the west, turn left at the Nu'uuli Family Mart and follow this side road, veering left at the pig farm. At the end, park on the grass to the left (you'll see a house downhill on your right); the start of the track is in front of you. If you see anyone, it's polite to ask their permission to continue on, but you shouldn't have to pay any money.

The narrow, rough track should take about 15 minutes. At the first juncture, veer left and continue until the trail reaches the stream. Stop here and look for the path leading steeply up the hill on the other side before wading across.

**Tia Seu Lupe** ARCHAEOLOGICAL SITE
(Map p148; Tafuna) The most accessible of American Samoa's fascinating star mounds is secreted behind a statue of St Mary near the huge Catholic cathedral in Tafuna. Tia Seu Lupe has a viewing platform where you get a good look at the two distinct tiers of the structure, without disturbing the ancient site. The name literally means 'earthen mound to catch pigeons'.

**Cathedral of the Holy Family** CHURCH
(Fatu-o-Aiga; Map p148; Tafuna) The exterior of Tafuna's imposing, snow white Catholic cathedral is striking, with a space-age bell tower and dissected dome, though a homier beauty lies in its Polynesian-meets-Western artworks, including an *'ava*-bearing, larger-than-life Samoan Christ, and a nativity featuring a *fale* as a stable and an *'ava* bowl as a manger.

**Turtle & Shark Site** HISTORIC SITE
(Map p148; Vaitogi; access fee US$2; ⏲Mon-Sat) The most famous of Tutuila's legends is set at this dramatic clifftop site. According to one version, an

old lady and her granddaughter were turfed out of their village during a famine, and jumped into the sea. The guilt-ridden villagers went to the shore and called their names; they appeared in the form of a turtle and a shark. The grandmother gave the villagers a song and promised they would come whenever it was sung; locals insist the song lures the pair to this day.

Whether the fabled creatures appear or not, you'll enjoy the rugged character of the place, with its black lava cliffs, heavy surf and blowholes. Don't swim here: this is a sacred site and the currents are treacherous.

**Leone** VILLAGE

The village of Leone welcomed the first missionary to Tutuila in 1832. John Williams subsequently erected the island's first **church**, garnishing it with three towers, a stunning carved ceiling and stained glass. Try to attend a service here on Sunday morning, when villagers congregate in their best whites to sing hymns before heading home for a lunchtime banquet.

Leone was hit exceptionally hard by the 2009 tsunami; there's a memorial monument and healing garden dedicated to the victims overlooking the sea.

**Cape Taputapu** AREA

For a memorable, perhaps romantic evening, this is a tough spot to beat: Tutuila's westernmost point is the last place on earth the sun sets each day.

Just past Amanave Village is the lovely, white-sand **Palagi Beach**. From there, a winding northern road brings you to a cluster of small villages, revealing spectacular coastline along the way.

## Eastern Tutuila

*Fale* have given way to clunky concrete-block houses; otherwise, the small villages cling to the shoreline as they've done for centuries.

**Rainmaker Mountain** MOUNTAIN

Also known as Mt Pioa, 523m-high Rainmaker Mountain traps rain clouds and gives Pago Pago the highest annual rainfall of any harbour in the world. From afar it looks like a single large peak, but a drive up Rainmaker Pass reveals a three-pronged summit. The mountain and its base area are national landmark sites due to the pristine tropical vegetation on the slopes.

**Masefau & Sa'ilele** AREA

A cross-island road leads from the village of Faga'itua up over a pass before winding slowly down to Masefau, a village that looks too idyllic to be true.

Back at the pass, a turn-off takes you down a narrow, potholed road to Sa'ilele, which has one of the island's loveliest swimming beaches. The sandy area below the large rock outcrop at the beach's western end is an excellent place for a picnic.

## Activities

Though its depths are home to hundreds of fish and coral species, **diving** is as yet a largely untapped market in American Samoa. On Tutuila, Pago Pago Marine Charters (p151) can organise dive trips.

### Hiking & Walking

Hiking is one of American Samoa's biggest drawcards, with decently maintained trails winding through thick, pristine rainforest and dazzling coastlines.



### AMERICAN SAMOA IN...

**Two Days**

Begin with breakfast at **DDW** in **Pago Pago** and then spend the day exploring the eastern end of Tutuila. Stop for a swim at **Alega Beach** and lunch at **Tisa's Barefoot Bar** before catching the ferry to **Aunu'u** for the afternoon. Head back to Pago Pago Harbor for dinner. Next morning, hit the **Mt Alava Trail** for a taste of Tutuila's dramatic landscapes, from forest to reef. That night catch the *fiafia* (traditional dance performance) at the **Equator** restaurant at the Tradewinds Hotel in Tafuna.

**Five Days**

Fly to **Ofu** and spend the first two days snorkelling, lying around the beach and exploring **Olosega** by foot. Catch a boat to **Ta'u** and explore the birthplace of Polynesia. Head back to Tutuila then follow the two days itinerary.

# Tutuila

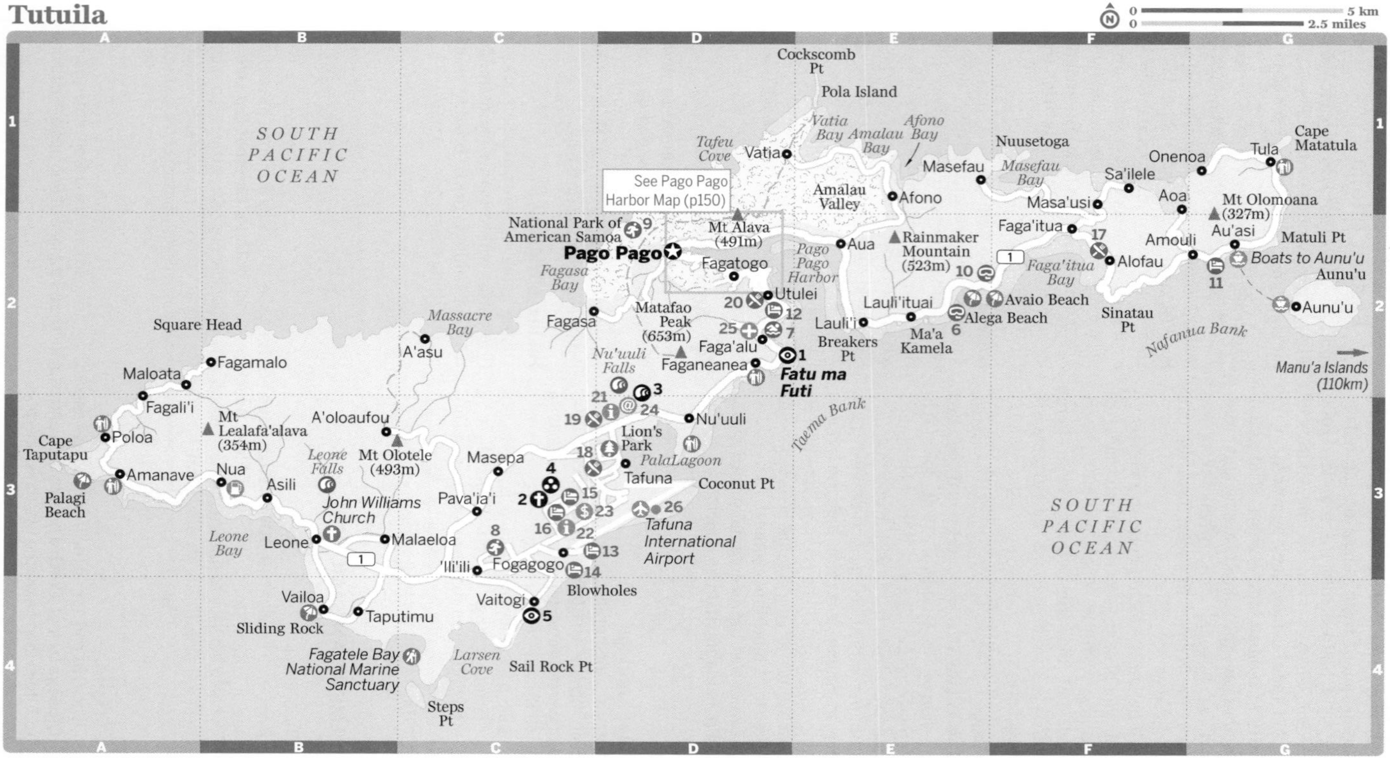

0 5 km
0 2.5 miles

SOUTH PACIFIC OCEAN
Cockscomb Pt
Pola Island
Vatia Bay
Amalau Bay
Afono Bay
Tafeu Cove
Vatia
Nuusetoga
Masefau
Masefau Bay
Onenoa
Sa'ilele
Tula
Cape Matatula
See Pago Pago Harbor Map (p150)
Amalau Valley
Afono
Masa'usi
Aoa
Mt Olomoana (327m)
National Park of American Samoa 9
Mt Alava (491m)
Faga'itua
17
Au'asi
Matuli Pt
Pago Pago
Aua
Rainmaker Mountain (523m)
Amouli
Alofau
Boats to Aunu'u
Aunu'u
Fagasa Bay
Fagatogo
Pago Pago Harbor
10
Faga'itua Bay
11
20
Utulei
Lauli'ituai
Avaio Beach
Sinatau Pt
Aunu'u
Square Head
Massacre Bay
Fagasa
Matafao Peak (653m)
12
25
7
Lauli'i
Alega Beach
6
Nafanua Bank
A'asu
Faga'alu
Breakers Pt
Ma'a Kamela
Nu'uuli Falls
Faganeanea
1
Fatu ma Futi
Manu'a Islands (110km)
Fagamalo
Maloata
21
3
Fagali'i
19
24
Nu'uuli
Taema Bank
Mt Lealafa'alava (354m)
A'oloaufou
Lion's Park
Cape Taputapu
Poloa
Leone Falls
Mt Olotele (493m)
18
PalaLagoon
Masepa
4
Tafuna
Coconut Pt
Amanave
Nua
Asili
15
Palagi Beach
John Williams Church
Pava'ia'i
2
23
26
16
22
Tafuna International Airport
SOUTH PACIFIC OCEAN
8
Leone Bay
Leone
Malaeloa
1
13
'Ili'ili
Fogagogo
14
Blowholes
Vailoa
Taputimu
Vaitogi
5
Sliding Rock
Fagatele Bay National Marine Sanctuary
Larsen Cove
Sail Rock Pt
Steps Pt

## Tutuila

**Top Sights**
1 Fatu ma Futi.......D2

**Sights**
2 Cathedral of the Holy Family.......C3
3 Nu'uuli Falls.......D2
4 Tia Seu Lupe.......C3
5 Turtle & Shark Site.......C4

**Activities, Courses & Tours**
6 Alega Beach.......E2
7 Faga'alu Park.......D2
8 'Ili'ili Golf Course Golf.......C3
9 National Park of American Samoa.......D2
Tisa's Tours.......(see 6)
10 Two Dollar Beach.......E2

**Sleeping**
11 Amouli Beach Fales.......G2
12 Le Falepule.......D2
13 Maliu Mai Beach Resort.......C3
14 Moana O Sina.......C3
15 Pago Airport Inn.......C3
Tisa's Barefoot Bar.......(see 6)
16 Tradewinds Hotel.......C3
Two Dollar Beach Apartments.......(see 10)

**Eating**
17 Da Tamalelei Seaside Grill.......F2
18 Mom's Place.......C3
Tisa's Barefoot Bar.......(see 6)
19 Toa Bar & Grill.......C3
20 Young's Mart.......D2

**Information**
21 American Samoa Historic Preservation Office.......D3
22 American Samoa Visitors Bureau.......C3
ANZ Amerika Samoa Bank ATM.......(see 25)
ANZ Amerika Samoa Bank ATM.......(see 16)
23 Bank of Hawai'i.......C3
24 Blue Sky.......D3
25 LBJ Tropical Medical Center.......D2

**Transport**
26 Avis Car Rental.......D3
Sir Amos Car Rental.......(see 26)
Tropical Car Rental.......(see 26)



### ★ National Park of American Samoa

NATIONAL PARK, HIKING

(Map p148; www.nps.gov/npsa) FREE Created in 1988, the territory's sole national park protects huge swathes of pristine landscapes and marine environments on Tutuila and the Manu'a Islands. The 1000-hectare Tutuila section follows the north coast between the villages of Fagasa and Afono. Trails within park boundaries are often very well maintained. Be sure to bring strong mosquito repellant.

The National Park Visitor Information Center (p156) in Pago Pago is an invaluable source of information and maps.

There are scores of hikes within the park to choose from: brochures available at the information centre (and online) list them all. In order of difficulty (easy to challenging), here are three popular hikes:

**➡ Pola Island Trail**

Vatia is a peaceful village situated on a lovely, coral-fringed bay. Guarding the mouth of the bay, tiny Pola Island has magnificent, sheer, 120m-high cliffs populated by seabirds. For a close-up of soaring rocks and birds, head through the village and park at the school, then walk 300m to reach the wonderfully isolated beach at the base of the cliffs.

**➡ Amalau Valley**

From Aua, a surfaced road switchbacks steeply up over Rainmaker Pass and down to Afono and Vatia. Between these two villages is the beautiful, secluded Amalau Valley, home to many forest-bird species and to two rare species of flying fox. Stop at the lookout point just past the western side of Amalau Bay for some wonderful views.

**➡ Mt Alava**

Hiking the trail that leads up Mt Alava (491m) and then down to the coast is a wonderful way to experience the park's lowland and mountain rainforests, its thriving birdlife, and the peacefulness that permeates it. On Mt Alava, a metal stairway leads up to a TV transmission tower and the rusted remains of a cable-car terminal that once ran 1.8km across Pago Pago Harbor to Solo Hill. The 5.5km ridge trail (1½ to two hours one way) starts from Fagasa Pass. Behind the rest *fale* at the end of this section, a very steep trail (including ladders in places) leads 2km down to Vatia; allow an additional two hours for the descent.

## Pago Pago Harbor

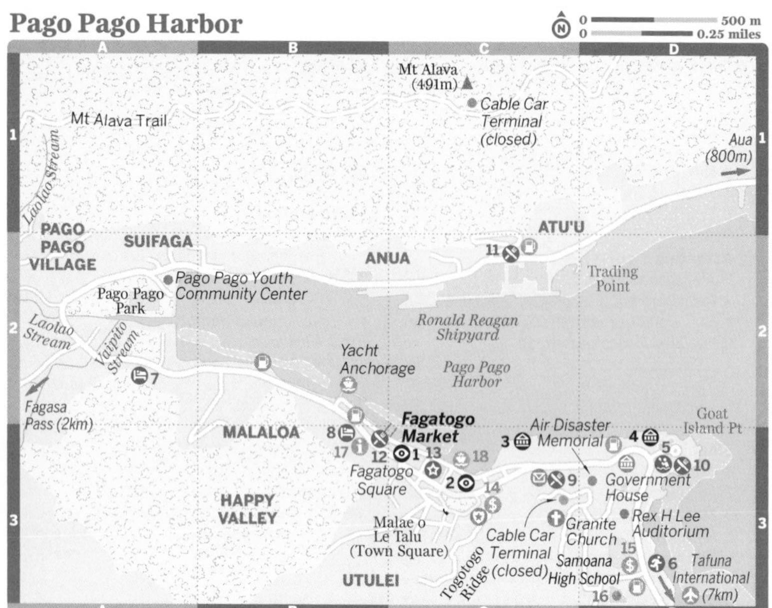




### Pago Pago Harbor

**Top Sights**
1 Fagatogo Market ... C3

**Sights**
2 Fono ... C3
3 Jean P Hayden Museum ... C3
4 Tauese PF Sunia Ocean Center ... D3

**Activities, Courses & Tours**
5 Sadie's by the Sea ... D3
6 South Pacific Watersports ... D3

**Sleeping**
7 Evalani's Motel ... A2
8 Sadie Thompson Inn ... B3
Sadie's by the Sea ... (see 5)

**Eating**
DDW Beach Cafe ... (see 6)
Evalani's Cantina ... (see 7)
9 Fia Fia Seafood Restaurant ... C3
10 Goat Island Cafe ... D3
11 Paradise Pizza ... C2
12 Sook's Sushi Restaurant ... B3

**Entertainment**
13 Regal Nu'uuli Place Twin ... C3

**Information**
14 ANZ Amerika Samoa Bank ... C3
15 Bank of Hawai'i ... D3
16 Immigration Office ... D3
17 National Park Visitor Information Center ... B3

**Transport**
18 Boats to Manu'a Islands & Samoa ... C3
Bus Station ... (see 1)

**Fagatele Bay National Marine Sanctuary** HIKING
(Map p148; ☎633 6500; www.fagatelebay.noaa.gov) A submerged volcanic crater, Fagatele Bay is fringed by Tutuila's last remaining stretch of coastal rainforest. Its depths house more than 140 species of coral, and are visited by numerous turtle species and migrating southern humpback whales (June to September). There are four marked trails here, two of which are less than 1km from the parking area at the bay's entrance.

The Tauese PF Sunia Ocean Center (p146) in Pago Pago has free maps detailing longer hiking routes.

**Massacre Bay** HIKING
A marvellous 4km hiking trail (allow four hours return) leads from the scenic village

of A'oloaufou down to A'asu on Massacre Bay. Its foreboding name was given after a deadly skirmish (1787) between French sailors and Samoan villagers.

The track begins near the community garden in A'oloaufou. It's often overgrown, extremely muddy and difficult to navigate, particularly on the climb back up. Hikers should consider hiring a guide in A'oloaufou (between US$5 and US$10).

### Swimming & Snorkelling

Many coastal areas are too rough or shallow for swimming but there are a number of easily accessible spots; you can get to the following beaches by bus. There's also a swimming beach in Utulei, just across from Samoana High School. In most cases swimsuits are a no-no – wear a T-shirt and long shorts or a *lava-lava* (wraparound sarong).

**Alega Beach** SNORKELLING, SWIMMING
(Map p148; admission US$5) A short drive east of Pago Pago, this is a lovely spot that gets crowded on the weekend. It's not only a great place to swim and snorkel (check currents and conditions with locals first), but it is also overlooked by Tisa's Barefoot Bar, the perfect spot for a cold drink. You can waive the access fee for the beach by buying a drink at Tisa's.

**Two Dollar Beach** SNORKELLING, SWIMMING
(Avaio Beach; Map p148; admission US$5; 7am-6pm) This well-maintained strip of white sand sits beside calm, shallow water that's great for snorkelling. There's a small rocky island just offshore for exploring. It's an excellent spot for a day trip, and has good facilities including barbecues, showers and clean toilets. Despite the name, it's now US$5 to use the beach.

**Faga'alu Park** SWIMMING
(Map p148) At the outer southern part of Pago Pago Harbor, this grassy park with picnic tables and a small white-sand beach is a good, central place for a dip. The water here is much cleaner than the interior of the bay and the corals are in surprisingly good shape.

### Kayaking & Canoeing

Some of the local outrigger canoe clubs welcome guests to paddle with them on Pago Pago Harbor; they often leave from the beach at Sadie's by the Sea. Ask around about times and availability.

**South Pacific Watersports** WATER SPORTS
(Map p150; 633 3050; www.southpacificwatersports.com; Utulei; 5am-7pm Mon-Fri, 6am-4pm Sat) The friendly folk here rent out stand-up paddle boards (per hour/half-day/day US$15/45/80), kayaks (US$10 per hour), snorkel gear (US$5 per hour) and outrigger canoes. They can also organise hiking and paddling tours; a modicum of fitness is required.

**Sadie's by the Sea** KAYAKING
(Map p150; 633 5981; www.sadieshotels.com; Utulei) Kayaks and paddle boats are free for hotel guests (US$10 per hour for nonguests), and are a highly recommended way to explore Pago Pago's scenic harbour. The beach fee for nonguests (where you'll have to launch from) is US$5 per day.

### Other Activites

**Pago Pago Marine Charters** FISHING
(733 0964; www.pagopagomarinecharters.com; Pago Pago Harbor) This professional outfit offers gamefishing and diving charters. A PADI dive centre, it rents and sells diving equipment; it also has the only re-compression chamber this side of Fiji. Email or phone for pricing.



### STAR MOUNDS

More than 140 distinctive stone or earthen mounds dating back to late prehistoric times have been found scattered across the Samoan archipelago. Dubbed 'star mounds', the structures range from 6m to 30m in length, are up to 3m high and have from one to 11 raylike projections radiating from their base. Forty star mounds have been discovered (though not yet excavated) in Tutuila's east on the road between Amouli and Aoa.

The prominent theory regarding the star mounds is that they were used for pigeon-snaring, an important sport of chiefs. However, some archaeologists believe they served a much more complex function in Samoan society, including as sites for rituals related to marriage, healing and warfare. Archaeologists also believe the star mounds came to reflect the position of the *matai* (family group leader) and the notion of *mana* (supernatural power).

**'Ili'ili Golf Course Golf** GOLF
(Map p148; ☎699 2995; 'Iii'ili; ⊙dawn-dusk) This is a 'very forgiving' 72-par course with great views. Green fees for nine/18 holes are US$4/7 on weekdays and US$5/10 on weekends. Club hire is US$20; carts are US$8/16 for nine/18 holes on weekdays and US$10/20 for weekends. Recap your game over a coldie at its Nighthawk clubhouse.

## Tours

History buffs should check out the American Samoa Historic Preservation Office's online walking tour (www.ashpo.org) of Pago Pago. Its detailed map links to fascinating titbits about the city's lesser-known landmarks.

**North Shore Tours** HIKING
(☎731 9294; rorywest@yahoo.com) Rory West has an impressive knowledge of and passion for the island's plants, legends and best secret spots. He caters to all levels but his tendency veers towards hard-core; be prepared for a real adventure.

**Tisa's Tours** TOUR
(Map p148; ☎622 7447; www.tisasbarefootbar.com) Island tours include lunch and swimming at Tisa's Barefoot Bar. Tisa can organise tailored tours for guests.

## Sleeping

Despite a surprising scarcity of waterside options, Tutuila has a handful of excellent – and occasionally quirky – places to stay.

### Pago Pago

**★Le Falepule** B&B $$
(Map p148; ☎633 5264; isabel@blueskynet.as; Faga'alu; s/d US$140/150; P❄📶) Sitting on the terrace of this luxury boutique B&B and gazing over the sublime ocean views, you may never want to leave. It's a wonderful place, with delightful staff, tropical breakfasts, elegant rooms and a private yet accessible location. Free laundry service is a bonus. It's at the end of a steep driveway 200m north of the hospital turn-off.

**Sadie Thompson Inn** HOTEL $$
(Map p150; ☎633 5981; www.sadieshotels.com; Fagatogo; r US$137; P❄📶) This wooden inn was – apparently – where the original Sadie Thompson (immortalised in Somerset Maugham's novel *Rain*) set up her red light. It's a bit less rollicking these days, but makes for a clean, central place to stay. The identikit rooms are – alas – not done in period style, but the verandah-edged building itself is quaint and charming. The restaurant is hit-or-miss.

**Evalani's Motel** HOTEL $$
(Map p150; ☎633 7777; www.evalanis.com; Pago Pago; r/ste/apt US$63/131/142; P❄📶) Also known as Motu-O-Fiafiaga Motel, this friendly place is owned by a former showgirl. Evalani may have left Vegas but Vegas never left Evalani: the fabulously retro decor here could best be described as brothel-chic. Head down the creaky, scarlet-carpeted corridors and you'll find that the bright rooms are very comfortable for the price. There's a lively bar–Mexican restaurant attached.

**Sadie's by the Sea** HOTEL $$$
(Map p150; ☎633 5900; www.sadieshotels.com; Utulei; r US$167; P❄📶🏊) 'By the sea' is the big drawcard here; this is one of the few places with a swimmable beach at its doorstep. Rooms are characterless in that midrange-hotel way, but are large and loaded with facilities. Shops, the harbour and other attractions are steps away. Other perks include the great on-site restaurant, Goat Island Cafe, and a well-stocked shop selling everything from souvenirs to booze.

### Western Tutuila

**Pago Airport Inn** HOTEL $
(Map p148; ☎699 6333; Tafuna; s/d US$78/99; P❄📶🏊) This friendly little hotel is a top option for those who need to be close to the airport (it's a three-minute drive away); that it's extraordinarily cheap – for Tutuila – is another bonus. There's a big pool, the rooms are clean and large, and its free shuttles go to the airport and nearby restaurants.

**★Moana O Sina** B&B $$
(Map p148; ☎699 8517; isabel@blueskynet.as; Fogagogo; s/d incl breakfast US$140/150; ❄📶🏊) This elegant seaside B&B makes for a stylish getaway, with gorgeous grounds and well-appointed, Polynesian-inspired rooms. The owners have made the most out of their stunning surrounds, with a delightful outdoor breakfast pavilion and two small swimming pools overlooking crashing waves and dramatic blowholes. Other than the three friendly dogs on-site, you may end up with this fantastic place all to yourself.

### AND GOD CREATED SAMOA

Samoans claim their land is the 'cradle of Polynesia', a place created by the sky god Tagaloa (Tangaroa). Before the sea, earth, sky, plants or people existed, Tagaloa lived in the expanse of empty space. He created a rock, commanding it to split into clay, coral, cliffs and stones. As the rock broke apart, the earth, sea and sky came into being. From a bit of the rock emerged a spring of fresh water.

At Saua in the Manu'a Islands, Tagaloa created man and woman, whom he named Fatu and 'Ele'ele ('Heart' and 'Earth'). He sent them to the region of fresh water and commanded them to people the area. He ordered the sky, called Tu'ite'elagi, to prop itself up above the earth.

Tagaloa then created Po and Ao ('Night' and 'Day'), which bore the 'eyes of the sky' – the sun and the moon. He sent their son, Manu'a, to be the people's chief. The Manu'a Islands were named after this chief, and from that time on, Samoan kings were called Tu'i Manu'a tele ma Samoa 'atoa (King of Manu'a and all of Samoa).

The world now consisted of Manu'a, Viti (Fiji), Tonga and Savai'i. Tagaloa then went to Manu'a and noticed that a void existed between it and Savai'i. Up popped Upolu and then Tutuila.

Tagaloa's final command was: 'Always respect Manu'a; anyone who fails to do so will be overtaken by catastrophe.' Thus, Manu'a became the spiritual centre of the Samoan islands and, to some extent, of all Polynesia.

**Maliu Mai Beach Resort** RESORT **$$**
(Map p148; ☎699 7232; maliumai@blueskynet.as; Fogagogo; r US$85-150; P ❄ ☜ ≋) Though a bit of a work in progress, this seaside resort is nevertheless a decent option, with helpful owners, a swimmable sea pool and a happening restaurant-bar attached. The new rooms are clean and serviceable; the pricier ones have lovely sea views.

**Tradewinds Hotel** HOTEL **$$$**
(Map p148; ☎699 1000; www.tradewinds.as; Main Ottoville Rd, Tafuna; r/ste from US$156/252; P ❄ @ ☜ ≋) Tradewinds has everything you'd expect from a large business hotel – including an enticing resort pool, day spa, car-rental/tour desk and an ATM – and like many such hotels, it's opted for a generic look for its spacious rooms and broad corridors. Its **Equator Restaurant** (⊙6am to 9.30pm) is fine, but fits the same homogeneous-hotel bill, though *fiafia* (traditional dance performance) nights on Fridays are worth attending.

## Eastern Tutuila

You may be able to arrange an overnight stay in Vatia through the homestay program of the National Park of American Samoa (p149).

★ **Tisa's Barefoot Bar** BUNGALOW **$**
(Map p148; ☎622 7447; www.tisasbarefootbar.com; Alega Beach; fale per person incl breakfast & dinner US$50) Tisa's is possibly the most popular place on Tutuila, and rightfully so. It's one of the rare spots to offer traditional *fale* (though these have proper beds instead of mattresses) and its superb setting on Alega Beach, brilliant bar-restaurant and the wonderful company of Tisa and her boyfriend Candyman combine to make this a very difficult place to leave.

**Amouli Beach Fales** BUNGALOW **$**
(Map p148; ☎254 2050; www.amoulibeachfales.com; Amouli; fale $25-75, electricity extra; P ☜) The open beachfront *fale* here are simple (electricity may be available, for an additional cost), and there's no restaurant (shops and eateries are but a stroll away), but who needs bells and whistles when you're parked on a glorious beach like this one? If you have kids, they'll love playing with the locals who come to take advantage of Amouli's top swimming.

**Two Dollar Beach Apartments** APARTMENT **$$**
(Map p148; ☎733 7011, 622 7656; www.twodollarbeach.com; Avaio Beach; apt US$150; P ❄ ☜) These two good-sized, two-bedroom self-contained apartments sit beside one of Tutuila's most popular beaches. If you don't feel like cooking indoors, pop down to the shore and crank up the barbecue; otherwise, there's a small bar-restaurant on-site.

## Eating & Drinking

American Samoa's reputation for fatty fried foods is not generally contradicted by the eateries on Tutuila. The main road leading from the airport is a tribute to America's fast-food giants and a testimony to the high esteem they hold in the Polynesian palate. A scattering of Asian restaurants provides a lighter alternative.

Many hotels have bars that are open to nonguests.

## Pago Pago

**Young's Mart** SUPERMARKET **$**
(Map p148; ☎633 2655; Utulei; ⏰7am-8pm) This well-stocked supermarket is in a convenient location, and is open on Sundays.

★**DDW Beach Cafe** AMERICAN **$$**
(Don't Drink the Water; Map p150; ☎633 5297; Utulei; mains US$6-30; ⏰7am-3pm Mon-Fri, 8am-2pm Sat) This bright waterfront cafe is a local favourite. Its huge breakfasts are legendary; lunches are equally gargantuan and span everything from well-cooked burgers to salads to seafood curries. It's also a top spot for a coffee.

**Goat Island Cafe** INTERNATIONAL **$$**
(Map p150; ☎633 5900; www.sadieshotels.com; Sadie's by the Sea, Utulei; mains US$10-35; ⏰6.30am-late) This popular restaurant has an incredibly extensive menu, offering everything from pizza and American-style sandwiches (its Philly 'steak bomb' is to die for) to the local version of haute cuisine. The outside dining *fale* overlook the beach. It's got the relaxed feel of an established hangout: you'll find plenty of locals and expats mixing it up, especially during happy hour (4pm to 6pm weekdays).

**Evalani's Cantina** MEXICAN **$$**
(Map p150; ☎633 7777; www.evalanis.com; Evalani's Motel, Pago Pago; mains US$5-22; ⏰7am-3pm & 5pm-late Mon-Sat) Attached to the flamboyant Evalani's Motel, this Mexican restaurant is no less gaudy, with over-the-top furnishings and flashing neon lights. The food is wonderfully cheesy too: the big burritos, enchiladas and nachos are fantastically fattening and so delicious that you won't care. It morphs into a fabulously kitsch nightclub as the evening wears on, and there's often live music. Don't miss it.

**Paradise Pizza** PIZZA **$$**
(Map p150; ☎731 6020; Satala, opposite Starkist Cannery; pizzas US$11-25; ⏰9am-10pm Mon-Sat) If you're craving big slices of American-style pizza, this is the place to indulge. It's got all the favourites, as well as those with interesting local toppings, including taro, Samoan pork sausage and one covered in tuna from the cannery across the road.

**Sook's Sushi Restaurant** ASIAN **$$**
(Map p150; ☎633 5525; GHC Reid Building, Fagatogo; mains US$7-20; ⏰9am-10pm Mon-Sat) Little has changed at this tiny seaside nook in the almost-20 years it's been running: that's a good thing. Fresh Japanese and Korean dishes – its beef *kalbi* (ribs) and tuna sashimi are locally famous – are prepared in an open kitchen beside the little dining room; there are small private rooms up the back if crowds aren't your thing.

**Fia Fia Seafood Restaurant** CHINESE **$$**
(Map p150; ☎633 0101; Fagatogo, Samoan News Building; mains US$6-25; ⏰10am-10pm) This clean, central place does Samoan-sized portions of Chinese food; thankfully, its quantity is matched by quality. While it's billed as a seafood restaurant, you'll find all the classics on the extensive menu.

### ILLUSTRATING SAMOA

The full-bodied *pe'a* (male tattoo), which extends from the waist to just below the knees, is a prized status symbol in Samoa. It can take weeks to complete and is a very painful process: anyone who undergoes the ritual is considered extremely brave. Any adult member can, in effect, receive a *pe'a* if the *'aiga* (extended family), *tufuga* (tattoo artist) and village leaders agree that it is suitable. The *tufuga* is usually paid with traditional gifts of *ie toga* (fine mats) and food.

Tattooing was discouraged when the missionaries came, but as young Pacific islanders take more pride in their heritage, there has been a revival of interest in the traditional designs. Contemporary tattoos – made with the modern machine or by the traditional comb – come without social and cultural restrictions, but designs often signify a person's *'aiga*, ancestors, or reference to nature.

## Western Tutuila

**Mom's Place** SAMOAN $
(Map p148; ☎699 9494; Tafuna; mains US$5-15; ⏰7am-2pm Mon-Sat) Mom's rich, diner-style cooking won't help keep your waistline under control, but to hell with it. Try your luck at getting through a plate of *panikeke* (the round doughnuts that Samoans call pancakes), or go island-style with corned-beef hash or spam and eggs.

**Toa Bar & Grill** INTERNATIONAL $$
(Map p148; ☎699 5099; cnr Nu'uuli St & Lion's Park Rd, Nu'uuli; US$8-25; ⏰4pm-midnight Mon-Thu, 2pm-2am Fri & Sat) Hungry locals congregate here for huge portions of seafood, steak and Samoan classics, as well as for the popular bar and regular screening of live sports. Toa rocks on into the night, with regular happy hours and live music throughout the week. It's friendly, but not fancy.

## Eastern Tutuila

**Da Tamalelei Seaside Grill** INTERNATIONAL $
(Map p148; ☎252 1488; Alofau; mains US$3-10; ⏰10am-7pm Mon-Sat) This humble seaside place dishes up gigantic serves of belt-busting grub for pocket change. Its burgers are legendary (even ravenous carnivores will battle to finish the two-patty, toppings-loaded 'Da Monster'), and it also cooks a variety of Asian and Samoan dishes; all meals come with rice, macaroni and vegetables. It does deliveries as far west as Pago Pago and Faga'alu.

**Tisa's Barefoot Bar** SAMOAN $$
(Map p148; ☎622 7447; www.tisasbarefootbar.com; Alega Beach; meals US$10-30) This social beachside restaurant specialises in super-fresh seafood with a Samoan twist. Opening hours can be sporadic, so it pays to call ahead. On Wednesday nights it fires up the *umu* (stone oven) for its legendary Samoan feast (US$40, bookings recommended), where traditional fare is given an international twist. Tisa's is also an exceptional spot for a cold beer or fruity cocktail.

## ☆ Entertainment

For an all-singing, all-dancing, thigh-slapping Samoan *fiafia*, head to the Equator restaurant at Tradewinds Hotel (p153) on a Friday night. A buffet dinner is included in the price (US$35).

### EATING PRICE RANGES

The following price ranges refer to a standard main course.

**$** less than US$10

**$$** US$10–US$20

**$$$** more than US$20

A handful of bars and cafes host local musicians (Sadie's by the Sea and Tisa's among them), while karaoke bars tend to cater to the seedier side of the fishing industry via Chinese prostitutes.

**Regal Nu'uuli Place Twin** CINEMA
(Map p150; ☎699 3456; Fagatogo; adult/child US$7.50/5) Head here for some smash-'em-up Hollywood action.

## Shopping

Tutuila's not quite Rodeo Drive, but you'll find what you need in the shopping centres and strip malls of Tafuna, Nu'uuli and Pago Pago. For souvenirs, head to Fagatogo Market (p146).

**Off Da Rock Tattoos** TATTOOS
(☎252 4858; www.offdarocktattoos.com; Nu'uuli; ⏰9am-4pm by appointment) The award-winning artists here specialise in clean, beautiful Polynesian designs; they take it easy on tourists with a modern electric needle.

## Information

Many of American Samoa's hotels offer free wi-fi. ATMs are found throughout commercial areas of the island.

**American Samoa Historic Preservation Office** (Ashpo; Map p148; ☎699 2316; www.ashpo.org; Nu'uuli) Excellent contact for history, sociology, anthropology and archaeology buffs. Its walking tours (info available online and in a pamphlet) offer insight into the region's colourful past.

**American Samoa Visitors Bureau** (Map p148; ☎699 9805; www.americansamoa.travel; Level 1, Fagaima Center One, Tafuna; ⏰8am-4pm Mon-Fri) Drop in if you're in the area, but you're better off with the National Park or National Marine Sanctuary info centres in town.

**ANZ Amerika Samoa Bank** (Map p150; Fagatogo) There are many branches around Tutuila, including in Fagatogo, Nu'uuli and Tafuna.

**Bank of Hawai'i** (Map p150; www.boh.com; Utulei; ⏰9am-3pm Mon-Fri, ATM 24hr) Has a branch in Utulei, plus one in Tafuna, on the main road from the airport.

**Blue Sky** (Map p148; www.bluesky.as; Laufou Shopping Centre; ⌚8am-4pm Mon-Fri) Blue Sky hot spots can be found all over Tutuila (see the website for a full list). Unlimited use for 24 hours/one week is US$10/20.

**LBJ Tropical Medical Center** (Map p148; ☎633 1222; Faga'alu; ⌚emergency 24hr) American Samoa's only hospital.

**National Park Visitor Information Center** (Map p150; ☎633 7082; www.nps.gov/npsa; 2nd fl, MHJ Building; ⌚8am-4.30pm Mon-Fri) This is the best place in American Samoa for tourist advice and information. It has excellent free maps, day-hikes pamphlets, information on WWII sites and a homestay program with choices on Tutuila, Olosega and Ta'u islands (US$35 to US$50 per night). Staff are helpful and professional.

**Post office** (Map p150; ⌚8.30am-3.30pm Mon-Fri, 9am-1pm Sat) American Samoa's main post office.



## Getting There & Away

All international flights and boats to American Samoa head to Tutuila.

A Pago Pago–bound ferry departs Apia (Samoa) every Thursday at 11pm; it departs Pago Pago the following day (also a Thursday, thanks to the bizarre dateline) at 4pm. The journey takes about seven hours. Prices (and currencies) vary, depending on which country you're leaving from; see the Samoa Shipping Corporation (p163) website for details.

## Getting Around

### TO/FROM THE AIRPORT

Frequent buses from Pago Pago Harbor to Tafuna International Airport are marked 'Tafuna' and stop right outside the terminal (US$2). If arriving at night you'll need to get a cab into Pago Pago (between US$15 and US$25). There's a taxi stand just outside the airport entrance.

### BUS

Riding Tutuila's colourful *'aiga* (extended family) buses is a must-do. These buses do unscheduled runs around Pago Pago Harbor and the more remote areas of the island from the main terminal at the market in Fagatogo. Fares range from US$1 to US$2.50.

Buses regularly head east to Aua and Tula, south to Tafuna and west to Leone. Less-frequent buses go to Fagasa, A'oloaufou on the central ridge, Amanave and Fagamalo in the far west; a trip to the northwest villages often means disembarking at Leone and catching another bus from there. Buses also head over Rainmaker Pass to Vatia.

### CAR

A 2WD is fine for motoring around Tutuila. Car hire is around US$80 per day.

**Avis Car Rental** (Map p148; ☎699 2746; www.avis.com; Tafuna International Airport)

**Sir Amos Car Rental** (Map p148; ☎256 4394; siramoscarrental@gmail.com; Tafuna International Airport)

**Tropical Car Rental** (Map p148; ☎699 1176; www.prtropicalcarrental.com; Tafuna International Airport)

### TAXI

Taxis are plentiful and convenient in Pago Pago, Nu'uuli and Tafuna. Fares vary wildly and meters aren't often used: be sure to agree on a price before getting in.

# MANU'A ISLANDS

POP 1160 / AREA 57 SQ KM

Ofu, Olosega and Ta'u, anchored about 100km to the east of Tutuila, are among the most ravishing – and remote – of all the Pacific isles.

The three share the same marvellous natural characteristics: enormous cliffs sheltering seabird colonies, expired volcanic cones, pristine lagoons stocked with a brilliant array of coral, and a soul-soothing sense of quiet. Ofu Beach ranks as one of the most splendid stretches of sand in the world.

The Manu'a Islands make the laid-back environs of Tutuila seem chaotic by comparison; be sure to pack plenty of extra reading material and a willingness to fall asleep in the middle of the day. While visitors are content to wallow in island inertia, the mosquitoes here are very active; bring repellent.

Plan to visit Manu'a near the beginning of your trip; any disruption in the weather could keep you here longer than you intended.

## Information

There are basic medical clinics in Ofu village and on Ta'u. There are post offices on each of the islands.

There are no banks in the Manu'a Islands (though one is apparently in the works for Ta'u), and most accommodation options don't take credit cards. Pack cash.

DON'T MISS

## AUNU'U

The 3-sq-km, tangled confines of Aunu'u are perfect for a half-day of exploring on foot. The walking tracks are manageable on your own, or you can arrange a guide when you get off the ferry (US$8 to US$10 is reasonable).

At the north end of the island is **Pala Lake**, a deadly looking expanse of quicksand whose fiery red hue is best appreciated at low tide. Within Aunu'u's central volcanic crater lies **Red Lake**, filled with eels and suffused by a preternatural glow at dusk. On the island's eastern shore is **Ma'ama'a Cove**, a rocky bowl pounded by large waves. Legend says that this is the site where two lovers, Sina and Tigila'u, were shipwrecked. You can make out bits of crossed 'rope' and broken 'planks' embedded in the rocks.

Below the western slope of Aunu'u's crater are the **Taufusitele Taro Marshes**. The safest place to swim on the island is in the little harbour, where the water's so clear that you can see the coral from the breakwater.

Small launches head to Aunu'u from the dock at Au'asi (at the eastern end of Tutuila). If you catch a boat with the locals, it's US$2 each way. If you charter a boat, a return trip is around US$10 to US$15. Boats don't run on Sundays.



## Getting There & Away

### AIR

Polynesian Airlines flies four times a week between Pago Pago and Ta'u Island (Fitiuta Airport) and once a week between Pago Pago and Ofu Airport.

**Manu'a Airways** (www.manuaair.com) – a new branch of **Inter Island Airways** (☎ in Pago Pago 699 7100, in Ta'u 677 7100; www.interislandair.com) – should be up and running by the time you read this, with direct flights between Pago Pago and Ofu and Ta'u islands, as well as flights between Ofu and Ta'u.

### BOAT

The **MV Sili** (☎ 633 4160; www.americansamoaport.as.gov/services/water-transportation-division.html; 1 way/return US$30/50) cargo ship departs Tutuila for Ofu and Ta'u every second Thursday morning, and returns the following morning. Book in advance: you'll need to call to do so, or ask your accommodation to help out. The journey takes between eight to 12 hours, and seas can get rough.

Take all of this with a grain of salt. The ageing ship often breaks down, and the Manu'a Islands have previously gone for weeks without it calling in. This is no fun for travellers, and even worse for locals: they depend on it for food and supplies.

## Getting Around

Ofu and Olosega are joined by a bridge; to get to Ta'u, you'll need to hop a boat or fly.

Flights between Ofu and Ta'u islands on new airline Manu'a Airways should have commenced by the time you read this.

The *Segaula* – an aluminum catamaran – regularly plies the waters between Ofu and Ta'u; the MV *Sili* creaks between the two fortnightly. Otherwise, charter boats can be arranged (about US$200 for four people).

Getting around on the islands themselves involves walking or sticking your thumb out; though there are only a handful of vehicles on the islands, few drivers will pass a walker without offering a lift.

# Ofu & Olosega

POP OFU 176, OLOSEGA 177 / AREA OFU 5.2 SQ KM, OLOSEGA 3 SQ KM

These twin islands, separated by a deep channel but linked by a bridge, are as close to paradise as it gets. Ofu's lone village crouches at its western end, leaving the rest of the island largely – and delightfully – uninhabited. Taking up its southern shoreline, exquisite **Ofu Beach** is 4km of shining, palm-fringed white sand, flanked by outrageously picturesque peaks that rise behind it like giant shark's teeth.

This, along with 140 hectares of offshore waters, comprises the Ofu section of the **National Park of American Samoa**. The reef here is considered to be one of the healthiest in all the Samoas. Huge schools of coloured fish dart through jaw-droppingly clear waters, occasionally pursued by reef sharks: they're harmless, to humans at least, but can induce heart palpitations for the novice snorkeller. Equally squeal-inducing (but just as benign) are the giant coconut crabs you'll likely see clattering around; they're the biggest land bugs in the world (not to mention very tasty).

## Ofu & Olosega

### Sights & Activities

Olosega shares the same marvellous encircling reef system as Ofu. The two islands look conjoined, but are separated from each other by the 137m-wide Asaga Strait. From the cyclone-proof **bridge**, the water is impossibly clear. Local kids regularly jump off, letting the current carry them to shore. This isn't advised for visitors – if you get the wrong tides you could easily be carried straight out to sea.

**To'aga Site** ARCHAEOLOGICAL SITE
(Ofu) While there's nothing to see here now, it was at this site (just behind Ofu Beach) where archaeologists found an unprecedented array of artefacts dating from early prehistory to the modern day. Samoans believe the bush between the road and the beach is infested with devilish *aitu* (spirits or ghosts), meaning you're likely to have one of the world's best beaches to yourself.

**Mt Tumutumu** HIKING
(Ofu) The 5.5km-long, often indistinct track (five hours return) to the summit of Mt Tumutumu (491m) begins just north of Ofu village wharf and twists up to the mountaintop TV relay tower. You'll need sensible shoes, long trousers (to protect from cutting plants), heavy-duty mosquito repellent and a knife to hack through the foliage.

**Maga Point** FISHING
(Olosega) The 1.5km walk to Maga Point on Olosega's southern tip offers unforgettable views of the point's steep cliffs, colourful reefs and distant Ta'u. To avoid local dogs, veer around Olosega village on the beach. After passing the rubbish tip, pick your way along the coral-strewn beach and look for the narrow hillside trail.

### Sleeping & Eating

Ofu and Olosega villages have basic stores where you can stock up on provisions.

★ **Vaoto Lodge** LODGE $
(☎655 1120; www.vaotolodge.com; Ofu; s/d US$80/90, cabins from US$120; 📶) This friendly, family-run place sits pretty at the base of Mt Tumutumu. Its beach – and those nearby – offers sensational snorkelling; it's also within strolling distance of some terrific hikes. Units are simple but comfortable; all have en suites. Delicious home-cooked meals (US$10 to US$20) are served communal-style.

**Asaga Inn** MOTEL $
(☎655 7791; www.asagainn.com; Ofu; r US$90; ❄📶) In a plum location right beside the Ofu–Olosega Bridge, this small motel offers good-sized rooms and air-conditioning (a rarity in the islands); the lovely family that owns it also runs the local mini-market. Full meal plans (US$36 per day) are available.

**Horizon Inn** INN $
(☎655 1302; www.horizoninn.yolasite.com; Olosega; s/d US$80/95; 📶) This new inn is small, simple and right on the sand. Rooms are basic but clean. The bridge connecting Ofa and Olosega, as well the Maga Point hike, are within walking distance. The meals at

its restaurant (5am to 9pm) are gigantic and fantastically fattening.

## Ta'u

POP 790 / AREA 39 SQ KM

On the dramatic south coast of this remote, sparsely populated volcanic island, some of the highest sea cliffs in the world rise 963m to Mt Lata, the territory's highest point.

The main settlement on Ta'u consists of the villages of Ta'u, Luma and Si'ufaga in the island's northwest. From Ta'u village there's a good walk south to secluded **Fagamalo Cove**. It was in Luma that Margaret Mead researched her classic anthropological work, *Coming of Age in Samoa*, in 1925. Despite the book's impression of a permissive society, Ta'u is the most conservative part of American Samoa.

The island's dense rainforests are home to flying foxes and numerous native birds. Ta'u is also the only habitat of the Pacific boa.

### Sights & Activities

**Saua Site** ARCHAEOLOGICAL SITE

This sacred site is where Tagaloa is said to have created the first humans before sending them out to Polynesia. Its volcanic boulders, wild surf and windswept beach lend it an ancient, supernatural atmosphere. Short trails lead to the main archaeological area, and *fale* have been erected for shelter. It's about 2.5km from Fiti'uta.

Keen hikers can continue from Saua via a rough track to Tufu Point. If you've arranged a guide, you could plug on for another 2km to a waterfall on the Laufuti Stream.

**Judds Crater** HIKING

(Luatele Crater) Treks to this gigantic volcanic crater should only be undertaken by very experienced hikers, and guides are a must; contact the National Park of American Samoa (p149) to arrange one well in advance of your trip. The hike should take about three hours (one way) from the road near Fiti'uta.

### Sleeping & Eating

At least three families on Ta'u offer village homestays (about US$80). These are facilitated by the National Park of American Samoa (p149): click on the 'homestay program' button on its website for more information.

**SUBSEA SPECTACLE: THE VALLEY OF GIANTS**

Ta'u, with its soaring sea cliffs, creation legends and preternatural sense of remoteness, is an extraordinarily exotic island. But its otherworldly feel isn't limited to land: Ta'u's surrounding waters are home to one of the largest, oldest and most mysterious coral colonies on the planet. Known as the Valley of Giants, this remarkable reef is populated by massive live boulder corals known as porites. The biggest is the gargantuan Big Momma, which looms 6.4m high, has a circumference of 41m and is believed to be at least 530 years old. How Big Momma and her colossal counterparts have managed to thrive despite centuries of climate change has baffled the few scientists that have been able to study this underwater wonder.

# UNDERSTAND AMERICAN SAMOA

## American Samoa Today

The two tuna canneries in Pago Pago account for 80% of American Samoa's employment, though the high costs of operating here makes their staying power shaky at best.

American Samoa's relationship with America is an unusual one. Though the people here are unquestionably Samoan, many speak with American accents and refer to the continental US as 'the mainland'. And whether due to patriotism or for economic reasons, American Samoa has the highest rate of military enlistment of any American state or territory. The 'American or not?' question was answered with some finality in 2015, when a court case (*Tuaua vs the United States*) pushing for full citizen rights for American Samoans was rejected.

## History

### Prehistory

Archaeological finds near the villages of Tula and Aoa at the eastern tip of Tutuila, and at To'aga on Ofu, reveal that the islands have been inhabited for more than 3000

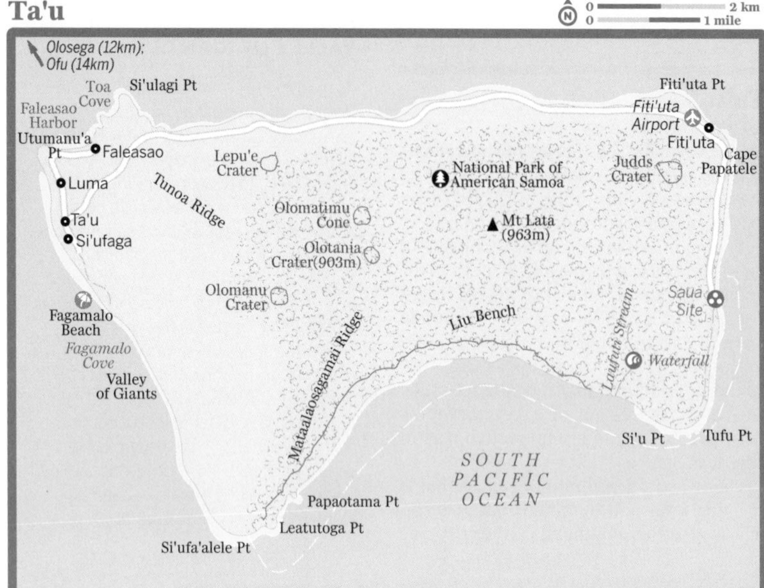


years. Traditionally Samoans believed that the Manu'a Islands were the first land to emerge at the hands of the god Tagaloa (see p153). The Tu'i Manu'a (paramount chief of the islands) was held in high esteem by Samoans. Although various conflicts ultimately split the islands, the paramount chief was still a powerful figure at the time of cession to the US at the beginning of the 20th century.

## European Contact

In 1722 Dutchman Jacob Roggeveen sighted the Manu'a Islands, but sailed on without landing. In May 1768 French explorer Captain Louis-Antoine de Bougainville bartered with the inhabitants of Manu'a, but merely sighted Tutuila. The first expedition to set foot on Tutuila was headed by Frenchman Jean-François de Galaup, comte de la Pérouse, who landed at Fagasa in 1787. The encounter had a tragic finish, with the French and the Samoans fighting each other at A'asu: 12 sailors and 39 villagers were killed, and A'asu was christened Massacre Bay.

## US Military Rule

A Samoan civil war in the 1870s and 1880s was co-opted by the US, Britain and Germany into an argument over which foreign power should rule the islands. By the time the dust had settled, control of western Samoa had been granted to Germany, and by 1900 the islands of eastern Samoa had been formally annexed to the US by a deed of cession signed by all local chiefs. Eastern Samoa became a naval station under the jurisdiction of the US Department of the Navy. In exchange, the US agreed to protect the traditional rights of indigenous Samoans. The inhabitants acquired the status of US nationals but were denied a vote or representation in Washington.

In 1905 the military commander of Tutuila was given the title of governor and the territory officially became known as American Samoa.

## Increasing Democracy

Until the 1960s American Samoa retained its traditional social structure and subsistence economy. But under President Kennedy, American Samoa was swiftly modernised, with European-style homes replacing traditional *fale*, electrification and the construction of an international airport and tuna canneries.

Through the 1960s and 1970s a series of referendums resulted in the adoption of a constitution, a democratically elected governorship and a two-chamber legislature. In 1980 American Samoans were allowed, for the first time, to elect a (non-voting) delegate to serve in the US House of Representatives.

### Recent Decades

In January 1987 the territory was hit by Cyclone Tusi, one of the worst storms in recorded history. Several more cyclones ploughed through the area between 1990 and 2009. In 2009 much of Tutuila was pummelled by a massive tsunami.

While American Samoa relies heavily on funding from the US government, the relationship isn't as one-sided as it seems: many American Samoans play for US sporting teams (particularly gridiron), and plenty more serve in the US military.

## The Culture

Samoans have maintained their traditional way of life and still closely follow the social hierarchies, customs and courtesies established long before the arrival of Europeans.

### Population

Most of the population lives on the main island of Tutuila. The birth rate is high but is offset by emigration to Hawai'i and the US mainland. Some 1500 foreigners reside in American Samoa, most of whom are Koreans or Chinese involved in the tuna or garment industries. About one-third are *palagi* (Westerners), many of whom hold government jobs, usually in the teaching or health fields.

## Arts

American Samoa shares its artistic traditions with Samoa, from the energetic song-and-dance routines called *fiafia* and the satirisation of their elders by village youth in the skit-based *Faleaitu* (meaning 'House of Spirits'), to the breezy architecture of the *fale,* intricate tattoos, and the lovely *siapo* (bark cloth) and *ie toga* (fine mats) used in customary gift exchanges.

## Environment

### Geography

American Samoa has a total land area of 197 sq km. The main island, Tutuila, is 30km long and up to 6km wide. The Manu'a group, 100km east of Tutuila, consists of the islands of Ta'u, Ofu and Olosega, all wildly steep volcanic remnants.

The easternmost part of the territory is tiny Rose Atoll, two minuscule specks of land (plus a surrounding reef) that were declared a Marine National Monument in 2009. This status helps protect the green turtle, as well as the extremely rare hawksbill turtle. Only scientific research expeditions are allowed to visit the atoll, though a charter there – at the discretion of the US Fish and Wildlife Service (www.fws.gov) – is theoretically possible

Equally tiny Swains Island (350km north-northwest of Tutuila) consists of a 3.25-sq-km ring of land surrounding a brackish lagoon. Both culturally and geographically, it belongs to Tokelau, but in 1925 the island's owners, the Jennings family, persuaded the US to annex it.

### Ecology

The wild inhabitants of American Samoa include two species of flying fox, *pili* (skinks), *mo'o* (geckos) and the harmless *gata* (Pacific boa), which is found only on Ta'u. The surrounding waters are home to pilot whales, dolphins and porpoises, while hawksbill turtles occasionally breed on remote beaches. Bird species include the nearly flightless banded rail, the barn owl and the superb *sega* (blue-crowned lory). While walking in rainforests, listen for the haunting calls of the rare multicoloured fruit doves (*manuma*) and the beautiful green-and-white Pacific pigeons.

Tutuila is characterised by its broadleaf evergreen rainforest. Ofu, Olosega and Ta'u host temperate forest vegetation such as tree ferns, grasses, wild coleus and epiphytic plants.

# SURVIVAL GUIDE

## Directory A–Z

### ACCOMMODATION

*Fale* accommodation for tourists has never quite caught on in American Samoa. With a few

## SLEEPING PRICE RANGES

The following price ranges refer to a double room with bathroom:

**$** less than US$100

**$$** US$100–US$150

**$$$** more than US$150

exceptions, lodgings here come in the form of generic motels, hotels and a handful of B&Bs.

The National Park of American Samoa (p149) operates a village homestay program.

### EMBASSIES & CONSULATES

All American Samoan diplomatic affairs are handled by the US. There are no consulates or embassies in American Samoa and no places that are able to issue visas for the US.

### EMERGENCY

☎911

### FESTIVALS & EVENTS

**Flag Day** (17 April) American Samoa's main public holiday commemorates the raising of the US flag over the islands in 1900 with an arts festival and traditional fanfare.

**Tisa's Tattoo Festival** (October) Showcase of traditional and modern *tatau* at Tisa's Barefoot Bar on Tutuila.

**White Sunday** (second Sunday of October) Celebration of Samoan childhood, with a heavy religious slant.

**Moso'oi Festival** (last week of October) A week of sporting and cultural events.

**Samoana Jazz and Arts Festival** (late October/early November) This new festival hosts local and international artists, and jumps between Tutuila and Apia.

### INTERNET ACCESS

Most hotels and guesthouses offer wi-fi.

### LANGUAGE

Samoan, English.

### MAPS

The tourism and national-park offices produce free brochures with maps.

### MONEY

The US dollar, divided into 100 cents, is the unit of currency in use in American Samoa.

ATMs are provided by the ANZ Amerika Samoa Bank and the Bank of Hawai'i on Tutuila.

Tipping is not expected or encouraged in American Samoa, though it's acceptable for exceptional service at finer restaurants.

### OPENING HOURS

The following are standard opening hours in American Samoa:

**Banks** 9am to 4pm Monday to Friday, some open 8.30am to 12.30pm Saturday

**Bars** noon to midnight

**Government offices** 9am to 5pm Monday to Friday

**Restaurants** 8am to 4pm and 6pm to 10pm

**Shops** 8am to 4.30pm Monday to Friday, 8am to noon Saturday (village stores keep longer hours)

### TELEPHONE

Blue Sky (p156) sells SIM cards and pre-paid mobile credit.

### TIME

The local time in American Samoa is GMT/UTC minus 11 hours. Therefore, when it's noon in American Samoa, it's 11pm the same day in London, 3pm the same day in Los Angeles, 9am the following day in Sydney and – just to be skull-crunchingly confusing for those booking flights to/from Samoa – 1pm the following day in Apia.

### USEFUL WEBSITES

**American Samoa Historic Preservation Office** (www.ashpo.org) This site includes information on Samoa's history and a good walking tour.

**American Samoa Visitors Bureau** (www.americansamoa.travel) Loads of information on attractions and accommodation in American Samoa.

**Busy Corner** (www.amsamoa-busycorner.blogspot.com.au) Online magazine focusing on the culture and highlights of American Samoa.

**Lonely Planet** (www.lonelyplanet.com/american-samoa) For planning advice, author recommendations, traveller reviews and insider tips.

**National Park of American Samoa** (www.nps.gov/npsa) This excellent site has a wealth of information on all aspects of the park, plus details of a territory-wide homestay program.

**Samoa News** (www.samoanews.com) For the latest American Samoan news.

### VISAS

US citizens equipped with a valid passport and an onward ticket can visit American Samoa visa-free. Nationals of Australia, New Zealand, Canada, the UK and some EU countries equipped with a passport (valid for at least 60 days) and an onward ticket will receive a free one-month visa on arrival. Other nationals must apply in advance for their one-month visa (US$40). It's a good idea to check your status before you go.

Visas can be issued by the **Attorney General's office** (☎633 4163; okboard.asag@gmail.com), but given that it has no official website, email queries often go unanswered and the phone connection can be dodgy, it's a better idea to ask your hotel if they can arrange a visa for you (fee about US$40).

Visa extensions are handled by the AG or the **Immigration Office** (Map p150; ☎633 4203; ground fl, Executive Office Bldg, Utulei; ⏰8am-4pm Mon-Fri), located within the government building in Pago Pago. Visas can only be extended by one month; the fee for this varies depending on what country you hail from. Again, larger hotels should be willing to play the middleman in what can be a confusing and convoluted procedure.

## Getting There & Away

### AIR

There's no better illustration of the physical isolation of American Samoa than the fact that you can only fly directly to Tutuila from Samoa and Hawai'i.

All flights go via Tafuna International Airport, 15km southwest of Pago Pago Harbor. The following airlines service American Samoa (telephone numbers here are for dialling from within American Samoa).

**Hawaiian Airlines** (☎699 1875; www.hawaiianair.com) Flies on Mondays and Fridays to/from Honolulu; return fare from US$955.

**Inter Island Airways** (☎699 7100; www.inter-islandair.com) Two daily flights to/from Samoa; return fares from US$170. It also runs flights to the Manu'a Islands.

**Polynesian Airlines** (☎699 9126; www.polynesianairlines.com) Runs frequent daily flights between Samoa and Pago Pago, plus some to the Manu'a Islands.

### SEA

#### Ferry

A car ferry/cargo ship called MV *Lady Naomi* runs between Pago Pago and Apia once a week. It departs Pago Pago each Thursday at 4pm for the trip (about seven hours). Return fares start at US$65. Tickets must be purchased at least one day in advance from **Samoa Shipping Corporation** (☎633 1211; www.samoashipping.com).

#### Yacht

Pago Pago's deep, spectacular harbour serves as the official entry point for private yacht owners.

All yachts and boats are required to contact the Harbour Master before entering American Samoan waters on VHF channel 16. Permission from Pago Pago is needed to sail to other islands in American Samoa. Yachts should be granted anchorage from US$7.50 per month in the harbour. Vessels arriving from Hawai'i need to present a US customs clearance document from Honolulu. See the **American Samoa Port Administration** (☎633 4251; www.americansamoaport.as.gov) website for full details.

## Getting Around

### AIR

Inter Island Airways and Polynesian Airlines fly between Tutuila and the Manu'a Islands. The new Manu'a Airways (p157) should be running flights between Ta'u and Ofu by the time you read this.

### BICYCLE

Tutuila is not very conducive to cycling. The island is mountainous, traffic can be heavy, and a complete circuit is impossible as there are no roads across the rugged north coast. Dogs can also be a major hassle here.

### BUS

Villages and towns on the island of Tutuila are serviced by *'aiga*-owned buses. Buses theoretically run until early evening, but don't test this theory after 2pm on Saturdays, or at all on Sundays. All buses display the name of their final destination in the front window. To stop a bus, wave your hand and arm, palm down, as the bus approaches. To signal that you'd like to get off the bus, either knock on the ceiling or clap loudly. Pay the driver; try to have the exact fare.

### CAR

Hiring a car allows you to explore Tutuila quickly and comfortably via the island's good sealed roads. That said, going it alone will rob you of the unique cultural experiences that public transport offers.

When hiring a vehicle, check for any damage or scratches before you drive off, and note everything on the rental agreement, lest you be held liable for damage when the car is returned.

Vehicles drive on the right-hand side of the road. The speed limit is 40km/h (25mph) islandwide. A valid foreign driving licence should allow you to drive in American Samoa.

#### Insurance

It's essential to have your hire car covered by insurance as repair costs are extremely high. Some local car-hire firms offer contracts where there's no option of accepting a collision/damage waiver (CDW). The lack of a CDW technically means that the car hirer is liable for *all* costs resulting from an accident, regardless of whose fault it is, so sign such contracts at your peril. You should insist on a CDW, for which you pay an extra fee of around US$12 per day.

### TAXI

Taxis on Tutuila are expensive and are only convenient for short trips.

# Tonga

☎676 / POP 106,000

**Includes ➡**



## Best Places to Stay

- Hideaway (p179)
- Port Wine Guest House (p190)
- Matafonua Lodge (p184)
- Sandy Beach Resort (p184)
- Nerima Lodge (p171)

## Best Places to Eat

- Friends Cafe (p173)
- Tiger Inn (p173)
- Mariner's Cafe (p183)
- Aquarium Café (p192)
- Bellavista Cafe & Restaurant (p192)

## Why Go?

Kiss the tourist hype goodbye – and say a warm *malo e lelei* (hello!) to the Kingdom of Tonga. Resolutely sidestepping flashy resorts and packaged cruise-ship schtick, Tonga is unpolished, gritty and unfailingly authentic. Life here ticks along at its own informal pace: church life is all pervasive, chickens and pigs have right of way, and there's nothing that can't wait until tomorrow. You don't have to seek out a cultural experience in Tonga – it's all around you!

Once you've shifted down into 'Tonga time', you'll find these islands awash with gorgeous beaches, low-key resorts, myriad snorkelling, diving, yachting and kayaking opportunities, hiking trails, rugged coastlines and affable locals (especially the kids!). Gear up for some active pursuits, then wind down with a cool sunset drink to the sound of waves folding over the reef. In Tonga, there really is nothing that can't wait until tomorrow.

## When to Go

**Nuku'alofa**

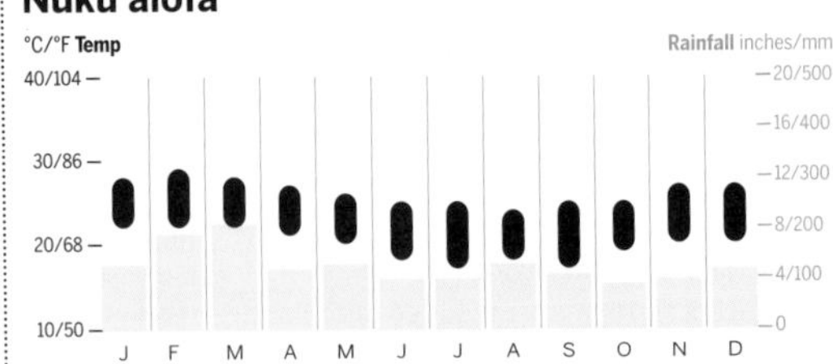


**Jun–Oct** Peak season: stable weather, warm seas and buzzy waterside restaurants.

**Apr–Aug** Cool, dry and less humid (winter) – when yachties turn up to play.

**Nov–Mar** Warm and wet in the South Seas summer, but fine for water sports.

176°W
174°W
8 Niuafo'ou
NIUA GROUP
Tafahi
Niuatoputapu
16°S
SOUTH PACIFIC OCEAN

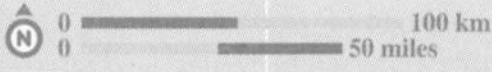


Fonualei
Toku
18°S
VAVA'U GROUP
11 Vava'u
1 7 Neiafu
Late
6 Swallows' Cave
20°S
'Ofolanga
Kao
Tofua
Pangai
Ha'ano
Foa
HA'APAI GROUP
Ha'afeva
1 Lifuka
Kotu
4 Uoleva
Tungua
'O'ua
'Uiha
Tokulu
Nomuka
Fonuafo'ou
Nomuk'iki
Telekivava'u
Hunga Tonga
Hunga Ha'apai
Ha'amonga a Maui Trilithon
Ha'atafu Beach 9
1 10 3
'Eue'iki
Tonga Trench
Nuku'alofa
5 Tongatapu
2 'Eua
TONGATAPU GROUP
'Ata
Same Scale as Main Map
Minerva Reef
Inset
'nerva Reef
0km, See Inset)

# Tonga Highlights

1 **Kayaking** (p168) between the reefs and islands offshore from Nuku'alofa, Neiafu and Pangai.

2 Hiking tropical rainforests and along sheer ocean clifftops on **'Eua** (p178).

3 Pondering Tongatapu's curious **Ha'amonga 'a Maui Trilithon** (p176), the 'Stonehenge of the South Pacific'.

4 Beach-bumming on the photogenic sands of **Uoleva** (p184), and (if you're lucky) watching whales breaching offshore.

5 Catching the cultural show at Tongatapu's **Oholei Beach & Hina Cave Feast & Show** (p176).

6 Swimming into **Swallows' Cave** (p194) on Kapa island in Vava'u.

7 Bouncing between bars and cafes in raffish **Neiafu** (p186).

8 Exploring far-off, doughnut-shaped **Niuafo'ou,** also known as Tin Can Island (p196) in the Niua Group.

9 Surfing the reef breaks at **Ha'atafu Beach** (p177) on Tongatapu.

10 Wandering aisles of produce and crafts at Nuku'alofa's **Talamahu Market** (p167).

11 **Sailing** (p187) through Vava'u's psychedelic web of waterways, islands and deserted beaches.

# TONGATAPU

POP 75,500 / AREA 260 SQ KM

Low-lying Tongatapu (Sacred South) is Tonga's main island – and the landing and launching pad for most adventures in Tonga. Around two-thirds of Tonga's 106,000 residents live here, most of them in the capital Nuku'alofa (Abode of Love – how romantic), also home to the royal family. Outside Nuku'alofa, the island is a patchwork of dark-brown agricultural plots, small villages, a few chilled-out resorts, wild stretches of coastline and more churches than a year full of Sundays. And smiling kids are everywhere!

Tongatapu's key archaeological sights – such as Mu'a and the Ha'amonga 'a Maui Trilithon – are on the isle's eastern side, which also features caves, calm sandy coves and the airport. To the west are the Mapu'a Vaca Blowholes and the most of the resorts and surf breaks. North of Nuku'alofa are some lovely little day-trip islands. Give yourself a good few days to check it all out.



## Getting There & Away

### AIR

**Fua'amotu International Airport** (Map p168; ☎35 415; www.tongaairports.com) is 21km southeast and a 30-minute drive from downtown Nuku'alofa. Air New Zealand, Fiji Airways and Virgin Australia all fly into Fua'amotu from overseas. In addition to local offices (p204), all are also bookable via Jones Travel (p175).

**Real Tonga** (Map p170; ☎23 777, 21 111; www.realtonga.to; Taufa'ahau Rd, Tungi Colonnade; ⌚8.30am-12.30pm & 1-5pm Mon-Fri, 9am-1pm Sat) is Tonga's domestic airline, flying between Tongatapu, 'Eua, Ha'apai, Vava'u and (occasionally) the Niua Group.

### BOAT

Regular ferries (p205) connect Tongatapu with Ha'apai, Vava'u and 'Eua.

## Getting Around

### TO/FROM THE AIRPORT

Taxis meet all incoming flights, charging around T$40 between the airport and Nuku'alofa. Watch out for drivers taking you to a different guesthouse than the one you asked for! Many hotels and guesthouses arrange transfers if you prebook (some for free).

The international and domestic airports are separate buildings; it's a short T$5 taxi fare between them.

### BICYCLE

Some guesthouses have bicycles for guest use. Rent a bike from Kingdom Travel Centre (p167) in Nuku'alofa.

### BOAT

Tongatapu's offshore island resorts all provide boat transport.

### BUS

Buses around Tongatapu are run privately. There are no public buses and no fixed timetables. Nuku'alofa's two bus terminals are on the waterfront on Vuna Rd. Buses to outlying areas of Tongatapu depart from the western bus terminal, close to Vuna Wharf. Local Nuku'alofa buses leave from the eastern bus terminal, opposite the Visitor Information Centre. Most fares fall into the T$1 to T$2 category. Bus services run from about 8am to 5pm; there are no buses on Sundays.

### CAR & SCOOTER

The following rental operators are all in Nuku'alofa.

**Avis** (Map p170; ☎21 179; www.avis.com; Asco Motors, Taufa'ahau Rd; ⌚8.30am-5pm Mon-Fri, to 12.30pm Sat) Cars from T$100 per day.

**Fab Rentals** (Map p170; ☎23 077; www.tongaholiday.com/listing/fab-rentals; Salote Rd; ⌚8am-5pm Mon-Fri, to noon Sat) Cars and vans from T$60 per day.

**Friendly Islander Cruisers** (☎849 2415; www.tongaholiday.com/listing/friendly-islander-cruisers; ⌚9am-6pm Mon-Sat) Scooter hire per half-/full day from T$35/50. Organise your pick-up/drop-off location when you book.

**Sunshine Rental** (☎23 848; www.tongaholiday.com/listing/sunshine-rental; cnr Laifone & 'Unga Rds; ⌚8am-5pm Mon-Fri, 8.30am-2pm Sat) Cars from T$80 per day.

### TAXI

Taxis are unmetered: ask for the fare to your destination before you agree to pay or get in. From the airport into Nuku'alofa should be about T$40. Taxis have a 'T' on the licence plate. They're not permitted to operate on Sunday, but some guesthouses know secret Sunday taxi suppliers.

**Holiday Taxi** (☎25 169)

**Wellington Taxi** (☎24 744)

# Nuku'alofa

POP 24,500

Raffish Nuku'alofa is the kingdom's seat of government and the home of the royal family. While it may not be a perfect Pacific paradise, Tonga's capital (aka 'Dirty Nuke') has hidden charm and promise if you blow the dust from the surface. The buzzy main street leads to the broad waterfront, from where there are impressive views across the bay to coral islands, a short boat ride away. The market here is a main line into Tongan life, there are a few good places to eat and drink, and you'll still see pigs and chickens careening around the back streets.

## Sights

**Royal Palace** PALACE

(Map p170; Vuna Rd) Encircled by expansive lawns and casuarina trees, the white weatherboard Victorian-style Royal Palace, erected in 1867, is the pinnacle of Tongan grandeur. The palace grounds are not open to visitors, but you can get a good look through the gates near the waterfront on the western side.

**Centenary Chapel** CHURCH

(Map p170; ☎23 522; www.fwc.to; Wellington Rd; free; ⊙daylight hours) Royal watchers and rubberneckers (regardless of denomination) head to this towering white church for a glimpse of Tonga's royal family at Sunday service, and to hear the congregation give its vocal chords a workout (you can hear the hymns a mile away). Dress sharp.

**Royal Tombs** CEMETERY

(Map p170; Taufa'ahau Rd) Mala'ekula, the large parklike area opposite the basilica, has been the resting place of the royals since 1893. The statue-studded white concrete tomb complex is off limits to the public, but you can peer across the lawns from the perimeter fence.

**★Talamahu Market** MARKET

(Map p170; ☎24 146; www.tongaholiday.com/listing/talamahu-marke; Salote Rd; ⊙8.30am-4.30pm Mon-Sat) Want to see the real Nuku'alofa? Wander through the aisles at Talamahu, Tonga's main fresh-produce hub. You'll find produce piled into handmade woven-frond baskets, branches of bananas, colourful pyramids of fruit and a few cooked-food stalls – plus outstanding (and affordable) Tongan arts and crafts. The whole place buzzes with talk and commerce, particularly on Saturday mornings.

## Activities

Tongatapu is relatively flat: exploring by bicycle is an option if you're brimming with energy.

You can also head out to the islands (p178) you can see from Nuku'alofa – Pangaimotu, Fafá or 'Atata – for a day trip that could include transfers, lunch, swimming and snorkelling (don't miss the wreck off Pangaimotu island). They're a good option on a Sunday, when Tonga takes a 24-hour time out, and good fun if you've got the kids in tow.

**Kingdom Travel Centre** BICYCLE RENTAL

(Map p170; ☎28 000; www.kingdomtraveltonga.to; cnr Vuna & Fatafehi Rds; ⊙8.30am-5pm Mon-Fri, 9am-12.30pm Sat) Bikes with helmets and locks for T$20 per day. On the Nuku'alofa waterfront.



### TONGA IN...

**One Week**

Acclimatise in the cafes in **Nuku'alofa**, then see the sights around Tonga's main island of **Tongatapu**: take a day tour or hire a car. Jet north to **Vava'u** and explore this magical maze of islands, beaches, reefs and sheltered waterways. Some time hanging out with the yachties in the waterside bars and restaurants in **Neiafu** is a must. Fly back to Tongatapu the day before your flight out.

**Two Weeks**

Throw in a visit to **Ha'apai** on your way back south from Vava'u. Lower than low-key, this is the place to be if you're really on the run from the stresses of life elsewhere. Sleep, read, eat, drink and strap on a snorkel at least once a day. Back on Tongatapu, fly out to nearby **'Eua**, an emerging ecotourism destination which offers up hiking trails, rainforest and raucous birdlife.

**One Month**

Consider using ferries to chug between the islands to really change down into 'Tonga time'. A stay out by the **Ha'atafu Beach** surf is a great family option on Tongatapu. Stretch out your stays in Vava'u, Ha'apai and on 'Eua (bring extra beach novels), or a trip to the **Niua Group** could even be on the cards.

## Tongatapu

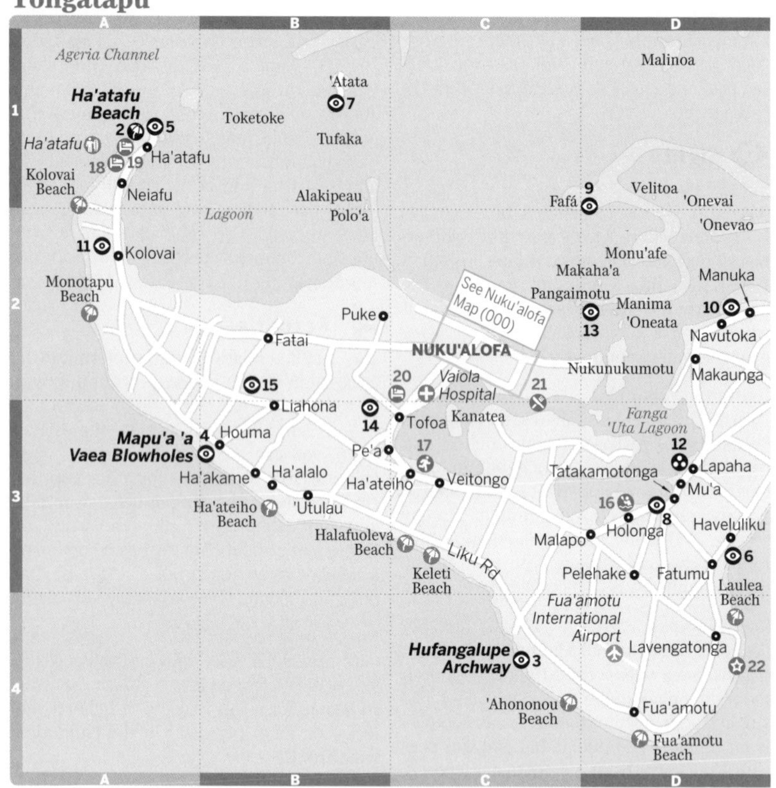




**Fatai Kayak Adventures** KAYAKING
(Map p168; ☎840 9175; www.tongaholiday.com/listing/fatai-kayak-adventures; Holonga Village) Based in Holonga Village in eastern Tongatapu, Fatai runs full-day kayak tours and offers kayak rentals. Its 'Island Hop Adventure Tour' takes paddlers out to Pangaimotu and Makaha'a islands (T$250). Single rental kayaks cost T$40/60 per half-/full day, doubles T$60/90.

**Ha'atafu Beach** SURFING, SNORKELLING
(Map p168; ☎41 088; www.surfingtonga.com; ) Tongatapu's best breaks are peeling over the reefs off Ha'atafu Beach in the island's northwest. Check out Steve Burling's excellent website for tips on what to bring and when to hit the waves. For the kids, an afternoon snorkelling in the shallows inside the reef isn't hard to take.

**Whale Swim, Fish & Dive** DIVING, SNORKELLING
(☎770 4984; www.whaleswimtours.com) Reliable small-group boat trips out into the briny sea to go diving (from T$325 full day), fishing (T$345 full day) or whale watching (T$195 half-day, T$325 with swimming). Boat tours with snorkelling also available ($T295 full day). Be aware that some animal welfare groups claim swimming with whales is disruptive to their behaviour and habitat: see (p193).

**Royal Tongan Golf Club** GOLF
(Manamo'ui Golf Course; Map p168; ☎24 949; Taufa'ahau Rd, Ha'ateiho; ⏲9am-4pm Mon-Sat) Take a swing at Tonga's only golf course, a relaxed nine-hole affair at Ha'ateiho on the way to the airport. Green fees are T$30/40 for nine/18 holes with rental gear included.

**Tonga Charters** FISHING, SNORKELLING
(☎771 5723; www.tonga-charters.com; half-day fishing/snorkelling per group T$1000/500) Fishing and snorkelling trips are on offer here. Good for groups; pricey for soloists.

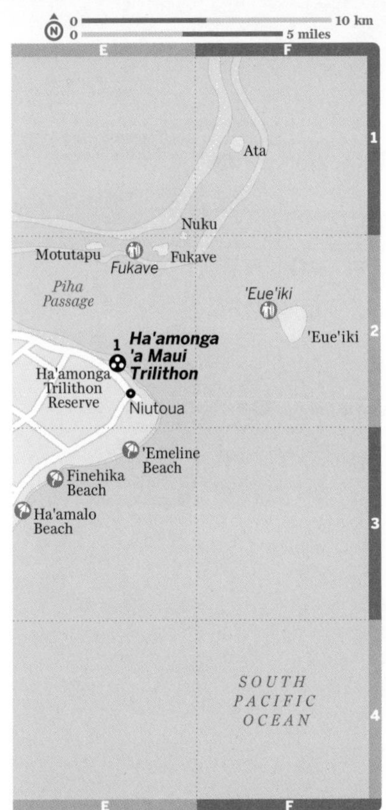


## Tongatapu

**Top Sights**

1 Ha'amonga 'a Maui Trilithon ............... E2
2 Ha'atafu Beach ............... A1
3 Hufangalupe Archway ............... C4
4 Mapu'a 'a Vaea Blowholes ............... B3

**Sights**

5 Abel Tasman Monument ............... A1
6 'Anahulu Cave ............... D3
7 'Atata ............... B1
8 Captain Cook Landing Site ............... D3
9 Fafá ............... D1
10 Fishing Pigs ............... D2
11 Flying Foxes ............... A2
12 Mu'a ............... D3
13 Pangaimotu ............... D2
14 Royal Residences ............... B3
15 Triple-headed Coconut Tree ............... B2

**Activities, Courses & Tours**

16 Fatai Kayak Adventures ............... D3
Ha'atafu Beach ............... (see 19)
17 Royal Tongan Golf Club ............... C3

**Sleeping**

18 Blue Banana Beach House ............... A1
19 Ha'atafu Beach Resort ............... A1
Heilala Holiday Lodge ............... (see 19)
Holty's Hideaway ............... (see 19)
20 Toni's Guesthouses ............... C2

**Eating**

21 Lunarossa Restaurant ............... C3

**Entertainment**

22 Oholei Beach & Hina Cave Feast & Show ............... D4

## Tours

Tongatapu's main sights can be comfortably covered in a day tour – a good option for an otherwise somnolent Sunday. Most local accommodation operators will have a tour guide they recommend. See also Teta Tours (p175).

**Ancient Tonga** CULTURAL TOUR
(786 3355, 25 510; www.ancienttonga.com; tours from T$140) Cultural full- and half-day tours around historic sites on Tongatapu, with activities that may include *umu* (earth oven), tapa- and mat-making demonstrations, *fale* (house) tours, dance performances and lunch. Call to discuss group numbers, options and prices.

**Toni's Tours** TOUR
(21 049, 774 8720; www.tonisguesthouse.com; tours from T$60) Pile into Toni's van and do a lap of the island's main sights (minimum three people). Bring a sun hat, sunscreen, swimming gear and a preparedness to weather Toni's acerbic Lancashire wit. Pick up/drop off at your accommodation.

**Supa Tours** TOUR
(771 6450; phlatohi@kalianet.to; tours from T$60) Big John's island tours operate daily, taking in all the main sights.

**Pacific Ocean Tours** BOAT TOUR, SURFING
(24 933; www.pacificoceantours.com) Based in Nuku'alofa, these guys run boat trips out to surf breaks on the outer reefs (T$180, BYO boards), and offer fishing (T$150) and whale-watching (T$300) trips.

## Sleeping

**Ola's Guest House** GUESTHOUSE $
(Map p170; 25 154; olakoloi@hotmail.com; off Tupoulahi Rd, Ngele'ia; d T$150, s/d/f without bathroom T$70/90/180, all incl breakfast; ) Formerly Ali Baba's, this out-of-the-way

## Nuku'alofa

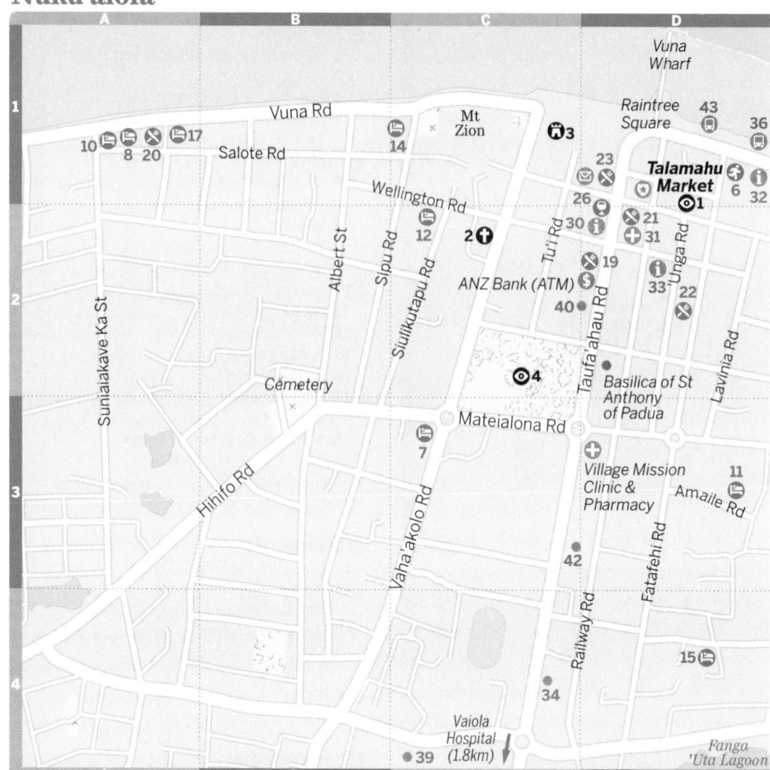


place is funky and friendly. Floors are chequered blue-and-gold, and the seven rooms (with two shared bathrooms) have TVs and their own colour schemes and themes. A welcoming host, Ola keeps things ultraclean and uptempo. It's about 1.5km from the post office.

**Noa Guest House** GUESTHOUSE **$**
(Map p170; ☎21 810; www.noaenterprises.com; Wellington Rd; dm/s/d without bathroom T$35/70/90, d with bathroom T$150; ❄📶) Not far from church, town and sea, yellow-painted, two-tier Noa has a plumb location and plenty of rooms, from dorms to basic singles and doubles and en-suite doubles. The best are upstairs; the cheaper ones are out the back. Air-con in some rooms only, but all are clean and shipshape. Beaut communal kitchen.

**Backpackers Townhouse** HOSTEL **$**
(Map p170; ☎771 6148; www.tongaholiday.com/listing/backpackers-townhouse-nukualofa; cnr Mateialona & Vaha'akolo Rds; dm/s/d T$25/60/80) This rickety hostel doesn't look like much from the dusty street out the front, but inside things quickly improve. There's a cheery communal kitchen-lounge, complete with beach books and a guitar to strum, free fruit from the owners' garden and reasonable rooms. The cheapest beds in downtown Nuku'alofa.

**Toni's Guesthouses** GUESTHOUSE, HOSTEL **$**
(Map p168; ☎774 8720, 21 049; www.tonisguesthouse.com; Tofua; dm/s/d/house from T$25/50/50/180) Toni's is a brightly coloured budget complex in Tofoa, 3km south of Nuku'alofa. On the list are kava sessions, airport pick-ups (T$20), shuttles into town (T$2) and island tours (p169) in Toni's van. There are a lot of sleeping options from dorms to full houses, so check out the website. Toni knows Tongatapu backwards (a wry font of advice).

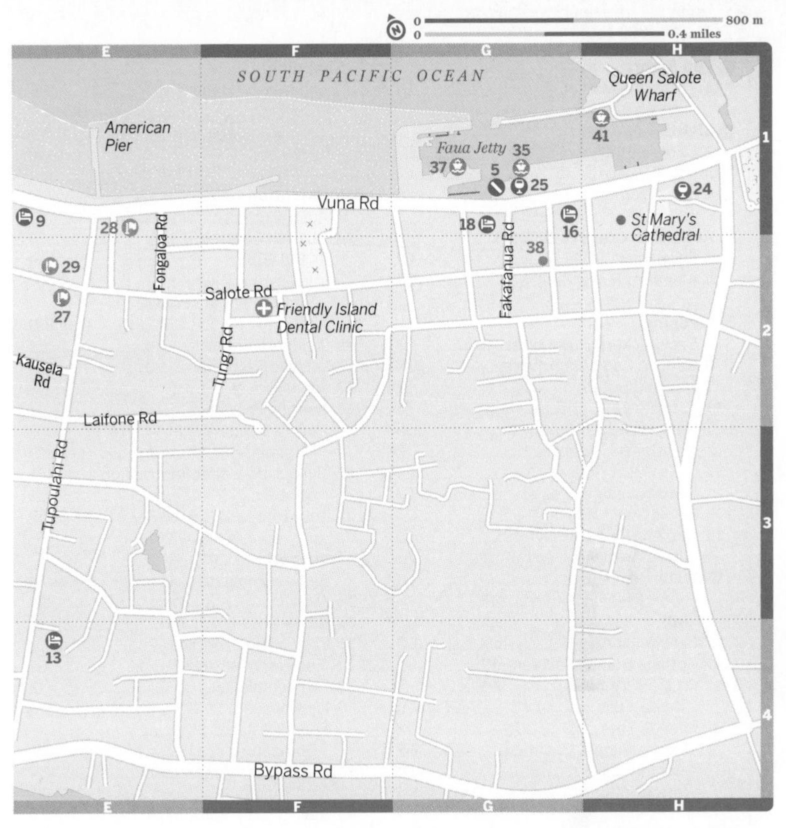




**Sela's Guest House** GUESTHOUSE **$**
(Map p170; ☎25 040; www.tongaholiday.com/listing/selas-guesthouse; Longoteme Rd; dm/s/d T$25/80/100; 📶) Sela's is a long-running, warren-like and very basic guesthouse that wouldn't comply with many Western building codes. Still, it's a cheap and cheery outfit, with lavish cooked breakfasts with fruit (T$15). It's about a 1.5km hike from the post office.

★**Nerima Lodge** GUESTHOUSE **$$**
(Map p170; ☎25 533; www.nerimalodge.com; Amaile Rd; s/d T$80/115, s/d/tr without bathroom T$65/100/135, all incl breakfast; 📶) Simple, quiet, clean, friendly and a short walk to town – just how any good South Pacific guesthouse should be. Downstairs is a sunny communal lounge and breakfast room, where the morning menu changes daily (pancakes, bacon and eggs, toast with pawpaw-and-coconut jam). Upstairs are one en-suite room and six tidy private rooms with shared bathrooms. Great value.

**'Utu'one Bed & Breakfast** B&B **$$**
(Map p170; ☎24 811; www.tongaholiday.com/listing/utuone-bed-and-breakfast; Vuna Rd; d incl breakfast T$150-250; ❄📶) Down near the ferry piers and the fish market, 'Utu'one is a bastion of cleanliness surrounded by things otherwise. It's a two-storey white hacienda, all rooms with en-suites or shared bathrooms across the hall. Free wi-fi and generous egg breakfasts, with a half-hour stroll into town to walk it off afterwards. Bit noisy on Saturday nights.

**Captain Cook Apartments** APARTMENT **$$**
(Map p170; ☎25 600; www.captaincooktonga.com; Vuna Rd; d T$160, extra person T$25; ❄📶) Trim two-bedroom serviced apartments with full kitchen and living area, peeking at the sea through casuarina trees. The complex (six apartments) has been around a

## Nuku'alofa

**Top Sights**
1 Talamahu Market....D1

**Sights**
2 Centenary Chapel....C2
3 Royal Palace....C1
4 Royal Tombs....C2

**Activities, Courses & Tours**
5 Deep Blue Diving....G1
6 Kingdom Travel Centre....D1

**Sleeping**
7 Backpackers Townhouse....C3
8 Captain Cook Apartments....A1
9 Emerald Hotel....E1
10 Little Italy....A1
11 Nerima Lodge....D3
12 Noa Guest House....C2
13 Ola's Guest House....E4
14 Seaview Lodge....C1
15 Sela's Guest House....D4
16 'Utu'one Bed & Breakfast....G1
17 Villa Apartments....A1
18 Waterfront Lodge....G1

**Eating**
19 Café Escape....D2
20 Cottage Breeze Restaurant....A1
Emerald Chinese Restaurant....(see 9)
21 Friends Cafe....D2
22 Marco's Pizza & Pasta....D2
23 Tiger Inn....D1
Waterfront Café....(see 18)

**Drinking & Nightlife**
24 Billfish Bar & Restaurant....H1
25 Ngutulei Bar & Restaurant....G1
26 Reload....D2

**Shopping**
Langafonua Handicrafts Centre....(see 21)
Tu'imatamoana Fish Market....(see 5)

**Information**
27 Australian High Commission....E2
28 Chinese Embassy....E1
Friends Cafe....(see 21)
Immigration Division, Department of Foreign Affairs & Trade....(see 29)
29 Japanese Embassy....E2
Jetsave Taufonua....(see 19)
30 Jones Travel....D2
31 Neeru's Pharmacy....D2
New Zealand High Commission....(see 26)
32 Nuku'alofa Visitor Information Centre....D1
33 Teta Tours....D2

**Transport**
Air New Zealand....(see 6)
34 Avis....C4
35 Boats to Pangaimotu....G1
36 Eastern Bus Terminal....D1
37 'Eua Ferry Terminal....G1
38 Fab Rentals....G2
Fiji Airways....(see 16)
Friendly Islands Shipping Company....(see 41)
39 Ministry of Infrastructure....C4
40 Real Tonga....D2
41 Vava'u & Ha'apai Ferry Terminal....H1
42 Virgin Australia....C3
43 Western Bus Terminal....D1

while and is showing its stylistic age, but it's still in good shape. Long-stay discounts.

**Waterfront Lodge** HOTEL $$$
(Map p170; ☎25 260; www.tongawaterfrontlodge.com; Vuna Rd; garden/sea-view d incl breakfast T$260/280, extra bed T$50; ❄📶) The rather boutiquey Waterfront is an elegant offering, with neat gardens and Victorian colonial aesthetics. The eight spacious rooms upstairs feature parquetry floors, teak and cane furnishings, tasteful prints and multihead showers to banish the Nuku'alofa dust from your bones. The Waterfront Café (p174) downstairs is also a good'un.

**Seaview Lodge** LODGE $$$
(Map p170; ☎23 709; www.seaview-lodge.com; Vuna Rd; d T$240-320, apt $320; ❄📶) This endearing fave a short stroll from town has large rooms with island vibes. The priciest rooms have balconies from which to absorb the namesake views. Out the back there's a bungalow apartment with a kitchen; out the front is the house restaurant, which is about as classy as dinner in Nuku'alofa gets (mains T$39 to T$46). Hit-and-miss hot water.

**Villa Apartments** APARTMENT $$$
(Map p170; ☎24 998; www.tongavilla.com/villa-apartments; Vuna Rd; 1-/2-bedroom apt from $265/395; ❄📶) Nuku'alofa's classiest beds? You could be right. These sassy New Zealand–owned apartments on Vuna Rd overlook the sea from a broad balcony, and tick all the upmarket boxes. It's a two-storey beige edifice with an air of exclusivity about it, and a big

fence keeping anything that might interrupt your holiday at bay.

**Emerald Hotel** HOTEL **$$$**
(Map p170; ☎22 888; www.emerald-tonga.com; Vuna Rd; d/tw/ste from T$250/250/349; ❄📶) One of Tonga's newer hotels has 20 bright, clean, spartan rooms over two levels. Air-con, friendly staff, in-room safe, wif-fi, minibar, the Emerald Chinese Restaurant (p174) downstairs, sea views from the best rooms... it's all here. A bit of soul is all that's lacking.

**Little Italy** HOTEL **$$$**
(Map p170; ☎25 053; www.littleitalytonga.com; Vuna Rd; garden/ocean-view r incl breakfast T$290/330; ❄📶) There are two floors of Tuscan-toned rooms atop the buzzy Little Italy restaurant. Expect superprofessional staff and knock-out sea views from the best rooms (look at the ocean instead of the decor, which is a tad dated). The restaurant is open for breakfast and dinner (mains T$18 to T$44): pizza, pasta, scaloppine, paintings of pine trees and crooner tunes.

## Eating

For self-caterers, Nuku'alofa's supermarkets stock a reasonable range of products (but not much fresh stuff: head to Talamahu Market, p167).

**★Tiger Inn** CHINESE **$**
(Map p170; ☎777 8666; Tonga Post Food Court, Taufa'ahau Rd; mains $6-10; ⏱9am-6pm Mon-Fri, to 5pm Sat; 📶) One of four quick-fire, perennially busy eateries on the ocean side of the Tonga Post building, Tiger Inn eschews the Western sausage-and-chips offerings of its neighbours and delivers authentic Chinese noodle soups. Order a spicy seafood version, laced with coriander, and slurp it down at one of the outside tables. Service can be surly.

**★Friends Cafe** CAFE **$$**
(Map p170; ☎22 390; breakfast from T$7, mains T$10-26; ⏱7.30am-10pm Mon-Sat; 📶) With a breezy charm, conversation, laughter and dependably good food, Friends is an irresistible social and culinary magnet for visitors and locals alike. Expect everything from panini to Thai beef curry to Moroccan spiced fish. Good coffee and free wi-fi to boot. There's also a tourist info (p175) wing off to one side.

**Marco's Pizza & Pasta** ITALIAN **$$**
(Map p170; ☎22 144; www.tongaholiday.com/listing/marcos-pizza-pasta; 'Unga Rd; mains $16-30; ⏱11am-2pm & 5-11pm Mon-Sat) Explore Nuku'alofa's back streets and you'll find plenty of places to eat: Korean, Singaporean, Indian, and Marco's – an unassuming little pizza and pasta joint. Chow down inside the modest shack, or sit out in the neat little garden area. Takeaways and occasional live music, too.

**Cottage Breeze Restaurant** INTERNATIONAL **$$**
(Map p170; ☎28 940; Vuna Rd; mains T$20-30; ⏱4-10pm Mon-Sat) Earning a glowing reputation, this place on Vuna Rd west of the palace offers cheery service and consistently good food: everything from pork ribs to seafood grills. Kick back at your mosaic-topped table on the broad terrace and see the sea across the road.



### SLEEPY SUNDAYS IN NUKU'ALOFA

Tonga comes to a screeching halt at midnight every Saturday night for 24 hours – Sunday is a day of rest and it's enshrined in Tongan law that it is illegal to work. There are no international or domestic flights, shops are closed, the streets are empty, sports are prohibited, and most Tongans are going to church, feasting and sleeping. Here are some suggestions to get you through till Monday morning:

- Go to church – magnificent singing and fiery sermons lift the soul (and almost the roof). At the Centenary Chapel (p167) you can tune your tonsils and worship alongside the king and the royal family.
- Take a round-the-island tour and explore Tongatapu's sights and attractions; try Toni's Tours (p169).
- Hire a bicycle and tootle around at your own pace.
- Visit one of the offshore island resorts for some sandy beaches and snorkelling.
- Truck out to Ha'atafu Beach and relax.
- Sleep and eat – that's what most of the locals will be doing!

**Café Escape** CAFE $$
(Map p170; ☎21 212; www.tongaholiday.com/listing/cafe-escape; Fund Management House, Taufa'ahau Rd; breakfast from T$7, mains T$10-25; ⏰7.30am-late Mon-Fri, to 4pm Sat; 📶) Slick Café Escape could be anywhere, but provides a refined air-conditioned retreat from the street and infuses the tropics into its mixed menu. Order the fab banana-and-pineapple porridge, or combat the starch in your diet with a big fruit salad. Free wi-fi, plus internet terminals and tourist brochures in the corner.

**Emerald Chinese Restaurant** CHINESE $$
(Map p170; ☎24 619; www.emerald-tonga.com; Vuna Rd; mains T$6-25; ⏰10.30am-10.30pm Mon-Sat, 10.30am-2.30pm & 5.30-10.30pm Sun) Part of the Emerald Hotel, this place gets the nod for top Chinese restaurant in town. Good value, it's licensed, takeaway is available and (best of all) it's open on Sunday. Try the fried Szechuan chicken.

**Waterfront Café** INTERNATIONAL, ITALIAN $$$
(Map p170; ☎25 260; www.tongawaterfrontlodge.com; Vuna Rd; mains T$22-43; ⏰6-10pm Mon-Sat) Downstairs at the Waterfront Lodge (p172), soak up the breezy South Seas vibes and chase a few sundowners with some Italian-style pasta, steak, lobster, lamb or seafood. It's a roomy room, spangled with colourful prints.

**Lunarossa Restaurant** ITALIAN $$$
(Map p168; ☎26 324; www.tongaholiday.com/listing/lunarossa-restaurant; Umusi Rd, Ma'ufanga; mains T$20-40; ⏰7-10pm Mon-Fri) You'll need a car or taxi to get to the 'Red Moon', but it makes for a reasonably classy experience. The vibe is intimate with authentic Italian cuisine, the focus on ultrafresh seafood (the creed: 'a passion to redesign Tongan seafood with Italian cuisine').

## Drinking & Nightlife

Tongans drink with gusto, but Nuku'alofa has a fairly limited bar scene. Ask a local about recommended kava circles (which you may be invited to join). Traditionally a male-only affair, both men and women are welcome around the kava bowl at Toni's Guesthouses (p170).

★ **Billfish Bar & Restaurant** BAR
(Map p170; ☎24 084; www.billfish.co; Vuna Rd; ⏰11am-late Mon-Sat) This chilled-out open-air place down by the wharves is a long-time locals' haunt. There are hefty pub-style meals (mains T$14 to T$38; try the fish curry or the Hawaiian burger), chipper staff, Steinlager on tap, Dire Straits on the stereo and occasional live bands (also playing Dire Straits).

**Reload** BAR
(Map p170; www.facebook.com/pages/reload-bar-tonga/156057704465308; Taufa'ahau Rd; ⏰noon-12.30am Mon-Fri, to 11.30pm Sat) 'Probably the best bar in Tonga' says the sign. We're not sure why it lacks confidence: the Ikale Lager is cold, the reggae is mellow and the upstairs balcony is surely the best spot for a beer in downtown Nuku'.

**Ngutulei Bar & Restaurant** BAR
(Map p170; ☎22 666; tongawater@gmail.com; Vuna Wharf; ⏰8am-12.30am Mon-Fri, 8am-11.30pm Sat, 11am-9pm Sun) You can order a bang-up steak, chicken, lobster or swordfish meal at Ngutulei (mains T$18 to T$45), but most folks are here for a cold beer overlooking the fishing boats. With a stylish woody fit-out inside, it sits in a cordoned-off compound on the edge of a concrete sea (just look at the real sea, not the concrete).

## Shopping

**Langafonua Handicrafts Centre** ARTS
(Map p170; ☎21 014; www.madeintonga.com/langafonua; Taufa'ahau Rd; ⏰9am-5pm Mon-Fri, to 1pm Sat) A nonprofit artists co-op representing 300-plus local artists. Inside you'll find brilliant Tongan jewellery, carvings, baskets, weavings, canvasses...and trashy second-hand beach books!

**Tu'imatamoana Fish Market** FOOD & DRINK
(Map p170; Vuna Wharf; ⏰5am-4.30pm Mon-Sat) Starts when the boats come in around 5am (get there early). There are trestle tables covered with bags of oysters, iridescent tropical fish, big crabs with taped-up claws, fish heads, slippery squid – a real briny bounty.

## Information

### EMERGENCY

**Police Station** (Map p170; ☎26 498, emergency 922; www.police.gov.to; Salote Rd) The local law-enforcement hub.

### INTERNET ACCESS

Nuku'alofa has a clutch of internet cafes, the best of which are Café Escape and Friends Cafe (p173). Most local accommodation has wi-fi access for guests.

### MEDICAL SERVICES

**Friendly Island Dental Clinic** (Map p170; ☎25 455; fidc@paluaviation.to; Fasi Village; ⏰5-7pm Mon-Sat)

**Neeru's Pharmacy** (Map p170; ☎21 810; www.neeruspharmacy.com; Wellington Rd; ⏱9am-7pm Mon-Fri, to 3pm Sat) Downtown pharmacy.

**Vaiola Hospital** (Map p168; ☎23 200; mohtonga@kalianet.to; Vaiola Rd, Tofoa; ⏱24hr) For emergencies and after-hours needs. There are also dentists here.

**Village Mission Clinic & Pharmacy** (Map p170; ☎27 522; www.villagemissionclinic.org; Patco Business Centre, Taufa'ahau Rd; ⏱8.30am-5pm Mon-Fri, 10am-1.30pm Sat) This pharmacy has a doctor on duty every Friday between 9am and noon (or by appointment).

#### MONEY

There are plenty of ATMs around Nuku'alofa's main drag, most of them ANZ or Bank of South Pacific (BSP took over Tonga's Westpac branches in 2015 – the rebranding process is ongoing). There are also ANZ and BSP ATMs on Vuna Rd near the ferry terminal, and there's a BSP ATM and several money-change booths at Fua'amotu International Airport.

#### POST

**Tonga Post** (Map p170; ☎21 700; www.tongapost.to; Taufa'ahau Rd; ⏱8.30am-4.30pm Mon-Fri, 9am-noon Sat) Down by the water in downtown Nuku'alofa.

#### TOURIST INFORMATION

**Friends Cafe** (Map p170; ☎26 323; www.friendstonga.com; Taufa'ahau Rd; ⏱7.30am-10pm Mon-Sat; 📶) This savvy little diner doubles up as a private tour-booking office, with plenty of details on what's happening around the kingdom. Also has internet access and books scooters for Friendly Islander Cruisers (p166).

**Nuku'alofa Visitor Information Centre** (Map p170; ☎25 334; www.thekingdomoftonga.com; Vuna Rd; ⏱8.30am-4.30pm Mon-Sat) A government-run bureau with info on the whole of Tonga, maps and neat racks of brochures.

#### TRAVEL AGENCIES

**Jetsave Taufonua** (Map p170; ☎23 052; inbound.taufonua@gmail.com; Fund Management Bldg, Taufa'ahau Rd; ⏱8.30am-4,30pm Mon-Sat) Books day tours, rental cars and domestic package holidays to all island groups.

**Jones Travel** (Map p170; ☎23 423; www.tonga-travel.travel; cnr Taufa'ahau & Wellington Rds; ⏱8.30am-4.30pm Mon-Sat) Flight bookings for Virgin Australia, Air New Zealand and Fiji Airways, plus local tours and scooter bookings for Friendly Islander Cruisers (p166).

**Teta Tours** (Map p170; ☎23 363; www.tongaholiday.com/listing/teta-tours-and-travel-ltd; cnr Wellington & Railway Rds; ⏱8.30am-4.30pm Mon-Sat) Myriad tour and activity bookings across Tonga, including trips to Anahulu Cave (p176).

## Around the Island

Buses are sporadic and taxis expensive, so the best way to see the sights is by island tour or rental car. The following points of interest run from Nuku'alofa in a clockwise direction around the island.

### Sights & Activities

#### Eastern Tongatapu

**Royal Residences** LANDMARK

(Map p168; Taufa'ahau Rd, Tofoa) South of Nuku'alofa, between Tofoa and Pe'a, you'll pass the private royal residences of the princess, adorned with white tigers and cannons, and the king, an austere European-style hilltop palace opposite (why are the princess's cannons pointing at the king?). After the 2015 coronation, it was unclear which royals would end up living in which houses (ask a passer-by!). No public access: views from the street only.

**Captain Cook Landing Site** HISTORIC SITE

(Map p168; Taufa'ahau Rd, Holonga) A modest cairn above a mangrove inlet near Holonga village marks the spot where Captain Cook came ashore in 1777 (on his third trip to Tonga) and where Queen Elizabeth II popped by to commemorate it in 1970. Up-close access



### JAPAN & CHINA: FUNDING FRENZY

Around Tongatapu you'll see neatly tarmacked roads emblazoned with 'China Aid' signs and hear people talking about the 'Japan road': they're referring to the sources of international funding used to construct these thoroughfares. China and Japan seem locked in a battle to see who can inject more money into Tonga's economy by financing civic projects: roads, hospitals, police stations, community health centres... Why? The international largesse is most welcome and Tonga is deeply indebted, but some cynical locals suggest that what China wants in return is to establish a naval base here, and that Japan is angling towards recommencing whaling in Tongan waters.

DON'T MISS

## OHOLEI BEACH & HINA CAVE FEAST & SHOW

The pinnacle of Tongatapu entertainment is this fab feast and show at **Oholei Beach & Hina Cave Feast & Show** (Map p168; ☎11 783; www.oholeibeachresort.com; buffet & show adult/child T$40/20; ⏲6pm Wed & Fri, buffet only 2pm Sun) in the island's southeast. The evening starts with a welcome on sandy Oholei Beach, followed by a hefty Tongan feast, including suckling pig roasted on a spit. The highlight is an enthusiastic traditional dance performance in the open-topped Hina Cave, culminating in an eye-popping fire dance.

There's a free shuttle to the show from Nuku'alofa. If you want to stay the night, bunk down in a *fale* at the resort (see the website).



was inhibited by a padlocked gate when we visited.

**Mu'a** ARCHAEOLOGICAL SITE
(Map p168; off Taufa'ahau Rd, Mu'a; ⏲24hr) The Mu'a area contains Tonga's richest concentration of archaeological remnants. In AD 1200 Tu'itatui, the 11th of the Tu'i Tonga kings, moved the royal capital from Heketa (near present-day Niutoua) to Mu'a. There are 28 royal stone tombs *(langi)* in the area, built with enormous limestone slabs. The most accessible of these are two monumental ancient burial sites off the dirt road towards the sea, just north of the Catholic church.

The structure closest to the main road is the Paepae 'o Tele'a (Platform of Tele'a), a pyramid-like stone memorial. Tele'a was a Tu'i Tonga who reigned during the 16th century. The other, the Langi Namoala, has a fine example of a *fonualoto* (vault for a corpse) on top.

**Fishing Pigs** LANDMARK
(Map p168; Taufa'ahau Rd, Manuka; ⏲daylight hours; 👪) As you round the coast to the north of Mu'a, keep an eye out for Tonga's famed fishing pigs. When the tide is out, these unusual porkers trot out into the shallows and snuffle around in search of seafood. The word is they taste saltier than their land-based brethren. Not something you see every day! There are more fishing pigs along Vuna Rd west of Nuku'alofa.

**★Ha'amonga 'a Maui Trilithon** ARCHAEOLOGICAL SITE
(Map p168; Taufa'ahau Rd, Niutoua; ⏲24hr) FREE The South Pacific's equivalent of Stonehenge, the Ha'amonga 'a Maui (Maui's Burden) trilithon near Niutoua is one of ancient Polynesia's most intriguing monuments. Archaeologists and oral history credit its construction to Tu'itatui, the 11th Tu'i Tonga. Others say it was built by ancient Chinese explorers. Either way, the structure consists of three large coralline stones, each weighing about 40 tonnes, arranged into a trilithic gate. Mortised joints ensure the top stone won't fall off, as per Stonehenge!

A walking track winds northward past several *langi* (tombs; known as the Langi Heketa), including **'Esi Makafakinanga**, supposedly Tu'itatui's backrest. Such chiefly backrests were common in Polynesia: apparently Tu'itatui used this one as a shield against attack from behind while he oversaw the trilithon's construction.

**'Anahulu Cave** CAVE
(Map p168; ☎23 363; www.anahulucave.to; off Liku Rd, Haveluliku; T$10; ⏲9am-4pm Mon-Sat) Tongatapu's most famous cave is an overloved, slightly eerie place full of stalactites and stalagmites, and blackened from the soot of flaming-frond torches and too much traffic. Inside is an underground freshwater pool where you can swim. The cave is managed by Teta Tours (p175): if there's no one from the company on site, the generator won't be working and you'll be venturing into the inky void (not advised).

## Western Tongatapu

**★Hufangalupe Archway** LANDMARK
(Map p168; off Liku Rd; ⏲daylight hours) Near nowhere in particular is this impressive arch, aka 'the pigeon's doorway' – a natural land bridge over the pounding Pacific waves, formed when the roof of a sea cave collapsed. Walk across the top and peer into the pit, then gaze west along the craggy coast. No fences – watch your step.

**★Mapu'a 'a Vaea Blowholes** LANDMARK
(Map p168; off Liku Rd, Houma; ⏲24hr) On an especially good day at Mapu'a 'a Vaea (Chief's Whistles), hundreds of blowholes spurt skywards at once. Time your visit for a windy day with a strong swell, when the surf, forced up through eroded vents in the coralline limestone, jets 30m into the air. The blow-

hole-riddled rocks stretch for 5km along the south coast, near the village of Houma.

**Triple-headed Coconut Tree** LANDMARK
(Map p168) If you think we must be scratching around for highlights to include a triple-headed coconut tree, then think again. Locals swear that this is the only coconut tree with three separate crowns in Tonga...some say in the whole South Pacific. Obligatory photo! The tree is on Loto Rd, just past Liahona.

**Flying Foxes** LANDMARK
(Map p168) While you'll get the opportunity to see flying foxes (aka fruit bats, or *peka*) in many places in Tonga, one spot renowned for their presence is the village of Kolovai, up near the western tip of the island. They cling to the trees upside down in their hundreds – if you haven't seen bats before, it's a mind-blowing scene.

**Abel Tasman Monument** HISTORIC SITE
(Map p168) At the northwestern tip of Tongatapu is a modest monument commemorating Dutchman Abel Tasman's 'discovery' of Tongatapu in 1643. He was on his way back to Batavia (present-day Jakarta) after firstly bumping into Tasmania, then New Zealand. With great European sensibility he named Tongatapu 'Amsterdam'.

**★Ha'atafu Beach** BEACH
(Map p168; ) On the sunset side of the island, Ha'atafu Beach is a sandy slice protected by a reef, where some of Tonga's best surf peels in (experienced surfers only need apply). There's sheltered swimming and snorkelling at high tide in the broad lagoon. If your timing is good (June to November), you can sometimes spy whales cavorting beyond the reef.

## Sleeping & Eating

### Western Tongatapu

There's a string of low-key (everything in Tonga is low-key) quasi-resorts facing onto Ha'atafu Beach in Tongatapu's northwest; the following are the pick of the bunch.

**Heilala Holiday Lodge** BUNGALOW **$$**
(Map p168; ☎41 600; www.heilala-holiday-lodge.com; Palm Ave, Ha'atafu Beach; s/d lodges T$78/98, s/d/tr bungalows from T$138/168/198, all incl breakfast; ) Photogenic thatched *fale* (sleeping three) are studded through tropical gardens at Heilala on fab Ha'atafu Beach. There's a restaurant for on-site dinners, or a communal kitchen if you'd rather DIY. Simple lodge rooms with shared bathrooms are a tad cheaper than the *fale*. Lots of free stuff (wi-fi, hammocks, snorkelling gear, bikes and books); airport pick-ups available. Nice one.

**Ha'atafu Beach Resort** BUNGALOW **$$**
(Map p168; ☎41 088; www.surfingtonga.com; off Hihifo Rd, Ha'atafu Beach; bungalows per adult/child from T$150/75; ) With a cosmic focus on surfing (owner Steve knows Tonga's waves backwards), this family-run set-up is laid-back and peaceful. Paths connect a range of thatched-roof *fale* to clean, shared facilities and the dining room (lots of organic stuff). Rates include breakfast and dinner. Free snorkelling gear,



### THE REPUBLIC OF MINERVA

The Minerva Reefs, Tonga's southernmost extremity, 350km southwest of Tongatapu, has long served as a rest point for yachts travelling between Tonga and New Zealand. Awash most of the time, it contains a safe anchorage in an almost perfect circle of reef, and has a colourful history. Tonga first claimed the unpopulated reef in 1972 after the Phoenix Foundation, founded by Las Vegas property developer Michael Oliver, tried to create the tax-free Republic of Minerva there, barging in tonnes of sand from Australia. Currency was even pressed, before the Tongan king himself sailed south to tear down the republic's flag.

More recently, yachties have been warned to keep away from Minerva after a fracas between neighbours Fiji and Tonga. In 2005 Fiji stated that it did not recognise Tonga's maritime water claims to the reefs, and filed a complaint with the International Seabed Authority. Tonga counterfiled in opposition. Then in 2010 and again in 2011, the Fijian Navy took potshots at navigation lights on the reefs, before their boats were chased away by Tongan patrol boats. The UN was called in to calm everybody down.

In a bid to resolve the dispute, in 2014 Tonga reportedly offered the Minerva Reefs to Fiji in exchange for the Lau Islands, with which many Tongans have an affinity. But at the time of writing the future of Minerva was as cloudy as ever: watch this space!

WORTH A TRIP

## DAY TRIPS TO TONGATAPU'S OFFSHORE ISLANDS

To the north of Tongatapu are a string of photoworthy islands that make for an interesting day trip (and a good way to fill a Sunday). All are only a short boat ride from Nuku'alofa. You can also visit some of these islands on a paddle tour with **Fatai Kayak Adventures** (p168).

**Pangaimotu** (Map p168; ☎771 5762; www.facebook.com/pangaimotu; day trip adult/child return incl lunch T$50/25; 👪) The closest island resort to Nuku'alofa, Pangaimotu makes an easy day trip. Daily departures (including Sunday) chug out from the wharf beside the Fish Market at 11am, returning at 4pm (Sundays departing hourly 10am to 1pm, returning 4pm, 5pm and 6pm). The trip takes about 10 minutes. There's a decent beach, a good restaurant and shipwreck snorkelling – bring the kids!

If you want to stay the night, Pangaimotu Island Resort has simple *fale* (doubles from T$100).

**Fafá** (Map p168; ☎22 800; www.fafaislandresort.com; day trip adult/child incl lunch T$92/46) Honeymooners, start your engines! Fronting onto a magnificent beach, Fafá Island Resort is the most elegant on Tongatapu's offshore islands, but it makes a great day trip from Nuku'alofa too. Day-trip boats to Fafá depart Faua Jetty at 11am and return at 4.30pm daily.

The resort's traditional-style *fale* are perfect in their simplicity, with wood-shingle roofs and walls of woven palm leaves. Accommodation starts at T$400 per double (extra person T$90, half/full board T$110/135).

**'Atata** (Map p168; ☎21 254; www.royalsunset.biz; day trip adult/child T$70/35) 'Atata, 10km from Tongatapu, has beaut beaches and a little island village to wander through. Snorkelling, diving and fishing are near-essential. There is a resort here, but day trips are the best bet for visitors, including lunch and a snorkelling trip. Boats leave Nuku'alofa wharf at 10am, returning 4pm (20 minutes; Sunday too!).

kayaks and rides into town if Steve is heading that way.

**Blue Banana Beach House** CABIN $$
(Map p168; ☎41 575; www.bluebananastudios.com; Ikalahi Rd, Ha'atafu Beach; d/q from T$170/350; 📶) Looking for a simple, fetching, self-contained studio nested into the trees on the shore, all to yourself? The beautifully decorated Blue Banana *fale* provide the beauty of an offshore island with the convenience of the Tongatapu mainland. Great for snorkellers and self-caterers: catch the bus into Nuku'alofa and stock up.

**Holty's Hideaway** LODGE $$$
(Map p168; ☎41 720; www.holtyshideaway.com; off Hihifo Rd, Ha'atafu Beach; d/f from T$350/400, extra person T$80; 📶🏊) Run by an expat Australian couple, Holty's is a simple, laid-back alternative to the resorts along Ha'atafu Beach. Book the large house (sleeping 10) or one of three *fale* (sleeping up to four). Great for groups of friends or families. There's also a cafe for weekend lunch, and surfboards and kayaks so you can paddle around at the beach.

# 'EUA

POP 5000 / AREA 87 SQ KM

Rugged 'Eua (pronounced 'a-wah'), 40km southeast of Tongatapu, is an unassuming slice of natural paradise. Known as 'the forgotten island', it's geologically the oldest island in Tonga (40 million years old!) and one of the oldest in the Pacific. There are steep hilly areas, cliff-top lookouts, hidden caves, sinkholes, a limestone arch and junglelike rainforest to explore. With its own species of plants, trees and the endemic *koki* (red shining parrot), 'Eua has a growing awareness of itself as a unique ecotourism destination.

'Eua's history is fascinating. In times past 'Euans had a reputation as the fiercest warriors in Tonga. Their sparsely populated island also became a haven for migrants moved from other islands. In 1860, when King Tupou I heard that European ships were capturing Tongans at the remote southern island of 'Ata for use as slaves, he resettled the island's entire population to 'Eua for their own protection. In 1946, after a nasty volcanic eruption at Niuafo'ou in the Niua Group, Queen Salote moved that island's population to 'Eua also.

## Sights & Activities

Activities on 'Eua are best booked via your guesthouse. Discuss what you want to do and everything will be arranged for you. 'Eua is the second-largest island in Tonga, and while fairly easy to navigate – just one long main road with a string of little villages along it – there's no public transport and distances are deceiving. Hideaway runs **4WD tours** to parts of 'Eua that are virtually inaccessible any other way. It's a great way to get the lay of the land: cliffs, forests, lookouts, beaches, rockpools...

For a cultural encounter, Hideaway also offers the chance for guests (and nonguests) to participate in community-orientated experiences such as **kava ceremonies** and **basket weaving** in the local village, as well as church visits and *umu* feasts on Sunday.

'Eua has some great **hiking** trails, particularly in **'Eua National Park** in the 'mountains' along the island's eastern coast. There are a number of options so discuss things with your hosts, get a map and organise a ride to the trailhead. Better yet, hire a guide for the day.

'Eua has some of the best **diving** in Tonga – its huge **Cathedral Cave** is becoming legendary. Book through your guesthouse. **Deep Blue Diving** (Map p170; ☎27 676; www.deepbluediving.to; Faua Jetty; snorkelling/diving from T$90/180), based in Nuku'alofa, also offers diving from its 'Eua base at Ovava Tree Lodge.

On the wildlife front, 'Eua is home to cacophonous **birds**, the star of which is the *koki* (red shining parrot). Others include *ngongo* (noddies), white-tailed *tavake* (tropic birds) and *pekapeka-tae* (swiftlets). The *peka* (fruit bat) also hangs around here (upside down in the trees). **Whales** come in very close to 'Eua. There are both whale-watching and whale-swim tours on offer between June and October, but it's very difficult to ensure that these are not intrusive or stressful experiences for the whales. Disruption to feeding, resting, nursing and other behaviour may have a long-term impact on populations.

## Sleeping & Eating

Accommodation on 'Eua is budget all the way, baby. There aren't any restaurants, so the only place for visitors to eat is at their accommodation, where cooked meals are available daily (lunch and dinner mains are around T$15 to T$30).

★ **Hideaway** GUESTHOUSE $
(☎50 255; www.hideawayeuatonga.com; West Coast Rd; s/d/tr incl breakfast T$65/95/120; wi-fi) Hideaway is a chilled-out, sound-of-the-surf kinda joint with two rickety rows of rooms, a breezy bar-restaurant and a viewing platform out over the rocky shore (good sunsets and whale spotting). Rooms have bathrooms and slow-spinning fans (no air-con). Optional tours (4WD, hiking, horse riding, cultural encounters etc) can be booked on the spot. Rates include continental breakfast and transfers.

**Ovava Tree Lodge** BUNGALOW $
(☎871 4536 22 840; www.deeplodge.to; Ohonua Village; bungalows s/d T$50/80, extra person T$15, all incl breakfast; wi-fi) Across the road from the ferry wharf, sociable Ovava is 'Eua's new kid on the block, with six handsome wood-and-iron en-suite cabins set in lush gardens. There's a pizza oven in the restaurant-bar, and plenty of diving and snorkelling trips on offer. Airport transfers T$20.

**Taina's Place** GUESTHOUSE $
(☎776 5002; www.tainasplace.com; Main Rd; camping per person T$20, cabins s/d/f T$45/60/110; wi-fi) A little way inland near the forest, the cute red-and-white cabins at family-run Taina's revolve around trim gardens and a communal kitchen and bathrooms. There are tours aplenty, plus bike hire and a disco (!) on Friday and Saturday nights. Breakfast is T$15; wharf/airport transfers are T$12/8 return.

## Information

### MONEY

There is a Westpac bank near the ferry terminal on 'Eua, plus a Western Union and a couple of other money-transfer agencies, but opening hours are sporadic. Bring cash and a credit card.

### TELEPHONE

There is mobile coverage in the villages but it's patchy on the hiking trails.

### TOURIST INFORMATION

Bone-up on 'Eua info at Nuku'alofa Visitor Information Centre (p175) before you go, and have a look at www.eua-island-tonga.com.

## Getting There & Around

### AIR

Real Tonga makes the 10-minute hop from Tongatapu, reputedly the world's shortest scheduled commercial flight (don't fall asleep), at least once daily Monday to Saturday (one way T$96).

### TOP TONGAN TRAVEL TIPS

- Patience is a virtue: in Tonga, time is a flexible entity! Slow down and chill out.
- Respectful dress is important to Tongans: Tongan law prohibits being in a public place without a shirt (avoid singlets too), and wear long pants to church.
- Swimsuits should be worn only at resorts. Tongans swim fully dressed.
- 'Keeping face' is extremely important in Tonga. If things don't meet your expectations, don't escalate the situation by waving and shouting about it.
- Tonga closes down on Sundays: plan ahead accordingly.
- Double- and triple-check your ferry and Real Tonga flight schedules – things change!

#### BOAT

It's a 2½-hour ferry trip (p205) between Tongatapu and 'Eua.

#### CAR & BICYCLE

Accommodation hosts will pick you up at the wharf or airport; there's no car hire on the island. You can hire a bike at Hideaway (T$30 per day) if the local guy who owns them isn't in the midst of a maintenance program.

# HA'APAI GROUP

POP 8200 / AREA 110 SQ KM

Isolated, thinly populated and untrammelled, the 62 Ha'apai islands – 45 of which are uninhabited – sprinkle themselves across the kingdom's central waters. Ha'apai appears on the horizon like a South Seas idyll: palm-fringed isles, vibrant reefs, breaching whales, deserted white beaches and even a couple of massive volcanoes.

That said, your initial arrival on Ha'apai may be a bit of a surprise, whether you arrive by plane or ferry. Simply put, there isn't much here, especially in the wake of category five Tropical Cyclone Ian, which lacerated the islands in 2014. If you were trying to get away from it all, pat yourself on the back – you've succeeded!

Online, have a look at www.haapai.to.

## History

Archaeological excavations in southern Lifuka island reveal settlement dating back more than 3000 years.

The first European to turn up was Abel Tasman in 1643. He stopped for supplies at Nomuka and called the island 'Rotterdam' (feeling homesick that day?). Later, several notable events in Tongan history took place in Ha'apai. Captain Cook narrowly avoided the cooking pot in 1777; the mutiny on the *Bounty* occurred just offshore from Tofua in 1789; and the *Port-au-Prince,* with William Mariner (p185) aboard, was ransacked in 1806.

In 1831 Ha'apai was the first island group in Tonga to be converted to Christianity, following the baptism of its ruler Taufa'ahau. He took the name of Siaosi (George) after the king of England, and adopted the surname of Tupou. His wife was baptised Salote after Queen Charlotte. As King George Tupou I he united Tonga and established the royal line that continues through to the present day. Nuku'alofa's main street, Taufa'ahau Rd, is named after him.

## Getting There & Away

#### AIR

Ha'apai's Pilolevu Airport is 3km north of Pangai on Lifuka. The island's main north–south road passes right through the middle of the runway, meaning that the road is closed when aircraft are arriving or departing.

Real Tonga flies daily (except Sunday) between Ha'apai and Tongatapu, and three or four times a week between Ha'apai and Vava'u.

#### BOAT

MV *'Otuanga'ofa,* operated by Friendly Islands Shipping Company, stops weekly at Pangai on both its northbound and southbound runs between Tongatapu and Vava'u.

There are protected anchorages along the lee shores of Lifuka, Foa, Ha'ano and Uoleva.

## Getting Around

#### TO/FROM THE AIRPORT & WHARF

Organise tranport to your accommodation with your hosts, most of whom will pick you up at the airport or Pangai wharf. Taxis charge T$10 between the airport and Pangai.

#### BICYCLE

Lifuka and Foa are flat – a bicycle is the perfect way to explore. Mariner's Cafe (p183) rents out bikes for T$20 per day. Guests can use the bikes at Sandy Beach Resort (p184) and Matafonua Lodge (p184).

#### BOAT

The Pangai Visitor Information Centre (p183) may have some info on arranging boat transport

## Ha'apai Group

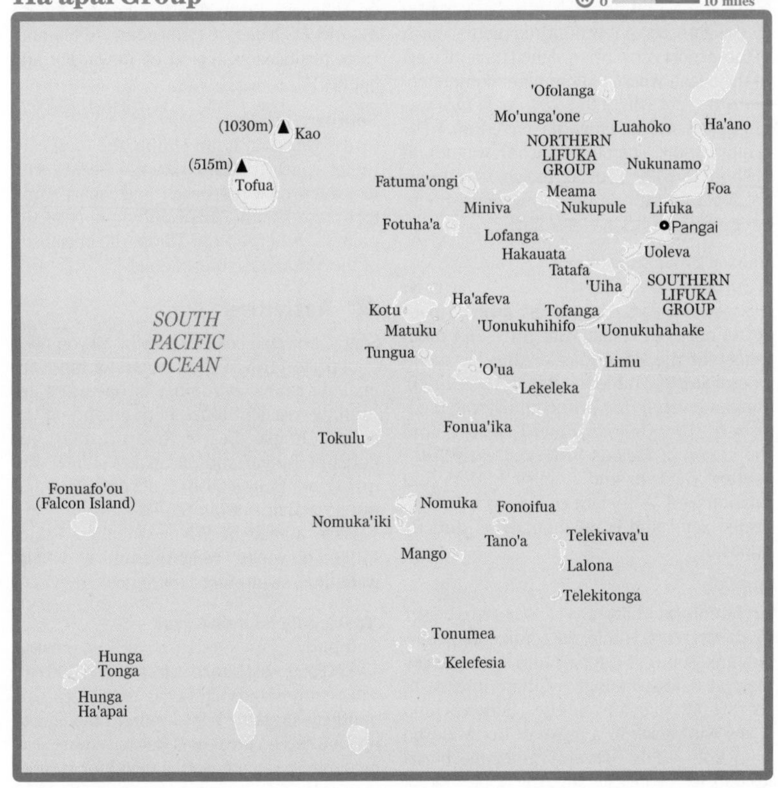


around the Ha'apai group...or they might just send you to Mariner's Cafe!

#### TAXI

There are a couple of taxis based on Lifuka: book through Mariner's Cafe or your accommodation.

## Lifuka Group

Most visitors to Ha'apai stay within the low-lying Lifuka Group of islands along the eastern barrier reef of Ha'apai. The airport, main ferry wharf and almost all of Ha'apai's accommodation and services are located here – with most of the action for visitors based on Lifuka, Foa and Uoleva islands.

It will take some serious planning, determination and rigour to get out to the remote Ha'apai islands, most of which are uninhabited: drop us a line and tell us about it if you do!

### Lifuka

Pangai, Lifuka's main town, has basic services and a cool cafe, but struggles to be described as attractive, particularly with wreckage and rooflessness wrought by 2014's Tropical Cyclone Ian still littered around everywhere. The eastern side of the island is wild and windy; the western side is calm and protected. On hot afternoons the Pangai wharf is a mass of cooling-down kids, splashing around in the brine.

#### Sights

The best way to get around the Lifuka island sights is by bicycle. The 14km (one way) ride to **Houmale'eia Beach** at the northern tip of Foa island is a good option.

**Port-au-Prince Massacre Monument** MONUMENT

(daylight hours) A few hundred metres north of the airport runway is a signed turn-off west to the beach where a monument commemorates the spot where the *Port-au-Prince* was ransacked and its crew massacred on 1 December 1806. The ship's anchor was found offshore in 2009; some of the ship's cannons are lined up outside the former British embassy on Vuna Rd in Nuku'alofa.

**Shirley Baker Monument & European Cemetery** CEMETERY

(Holopeka Rd, Pangai; daylight hours) About 800m north of Pangai, the grave and monument of the imperious-looking Reverend Doctor Shirley Waldemar Baker (1836–1903), Tonga's revered first prime minister and adviser to King George Tupou I, stands amid the graves of various 19th- and early-20th-century German and English traders and missionaries. A Tongan cemetery, with decorated sand and coral mounds, is directly opposite.

**Hihifo's Archaeological Sites** ARCHAEOLOGICAL SITE

(daylight hours) Hihifo, the contiguous suburban area south of Pangai, hides some archaeological relics seemingly of more interest to rooting pigs than anyone else. Hidden behind a low wire fence in a grove of ironwood on Loto Kolo Rd is **Olovehi Tomb**, the burial ground for people holding the noble title of Tuita.

Turn east at the Free Wesleyan Church on Holopeka Rd to find the circular **Velata Mound Fortress**, a 15th-century ditch-and-ridge fortification, typical of Tonga, Fiji and Samoa.

**Southern Lifuka** AREA

(daylight hours) From Hihifo, the road continues south to **Hulu'ipaongo Point**, with its sweep of white beach and views south to Uoleva island. About 200m short of the point is **Hulu'ipaongo Tomb**, the burial site of the Mata'uvave line of chiefs.

## Activities

Sandy, deserted beaches may be all you need for a perfect trip to Ha'apai, but for more animated visitors, a number of operators are running excellent tours, both on and off the water. Ha'apai Beach Resort (p183) just north of Pangai and Ha'apai Whale & Sail (p184) on Uoleva also run boat trips and watery activities from Lifuka.

Have a read of Whale-Watching Ethics (p193) if you're weighing up a whale-watching/-swimming experience.

★ **Friendly Islands Kayak Company** KAYAKING

(874 8506; www.fikco.com; trips from T$1100; ) Friendly Islands Kayak Co runs all-inclusive, multiday kayaking trips around Lifuka: sign up for a seven-, nine- or 11-day adventure. The moderate seven-day option (good for families with older kids) includes accommodation and

### FONUAFO'OU: NOW YOU SEE IT, NOW YOU DON'T

The Ha'apai group is home to Tonga's mysterious disappearing island, Fonuafo'ou. From 1781 to 1865 there were repeated reports of a shoal 72km northwest of Tongatapu and 60km west of Nomuka in the south of the Ha'apai group. An island was confirmed by the HMS *Falcon* in 1865 and given the name Falcon Island. In 1885 the island was 50m high and 2km long. Amid great excitement, Tonga planted its flag and claimed it as Fonuafo'ou, meaning 'New Land'.

Then in 1894 Fonuafo'ou went missing! Two years later it reappeared at 320m high before disappearing again. In 1927 it reemerged and in 1930 was measured at 130m high and 2.5km long! By 1949 there was again no trace of Fonuafo'ou, which had once more been eroded by the sea. Fonuafo'ou came back again, but at last report this geographical freak had once more submerged.

The island is a submarine volcano that alternates between building itself up above sea level and being eroded down below it. At present, its summit elevation is estimated at 17m below sea level. If the 'New Land' does come back, your best chance of spotting it is if you are on a yacht.

In early 2015 volcanic hubbub 65km northwest of Nuku'alofa created another new black-ash island, 2km long by 1km wide. Tongan officials have decided not to name it (yet), with the expectation that, like Fonuafo'ou, the South Pacific surf will soon reclaim it. What the sea wants, the sea shall have...

meals at Serenity Beaches Resort (p185) on Uoleva island; all the trips include snorkelling, a bit of hiking and plenty of beach time. Also runs trips in Vava'u (p188).

**Whale Discoveries** BOAT TOUR
(☎873 7676; www.whalediscoveries.com; day trips from T$200) Excellent snorkelling day tours with lots of time in the water, some beach and bush walking, birdwatching, picnicking and Tongan cultural insights. Multiday live-aboard sailing trips and whale-watching/-swimming trips also available.

## Sleeping

**Fifita Guesthouse** GUESTHOUSE $
(☎731 8159, 60 213; www.tongaholiday.com/listing/fifita-guesthouse; Fau Rd, Pangai; s & d from T$70, s/d without bathroom from T$40/55, all incl breakfast) Morphing into the building upstairs/behind Mariner's Cafe and just a short walk from the wharf, red-and-white Fifita's remains a popular choice. It's rudimentary but friendly and clean enough, with back-and-forth travel banter flying around the communal kitchen. Rates include breakfast (or go downstairs to the cafe).

**Lindsay Guesthouse** GUESTHOUSE $
(☎888 3531; www.tongaholiday.com/listing/lindsay-guesthouse; cnr Loto Kolo & Tuita Rds, Pangai; s/d/f T$60/60/75) A clean and friendly spot walking distance to downtown Pangai, with a broad verandah and communal sitting room and kitchen. Beds are distributed through sundry basic rooms: ask for a private one if you're not into dorm life. Breakfast is T$10. The scent of baking bread wafts across the lawn from the Matuku-ae-tau Bakery next door.

**Ha'apai Beach Resort** BUNGALOW $$
(☎60 051; www.haapaibeachresort.com; Holopeka Rd, Lifuka; d T$190, s without bathroom T$85; 📶) Halfway between the airport and Pangai (about 1.5km from each), Ha'apai Beach Resort is chilled-out enclave of blue-and-white cabins on a grassy verge above the sand. Snorkelling, diving, kayaking, island trips, free wi-fi...it's all on offer. Head to the bar for a big TV and big breakfasts. Love the vintage *Mutiny on the Bounty* poster!

## Eating

There's an informal market on the Pangai waterfront and a few shops with limited food supplies around town, but it would be a stretch to call them supermarkets. Plan ahead accordingly.

**Matuku-ae-tau Bakery** BAKERY $
(cnr Loto Kolo & Tuita Rds, Pangai; items from T$1; ⏲8am-5pm Mon-Sat, 5-8pm Sun) This basic bakery has two ovens to keep the island in bread, jam-filled rolls and *keki* (similar to doughnuts). There's a mad rush on Sunday afternoon.

★**Mariner's Cafe** CAFE $$
(☎60 374; www.tongaholiday.com/listing/mariners-cafe; Fau Rd, Pangai; mains $10-20; ⏲9am-late Mon-Sat, 6-9pm Sun; 📶) Pangai's prime dining option, cheery Mariner's is just off the main street. The menu, chalked up on little blackboards, features burgers, soups, stews and pastas, served to a soundtrack of Bryan Adams or Robbie Williams. Sit down with a beer or an iced coffee and soak up some local knowledge before heading on your adventures. Wi-fi is T$6 per hour.

## Information

Tap water in Ha'apai is only fit for washing clothes and getting the sand off your bod. Drink bottled or rain water.

For money exchange and credit-card advances, there's a Western Union branch next to the visitor centre, and a Westpac bank branch on Holopeka Rd. There are no ATMs in Ha'apai (bring cash).

**Niu'ui Hospital** (☎60 201; Holopeka Rd, Hihifo; ⏲24hr) Basic facilities and a pharmacy; for emergencies only.

**Pangai Visitor Information Centre** (☎60 733; www.thekingdomoftonga.com; Holopeka Rd, Pangai; ⏲8.30am-4.30pm Mon-Fri, to 12.30pm Sat) Can assist with accommodation bookings, boat transport and directions (does it have a Pangai town map yet?). Next to the Western Union office.

## Foa

To the north of Lifuka and connected by a wind-buffeted concrete causeway you can cycle over, Foa is a heavily wooded island. **Houmale'eia Beach**, on the western side of the northern tip, is the best beach on the Ha'apai 'mainland', with coral close to the shore, sublime views of Nukunamo and terrific snorkelling (or just a sunny patch of sand on which to sit and do nothing). On the eastern side of the northern tip, there are some ancient **petroglyphs** carved into a rocky ledge just offshore (only visible at low tide). Ask the bar staff at Matafonua Lodge to point you in the right direction.

## Sleeping

**★Matafonua Lodge** BUNGALOW $$$
(☎69 766; www.matafonua.com; Faleloa, Foa; s & d bungalows T$210, extra adult/child T$60/30, all incl breakfast; 📶) Right on the sandy northern tip of Foa, gazing across at Nukunamo island, family-friendly Matafonua was hammered by Tropical Cyclone Ian in 2014 but has been fully resurrected. Lovely water-view *fale* are totally comfortable, with freshwater showers in well-designed shared bathrooms. There's also an all-day cafe-bar, lagoon swimming and snorkelling, kayaks, bicycles and cultural tours to Ha'ano island.

**★Sandy Beach Resort** RESORT $$$
(☎69 600; www.sandybeach-tonga.com; Faleloa, Foa; s & d per person incl breakfast & dinner T$540; 📶) Arguably Tonga's best resort, Sandy Beach really delivers (this is where the king stays when he's in Ha'apai). A row of elegant bungalows are oriented for sunset views over the sublime white-sand Houmale'eia Beach. The resort can organise activities daily, bookended by breakfast and dinner in its excellent restaurant. A library and open-air bar complete the experience. Paradise found.

## Getting There & Around

If you're staying at either of the sleeping options, the operators will arrange to get you there. By bicycle from Pangai it takes around one hour; the taxi fare is about T$35.

# Nukunamo

The small picture-postcard island you can see from the tip of Foa is Nukunamo, an uninhabited isle with a shining white beach littered with beautiful shells. You can kayak to Nukunamo across the channel from Foa, but don't try and swim over – the current ripping through here is truly powerful. If you're staying at Matafonua Lodge or Sandy Beach Resort, they have kayaks you can use.

# Ha'ano

Travellers will get a dose of traditional Tongan life on the strikingly clean and friendly island of Ha'ano that lies to the north of Foa and Nukunamo.

Ask at Matafonua Lodge about occasional **cultural day tours** here, working in unison with the Ha'ano Women's Group. Trips include boat transfers, a school visit, a kava ceremony, handicraft demonstrations, a Tongan feast, some snorkelling and transport in a horse and cart around the island (there are only two cars on Ha'ano!).

# Uoleva

Robbed a bank? On the run from tax-evasion allegations back home? The island of Uoleva, just south of Lifuka, is the perfect place to hide. Uninhabited apart from the accommodation providers (there are no villages here), it offers up an uncluttered, unharried South Pacific experience with little to do other than swim, snorkel, fish, read and relax (and figure out your escape route if the cops do come knocking). Whales swim close to the shore here during the migration season (June to October) – you can sometimes see them breaching just offshore.

## Activities

Activity operators based on Lifuka will pick you up here if you're booked on one of their tours. See also Fanifo Lofa Kitesurf Tonga.

**Ha'apai Whale & Sail** SAILING
(☎888 5800; www.uoleva.com; trips per half-/full day from T$70/155) Let the breeze sail you out into the day with Ha'apai Whale & Sail, based on Uoleva (it can also pick you up from Lifuka). Island-hopping and snorkelling are the names of the games. Whale-watching/-swimming trips are also available: have a read of Whale-Watching Ethics (p193) before you book.

## Sleeping & Eating

There are no shops or restaurants on Uoleva – BYO food or eat at your accommodation.

**Taiana's Resort** BUNGALOW $
(☎883 1722; www.tongaholiday.com/listing/tiannas-resort; Uoleva; bungalows s/d/f T$35/45/75, breakfast/dinner T$10/15) Ponder the stars and lapping west-coast waves at this budget beach-bum paradise. Simple tapa-lined *fale* have mats over sandy floors, comfy beds, mosquito nets, enclosed sitting areas, hammocks...and the sea is just 50m away! Homespun cooking completes the package (or you can BYO food if you like). Transfers from Pangai are T$30 one way.

**Talitali'anga Eco Resort** SAFARI TENT $$
(☎868 5800; www.talitalianga.com; Uoleva; d T$185) 🍃 About halfway down Uoleva's becalmed west coast, this outfit comprises just two private, elevated safari tents, each with a bathroom (self-composting toilets), deck

## WILLIAM MARINER

Thanks to a series of serendipitous events, the world has an extensive account of the customs, language, religion and politics of pre-Christian Tonga.

In 1805 15-year-old William Mariner went to sea on the privateer *Port-au-Prince*. The voyage took the ship across the Atlantic, around Cape Horn, up the west coast of South America, to the Sandwich (Hawaiian) Islands and finally into Tonga's Ha'apai Group. The crew anchored at the northern end of Lifuka and was immediately welcomed with yams and barbecued pork. The reception seemed friendly enough, but on 1 December 1806 an attack was launched, the crew murdered and the ship burned to the waterline.

Young Mariner, however, dressed in uniform, was captured and escorted ashore. Finau 'Ulukalala I, the reigning chief of Ha'apai, seeing the well-dressed young man, assumed that Mariner was the captain's son and ordered that his life be spared.

Mariner was taken under the wing of Finau and became privy to most of the goings-on in Tongan politics over the following four years. He learned the language well and travelled with the chief, observing and absorbing the finer points of Tongan ceremony and protocol.

After the death of Finau, the king's son permitted Mariner to leave Tonga on a passing English vessel. Back in England, an amateur anthropologist, Dr John Martin, was fascinated with Mariner's tale and suggested collaboration on a book. The result, *An Account of the Natives of the Tonga Islands,* is a masterpiece of Pacific literature.

The Port-au-Prince Massacre Monument (p182) is just north of the airport, near to where the wreck of the *Port-au-Prince* was found in 2012.

and sunset views as far as Foa. Drinks and meals at the sandy-floor bar (not included in accommodation prices); transfers from Pangai per person $T35 one way. And there's a resident turtle in the lagoon!

**Serenity Beaches Resort** BUNGALOW **$$$**
(☎873 4934; www.serenitybeaches.com; Uoleva; bungalow d with/without bathroom T$330/190, half/full board T$75/100; wifi) At the southern end of Uoleva, Serenity Beaches features beautifully constructed octagonal *fale* on both sides of the island. Food utilises fresh local ingredients (vegetarians rejoice!). There are free kayaks and snorkelling gear to entice you into the sea. Transfers from Pangai cost T$50 per person one way. If you've got the loot, stay here.

**Fanifo Lofa Kitesurf Tonga** BUNGALOW **$$$**
(☎845 8188; www.kitesurftonga.com; Uoleva; bungalows per person incl meals T$140; wifi) On the northern end of Uoleva, Fanifo Lofa is geared towards kitesurfers, but anyone can stay here regardless of whether they're prone to flying across the ocean waves or not. Elevated timber *fale* are solar-powered and supercomfortable. Rates include all meals and transfers, use of kayaks and stand-up paddle boards, and transport to kitesurfing hot spots (BYO equipment).

### 'Uiha

The conservative, traditional island of 'Uiha, to the south of Uoleva, is a friendly place with two little villages: 'Uiha, with a wharf, and Felemea, about 1.5km south.

In the centre of 'Uiha village is a large, elevated burial ground containing several **royal tombs**, once the official burial ground of the Tongan royal family until they moved to Nuku'alofa. At the village church are two **cannons**, souvenirs taken from a Peruvian blackbirding (slaving) ship that was attacked and destroyed by the locals in 1863.

A day trip to the island is good fun. Talk to the Pangai Visitor Information Centre (p183) about boat transport, or see if the folks at Ha'apai Beach Resort (p183) will ship you here.

## VAVA'U GROUP

POP 18,000 / AREA 119 SQ KM

Shaped like a giant jellyfish with its tentacles dangling south, gorgeous Vava'u (va-vuh-ooh) is a photo opportunity at every turn. Those tentacles comprise myriad islands (61 of them!) intertwined with turquoise waterways and encircling reefs – one of the most famed sheltered yachting grounds on the planet.

To really experience it, get out onto the water. Vava'u has it all: charter sailing, sea kayaking, game fishing, surfing, diving and swimming with whales are the names of the games. Bunk down in town or head out to one of the islands for a remote tropical stay.

Vava'u plays host to around 500 visiting yachts each year, mainly during the May-to-October season as trans-Pacific yachts blow through heading west. Port of Refuge is one of the safest harbours in the South Pacific, attracting more than its share of yachts during cyclone season (November to April).

Online, have a look at www.vavau.to.

## History

Vava'u is believed to have been settled for around 2000 years. The capital, Neiafu, looks out onto Port of Refuge, christened by Spaniard Don Francisco Antonio Mourelle, who sighted Vava'u on 4 March 1781 en route from Manila to Mexico. Mourelle claimed the new-found paradise, one of the last South Pacific island groups to be contacted by Europeans, for mother Spain. Captain Cook missed it a decade earlier when the Ha'apai islanders convinced him that there were no safe anchorages north of Ha'apai (ha-ha, Ha'apai).

William Mariner spent time here during Finau 'Ulukala I of Ha'apai's conquest of Vava'u in 1808. Later, on the death of 'Ulukala III, King George Tupou I added Vava'u to his realm when he formed a united Tonga in 1845.

## Getting There & Away

### AIR

Lupepau'u Airport is a 15-minute drive north of Neiafu.

**Real Tonga** (Map p191; ☎71 115; www.realtonga.to; Tu'i Rd; ⏲8.30am-5pm Mon-Fri, 9am-1pm Sat) has a local office (domestic flights).

### BOAT

The Friendly Islands Shipping Company runs long-haul ferries between Vava'u and Tongatapu, Ha'apai and occasionaily the Niua Group.

## Getting Around

### TO/FROM THE AIRPORT

Some accommodation, including island resorts, offers airport transfers for a price (from around T$15). Taxis charge T$30 for the airport–Neiafu trip.

### BICYCLE

Vava'u is hilly but fairly manageable by bicycle. Café Tropicana (p190) in Neiafu rents out decent bikes with helmets from $15 per day.

### BUS

Buses run from central stops on Tu'i Rd and Fatafehi Rd in Neiafu to most parts of Vava'u and its connected islands, leaving when full. They usually make the run into town in the morning and return in the afternoon, so they're not much good for day trips from town. Most fares are under T$2.

### CAR

Rental cars are available in Neiafu. A Tongan visitor's driver's licence is probably prudent (T$40 from the police station) but operators may turn a blind eye if you don't have one. Don't park under coconut trees, and watch out for the usual maelstrom of kids, pigs, chickens and dogs throwing themselves into the road.

**Coconut Car Rentals** (☎755 6667; www.coconutcarrental.net) has a couple of small cars and a big Nissan pickup truck for rent, both from T$60 per day. Pick up and delivery anywhere in Neiafu.

### TAXI

Taxis charge T$5 to T$10 around Neiafu, and T$30 to the airport, 'Ano and Hinakauea Beaches. You'll usually find one parked along Fatafehi Rd, across from the Westpac bank.

# Neiafu

POP 6000

Strung around the fringes of Port of Refuge, surely one of the world's most photogenic harbours, Neiafu has a dishevelled charm. Home to a slew of decent restaurants and bars along the waterfront, the town itself is ramshackle and rakish (a great place to drink rum and write a novel). Over winter (June to October), with visiting yachties and a steady flow of visitors winging in, the ol' town buzzes with accents and activity.

## Sights

**★St Joseph's Cathedral** CATHEDRAL

(Map p191; Fatafehi Rd; free; ⏲daylight hours) A vision of colonial piety above Port of Refuge, St Joe's is Neiafu's defining piece of archiecture. Inside, the hypercoloured crucifixion scene behind the altar is something to behold. The stretch of Fatafehi Rd below the cathedral is called **Hala Lupe** (Way of Doves), named for the mournful singing of the female prisoners (convicted adulterers) who constructed it.

OFF THE BEATEN TRACK

## TOFUA & KAO

About 70km west of Lifuka are pyramidal Kao (1030m) and its smoking partner, Tofua (515m). On a good day this uninhabited pair is clearly visible from Lifuka.

Tofua is a flat-topped volcanic island that, like Niuafo'ou in the Niua Group, looks not unlike a huge floating life ring when viewed from above. It started life as a classic cone-shaped volcano but the top blew off in a violent eruption, creating a caldera, in the middle of which is a freshwater lake 38m above sea level. The crater rim is a tough one-hour climb from the Hokala landing site on the northern side of the island.

Adding to Tofua's intrigue, champion Swiss snowboarder Xavier Rosset decided to play modern-day Robinson Crusoe here in 2008 and spent 10 months on the island in survival mode. He took a satellite phone and blogged about his adventures – have a look online at www.xavierrosset.ch.

The four-hour hike up uninhabited Kao, a perfect volcanic cone 4km north of Tofua, is not recommended without a guide. The summit is the highest point in Tonga, but there is no marked track and the vegetation closes in around you in a green tropical embrace.

Unless you're on a yacht, reaching Tofua and Kao is not easy. Talk to the Pangai Visitor Information Centre (p183) or the boat-tour operators around Lifuka if you're keen. It should be considered a major expedition, not a day trip: taking along a local guide is a smart move.

**Mt Talau National Park** MOUNTAIN
(Map p188; off Tapueluefu Rd; ⏲daylight hours) FREE A flat-topped mountain looming behind Port of Refuge, 131m Mt Talau (Mo'unga Talau) is protected as part of Mt Talau National Park. To check it out, from the centre of Neiafu truck west along Tapueluefu Rd for around 2km, where the road narrows into a bush track to the summit. Keep an eye out for flying foxes, the Tongan whistler and the *fokai* (banded lizard) en route.

**Old Harbour** HARBOUR
(Map p191; off Naufahu Rd; ⏲24hr) Head north on Tokongahahau Rd from the cathedral then turn east onto Naufahu Rd and you'll reach the low-key Old Harbour. It's much less developed than the main harbour over the hill: just a few houses, strings of *tapa* drying in the wind and the launch pad for boats to some of Vava'u's eastern islands.

## Activities

### Sailing

Vava'u is a world-famous yachtie hang-out. Charter a yacht, either bareboat or skippered, and cruise around the islands, stopping to snorkel and explore beaches as the mood strikes you (not a bad life).

**Moorings** BOATING
(Map p191; ☎70 016; www.tongasailing.com; waterfront, off Fatafehi Rd) Charters out catamarans and monohulls, sleeping up to 10 South Seas rapscallions. Prices vary with the seasons. Check the website for details, plus a handy Crusing Guide, maps and downloadable yachting info.

**Melinda Sea Adventures** BOATING
(Map p191; ☎889 7586; www.sailtonga.com; waterfront, off Fatafehi Rd) Fully crewed, full-day sailing trips on a luxury yacht, or three-night all-inclusive sailing experiences (beds, meals, skipper and cook). Rates depend on the season and number of passengers; check the website.

**Vava'u Yacht Club** BOATING
(Map p191; ☎70 650, 70 016; Mango Cafe, waterfront, off Fatafehe Rd; ⏲Fri Jun-Nov) On a balmy Friday afternoon, you can't beat knocking back some beers as the yachts race around Port of Refuge. If you want to crew, turn up at the Mango Cafe (p192), where the skippers meet around 4pm (5pm race start). Tons of fun at the bar, whether you're racing or not.

### Diving

Vava'u's dive sites range from hard and soft coral gardens to barnacle-encrusted wrecks and vast sea caves – plenty of options for all levels and abilities. Most dive operators also offer whale-swim and snorkelling tours.

**Beluga Diving** DIVING
(Map p191; ☎70 327; www.belugadivingvavau.com; waterfront, off Fatafehi Rd; snorkelling/diving trips from T$200/350) With 25 years' experience, Beluga knows a thing or two about Tonga's undersea terrain. Diving, snorkelling, whale-watching and PADI dive courses available, plus occasional camping trips.

## Vava'u Group

**Dolphin Pacific Diving** DIVING
(Map p191; ☎70 292; www.dolphinpacificdiving.com; waterfront, off Fatafehi Rd; full-day snorkelling/diving trips from T$330/220) Dolphin Pacific prides itself on being a relaxed, friendly operation. Down on the waterfront near the white-elephant Puataukanave Hotel.

### Fishing

If you're keen to bag a marlin, tuna or sailfish (then let it go), Vava'u is one of the best game-fishing destinations in the Pacific (more than 1km deep not far offshore).

**Hakula Sport Fishing Charters** FISHING
(Map p188; ☎70 872; www.fishtonga.com; full-day trips per 4 people from T$2000) Fishing trips for experienced anglers on the MV *Hakula*. Operates out of Hakula Lodge (p190).

**Poppin' Tonga** FISHING
(☎873 3347, 71 075; www.talihaubeach.com; half-/full day per 3 people incl equipment T$600/1000) Operating out of Lucky's Beach Houses (p194), and specialising in hooking giant trevally (catch-and-release), either from land or boat.

### Water Sports

Island resorts and beachside accommodation operators around Vava'u often provide kayaks for guest use. There are some remote reef surf breaks here, for expereinced wave hounds.

**Friendly Islands Kayak Company** KAYAKING
(Map p188; ☎874 8506; www.fikco.com; 👪) 🍃 These ecofriendly paddlers run magical three- to 10-day kayaking expeditions around Vava'u (and Ha'apai, p182) with knowledgeable local guides. Expect plenty of snorkelling, beachcombing and village-visit action, with myriad add-on options (whale watching, mountain biking, diving...). Accommodation can be either camping out or sleeping under more rigid roofs; check the website for options.

## Vava'u Group

**Top Sights**

1 Mariner's Cave....B4
2 Swallows' Cave....C3

**Sights**

3 'Ano & Hinakauea Beaches....D4
4 Ark Gallery Vava'u....D4
5 'Ene'io Botanical Garden....F2
6 Mt Talau National Park....D3

**Activities, Courses & Tours**

7 Friendly Islands Kayak Company....D3
8 Hakula Lodge Tours....D3
Hakula Sport Fishing Charters....(see 8)

**Sleeping**

9 Blue Lagoon Resort....A4
10 Flying Annie Moa B&B....D3
Hakula Lodge....(see 8)
11 Harbourview Resort....D3
12 Lucky's Beach Houses....D3
13 Mafana Island Beach Backpackers....E3
14 Mandala Resort....E3
15 Mystic Sands....D3
16 Reef Resort....C4
17 Tongan Beach Resort....D3
18 Vava'u Villa....D3



### Whale Watching

With a passing parade of humpback whales, Vava'u has become one of the world's top whale-watching destinations. The activity is not without controversy: see Whale-Watching Ethics (p193) for more.

There are 19 commercial whale-watching/-swimming licensees in Vava'u, all with similar prices (around T$350 to T$450 per person per day). The whales are generally here from June to late October.

## Tours

Land-based tours are the best way to see the main island of Vava'u, while several operators run day boat excursions that typically include Swallows' Cave, Mariner's Cave, lunch on an uninhabited island and snorkelling at an offshore reef.

**Hakau Adventures** BOAT TOUR
(755 8164; www.hakauadventures.com; tours per adult/child incl lunch T$140/70; ) Casual full-day boat trips that include a visit to Swallows' Cave on Kapa, reef snorkelling, swimming and picnic lunch on a remote beach (home-made chocolate brownies!). Trips to Vava'u's eastern islands also available.

**Hakula Lodge Tours** TOUR
(Map p188; 755 9279, 70 872; www.hakulalodge.com/tour; Fatafehi Rd; tours from T$70) Hakula Lodge (p190), just south of Neiafu, is a one-stop shop for tours and activities, both guided and unguided: fishing, snorkelling, sailing, bike-riding, diving, driving... Give them a call to discuss what you'd like to do: if they don't offer what you want, they'll suggest someone who does!

**Vava'u Tours** TOUR
(771 6148, 874 0000; www.vavau.to/portofrefugevillas) Salesi proudly shows visitors around his home island for T$75 (minimum two people). Island-hop boat tours also available (T$150).

### COCK-A-DOODLE-DOO

Forget to set your alarm for your early flight? Don't worry: as per most South Pacific islands, Vava'u's roosters will ensure you're awake well before dawn even thinks about cracking. In a scrambled interpretation of International Date Line protocol, the birds here start crowing around 4am. Cock-a-doodle-don't... Bring your earplugs.

**Vava'u Adventures** ADVENTURE TOUR
(Map p191; ☎751 2984, 874 6248; www.vavauguide.com/vavau-adventures-ltd-kart-safaris; s/d kart T$200/300) Upbeat, three-hour, 40km guided kart tours all over the main island. Take it all in (including wind-blown dust and dirt) while driving your own one- or two-seater petrol-powered kart.

## Festivals & Events

**Regatta Vava'u** SPORTS
(www.regattavavau.com) Held in early September each year, Regatta Vava'u is a blossoming party week with all sorts of action for yachties and landlubbers alike.

## Sleeping

For rental houses, see www.vavauholidayhomes.com.

★ **Flying Annie Moa B&B** B&B $
(Map p188; ☎842 0325, 71 463; www.flyinganniemoavavau.com; Fatafehi Rd; r $T60-220; wifi) Moas were flightless, weren't they? Regardless, this newish B&B soars above most Neiafu accommodation. It's immaculately clean for starters, without a cracked tile or broken fan in sight. Over two levels are a lovely lounge and broad balcony, bright singles and doubles (four en-suite), tidy bathrooms and a five-berth self-contained unit. Breakfast is eggs, cereal, toast and coffee. Nice one!

**Backpackers Vava'u** HOSTEL $
(Map p191; ☎883 7080, 70 149; www.backpackersvavau.com; Fatafehi Rd; dm/d T$35/200, s/d without bathroom T$75/100) This modern hostel in the middle of Neiafu makes a decent budget base from which to propel yourself into Vava'u's myriad activities and after-dark indulgences. Fan-cooled rooms are bright, clean and secure. The shared kitchen sees plenty of action, as does the sun-swathed terrace overlooking buzzy 'Utukalongalu Market.

★ **Port Wine Guest House** GUESTHOUSE $$
(Map p191; ☎70 479; www.portwineguesthouse.com; Ha'amea Rd; s/d T$120/180, s/d without bathroom T$60/100, s/d bungalows T$180/250; wifi) For a cheery Tongan family experience, head to smart-looking Port Wine, run by Lu'isa Tuiniua and her son Tai. Sleeping options include original guesthouse rooms (shared bathrooms), newer en-suite guesthouse rooms, and two private en-suite *fale* – all of which are superclean and proudly maintained. There's always a cold coconut in the fridge and fruit comes direct from the lush gardens.

**Boathouse Apartments** APARTMENT $$
(Map p191; ☎70 016; www.boathousetonga.com; Fatafehi Rd; d/q from T$160/210; air-con) Propped up on the cliff above the harbour, this sky-blue apartment complex offers fabulous water views and four ship-shape apartments with kitchens – great for families and self-catering couples. Super location too, close to the cafes and the town hubbub.

**Harbourview Resort** BUNGALOW $$
(Map p188; ☎70 687, 751 2149; www.harbourviewresort.com; off Fatafehi Rd, Toula; d/f from T$180/230; wifi) The dodgy dirt road leading you here doesn't inspire, passing an old gas storage facility, but once you're ensconced in your motel-style cabin at Harbourview, you'll soon forgive. Set in immaculate tropical gardens (pink hibiscus blooms!) about 3km south of Neiafu, these nine units have kitchenettes and verandahs. Self-catering and family terrain. Taxis are T$10 from Neiafu.

**Hakula Lodge** LODGE $$$
(Map p188; ☎70 872; www.hakulalodge.com; Fatafehi Rd; s/d/f T$195/275/350; air-con wifi) Top-end, terracotta-tiled units opening onto a full-length verandah overlooking Port of Refuge (good sunsets). Wander down through the tropical gardens to swim off the private jetty, from which the owners' various boat trips (p189) set sail. The lodge is about 2km south of Neiafu.

## Eating

There are a few no-frills supermarkets and bakeries around town for self-caterers, plus the 'Utukalongalu Market (p192).

**Café Tropicana** CAFE $
(Map p191; ☎71 322; www.vavau.to/tropicana; Fatafehi Rd; mains $5-16; ⏰8am-9pm Mon-Sat; wifi vegetarian) Nab a seat in the shady interior or slouch into a deckchair on the terrace at this

# Neiafu

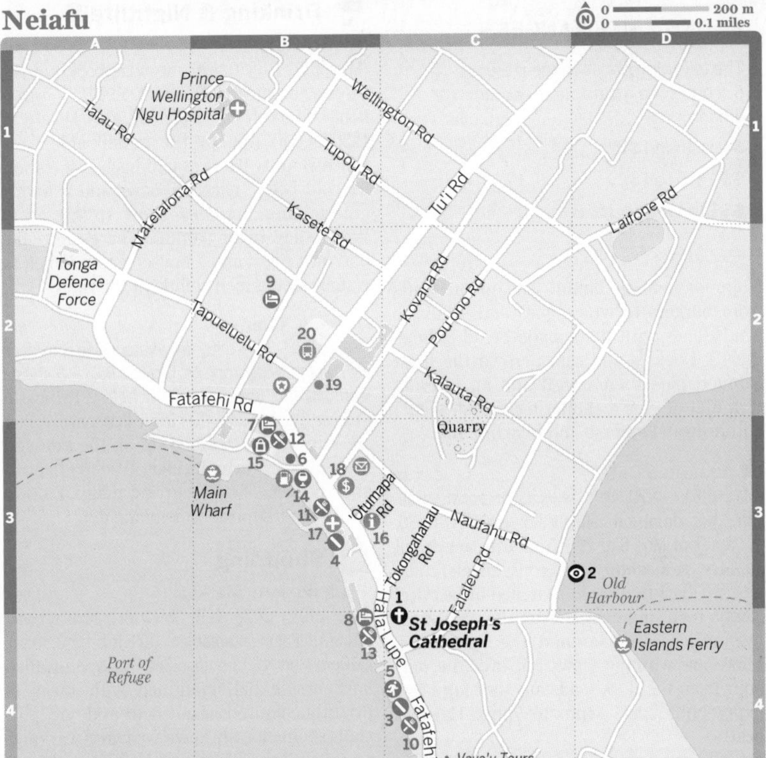


## Neiafu

**Top Sights**
1 St Joseph's Cathedral ........ C4

**Sights**
2 Old Harbour ........ D3

**Activities, Courses & Tours**
3 Beluga Diving ........ C4
4 Dolphin Pacific Diving ........ B3
Melinda Sea Adventures ........ (see 10)
5 Moorings ........ C4
6 Vava'u Adventures ........ B3
Vava'u Yacht Club ........ (see 13)

**Sleeping**
7 Backpackers Vava'u ........ B3
8 Boathouse Apartments ........ B4
9 Port Wine Guest House ........ B2

**Eating**
10 Aquarium Café ........ C4
11 Bellavista Cafe & Restaurant ........ B3
12 Café Tropicana ........ B3
13 Mango Cafe ........ B4

**Drinking & Nightlife**
14 Bounty Bar ........ B3
Dancing Rooster ........ (see 11)

**Shopping**
15 'Utukalongalu Market ........ B3

**Information**
ANZ Bank (ATM) ........ (see 6)
16 Neiafu Visitor Information Centre ........ B3
17 Universal Clinic & Pharmacy ........ B3
18 Westpac Bank (ATM) ........ B3

**Transport**
Fatafehi Rd Bus Stop ........ (see 15)
19 Real Tonga ........ B2
20 Tu'i Rd Bus Stop ........ B2

**EATING PRICE RANGES**

The following prices ranges refer to the price of a main course, for lunch or dinner.

**$** less than T$15

**$$** T$15 to T$25

**$$$** more than T$25

troppo-bohemian haunt. The menu wafts from burgers to wraps, pies and salads to sandwiches with homemade bread (wholemeal!). Cookies and cakes crowd the front cabinet, plus there's wi-fi and an internet terminal if you're suffering social media withdrawal. Espresso and bike hire too.

★ **Aquarium Café** CAFE **$$**

(Map p191; ☎70 493; www.aquariumcafevavau.com; waterfront, off Fatafehi Rd; mains T$10-30; ⊙9am-9pm Mon-Sat; ) You can get it all at airy Aquarium: generous meals, fully stocked bar, free wi-fi, switched-on service, classic rock soundtrack, even the occasional live-music session around the kava bowl. There are winning views out over the harbour from the deck – a beaut spot for a few happy-hour beers (4pm to 7pm). Hard to beat!

★ **Bellavista Cafe & Restaurant** ITALIAN **$$**

(Map p191; ☎71 035; www.tongaholiday.com/listing/bellavista-cafe-restaurant; Gutenbeil Plaza, Fatafehi Rd; mains $19-26; ⊙11am-2pm & 5-9pm Mon-Sat; ) Quiz a local about their favourite Neiafu eatery, and they'll most likely point you towards Bellavista – a romantic, top-floor Italian restaurant, complete with candlelight and red-and-white checked tablecloths. Terrific harbour views, attentive staff and disco hits (when was the last time you heard Andy Gibb?). Ask for some of the house-made chilli sauce on your pizza. Very kid-friendly, too.

**Mango Cafe** CAFE **$$**

(Map p191; ☎70 664; waterfront, off Fatafehi Rd; mains T$10-30; ⊙9am-9pm Mon-Sat) This curvy-roofed, clubby cafe is right on the water (literally – you can see the sea through floorboards!) and is a fave with yachties who tie up their tenders out the front. Check the blackboard for daily offerings (the sesame-seed wasabi tuna is a knockout). Don't miss the yacht racing (p187) and a few ales here on Friday evenings (June to November).

## Drinking & Nightlife

**Bounty Bar** BAR

(Map p191; ☎70 576; www.facebook.com/pages/vavau-bounty-bar/728610520519671; waterfront, off Fatafehi Rd; ⊙10am-12.30am Mon-Fri, to 11.30pm Sat) Run by the unflappable Lawrence, Bounty Bar is as laid-back as it comes; ice-cold beers, harbour views and a highly entertaining *fakaleiti* show (p199) every Wednesday night (10pm). There's also the odd quiz night and a big screen on which to watch the big men collide in the rugby.

**Dancing Rooster** BAR

(Map p191; ☎70 886; www.vavauguide.com/dancing-rooster; waterfront, off Fatafehi Rd; ⊙9am-late Mon-Sat) On the waterfront below Bellavista Cafe & Restaurant, this joint is usually full of sea-salty expats, washed up on the tide and in need of a rum and a cigar. The food's passable (burgers, steaks, curries; mains T$10 to T$30) but it's mostly a drinking den.

## Shopping

**'Utukalongalu Market** MARKET

(Map p191; ☎70 406; www.tongaholiday.com/listing/utukalongalu-market; Tu'i Rd; ⊙8.30am-4.30pm Mon-Fri, 7am-noon Sat) An open-walled harbourside hall crammed with racks of brightly coloured island fruit and veg, plus stalls selling locally hewn weavings, carvings and jewellery. There's a budget takeaway food arcade here too.

## Information

There are Westpac and ANZ banks on Fatafehi Rd, both with ATMs.

The Aquarium Café has free wi-fi for customers; at Café Tropicana (p190) it's T$6 per hour (it also has an internet terminal).

**Neiafu Visitor Information Centre** (Map p191; ☎70 115; www.thekingdomoftonga.com; cnr Fatafehi & 'Otumapa Rds; ⊙8.30am-4.30pm Mon-Sat) An open-walled, lime-green office stocked with neatly piled brochures. Helpful staff can assist with bookings, maps and accommodation reservations.

**Police Station** (Map p191; ☎26 498, emergency 922; www.police.gov.to; Tu'i Rd; ⊙24hr) Ask about getting a Tongan visitor's drivers licence if you're renting a car.

**Post Office** (Map p191; www.tongapost.to; Pou'ono Rd; ⊙8.30am-4.30pm Mon-Fri) Hard to find on the end of a little bank of shops, up a set of stairs.

**Prince Wellington Ngu Hospital** (Map p191; ☎70 201; Mateialona Rd; ⊙24hr) On the hill behind town. For emergencies.

**Universal Clinic & Pharmacy** (Map p191; ☎70 213; Fatafehi Rd; ⊙8.30am-5pm Mon-Fri, 11am-noon Sat) Pharmacy with a doctor on site between 9am and 4pm Monday, Thursday and Friday.

# Around Vava'u

Neiafu is where everybody hangs out, but it's not at all typical of wider Vava'u, which is laced with farmland, little villages, some impressive lookouts and empty beaches. Take an island tour or hire a car for a day or two to get the true lay of the land.

South of the main island, **Pangaimotu** is a largish isle connected to the 'mainland' by A'hanga Causeway. Long, thin **'Utungake** is in turn connected to Pangaimotu via another causeway.

## Sights

**'Ene'io Botanical Garden** GARDENS
(Map p188; ☎71 048; www.eneio.com; 'Ene'io Beach, Tu'anekivale, Vava'u; ⊙tours available 9am-5pm Mon-Sat) Developed by Tonga's former Minister of Agriculture, these gardens are brimming with botany (550 different plant varieties!). Access is via guided tour: book yourself onto a short garden walk (T$35), a three-hour birdwatching and hiking tour (T$85) or a full-day cultural tour (T$180). The cafe–gift shop sells everything from handicrafts to organic taro chips. 'Ene'io Beach is on the main island's eastern fringe – transport by arrangement. Bookings essential.

**'Ano & Hinakauea Beaches** BEACH
(Map p188) Near the southern end of Pangaimotu are these two beaut beaches backed by vegetation, with sheltered waters, good snorkelling and a safe spot to anchor your yacht. A rewarding bike ride from Neiafu.

**Ark Gallery Vava'u** GALLERY
(Map p188; ☎888 7998; www.tongavavauholiday.net/arkgalleryofvavau.htm; Anchorage 11, 'Ano Beach; ⊙by appointment) Paintings, prints, local arts and crafts...on a boat! If you're keen to visit, phone first, then take a taxi to 'Ano Beach – you'll be picked up there. Or if you're on a yacht, sail up and use one of the Ark's moorings (one night for free with a

### WHALE-WATCHING ETHICS

Tonga is an important breeding ground for humpback whales, which migrate to its warm waters between June and October. They can be seen raising young in the calm reef-protected waters and engaging in elaborate mating rituals. Humpbacks are dubbed 'singing whales' because the males sing during courtship routines. The low notes of their 'songs' can reach 185 decibels and carry 100km through the open ocean.

Humpback populations around the world have declined rapidly over the past 200 years, from 150,000 in the early 1800s to an estimated 12,000 today. The same predictable migration habits that once made the giants easy prey for whalers nowadays make them easy targets for whale watchers.

As Tonga's whale-watching industry has grown, so has concern over its impact. At the centre of the debate is the practice of swimming with whales. While it's undoubtedly one of the more unusual experiences you can have on the planet, some suggest that human interaction with whales – especially mothers and calves when they are at their most vulnerable – has a disruptive effect on behaviours and breeding patterns. Taking a longer view, others say that given humanity's historic propensity for slaughtering humpbacks by the tens of thousands, it's time we gave them a little peace and quiet.

In response to these concerns, in 2013 the Tongan government enacted a strict code of conduct for whale-watch operators and noncommercial yachts in the nation's waters, prohibiting unlicenced vessels within 300m of any whale, and banning swimming, diving, kayaking or jet-skiing near whales for anyone other than licenced operators.

If whale watching is a bucket-list essential for you, there are whale-watch and whale-swim operators in all of Tonga's island groups. Vava'u has most of the operators, but Ha'apai is probably a safer bet: there are only five operators here, which equates to less pressure on the whales. Make sure you go with a licensed operator – ask at the Nuku'alofa (p175) or Neiafu (p192) visitor information centres – and give yourself a few days to do it so that there is no pressure on the operator to 'chase' whales in order to keep you happy. If you feel your whale-swim operator has breached the boundaries and 'hassled' the whales in any way, make sure you report this to the info centres.

purchase from the gallery). The Ark was for sale at the time of writing – let us know if it has sailed away into the sunset!

## Sleeping & Eating

**Lucky's Beach Houses** BUNGALOW **$**
(Map p188; ☎71 075; www.luckysbeach.com; Talihau Village, 'Utungake; d bungalows/beach house from T$75/170; 📶) Lucky's overlooks the water at Talihau Beach at the tip of causeway-connected 'Utungake. Set up for self-caterers, there are two houses and two *fale* right by the water. Launch a kayak off the beach to explore 'Utungake, or paddle over to nearby Mala. Meals by request; two-night minimum stay. Lucky's also runs Poppin' Tonga (p188) fishing carters.

★ **Vava'u Villa** GUESTHOUSE **$$**
(Map p188; ☎71 010; www.vavauvilla.com; A'hanga Causeway, Pangaimotu; d incl breakfast from T$190; 📶) Just across the causeway a short drive south of Neiafu, this bright white villa is run by an Australian couple (who also run the vanilla bean processing plant across the road – ask for a tour!). There are nine renovated en-suite rooms, upstairs and down, plus an airy terrace restaurant (mains T$8 to T$22 – terrific pancakes). 'Beer o'clock is any time'.

**Mystic Sands** MOTEL **$$$**
(Map p188; ☎758 4148, 758 4027; www.mysticsands.net; 'Utungake Village, 'Utungake; d/f from T$345/365, 2-bedroom house T$555; 📶🏊) Up-market (if not mystical) beachfront motel-style units on the northern end of 'Utungake, with one family-sized room and a two-bedroom house sleeping four (with kitchen). There isn't a restaurant on site; order room service, or taxi it back to Neiafu (10 minutes back over the causeway). Activity operators will pick you up from the jetty out the front.

**Tongan Beach Resort** RESORT **$$$**
(Map p188; ☎70 380; www.thetongan.com; 'Utungake Village, 'Utungake; bungalows incl breakfast from T$590; 📶🏊) Right on Hikutamole Beach on 'Utungake, this relaxed resort gazes out onto the main channel into Port of Refuge (as many whales as yachts, at times). Up-tempo staff, decent rooms, a sandy-floor *fale* bar, beachfront restaurant and – that Tongan rarity – a swimming pool! Good for families.

# Southern Vava'u Islands

Vava'u has an astounding number of islands and waterways weaving towards the south. Visitors can head out to one of the growing number of island resorts, take it all in by boat, or sign up for a multiday kayak tour with Friendly Islands Kayak Company (p188). The resorts here can arrange all transfers.

## Mala

Just south of 'Utungake, itself connected to 'mainland' Vava'u by causeways, the wee isle of Mala is just a few minutes' chug by boat from the road end (day-trip territory; talk to the Neiafu Visitor Information Centre, p192, about getting there). The island has a sandy swimming beach, a small resort and the **Japanese Gardens** – a brilliant snorkelling area between Mala and Kapa (though beware the strong current churning between these two islands and 'Utungake).

## Kapa

Kapa island's big-ticket attraction is **Swallows' Cave** ('Anapekepeka; Map p188), cutting into a cliff on the west side of the island. It's actually inhabited by hundreds of swiftlets (not swallows) and you can swim right into it. The water is gin-clear, with the floor of the cave 18m below the surface. A regular inclusion in day tours, the only access is by boat.

### Sleeping

**Reef Resort** RESORT **$$$**
(Map p188; ☎755 9279; www.reefresortvavau.com; Otea; d T$480-550, extra person T$100-130, full board T$150; 📶) This German-run honeymooner is a top boutique outfit with perfect beach frontage and five roomy suites, decked out in classy castaway style. Euro-Polynesian meals are a real highlight, featuring fresh organic and local produce (seafood steals the show: expect lots of tuna, lobster, coral trout and snapper). Kayak to Swallows' Cave. Transfers T$60 per person.

## Hunga & Foe'ata

In Vava'u's western fringes, the large, sheltered lagoon embraced by Hunga, Kalau and Fofoa islands offers safe anchorage and brilliant **snorkelling**. There's more good snorkelling off the island of Foe'ata, immediately south of Hunga, which has some glorious arcs of white sand.

### Sleeping

**Blue Lagoon Resort** BUNGALOW **$$$**
(Map p188; ☎867 1300; www.tongabluelagoon.com; Foe'ata; bungalows T$360-460, full board

T$140, transfers return T$175; ) One-of-a-kind Blue Lagoon has a show-stopping position on Foe'ata's northern tip. Each of the five en-suite bungalows here is uniquely constructed from local materials (lots of timber), with four of them on stilts over the water. Multiday package deals including accommodation, meals, transfers and whale watching from T$1750 per person. Wi-fi in the restaurant. No sign of Brooke Shields...

### Nuapapu

Nuapapu is best known for **Mariner's Cave** (Map p188), a hidden underwater cave at the island's northern end. The main entrance is a couple of metres below the surface and the tunnel is about 4m long; use the swell to pull you towards it, then exit when the swell surges back out. Make sure you're with someone who knows what they are doing (this is dangerous stuff); snorkelling gear is essential.

### 'Eua'iki & 'Euakafa

In Vava'u's far southern reaches, the small atoll of 'Eua'iki has an amazing bright-white sandy beach, with a coral garden off the north shore (snorkelling supremacy).

A sandy beach also rings the north side of uninhabited 'Euakafa. From the island's eastern end a trail leads through the forest and mango trees to the summit (100m) and the overgrown tomb of Talafaiva, and ancient Tongan queen.

#### Sleeping

**Treasure Island Eco-Resort** BUNGALOW **$$$**
(847 6200; www.tongaislandresort.com; 'Eua'iki; bunglalows d T$460, full board T$150; ) Want to see whales cavorting while you chew your breakfast? This solar-powered resort on 'Eua'iki features traditional thatched-roof *fale* spaced along the beachfront. There are deep sea channels on both sides of the island – whale commuter lanes. If your timing's good, they'll be trucking past while you sip your coffee. Snorkelling equipment and kayaks available.

### Mounu & 'Ovalau

Almost as far south as Vava'u extends, little Mounu and 'Ovalau are perfectly far-flung sand-fringed islands. If you're looking for a romantic bolt-hole in which to express your amorous affections, look no further.

#### Sleeping

**Mounu Island Resort** RESORT **$$$**
(886 6403; www.mounuisland.com; Mounu; d T$430-670, full board T$150; ) On a tiny southern Vava'u atoll (just 6.5 acres), Mounu Island Resort comprises four wooden *fale* spaced around the island for perfect privacy (do your Tom-Hanks-in-*Castaway* impersonation at full volume). Meals and drinks at the bar; swimming, snorkelling and beach-bumming everywhere else. Good stuff.

## Eastern Vava'u Islands

### Mafana & 'Ofu

A short boat ride from Neiafu's Old Harbour, Vava'u's eastern islands are isolated without being too remote. 'Ofu's surrounding waters are the primary habitat of the prized but endangered *'ofu* shell (needless to say, we don't suggest you buy any).

#### Sleeping

**Mafana Island Beach Backpackers** HOSTEL **$**
(Map p188; 889 7679; www.mafanaisland beach.com; Mafana; bungalows s/d from T$55/80) Budget accommodation on Vava'u's outer islands is as rare as turtle's teeth! Mafana offers treehouse-style bamboo and beachside *fale,* with a maximum of eight guests (book well ahead!). Guests self-cater, with a communal cooking area on the beach, and there are beach showers. Swim, snorkel, kayak, hike – great for families. Boat transfers T$15.

**Mandala Resort** BUNGALOW **$$$**
(Map p188; 849 1270; www.mandalaisland.com; Fetoko; s & d T$395-495, extra person T$65, half/full board T$70/100; ) Need an unpretentious, private Tongan island escape? Mandala fits the bill. Miniscule Fetoko Island is adrift midway between Mafana and 'Ofu, and plays host to Mandala's four brilliant en-suite bungalows. The tree house is built for couples; the two-bedroom villa is a winner for families. Meals are in the open-walled restaurant/bar. Transfers from T$17 one way.

## NIUA GROUP

Tongan tradition is alive and kicking on these three small volcanic islands in Tonga's extreme northern reaches. The Niua group were the first Tongan islands to be eyeballed by Europeans (Dutchmen Schouten and Le

OFF THE BEATEN TRACK

### TAFAHI

Its fair to say that the Niua Group is 'OTBT' by definition, but that goes double for Tafahi. Nine kilometres north of Niuatoputapu, the perfect 560m cone of this extinct volcano (population 100) rises up from the sea. On the right tide you can cross by boat from Niuatoputapu to Tafahi in the morning and return in the afternoon. It's a good climb to the summit, from which on a good day you can see Samoa! Negotiate boat transfers with the local fishers if you're keen.

Maire in 1616); it may seem like little has changed since. The main islands of Niuatoputapu and Niuafo'ou are about 100km apart.

Unless you're on a yacht, any trip to the Niua Group should be approached with flexibility in mind as weather conditions often cause delays and cancellations of flights and ferry services.



##  Getting There & Away

### AIR

From Vava'u, Real Tonga flies to the grassy runways at Niuatoputapu (T$350 one way, weekly) and Niuafo'ou (T$420 one way, fortnightly).

### BOAT

The ferry supposedly makes a trip from Vava'u to Niuatoputapu and Niuafo'ou, then back to Vava'u once a month. Sailings are reliant on unpredictable factors (ie there is no schedule): contact Friendly Islands Shipping Company (p205) for info.

Many visitors arrive on private yachts. Both islands are ports of entry to Tonga, but Niuafo'ou lacks a decent anchorage or landing site. Niuatoputapu has a pass in the reef on the northwest side of the island.

## Niuatoputapu

POP 1300 / AREA 18 SQ KM

Niuatoputapu (Very Sacred Coconut) has a squashed sombrero shape, comprising a steep and narrow central ridge (a 157m-high eroded volcano) and surrounding coastal plains. The north coast is bounded by a series of reefs, and the island is surrounded by magnificent white beaches, easily circumnavigated on foot.

In 2009, following the Samoa earthquake, Niuatoputapu suffered extensive tsunami damage and nine people died.

**Hihifo**, the Niua Group's 'capital', has a police station, a post office and a small store. Cash and travellers cheques can be changed at the Treasury, though it sometimes runs out of cash: BYO *pa'anga* is a better idea. There is no ATM on the island.

**Boat trips**, including to nearby Tafahi, can be negotiated with local fishers. There's good **diving** outside the reef, but no diving equipment is available on the island.

**Kalolaine Guesthouse** (☎758 5803; s/d from T$30/40) offers up warm hospitality in a village home with a spacious lounge and neat rooms. Guests can use the kitchen or book meals in advance. To find it, just ask a local to point the way.

## Niuafo'ou

POP 735 / AREA 49 SQ KM

Remote Niuafo'ou, about 100km west of Niuatoputapu, looks like a huge doughnut floating in the ocean. But it's not fast food for giants – it's a collapsed volcanic cone (caldera), thought to have once topped 1300m in height. Today, the highest point on the caldera is 210m, and the lake it encloses is nearly 5km wide and 23m above sea level.

During the past 150 years, Niuafo'ou has experienced 10 major volcanic eruptions. After a particularly nasty one in 1946, the government evacuated the 1300 residents to 'Eua island, and Niuafo'ou was uninhabited until 200 homesick locals returned in 1957.

Niuafo'ou has no coral reef and no sandy beaches, just open ocean surrounds. A track leads right around the caldera and its impressive freshwater lake, **Vai Lahi** (Big Lake). Keep an eye out for Niuafo'ou's most unusual inhabitant, the turkeylike **Tongan megapode**, which uses the warm volcanic soil to incubate its eggs. Efforts to save this threatened bird have included transplanting chicks to the uninhabited volcanic islands of Late and Fonualei, two of Vava'u's outlying islands.

Real Tonga lands on Niuafo'ou Airport's grassy strip, winging in from Vava'u. There are a few campsites on the crater, although you should ask for permission from locals first. A handful of village houses offer guest rooms; contact the Nuku'alofa Visitor Information Centre (p175) in Tongatapu for details. There are several small shops scattered through the villages, but bring plenty of food and cash with you (no ATMs).

# UNDERSTAND TONGA

## Tonga Today

Politically, Tonga is in the midst of exciting times.

Before King George Tupou V was crowned in 2008, his lord chamberlain announced that the new king would relinquish much of his power to meet the democratic aspirations of his people. Changes were subsequently made to the electoral system, and in the November 2010 elections the people of Tonga gained the right to vote for 17 spots out of 26 in parliament. The other nine members are elected by the noble class from among themselves (there are 33 noble titles in Tonga).

Around 89% of eligible voters cast their ballots in this historic election. The Democratic Party of the Friendly Islands, led by long-term pro-democracy leader Akilisi Pohiva, won 12 of the 17 seats available to commoners. This wasn't quite enough, however: the other five seats were won by independents and they joined the nine nobles for a 14 to 12 majority in parliament and elected a noble, Lord Tu'ivakano, to be prime minister. This irked a number of political commentators, but democracy had taken root.

In 2014, after the unexpected death of King George Tupou V in 2012 and with his brother Tupou VI at the helm, all 26 seats were up for election, although the king retained the right to appoint nobles, nine of which again gained seats, with independents pinching three seats from the Democratic Party of the Friendly Islands to boost independent representation to eight seats. 'Akilisi Pohiva is now serving as prime minister.

Economically, Tonga is in the doldrums, reliant on limited tourism, agriculture and fishing. Remittances from Tongans living abroad are dropping as second-generation Tongans abroad need their hard-earned cash to raise their own families – rather than sending it back to Tonga. International aid is also apparently dropping, though aid work from China and Japan (p175) remains plainly visible.

Psychologically, however, Tongan national pride is soaring, with the lavish 2015 coronation of King Tupuo VI and Queen Nanasipau'u making global headlines and captivating the whole country (Tongans adore their royals). Still glowing from its historic defeat of France in the 2011 Rugby World Cup, the Tongan team went into the 2015 fixture in England with high hopes. A win over Namibia and a loss to eventual champions New Zealand was a reasonable return. All this excitement has done much to gloss over Tonga's various problems.

## History

Tonga has a rich mythological tradition, and many ancient legends relate to the islands' creation. One tells that the Tongan islands were fished out of the sea by the mighty Polynesian god Tangaloa. Another story has Tonga plucked from the ocean by the demigod Maui, a temperamental hero well known throughout the Pacific.

The earliest date confirmed by radiocarbon testing for settlement of the Tongan group is 1100 BC. On Tongatapu, the Lapita people had their first capital at Toloa, near present-day Fua'amotu International Airport. Archaeological excavations in the village of Hihifo in Ha'apai unearthed Lapita pottery that has carbon dated settlement of this area to more than 3000 years ago. The Vava'u Group has been settled for around 2000 years.

The first king of Tonga, known as the Tu'i Tonga, was 'Aho'eitu. He came to power some time in the middle of the 10th century



### COOK'S 'FRIENDLY ISLANDS'

On Captain James Cook's third voyage – he later died in Hawai'i on this same trip – he spent from April to July 1777 in the Tongan islands. While visiting Lifuka in the Ha'apai Group, Cook and his men were treated to lavish feasting and entertainment by chief Finau, inspiring Cook to name his South Seas paradise the 'Friendly Islands'.

It was later learned, through William Mariner (p185), that the celebration had been part of a conspiracy to raid Cook's two ships *Resolution* and *Discovery* for their plainly visible wealth. The entertainment had been planned in order to gather the Englishmen in one spot so that they could be quickly dispatched and their ships looted. There was, however, a last-minute dispute between Finau and his nobles, and the operation was abandoned. Cook never learned how narrowly they had escaped! Not so friendly now, eh James?

AD and was the first in a line of almost 40 men to hold the title.

During the 400 years after the first Tu'i Tonga, the Tongans were aggressive colonisers, extending their empire over eastern Fiji, Niue and northward as far as the Samoas and Tokelau.

## European Arrival

The first European arrivals in Tonga were Dutch explorers Willem Schouten and Jacob Le Maire, who bumped into the Niua Group in 1616.

Tongatapu's first European visitor was Dutchman Abel Tasman, who spent a few days trading with the locals in 1643. He named the island 'Amsterdam' (it didn't stick). In the same year, Tasman was also the first European to visit the Ha'apai Group.

The next European contact came in 1773 with James Cook, who buddied up with the 30th Tu'i Tonga, Fatafehi Paulaho.

Vava'u remained unseen by Europeans until Spaniard Don Francisco Antonio Mourelle showed up in 1781, making it one of the last South Pacific island groups to be contacted by Europeans.

## House of Tupou

In 1831 missionaries baptised the ruling Tu'i Tonga, who took the Christian name George. As King George Tupou I, he united Tonga and, with the help of the first prime minister, Reverend Shirley Baker (yes, he was a man), came up with a flag, a state seal and a national anthem, then began drafting a constitution, which was passed in 1875. It included a bill of rights, a format for legislative and judicial procedures, laws for succession to the throne and a section on land tenure. It is also responsible for Tonga's heavily Christian laws today.

The second king, George Tupou II, who took over in 1893, lacked the charisma and fearlessness of his predecessor. He signed a Treaty of Friendship with Britain in 1900, placing Tonga under British protection and giving Britain control over Tonga's foreign affairs. When he died at the age of 45 in 1918, his 18-year-old daughter Salote became queen.

## Queen Salote

A popular figure, Queen Salote's primary concerns for her country were medicine and education. With intelligence and compassion she made friends for Tonga throughout the world and was greatly loved by her subjects and foreigners alike. Her legendary attendance at Queen Elizabeth's coronation in 1953 won many hearts as she took part in the procession bareheaded in an open carriage through London, smiling resolutely at the crowds despite the pouring rain.

## The World's Heaviest Monarch

King Taufa'ahau Tupou IV took over as ruler of Tonga on his mother's death in 1965. He reestablished full sovereignty for Tonga on 4 June 1970 and oversaw Tonga's admission to the Commonwealth of Nations and to the UN. In his later years, however, he made a number of unpopular decisions, including selling Tongan passports to anyone who wanted one and appointing an American to the dual role of financial advisor and official court jester, who oversaw the loss of T$50 million in funds.

An imposing figure who was renowned as the world's heaviest monarch, the 210kg king became a health role model for Tongans when he shed more than 75kg in weight. He was 88 when he died in September 2006.

In the last years of his life, the king resisted growing calls for democracy, which peaked in a 2005 strike by public servants that lasted for months and resulted in a huge growth of pro-democracy sentiment. Two months after his death, riots in Nuku'alofa killed eight, destroyed much of the business district, shocked the world and led to Australian and

### TIN CAN ISLAND

Niuafo'ou is the 'Tin Can Island' legendary for its unique postal service. In days of old, since there was no anchorage or landing site, mail and supplies for residents were sealed up in a biscuit tin and tossed overboard from a passing supply ship. A strong swimmer from the island would then retrieve the parcel. Outbound mail was tied to the end of metre-long sticks, and the swimmer would carry them balanced overhead out to the waiting ship. This method persisted until 1931, when the mail swimmer became lunch for a passing shark.

In keeping with its postal tradition, special Niuafo'ou postage stamps, first issued by the Tongan government in 1983, are highly prized. To stamp collectors, Tin Can Island is legendary. The mail must go through...

**FAKALEITI**

One of the most distinctive features of Tongan culture are *fakaleiti*, a modern continuation of an ancient Polynesian tradition, known as *fa'afafine* in Samoa and *mahu* or *rae rae* in French Polynesia.

The term *fakaleiti* is made up of the prefix *faka-* (in the manner of) and *-leiti* from the English word 'lady'. Traditionally, if a Tongan woman had too many sons and not enough daughters she would need one of the sons to assist with 'women's work' such as cooking and housecleaning. This child would then be brought up as a daughter. These days, becoming a *fakaleiti* can also be a lifestyle choice. There is little stigma attached to *fakaleiti*, and they mix easily with the rest of society, often being admired for their style.

On Tongatapu, the Tonga Leitis' Association (TLA) is an active group – members prefer to call themselves simply *leiti* (ladies). The association sponsors several popular, well-attended events, including the international Miss Galaxy competition in July. On Vava'u, check out the *fakaleiti* show every Wednesday night at the Bounty Bar (p192).

New Zealand troops being sent to the supposedly peaceful Pacific paradise.

## King George Tupou V

Following in the footsteps of his father, King George Tupou V was crowned in a lavish ceremony on 1 August 2008. The monocled bachelor, a graduate of Oxford and Sandhurst, came to power with the lord chamberlain making the following statement before his coronation: 'The sovereign of the only Polynesian kingdom…is voluntarily surrendering his powers to meet the democratic aspirations of many of his people…the people favour a more representative, elected parliament. The king agreed with them. He planned to guide his country through a period of political and economic reform for the 21st century.'

## The King is Dead: Long Live the King!

In what was a shock to all Tongans, King George Tupou V died suddenly in Hong Kong in 2012. A hundred and fifty pallbearers carried him to his grave and the country mourned. His deeply religious and staunchly conservative younger brother is the new King Tupou VI, and was officially coronated in 2015, along with his wife Queen Nanasipau'u. The former crown prince, the new king previously voiced his opposition to democracy for Tonga and has a chequered history in charge, including a stint as prime minister that ended in his resignation. Tonga's economy plummeted during his leadership, leading to the calls for democracy his brother heeded. He was also involved in the demise of Royal Tongan Airlines, which lost the country millions. While many worry about the future under the new king, others feel that as a family man with a wife and children (his brother was a bachelor) he will be a more caring king. And if his lengthy, hyperfestive coronation is any indication, he will be much adored!

# The Culture

Tonga is a largely homogenous, church- and family-oriented society. Although most Tongans are open and extremely hospitable, due to cultural nuances foreigners can often feel a bit at arm's length.

## Population

Tongans are proud Polynesians with a unique culture, different from other South Pacific nations. Tongans make up the vast majority of the people; there are a few *palangi* (Westerners) and a small but significant population of Chinese immigrants.

Tonga's total resident population is around 106,000. Tongatapu has more than 65% of the total population, with approximately 30% of the total living in and around Nuku'alofa (the island's and the nation's capital).

Estimates suggest there are as many Tongans living abroad as there are in the kingdom, mostly in New Zealand, Australia and the US. There are now many second- and third-generation Tongans living in these countries.

## Religion

Tonga is, on the surface at least, a very religious country. Around 99% of the population identifies as being of Christian faith. The Free Wesleyan Church (the royal family's church of choice) claims the largest number

### AMERICAN WWII SERVICEMEN: TONGA'S SAVIOURS?

Within 24 hours of the Japanese bombing of Pearl Harbour in 1941, Tonga declared war on Japan. Waves of fear swept the South Pacific: how far south would the Japanese war machine march? Between 1942 and 1945 it's estimated that 30,000 US servicemen passed through Tongatapu, either stationed here or en route to other regional bases. At the time, Tonga was a closeted nation of little more than 30,000 people itself, and was still reeling from the 1918 flu pandemic. Some suggest that the new bloodlines these thousands of GIs introduced into Tongan society were the saviour of Tonga, deepening the gene pool, bolstering immunity and building a platform for population growth.

of adherents, followed by the (Methodist) Free Church of Tonga, the Church of England, the Roman Catholics, Seventh Day Adventists and the wealthy and increasingly prominent Mormons (look for their tidy cream-and-blue complexes around the country).

Churches are central to everyday life and, as they are seen as social and community organisations, Tongans donate a lot of money to them. Because of this, Tongans are very conservative and bring religion into all kinds of aspects of their daily lives. For example, public displays of affection between the sexes are a no-no. Many Tongans, especially women, may go to church two, three or even four times every Sunday.

Many Tongans still believe in the spirits, taboos, superstitions, medical charms and gods of pre-Christian Polynesia. One such belief is that if a family member is suffering a serious illness, it is because the bones of their ancestors have been disturbed. Many will return to old family burial sites, dig up remains and rebury relatives to remedy their own ill health.

## Lifestyle

Family is very important in Tongan life, with each member playing a role and elders commanding respect. A family unit often consists of extras including adopted children, cousins and other relatives living alongside the parents, children and grandparents. Everything is communal, from food to sleeping arrangements, and everyone is looked after. The patriarch is usually the head of the family and jobs are distributed according to gender.

You'll often see Tongans in conservative dress wearing distinctive pandanus mats called *ta'ovala* around their waists. In place of a *ta'ovala,* women often wear a *kiekie,* a decorative waistband of woven strips of pandanus. Men frequently wear a wraparound skirt known as a *tupenu* and women an ankle-length *vala* (skirt) and *kofu* (tunic).

## Education

Tongans highly value education. The literacy rate is 99%, reflecting the large investment that Tonga – and some highly visible religious groups – have made in the people. English is taught in schools throughout the islands. At tertiary level, the University of the South Pacific (USP) has a large campus outside Nuku'alofa.

Check out the colourful school uniforms worn by Tongan kids, standard throughout the country. Children at government primary schools wear red and white, government secondary school students wear maroon, blue is the colour for Wesleyan schoolkids, orange is for Church of Tonga schools, and Mormon school students wear green.

# Arts

## Handicrafts

Tongan handicrafts are handmade from local materials and each piece is unique, not mass produced. A lot of time and effort has gone into making all those carved necklaces, wooden carvings, woven baskets, mother-of-pearl earrings and tapa mats that you're ogling in the markets and handicraft shops.

Women's groups often work together making handicrafts and especially tapa and woven mats, which are treasured possessions in every household and used for important occasions like weddings and funerals.

Tapa is made from beaten bark of the mulberry tree, and as women usually work together in a mat-making group to produce a large piece, it is often divided up later. Woven mats are made from pandanus leaves and used for floor coverings or as *ta'ovalas,* to be worn around the waist.

Visitors should avoid buying handicrafts made from turtleshell or whalebone while in Tonga – certainly nonsustainable materials.

## Music & Dance

Tongans love to sing, and conjure up some seriously sweet South Seas harmonies. They enthusiastically launch into song in church, at festivals, in cafes and bars, at dances, and with guitars and ukeleles around the kava bowl. They also love brass marching bands and every high school has one. Young Tongans, however, increasingly listen to imported Western music: hip hop is de rigeur and appropriately badass (but inexplicably, Elton John seems to emanate from every cafe, bar, car and construction site).

The most frequently performed traditional dance in Tonga is called the *lakalaka*. The *tau'olunga,* a female solo dance, is the most beautiful and graceful of all Tongan dances, while the most popular male dance is the intimidating *kailao* – the war dance (something akin to the famous Maori haka, but more kinetic).

At traditional feasts that visitors may attend, female dancers are often lathered in coconut oil and, as they dance, members of the audience approach and plaster paper money to their sticky bods. Far from an erotic prelude, this is good form and 'tips' given in this manner will be greatly appreciated.

# Environment

The Kingdom of Tonga comprises 177 islands, scattered across 700,000 sq km of the South Pacific Ocean. Geographically Tonga is composed of four major island groups, which are, from south to north: Tongatapu and 'Eua, Ha'apai, Vava'u and the Niua Group.

Tonga sits on the eastern edge of the Indo-Australian plate, which has the Pacific tectonic plate sliding under it from the east, creating the Tonga Trench. This 2000km-long oceanic valley that stretches from Tonga to New Zealand is one of the deepest in the world – if Mt Everest was placed in the deepest part of the Tonga Trench, there would still be more than 2km of water on top of it. Tonga is moving southeast at 20mm a year (geologically speaking, that's really truckin'!), meaning that the region is a particularly volatile area for volcanic and earthquake activity.

## Flora & Fauna

Tonga's national flower is the *heilala,* a small, pudgy pink-red bloom. The *heilala,* plus colourful and sweet-smelling hibiscus, frangipani and bird-of-paradise blooms, create dazzling roadside colours. There are coconut groves and banana plantations amid fields of taro, *cassava* and yams. Papaya are everywhere. Huge rain trees (*kasia*), mango trees and banyans dot the landscape, while mangroves smother the mudflats.

Dolphins and migrating humpback whales swim in the waters around Tonga. The humpbacks come from June to October and can often be seen offshore from the major islands.

The only land mammal native to Tonga is the flying fox (fruit bat; *peka*). Interesting birdlife includes the *henga* (blue-crowned lorikeet); the *koki* (red shining parrot) of 'Eua; and the *malau* (megapode or incubator bird), originally found only on the island of Niuafo'ou, but introduced in recent years to uninhabited Late Island west of Vava'u in an effort to save it from extinction. Butterflies are a constant delight, right across the country.

## Conservation Issues

A number of murky conservation issues cloud the waters of Tonga. These are mainly based around the environment being compromised for economic gain and include the following:

**Swimming with dophins and whales** There are arguments that swimming with whales alters their behaviour and habitat, and has a detrimental affect on both mothers and babies.

**Green turtle conservation** Tongans eat green turtles, often as part of religious ceremonies, and use turtle shell for jewellery, but turtle numbers are dwindling.

**Sea cucumbers** Asian culinary tastes mean that big dollars can be earned by exporting sea cucumbers to Asia. There is a fear that they are being overfished.

**Aquarium fish** It has been suggested that exporting brightly coloured aquarium fish to the USA is to the detriment of populations around Tongan reefs.

**Litter** Everywhere you go in Tonga you'll see piles of rubbish and non-biodegradable junk strewn along the roadsides. What a mess!

## National Parks

Tonga has eight officially protected areas, including six national marine parks and reserves, Ha'atafu Beach Reserve on Tongatapu, and two national parks: the

449-hectare 'Eua National Park and Mt Talau National Park in Vava'u.

## Food & Drink

Tonga is surrounded by the sea and Tongans will eat just about anything that comes out of it, from shellfish to shark to sea turtle. *'Ota'ika*, raw fish in coconut milk, is a favourite across the islands.

Pigs are prized family possessions and roam the streets, along with myriad chickens. For feasts, smaller pigs are roasted on spits over open fires while bigger ones are cooked in *umu* (underground ovens).

Starchy root crops such as taro, sweet potato and yams are easy to grow in Tonga, so take precedence over vegetables which are more high-maintenance.

Tropical fruits are everywhere, with coconuts, bananas and papaya available year-round. Summer is the season for mango, pineapple, passionfruit and guava.

Unfortunately, imported goods are having detrimental effects on Tongan diets and obesity is a problem. Canned meats from Australia and New Zealand, packets of chips (crisps), sugary drinks and high-carb instant noodles are some of the worst offenders.

There are bakeries throughout Tonga producing a wide variety of goodies. Tongans love *keki* (doughnuts).

Tongans have a growing taste for imported wine (mostly from Australia and New Zealand) and beer is available everywhere, also mostly imported (fine if you like Heineken). Look for the excellent Tongan-brewed Outrigger lager and Popao ale in bars and bottle shops.

As in other South Pacific countries, Tongan men drink kava, made from pepper roots. This is done as a social activity by groups of men in kava circles, usually in the evenings and late into the night.

### SLEEPING PRICE RANGES

The following price ranges refer to a double room with bathroom: prices don't tend to vary much between seasons. Unless otherwise stated tax is included in the price.

**$** less than T$100

**$$** T$100 to T$200

**$$$** more than T$200

Coffee grows well in Tonga's climate, but local cafes and restaurants haven't quite mastered the dark art of espresso. Weak and watery is the norm.

# SURVIVAL GUIDE

## Directory A–Z

### ACCOMMODATION

By lofty Western standards, accommodation in Tonga is basic, and maintenance is something to do tomorrow. The golden rule: even if prices seem expensive (and they often are), don't expect too much.

Tonga doesn't have much range in terms of international-style hotels, resorts or backpacker hostels. Instead, B&Bs and small boutique-style guesthouses have the market cornered, often with shared bathrooms and cooking facilities. Many of these are run by European expats.

Camping is generally discouraged and is illegal in Ha'apai and Vava'u unless part of a guided trip. Some guesthouses allow camping on their property.

### CUSTOMS REGULATIONS

You may bring two cartons of cigarettes and 2.25L of spirits or 4.5L of wine or beer into Tonga duty free.

### EMBASSIES & CONSULATES

The following foreign diplomatic representatives are all in Nuku'alofa. The nearest UK and US consulates are in Suva, Fiji.

**Australian High Commission** (Map p170; ☎23 244; www.tonga.embassy.gov.au; Salote Rd, Nuku'alofa; ⏲8.30am-4.30pm Mon-Fri) For visa applications head to the Australian Visa Application Centre in the Tonga Post (p175) building in Nuku'alofa.

**Chinese Embassy** (Map p170; ☎24 554; http://to.chineseembassy.org/eng; Vuna Rd, Nuku'alofa; ⏲9am-noon & 2.30-5pm Mon-Fri) On the waterfront.

**Japanese Embassy** (Map p170; ☎22 221; www.ton.emb-japan.go.jp; Salote Rd, National Reserve Bank Bldg, Nuku'alofa; ⏲8.30am-12.30pm & 1.30-4.30pm Mon-Fri)

**New Zealand High Commission** (Map p170; ☎23 122; www.nzembassy.com/tonga; Taufa'ahau Rd, Nuku'alofa; ⏲9am-3pm Mon-Fri)

### EMERGENCY

☎911

### FOOD

As per most South Pacific nations, food in Tonga is heavy on the protein and carbs: big serves, big people. See Food & Drink (p230) for more.

### REAL TONGA SCHEDULING CHAOS

No doubt, Real Tonga plays a vital role in flying people between the isles of the Kingdom. But when it comes to concrete departure times, forget about it! Real Tonga's flight schedules are a movable feast, changing even within 24 hours of your next flight. They do try and email and phone your accommodation (if you've told them where you'll be!) to let you know, but otherwise beware. Reconfirm your booking as close as possible to your departure time, then arrive at the airport early – otherwise you may find yourself missing your flight, or with a long, desultory wait in a remote airport with nothing but bitterness to keep you company.

## GAY & LESBIAN TRAVELLERS

Homosexuality is technically illegal but remains an accepted fact of life in Tonga: you'll see plenty of gay men around. The fine old Polynesian tradition of fakaleiti (p199) is alive and well, but the lesbian population is much more underground. Public displays of sexual affection are frowned upon, whether gay or straight.

## INSURANCE

A comprehensive travel-insurance policy is a no-brainer for Tonga: check whether you're covered for 'dangerous' activities like surfing, snorkelling, diving etc.

Worldwide travel insurance is available at www.lonelyplanet.com/travel-insurance. You can buy, extend and claim online anytime – even if you're already on the road.

## INTERNET ACCESS

Internet cafes crop up in Nuku'alofa and Nieafu. Charges are around T$6 per hour. Most guesthouses have wi-fi, often for free, but often with dazzlingly censorious browsing blockers in place (Tonga is a churchgoing nation – you're not supposed to be watching YouTube on a Sunday morning).

## LEGAL MATTERS

Tonga is generally a very law-abiding country, and it's unlikely you'll need to have anything to do with the police. Watch out for speed cameras when driving on Tongatapu, especially between the airport and Nuku'alofa.

## MONEY

Cash is king in Tonga (dig the new plastic notes to celebrate King Tupou VI's coronation): be sure to take plenty with you to Ha'apai and 'Eua, which are ATM-free. There are ATMs, however, in Tongatapu and Vava'u, and it's easy to change major currencies at local banks.

Credit cards are accepted at many tourist facilities but often attract a 4% to 5% transaction fee. Visa and MasterCard are the most common.

Tongans don't expect tips but you won't cause offence by rewarding good service with a few *pa'anga*.

## OPENING HOURS

Following are some standard opening hours, but remember, time is a flexible entity in Tonga! Virtually everything is closed on Sundays.

**Banks** 9am to 4pm Monday to Friday

**Bars** 11am to 12.30am Monday to Friday, to 11.30pm Saturday

**Cafes** 7am to 10.30pm Monday to Saturday

**Post Offices & Government Offices** 8.30am to 4pm Monday to Friday

**Shops** 8am to 5pm Monday to Friday, to 1pm Saturday.

## PUBLIC HOLIDAYS

In addition to New Year's Day, Easter, Christmas Day and Boxing Day, public holidays in Tonga include the following:

**Anzac Day** 25 April

**Emancipation Day** 4 June

**King Tupou VI's Birthday** 4 July

**Crown Prince Tupouto'a-'Ulukalala's Birthday** 17 September

**Constitution Day** 2 November

**King George Tupou I Commemoration Day** 4 December

## SAFE TRAVEL

Tonga, in general, is a safe country to visit, though late nights and booze can be a bad mix: the big boys sometimes brawl in the bars.

Dogs can be aggressive: cross the street to avoid packs.

Watch out for coral cuts (p239), which tend to get infected.

## TELEPHONE

The country code for Tonga is ☎676; there are no local area codes. Dial ☎913 for the international operator and ☎910 for directory enquiry.

There are public phones throughout Tonga (buy a phonecard to make calls), but a mobile (cell) phone is a more reliable bet. Most foreign phones set up for global roaming work here and coverage is reasonably good throughout the islands.

The two telecommunication companies are **Tonga Communications Corporation** (TCC; ☎27 006; www.tcc.to) and **Digicel** (☎876 1000;

## PRACTICALITIES

- **Currency** The Tongan *pa'anga* (T$) comes in one, two, five, 10, 20 and 50 *pa'anga* notes, and coins in denominations of one, five, 10, 20 and 50 *seniti.*
- **Language** Tongan is the official language, but English is taught in schools and is widely spoken and understood.
- **Photography** Politeness goes a long way: always ask before taking pictures of people. Check out Lonely Planet's *Travel Photography* guide for inspiration.
- **Time** Tonga is 13 hours ahead of Greenwich Mean Time, making it the first country in the world to start each new day. Tonga does not observe daylight savings.

www.digiceltonga.com); a cheap local phone, including SIM, will cost you around T$60. Digicel also offers a T$20 Visitor SIM that expires after 30 days.

### TOILETS

Tongan toilets are of the sit-down Western variety. Public toilets are few and far between, and are often closed for repairs.

### TOURIST INFORMATION

Online, check out www.lonelyplanet.com/tonga for planning advice, recommendations and reviews.

The official Tongan tourism websites are www.thekingdomoftonga.com and www.tongaholiday.com.

**'Eua Island** (www.eua-island-tonga.com)
**Ha'apai Islands** (www.haapai.to)
**Matangi Tonga** (www.matangitonga.to)
**Vavu'a Islands** (www.vavau.to)

### TRAVELLERS WITH DISABILITIES

Tonga isn't an easy place to visit for mobility- or vision-impared travellers: footpaths (sidewalks) are almost nonexistant, roadsides are potholed and dusty/muddy, and most accommodation, tours and transport aren't set up for wheelchairs.

### VISAS

Most countries' citizens are granted a 31-day visitors' visa on arrival. You'll need a passport valid for at least six months and an onward ticket. One-month extensions are granted for up to six months at T$69 per month: contact the **Immigration Division, Department of Foreign Affairs & Trade** (Map p170; ☎26 970; www.mic.gov.to; Salote Rd, Nuku'alofa).

Those intending to fly in and depart Tonga by yacht require a letter of authority from a Tongan diplomatic mission overseas or the Immigration Division.

### VOLUNTEERING

Volunteering opportunities in Tonga are best organised through international agencies. See also Lonely Planet's *Volunteer: A Traveller's Guide to Making a Difference Around the World* for useful information about volunteering.

### WOMEN TRAVELLERS

Tonga is generally a safe and respectful place for women travelling solo, but exercise the usual precautions: don't walk around alone at night, avoid the bars at closing time, don't bother with hitchhiking etc.

### WORK

There are penalties in place for working in Tonga whilst visiting on a tourist visa. Contact the Immigration Division, Department of Foreign Affairs & Trade for information before you arrive if you plan to conduct business or gain employment in Tonga.

## Getting There & Away

### AIR

Three international airlines fly into Tonga, with direct flights from New Zealand, Australia and Fiji.

**Air New Zealand** (Map p170; ☎23 192; www.airnewzealand.co.nz; Vuna Rd, Kingdom Travel Centre, Nuku'alofa; ⏲8.30am-5pm Mon-Fri, 9am-12.30pm Sat) Based at Kingdom Travel Centre on the Nuku'alofa waterfront. Jets into Tongatapu from Auckland.

**Fiji Airways** (Map p170; ☎24 021; www.fijiairways.com; Vuna Rd, 'Utu'one B&B, Nuku'alofa; ⏲8am-5pm Mon-Fri, 9am-noon Sat) Based at 'Utu'one B&B opposite the Nuku'alofa wharves. Flies Fiji to Nuku'aloka, and also operates some Real Tonga code-share flights between Nuku'alofa and Vava'u.

**Virgin Australia** (Map p170; ☎26 033; www.virginaustralia.com; Taufa'ahau Rd, Nuku'alofa; ⏲8.30am-5pm Mon-Fri, 9am-noon Sat) On Nuku'alofa's main street. Flies into Tongatapu from Australia via Auckland.

### SEA

Trans-Pacific yachts ride the trade winds from Samoa, the Cook Islands and French Polynesia. Others come north from New Zealand. All vessels calling on Tonga must give customs 24-hour advance notice of arrival. To summon the harbour master and for emergencies in Tonga use VHF Channel 16.

Official entry ports include Nuku'alofa (Tongatapu), Neiafu (Vava'u), Pangai (Ha'apai), Falehau (Niuatoputapu) and Futu (Niuafo'ou). Contact **Ports Authority Tonga** (☎ 21 168; www.portsauthoritytonga.com) and see www.noonsite.com for more info.

## Getting Around

### AIR

Flying is by far the easiest, fastest and most comfortable way to get around Tonga.

Real Tonga (p166) operates most of the domestic flights in Tonga. Fiji Airways (p204) also flies between Nuku'alofa and Vava'u, often as a code-share flight with Real Tonga. Flights are scheduled to work in with arriving and departing international flights (no flights on Sundays). Typical fares:

| Route | Fare | Duration | Frequency |
|---|---|---|---|
| Ha'apai–Vava'u | T$204 | 30min | 3-4 weekly |
| Tongatapu–'Eua | T$96 | 10min | 1–2 daily |
| Tongatapu–Ha'apai | T$214 | 40min | 2–3 daily |
| Tongatapu–Vava'u | T$310 | 1hr | 2-3 daily |
| Vava'u–Niuafo'ou | T$420 | 1½hr | fortnightly |
| Vava'u–Niuatoputapu | T$350 | 70min | weekly |

### BOAT

The Nuku'alofa Visitor Information Centre (p175) lists ferry schedules, which must be rechecked prior to intended travel. See also www.tongaholiday.com/islands/transport.

Subsequent to the tragic sinking of the *Princess Ashika* in 2009 with the loss of 74 lives, all Tongan ferries and aircraft have come under intense scrutiny, and safety standards have risen dramatically.

#### Ferries to Ha'apai, Vava'u & the Niua Group

**Friendly Islands Shipping Company** (Map p170; ☎ 22 582; www.fisa.to; Queen Salote Wharf, Nuku'alofa) operates the MV *'Otuanga'ofa*, donated by the Japanese government in 2011. Once a week it plies the waters between Tongatapu, the Ha'apai Group and Vava'u (departing Tongatapu on Thursdays, getting back there on Saturdays), and occasionally heads to the Niua Group (unscheduled).

The following are adult fares; children aged 4–12 years pay half-price.

| Route | Fare |
|---|---|
| Nuku'alofa–Neiafu (Vava'u) | T$99 |
| Nuku'alofa–Pangai (Ha'apai) | T$79 |
| Pangai (Ha'apai)–Neiafu (Vava'u) | T$71 |
| Neiafu (Vava'u)–Niuafo'ou (Niuas) | T$121 |
| Neiafu (Vava'u)–Niuatoputapu (Niuas) | T$121 |

#### Ferries to 'Eua

On a calm day the 2½-hour ferry trip between Tongatapu and 'Eua (T$23 one way) is a breeze. The **MV 'Onemato** (☎ 24 755) leaves Nuku'alofa daily Monday to Saturday, returning from 'Eua the same day (sometimes it stays docked overnight in 'Eua; check when you buy your ticket). The **MV 'Alaimoana** (☎ 21 326) sails for 'Eua on Tuesday and Thursday, returning from 'Eua the following morning.

The schedule does shift from time to time: check www.tongaholiday.com/islands/transport for the latest. Tickets are sold either at the ferry terminal or on board; get there an hour before sailing.

### BUS

Tonga's privately owned buses have a handy interpretative 'B' at the start of their licence plates. They run on Tongatapu, and in a more limited capacity on Vava'u and its causeway-linked islands. Fares range from T$0.70 to T$2 depending on distances travelled. Don't expect to get where you're going in a hurry...but riding a local bus is a cultural experience in itself!

### CAR

The official line is that to drive in Tonga you need a visitor's driving licence (T$40) from the **Ministry of Infrastructure** (Map p170; ☎ Nuku'alofa 23 201, Vava'u 70 100; www.infrastructure.gov.to; Bypass Rd, Nuku'alofa; ⏱ 8.30am-4pm Mon-Fri), valid for three months (bring your passport, home drivers licence and international driving permit if you have one). But if it's only a one-day rental, some operators may turn a blind eye and require only your home licence.

People drive *veeery slooowly* on the left-hand side of the road. The speed limit is 50km/h in villages, 70km/h elsewhere. On the road, watch out for children, dogs, chickens and pigs, and don't park under coconut trees!

At the time of writing, petrol cost around T$2.50 per litre.

### TAXI

Tonga's scrappy-looking taxis have a 'T' on their licence plates. There are plenty of taxis on Tongatapu and Vava'u, though it may not be an 'official' taxi that picks you up: if you ask someone to organise a taxi, it may be their husband, brother or nephew who comes to get you. Just pay the going rate; ask at your accommodation so you have a ballpark figure.

# Understand Rarotonga, Samoa & Tonga

# Rarotonga, Samoa & Tonga Today

**These island nations have much in common, but – strewn across a vast span of the South Pacific – they remain a varied bunch. It's not all kava, cocktails and good times here: political change is par for the course, and the complex ties between regional allies, both old and new, are strengthened and weakened all the time. Locals are proving resourceful, though, upping the tourism ante with innovative enticements to visitors.**

### Best in Print

**Pacific Tsunami Galu Afi** (Lani Wendt Young; 2010) Details the impact of the 2009 tsunami that devastated parts of Samoa, American Samoa and Tonga.

**Patterns of the Past: Tattoo Revival in the Cook Islands** (Therese Mangos and John Utanga; 2011) Getting inked in the Cooks, from past to present.

**Blue Latitudes** (Tony Horwitz; 2002) Retraces Captain Cook's epic voyages through the South Seas.

**The Happy Isles of Oceania** (Paul Theroux; 1992) Theroux kayaks through the South Pacific (try to overlook the mildly patronising title…).

### Best on Film

**Sione's Wedding** (director Chris Graham; 2006) Four Samoan lads get up to mischief in Auckland.

**The Orator** (director Tusi Tamasese; 2011) Love, courage and honour: the first 100% Samoan feature film.

**My Lost Kainga** (director Tony Fuemana; 2011) Tongan film exploring the loss of language and culture.

**Mutiny on the Bounty** (directors Frank Lloyd, Lewis Milestone and Roger Donaldson; 1935, 1962 and 1984, respectively) Captain Bligh and Fletcher Christian disagree.

## The Political Landscape

Samoa staged its most recent general election in March 2016 – the country's first election since it hopped west of the International Date Line at the end of 2011 to align with key trading partners Australia and New Zealand. Sitting prime minister Tuila'epa Sa'ilele Malielegaoi of the Human Rights Protection Party, the top dog since 1998, was returned to power in a landslide victory. Electoral integrity in the 2016 election was bolstered by the 10,000-plus Samoans who registered to vote for the first time, many of whom were no doubt encouraged by new laws to improve voting confidentiality. In the lead-up to the election, penalties for illicit coercion, infringement on voting secrecy or otherwise cooking the electoral books were upped from a minimum of three months' to 12 months' imprisonment.

In Tonga, new King George Tupou VI has been settling into the hot seat. Tonga was rocked in 2012 by the sudden death of the new king's brother, King George Tupou V, aged 65, while visiting Hong Kong. Crowned only in 2008, he ceded many of his powers after ascending the throne to pave the way for democratic reform in the country. Some say this magnanimous move betrayed a lack of enthusiasm for the top job, suggesting that the king – something of a footloose bachelor – was more at home travelling overseas than, well…at home. But new King George VI, a deeply religious family man, has a much more earnest and caring reputation. His coronation in 2015 (postponed until this time so the country could raise the coin to bankroll the event with sufficient pomp) was a lavish affair, and he's been very well received by an adoring public. And in the wake of the 2014 general election, where Tonga's own brand of democracy again withstood the test of the proletariat, the pro-democracy riots of 2006 that tore up downtown Nuku'alofa seem a distant memory.

Meanwhile in the Cook Islands, in 2015 the country celebrated 50 years of self-governing independence from New Zealand. New Zealand prime minister John Key turned up for the party, which involved typically effervescent dancing displays and much feasting. In his address to the nation, Key pledged a donation of NZ$11.7 million towards the redevelopment of Rarotonga's national secondary school, on top of the NZ$42 million NZ will be contributing over the next three years towards infrastructure and health projects in the Cooks. That's good news for local prime minister Henry Puna, who is still pushing for the Cook Islands to gain a seat in the UN. As an aside to his address, Key suggested that while the Cooks remain so reliant on foreign aid from NZ, Australia and China, the chances of the UN acceding to Puna's proposal remain slim.

To keep up to speed with the often fast-changing political landscape right across the South Pacific, check out the comprehensive Pacific Islands Report (www.pireport.org), which includes updates on the Cook Islands, Samoa, American Samoa and Tonga.

## Influences from Afar

New Zealand and Australia remain key foreign-aid donors to the Cook Islands, Samoa and Tonga. Recent projects in the region funded by NZ/Australian aid money include investments in solar and wind power; upgrading police infrastructure, training and equipment; and efforts to improve attendance and educational outcomes in island schools. However, the impact of Chinese and Japanese aid throughout this part of the South Pacific should not be underestimated. Japan has invested millions in services and infrastructure right across the South Pacific and China's influence is becoming increasingly visible. Chinese road workers are a common sight in Tonga (look for the signs saying 'China Road'); aid money from Beijing has funded several public buildings in the Samoan capital of Apia; and the main road and water systems on Rarotonga are currently being overhauled using Chinese money.

But this investment definitely comes with strings attached – namely, via the enactment of so-called Chinese 'soft power'. In the Cook Islands, for example, a Chinese workforce must be used for construction projects, and the Cooks must purchase equipment and goods from China to get the job done. Other perks for the Chinese include fishing licences and access to regional mineral and timber resources being subsequently granted to Chinese companies. Some Tongans we spoke with suggest that China's motives are also poli-military, looking to undermine regional ties between the South Pacific nations and Australia, Japan and the USA, with an eye to tactical naval expansion in the South Seas.

COMBINED AREA: **4131 SQ KM**

COMBINED POPULATION: **373,750**

MOST ISLANDS: **TONGA (176)**

BIGGEST CITY: **APIA, SAMOA (POP 36,735)**

HIGHEST POINT: **MT SILISILI, SAMOA (1858M)**

### if these countries were 100 people

5 would be Cook Islanders
51 would be Samoan
16 would be American Samoan
28 would be Tongan

### national parks & reserves

(% of country)

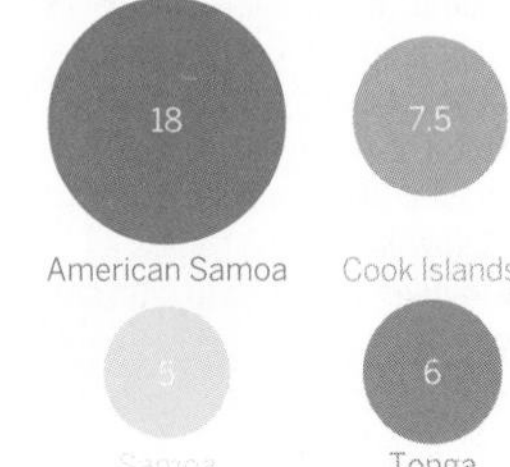


### population per sq km

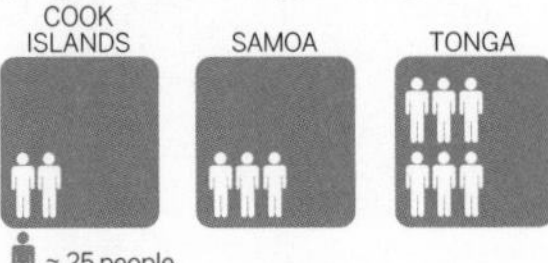

### Saying Hello

**Kia orana** (Cook Islands)
**Talofa** (Samoa)
**Malo e lelei** (Tonga)

### Top Blogs

**Sleepless in Samoa** (www.sleeplessinsamoa.blogspot.co.nz)
**Raro Lens: A Look at the Cooks** (www.rarolens.com)
**Samoa Food** (www.samoafood.com)
**Fagogo mai Samoa...aue!** (www.savaii.blogspot.co.nz)

### Etiquette

**Beaches** Beach access is often via local family land: ask permission before you barge through.
**Souvenirs** Don't buy items made from endangered resources like black coral or sandalwood.
**Turtle** Don't eat it – it's endangered and you'll be promoting illegal trade.
**At the table** Don't just dig in: many locals say grace before a meal.

### Sports Stars

**Kevin & Tony Iro** The former rugby-league players have Cook Islands heritage.
**Dwayne 'The Rock' Johnson** The wrestler and chiselled Hollywood actor has a Samoan mum.
**Jonah Lomu** The former NZ All Blacks rugby-union superstar (RIP) had a Tongan background.
**Tim Cahill** The Australian soccer (football) star has a Samoan mum.
**Sonny Bill Williams** The badass All Black with the killer Samoan tatts has a Samoan dad.

But regardless of criticism, it's undeniable that this investment is very welcome and very timely. This is especially true in countries like Tonga, Samoa and American Samoa, where the local economies lean heavily on remittances sent home from family members living overseas. When times get tough for these second-generation families in Auckland, Sydney and Los Angeles, the natural inclination is to send less money back to their home islands, which seem increasingly far away and in time increasingly detached from day-to-day concerns.

## Isolation Breeds Innovation

The global financial realm may remain a tad shaky in the wake of the crisis of 2007–08, but visitor numbers are still increasing year on year for the isolated isles of Samoa, the Cook Islands and Tonga. Within these countries, specific islands are developing innovative attractions to inspire traveller interest. 'Atiu in the Cook Islands and the Tongan island of 'Eua, for example, are becoming popular for birdwatching and ecotourism (hiking, diving and caving). Rarotonga is growing as a destination for foodies by moving away from a dependence on imported foodstuffs, while sea kayaking in the Ha'apai and Vava'u island groups in Tonga entices adventurous travellers. More broadly, Samoa has lately been garnering international attention as a sporting destination, with triathlons and ocean-swimming events luring fit bods from all over the planet. Across the region there's also a general move towards enabling visitors to have more authentic experiences, often by focusing on local food and accommodation. The feeling is that travellers want to break free of the confines of their resorts and really experience village life.

# History

**Arrayed across the Polynesian heart of the world's largest ocean, the Cook Islands, Samoa and Tonga have been at the hub of Pacific history for many centuries. Exploration, conquest and trade connected the diffuse island groups well before the arrival of European explorers and missionaries, and the nations' experiences with the impact of colonialism and Christianity have been both shared and unique.**

The Cook Islands remains closely aligned to former colonial guardians New Zealand (NZ), Samoa is divided between independence and the US, and Tonga is the Pacific's last remaining monarchy.

Since independence, geographical isolation and limited population bases have meant that economic and stability goals have been hard to reach, but tourism is increasingly seen as a positive force for future growth.

Emigration and improved transport links have made islands like Rarotonga more modern and cosmopolitan, but the region's outlying islands all still proudly and robustly showcase traditional Polynesian values.

## Polynesian Settlement

Polynesia ('Many Islands') is scattered across a vast triangle of the Pacific Ocean with its three points at Hawai'i, Easter Island (off the west coast of South America) and NZ.

### A Gradual Journey East

Although the Norwegian explorer and archaeologist Thor Heyerdahl theorised in the 1940s that the earliest Polynesians migrated from Peru via Easter Island on balsa-wood rafts, it is now commonly accepted that humans first entered the Pacific from the west via the East Indies and the Malay Peninsula. This idea is reinforced by linguistic and DNA studies, archaeological evidence and oral histories.

About 50,000 years ago the first people arrived in New Guinea from southeast Asia via Indonesia. These people, now known as Papuans, share ancestry with Australia's Aborigines. Moving slowly east, the Papuans' progress halted in the northern Solomon Islands about 25,000

**Archaeological Sites**

*Avana Harbour (Cook Islands)*

*Ha'amonga 'a Maui Trilithon (Tonga)*

*Pulumelei Mound (Samoa)*

*Hihifo's Archaeological Sites (Tonga)*

**TIMELINE**

**3100–3000 BC**

Descendants of the Lapita people first arrive in Polynesia, travelling from East Asia, down the Malay Peninsula and through the islands of Melanesia.

**1500 BC**

The Samoan islands are inhabited by the first Polynesians, exploring this part of the South Pacific and discovering new island groups.

**200 BC – AD 200**

Polynesian pioneers reach the Society and Marquesas Islands (now French Polynesia), honing their ocean-going navigational skills for longer journeys.

years ago, due to the lack of boats able to cross the increasingly wide stretches of ocean. Subsequent people, collectively known as Austronesians, moved into the area from the west, mingling with the Papuans and eventually becoming the highly diverse group of people known as Melanesians. New Guinea and the Solomons were the only inhabited islands in the Pacific for many thousands of years.

## Onwards to Polynesia

*Vaka: Saga of a Polynesian Canoe*, by Sir Tom Davis, is a historical novel based on the story of the *Takitumu* canoe (one of the canoes of the 'great migration' to NZ in the 14th century) over a span of 12 generations.

The wider seas from the Solomons to Vanuatu were crossed in about 1500 BC. An Austronesian people now known as the Lapita finally developed the technology and skills to cross the open seas to New Caledonia. Heading east, they quickly expanded through Fiji, Tonga and Samoa, where they developed the culture we now know as Polynesian. The Lapitas' Polynesian descendants waited on Samoa and Tonga for 1000 years or so, until more-advanced ocean vessels and skills were developed. Some time around 200 BC they crossed the longer ocean stretches to the east to the Society and Marquesas island groups (in modern French Polynesia). From there, voyaging canoes travelled southwest to Rarotonga and the southern Cook Islands, southeast to Rapa Nui (Easter Island) in AD 300, north to Hawai'i around AD 400 and southwest past Rarotonga to Aotearoa (New Zealand) in AD 900.

### Canoes

The term 'canoe' (*vaka* or *va'a*) can be misleading. Across the South Pacific, the same word describes small dugouts used for river navigation, giant war vessels accommodating hundreds of men and 25m-long

### THE ANCIENT LAPITA CULTURE

The ancient race of people known as the Lapita is thought to be responsible for the wide distribution of Polynesian culture and Austronesian languages in the Pacific. It was in Tonga and Samoa that the Lapita developed into the people we now call Polynesians.

From 1500 BC to 500 BC, the Lapita held sway over a vast area of the Pacific, where their influence can be traced through the far-flung dispersal of their unique pottery. Lapita pottery has been found in Papua New Guinea (PNG), New Caledonia, parts of Micronesia, Fiji, Tonga, Samoa, and Wallis and Futuna.

The Lapita were skilled sailors and navigators, able to cross hundreds of kilometres of open sea, and trade and settlement were important to them. They were also agriculturists and practised husbandry of dogs, pigs and fowl. Regarded as the first cultural complex in the Pacific, they were an organised people who traded obsidian (volcanic glass used in tool production) from New Britain (an island off PNG) with people up to 2500km away in Tonga and Samoa.

**500**

Settlers arrive on Rarotonga and begin the process of colonising the other islands, eventually travelling south to the islands of NZ.

**950**

Samoan warriors, led by Chief Savea, defeat Tongan invaders and the victorious chief is rewarded with the title of Malietoa.

**1300s**

Tangi'ia and Karika, two chiefs from Tahiti and Samoa, conquer Rarotonga and divide the island's population into six different tribes.

**1773**

James Cook sights Manuae and the 'Hervey Group' in the Cook Islands, and Tonga for the first time. Six years later he'll be killed in Hawai'i.

ocean-voyaging craft. These ocean-voyaging craft – either double canoes or single canoes with outriggers – carried one or more masts and sails of woven pandanus. Captain James Cook and contemporary observers estimated that Pacific canoes were capable of speeds greater than their own ships, probably 150km to 250km per day, so that trips of 5000km could be comfortably achieved with available provisions.

Published in 1884, *Samoa – A Hundred Years Ago and Long Before*, by George Turner, features myths, legends and stories revealing the pre-colonial society and culture of the Samoan islands.



### Navigation Techniques

Initial exploratory journeys often followed the migratory flights of birds. Once a new land had been discovered, the method of rediscovery was remembered and communicated mostly by which stars to follow. Fine-tuning of these directions was possible by observing the direction from which certain winds blew, the currents, wave fronts reflecting from islands and the flight of land birds.

## European Contact

### Searching for Terra Australis

Like Pacific islanders, European explorers came in search of resources (gold and spices initially), and they were driven by curiosity or national pride. Europeans were also inspired by one overpowering myth: the search for the great southern continent, Terra Australis.

Since the time of Ptolemy (around AD 100), scientists predicted the presence of a huge land mass in the southern hemisphere to counter the earth's northern continents. Otherwise, it was believed, the globe would be top-heavy and fall over. Belief in this southern continent was unsubstantiated, and to confirm its existence, explorers were dispatched to chart its coasts and parley with its people. In the absence of hard facts, Terra Australis was believed to be peopled by strange heathens and magical creatures, and rumoured to be rich in gold.

### Dutch & French Exploration

Dutch explorers Jacob Le Maire and Willem Schouten's 1616 search for Terra Australis introduced Europe to the Tongan islands and Futuna. Another Dutchman, Jacob Roggeveen, spotted Bora Bora in the Society Islands in 1722, and Tutuila and Upolu in Samoa. Abel Tasman became the most famous Dutch explorer after charting Tasmania and the east coast of NZ in 1642, then landing on the islands of Tonga and Fiji.

The most famous French explorer, Louis-Antoine de Bougainville, came upon Tahiti and claimed it for France in 1768. He went on to the Samoan islands, then continued to Vanuatu and discovered Australia's Great Barrier Reef. Bougainville's impact was greater than dots on a map, however: his accounts of the South Pacific sparked massive European interest and created the myth of a southern paradise.

**1789**

Captain William Bligh and 18 crewmen are set adrift off the volcanic Tongan island of Tofua after the crew of HMS *Bounty* mutiny.

**1823**

Rev John Williams of the London Missionary Society (LMS) lands on Rarotonga and the conversion of Cook Islanders to Christianity begins.

**1830**

Rev Williams arrives on the Samoan island of Savai'i during a civil war.

**1845**

King George Tupou I begins his reign over a united Tonga, assuming his new first name as a tribute to British monarch King George IV.

### CROWNING A COOK ISLANDS CHIEF

Traditionally the *ariki* (high chief) in the Cook Islands was the first-born son in the royal line and held the highest rank in the tribe. The *ariki* was believed to be a direct descendant of the gods, and during ritual ceremonies was seen as an intermediary between heavenly and earthly realms. The *ariki* commanded huge power, sitting in judgement over family disputes, declaring war and peace with other tribes, and ensuring the continuing welfare of his people.

These days, with a modern democratic system in place in the Cook Islands, the *ariki* is more a figurehead than an actual ruler, but they still command considerable moral authority. The House of Ariki, which consists of all the 24 *ariki* in the Cook Islands, serves to advise the elected government on issues of custom and tribal tradition, but it has little say in the actual day-to-day running of the country. The title has also lost its sexist overtones: today the *ariki* is just as likely to be a woman as a man.

The investiture of a new *ariki* is still an important ceremony in the Cook Islands. The new *ariki*, *mataiapo* (sub-chiefs) and all the other attendants are clad in the traditional ceremonial dress, and the ancient symbols of office (including a spear, woven shoes, a feather headdress, a woven fan and a huge mother-of-pearl necklace) are presented. The ceremonies are also packed with strange quirks: on Rarotonga, the investiture of the *ariki* is for some reason not considered complete until he or she has bitten the ear of a cooked pig...but no one can quite remember why.

## The Arrival of the English

For a cracking rendition of the story of the HMS *Bounty*, catch a debonair Marlon Brando as Fletcher Christian and Trevor Howard as the despicable William Bligh in *Mutiny on the Bounty* (1962).

In 1767 Samuel Wallis – *still* searching for Terra Australis – landed on Tahiti, but the greatest of the English explorers was James Cook. His three journeys into the region – the first, in 1768, most famously 'discovered' Australia and NZ – saw detailed mapping and exploration that would later allow others to follow. His third and final journey was the first European visit to Hawai'i, where Cook was killed in a skirmish. His legacy can be seen throughout the Pacific, with his detailed maps used up until the 1990s, and several places – most notably the Cook Islands – bearing his name.

Following the most famous of maritime mutinies, Fletcher Christian captained the *Bounty* to discover Rarotonga in the southern Cook Islands in 1789.

# Arrival of the Missionaries

## Protestant Power

After a few largely unsuccessful Spanish Catholic forays into Micronesia during the 17th century, the first major attempt to bring Christianity to the Pacific was by English Protestants. The newly formed London Mis-

**1879**

French explorer La Pérouse sets off to explore the South Pacific, visiting Tonga, Samoa and Australia before mysteriously disappearing. His wrecked ship is discovered in the Solomon Islands in 2005.

**1888**

The Cook Islands are established as a British protectorate to avoid French invasion. Within 13 years, the Brits will be ready to offload the Cooks to NZ.

**1889**

Robert Louis Stevenson abandons the chilly moors of Scotland for his own 'Treasure Island' and the warm delights of Samoa.

**1894**

'Here he lies where he longs to be' – Tusitala (Teller of Tales) Robert Louis Stevenson dies of a stroke and is buried at Vailima.

sionary Society (LMS) outfitted missionary outposts on Tahiti and Tonga, and in the Marquesas in 1797. These first missions failed – within two years the Tongan and Marquesan missions were abandoned. The Tahitian mission survived, but its success was limited. For a decade there were only a handful of islanders who were tempted to join the new religion.

Other Protestants soon joined the battle. The new players in the South Pacific were the Wesleyan Missionary Society (WMS), fresh from moderate success in NZ, and the American Board of Commissioners for Foreign Missions (ABCFM), following their Christianising of Hawai'i. The WMS and ABCFM both floundered in the Marquesas, but they fared better in Tonga.

Despite the slow start, missionary success grew. By the 1820s missionary influence was enormous. A Protestant work ethic was instilled and tattooing was discouraged. Promiscuity was guarded against by nightly 'moral police' and practices such as cannibalism and human sacrifice were forbidden. From Tahiti, Tonga and Hawai'i, Christianity spread throughout the Pacific.

When Captain James Cook dined on locally prepared fish cooked in coconut cream with the Ha'apai chief Finau, he was so impressed that he ordered his own chef to try to cook fish the Tongan way.



## The Expansion of Christianity

The missionaries' success was due to three major factors. First, politics played a part, particularly the conversion of influential Tongan chief Taufa'ahau. After conversion, he went on to seize control of Ha'apai from its rightful heir, Laufilitonga. Baptised in 1831, Taufa'ahau took on the first name Siaosi, or George, after the king of England, and adopted the surname Tupou.

Under his influence, all of Ha'apai in Tonga converted to Christianity. When George's cousin, King 'Ulukalala III of Vava'u, followed suit, so did the people of Vava'u. On Tongatapu, Wesleyan missionaries were gaining momentum, and secured the conversion of George's great-uncle Tu'i Kanokupolu. Upon his death, George Tupou assumed his title and became the sole king of a now united Tonga.

The second factor was the perceived link between European wealth and Christianity also played a part in the spread of the religion. Missionaries 'civilised' as well as Christianised, and islanders obtained European tools and skills such as literacy.

The third and final catalyst for the expansion of Christianity throughout the Pacific was that the message of afterlife salvation fell on attentive ears: European arrival coincided with massive depopulation through the spread of disease.

Missionaries also shielded islanders from the excesses of some traders, and it was missionary pressure that finally put an end to the 'blackbirding' slave trade that forced Pacific islanders to work in the mines of South America.

**1899**

The Tripartite Treaty gives Western Samoa to Germany and Eastern Samoa to America; Samoans hand in their guns, and full independence for Western Samoa won't occur until 1962.

**1900**

Tonga becomes a protectorate of the British Empire, an understanding that will linger until 1970, when full sovereignty is declared and Tonga joins the UN.

**1901**

NZ annexes the Cook Islands and more than a century of close association begins for the two countries.

**1905**

Mt Matavuno on the Samoan island of Savai'i erupts – lava destroys a village but no one is killed.

Putting Pacific languages into written form, initially in translations of the Bible, was another major contribution. While many missionaries deliberately destroyed 'heathen' Pacific artefacts and beliefs, others diligently recorded myths and oral traditions that would otherwise have been lost. A substantial portion of our knowledge of Pacific history and traditional culture comes from the work of missionary-historians.

## Colonial Expansion

Once European traders were established in the Pacific, many began agitating for their home countries to intervene and protect their interests. Missionaries also lobbied for colonial takeover, hoping that European law would protect islanders from the lawless traders. European powers began following a policy of 'flag following trade' by declaring protectorates and then by annexing Pacific states.

Despite the fact that the Cook Islands bear his name, James Cook never actually laid eyes on Rarotonga and only ever set foot on tiny Palmerston Atoll.

Colonialism brought peace between warring European powers but an increase in tensions with islanders. The arrival of settlers brought many diseases that had been unknown in the Pacific or had been experienced only in limited contact with explorers or traders, and these diseases took a horrific toll. Cholera, measles, smallpox, influenza, pneumonia, scarlet fever, chickenpox, whooping cough, dysentery, venereal diseases and even the common cold all had devastating effects. Most Polynesian populations were halved, while some islands of nearby Vanuatu dropped to just 5% of their original populations.

### Protecting the Cook Islands from France

The late 19th century saw a headlong rush of colonial expansion over much of the South Pacific. Following several requests for British protection from Makea Takau, the ruling *ariki* of Avarua, Rarotonga was officially made a British overseas protectorate in 1888, mainly in order to avoid a French invasion. The first British Resident (the representative of the British government in a British protectorate) arrived in 1891, but the relationship soon went sour. As a tiny country of little strategic or economic importance, the Cook Islands held little interest for the British, and, following a request from NZ prime minister Richard Seddon, the Cook Islands was annexed to NZ in 1901.

### A Three-Country Stand-Off for Samoa

Following a civil war between two rival Samoan ruling families, the British, North Americans and Germans then set about squabbling over Samoan territory, and by the late 1880s Apia's harbour was crowded with naval hardware from all three countries. Most of it subsequently sank – not because of enemy firepower but because of a cyclone that struck the harbour in March 1889. After several attempted compromises, the

**1914**

NZ troops occupy German-run Western Samoa without opposition at the beginning of WWI. In 1916 New Zealanders and Germans will face off in the Battle of the Somme.

**1918**

Spanish influenza, an H1N1 virus that caused one of the biggest pandemics in history, ravages Tonga and Samoa, wiping out approximately 20% of their populations.

**1929**

On 28 December, Black Saturday, armed NZ police in Apia gun down 11 Mau protesters seeking Samoan independence.

**1962**

Western Samoa celebrates becoming the first South Pacific island group to gain independence. By 1997 the country will have dropped the 'Western' tag.

Tripartite Treaty was signed in 1899, giving control of Western Samoa to the Germans and Eastern Samoa to the Americans.

### Christianity Brings Unity to Tonga

Tonga was largely spared this superpower squabbling and colonial annexation, and following the 1831 baptism of the ruling Tu'i Tonga, Tonga was united under King George Tupou I. A constitution, a flag and a national anthem were introduced in 1875. The constitution included a bill of rights, a format for legislative and judicial procedures, laws for succession to the throne and a section on land tenure. It is also responsible for Tonga's heavily Christian laws today.

The second king, George Tupou II, who took over in 1893, lacked the charisma, character and fearlessness of his predecessor. He signed a Treaty of Friendship with Britain in 1900, placing Tonga under British protection and giving Britain control over Tonga's foreign affairs. However, Tonga is still the Pacific's only kingdom.

## Moving Towards Independence

### Annexation & Administration

Following the annexation to NZ in 1901, the next six decades were largely quiet years for the Cook Islands. In the 1960s, as colonies became increasingly unfashionable, NZ jumped at the chance to offload its expensive overseas dependency and in 1965 the Cook Islands became internally self-governing.

In 1914, at the outbreak of WWI, Britain persuaded NZ to seize German Samoa. Preoccupation with affairs on the home front prevented Germany from resisting. Under the NZ administration, Samoa suffered a devastating (and preventable) outbreak of influenza in 1919; more than 7000 people (one-fifth of the population) died, further fuelling anger with the foreign rulers. Increasing calls for independence by the Mau movement culminated in the authorities opening fire on a demonstration at the courthouse in Apia in 1929, killing 11.

As a 14-year-old in 1932, Tonga's King Taufa'ahau Tupou IV achieved the national pole-vaulting record in his age group. The record remained unbroken until 1989.



### WWII in the South Pacific

While WWI had little impact on the Cook Islands, Samoa and Tonga (other than the transition of German Samoa to NZ's administration), WWII was a different story. Much of the conflict between Japanese and Allied forces happened through Micronesia, but many islands in Polynesia became key strategic posts. Soldiers from Samoa and Tonga – and many more from Fiji, the Solomons, French Polynesia and New Caledonia – also served in the Allied forces.

The war with Japan was fought through the Micronesian territories Japan had won from Germany in WWI, in Papua New Guinea and in

**1965**

The Cooks become a 'self-governing nation in free association with New Zealand'. Cook Islanders start eyeing up the bigger pay packets of Auckland and Wellington.

**1991**

Samoa beats Wales and Argentina at the Rugby World Cup, signalling the arrival of Pacific players onto the world stage.

**1996**

A Cook Islands 'economic crisis' sees 50% of public-service workers sacked and a NZ rescue package implemented.

**2002**

NZ prime minister Helen Clark formally apologises to Samoa for her country's poor treatment of Samoan citizens during colonial times.

the Solomon Islands. Initially Japan expanded south from its Micronesian territories almost unhindered and captured the Solomon Islands in 1942. It began building an airfield on Guadalcanal (which today is Henderson Airport) that would supply further advances south. Allied forces staged a huge offensive that saw more than 60 ships sunk in the surrounding waters that became known as Iron Bottom Sound. From 1944, US and Australian forces pushed the defending Japanese back, island by island. US bombers based in the Marianas punished Japanese cities for 10 months until 6 August 1945, when *Enola Gay* took off from Tinian (in the Northern Marianas) to drop an atomic bomb on Hiroshima. Days later, another was dropped on Nagasaki and the Pacific war was over.

*Lagaga – A Short History of Samoa*, edited by Malama Meleisea, is the definitive history and covers everything from legends and the infinite complexities of the *matai* (family-group leader) system to colonial rule and beyond from a Samoan perspective.

WWII had a lasting effect on the region. Most obviously, Japan's Micronesian colonies were taken over by the US, becoming the Trust Territory of the Pacific Islands. However, the war also left a legacy of more widespread and subtle effects. There was a huge improvement in roads and other infrastructure on many islands. There was also an input of money, food and other supplies. Some say that the many thousands of American GIs stationed in Tonga in WWII expanded the local gene pool, thereby bolstering immunity and providing a platform for sustained population growth.

WWII also hastened the end of traditional colonialism in the South Pacific, the relative equality between white and black US soldiers prompting islanders to question why they were still subservient to the British and the French. Many independence leaders were influenced by wartime experiences.

## Postcolonial Transitions

Following a change of government (and policy) in NZ, Western Samoa's independence was acknowledged as inevitable and on 1 January 1962 independence was finally achieved. Following Samoa, most Pacific island states gained independence (or partial independence) from their former colonial rulers.

Some Pacific territories remain fully or partially under the auspices of the US (American Samoa), France (New Caledonia, Wallis and Futuna, French Polynesia), Chile (Easter Island) and NZ (Cook Islands), and some of these are gradually returning power to islanders.

Tonga, which was never officially colonised, remains the last monarchy in the Pacific, though the royal family has begun relinquishing power in favour of democracy. It continued as a British Protectorate until 1970, when King Taufa'ahau Tupou IV re-established full sovereignty for the country, and subsequently joined the Commonwealth of Nations and the UN.

**2005**

A record five cyclones strike the Cook Islands, causing widespread damage; the Unit Titles Act is passed on Rarotonga but rejected by Aitutaki.

**2006**

Tongan capital Nuku'alofa is struck by pro-democracy riots after the death of King Taufa'ahau Tupou IV. Incoming King George Tupou V lessens his powers to progress Tongan democracy.

**2007**

Samoa's King Malietoa Tanumafili II dies and the nation becomes a republic, electing Tuiatua Tupua Tamasese Efi as head of state for a five-year term.

**2009**

The southern and eastern coasts of Upolu in Samoa and the southern coast of Tutuila in American Samoa are struck by a tsunami, killing approximately 190 people.

# Trials of Independence

## Instability in the Cook Islands

The first leader of the newly independent Cook Islands was Albert Henry, leader of the Cook Islands Party (CIP), and a prime mover in the push for self-rule. Henry did much to unify the country in the initial years of independence, but he fell spectacularly from grace during the 1978 elections, in which he became embroiled in a massive scandal involving overseas voters. The election was handed to the opposition party, the Cook Islands Democratic Party, and Henry was stripped of his knighthood. Power seesawed over the ensuing years between the two rival parties, and the Cook Islands political landscape of the period is littered with spats, scandals and larger-than-life personalities.

In the mid-1990s, foreign debt spiralled out of control and, with bankruptcy looming, the government was forced to take radical action. A 1996 economic-stabilisation program resulted in the sacking of about 2000 government employees – 50% of the public service – a huge proportion of the working population in a country of just 20,000 inhabitants. Masses of redundant workers left the country for NZ or Australia and never returned, and the Cooks were only saved from the brink thanks to an emergency aid package implemented by the NZ government.

## Tourism the Way Ahead for Samoa

In Samoa, the Human Rights Protection Party (HRPP) has mainly been in power since independence. Economic development remains excruciatingly slow or nonexistent, and far below population growth, but unlike neighbours Tonga and Fiji, the country has been politically stable. Fish and tropical produce such as cocoa, coffee, bananas, coconuts and taro were expected to become big export earners, but due to mismanagement, crop diseases and destructive cyclones, this has not happened. Nowadays container ships arrive piled with imports, but they leave almost empty. Increased tourism provides a ray of hope for a brighter economic future.

## Overseas Remittances Fuel Tonga

Tonga tends to lurch from one economic crisis to another; standards of living are generally dependent on investment from China, Japan and others, and remittances – money sent home from relatives living and working overseas. As in Samoa, tourism has been slow to take off here: when family ties between Tongans at home and abroad become weaker and the money dries up, the Tongan economy tends to suffer.

**2010**

Tonga holds its first democratic elections and nobles from the monarchy that has ruled for generations win when fringe parties join their ranks; 2014 delivers much the same result.

**2012**

King George Tupou V of Tonga dies while visiting Hong Kong. His brother George Tupou VI steps into the role.

**2015**

The popular George Tupou VI is officially crowned King of Tonga in a lavish week-long coronation celebration.

**2015**

In a disappointing Rugby World Cup for the South Pacific nations, Samoa and Tonga win one match each but fail to advance to the second stage of matches.

# Culture, Religion & Tradition

## The Local Psyche

Throughout the Cook Islands, Samoa and Tonga, visitors will experience a relaxed and easy-going welcome. While a 21st-century modernity is often evident, just scratching the surface will reveal traditional values and customs, and family and island alliances from earlier times.

### The Cook Islands

*Hongi* – the traditional New Zealand Maori custom of pressing noses together – was once practised in the Cook Islands too. *Hongi* literally means 'to smell the fragrance', and it was customary to sniff hands, shoulders, bodies and even feet as a form of greeting.

Beneath the Cook Islands' Westernised veneer (especially on Rarotonga), many aspects of traditional islander culture survive and inform everyday life and society. This culture is evident in the way land is inherited, managed and leased (but never sold), and lives on in dance, music and celebration.

However, it's important to remember that the Cook Islands has only been a unified country for a relatively short while. Previously, each island celebrated distinct customs, traditions and tribal structures. Many proud Cook Islanders still refer to their own 'home island' and can explain exactly how its people are different from those from other islands.

In the few short decades since independence, the Cook Islands has harnessed a remarkably strong sense of national pride. Politics, sport, dance and music are cohesive passions, and Cook Islanders share a collective belief in community, family and the preservation of traditional values.

### Samoa

Beyond the friendly and laid-back nature Samoans present to visitors, the strict conventions of *fa'a Samoa* (the Samoan way) are rigorously upheld throughout society.

At the heart of *fa'a Samoa* are *'aiga* (extended family groupings), which give life, culture, education, dignity and a purpose to individuals from the cradle to the grave and beyond. Each *'aiga* is headed by a senior *matai* (family group leader), who is supported by a junior *matai* and

#### ISLAND TIME

If you're keen for a break from schedules, meetings and generally having to be on time, all the time, a few weeks in the Cook Islands, Samoa or Tonga could be just what the doctor ordered. Patience is definitely a virtue in these laid-back South Pacific lands, where time is often a somewhat flexible concept.

Perhaps it's the tropical climate, the relaxed lifestyle or the fact that you can circumnavigate some of the islands in less than an hour, but local attitudes to time can be quite different from those in the West. If you're genuinely in a hurry (ie catching a plane), it can be extremely frustrating, but you'll get there faster if you learn to take it in your stride. So sit back, order another smoothie and make sure you book your taxi half an hour earlier than you think you'll need it. Come to think of it, better make that an hour...

who represents the family on the *fono* (village council). The *fono* punishes such crimes as theft, violence and insubordination with fines, reparation or ostracism. Punishments by the local *fono* are taken into account if the case also comes before the *palagi* (Western-style) court system.

In theory, all wealth and property is owned communally by caring, sharing *'aiga,* and decisions about these matters are always made by the *matai*. You serve and give your wages to your *matai,* and in return your *matai* helps you if you become sick or need money for school fees or a trip to New Zealand. *'Aiga* members share their wealth and provide welfare services to needy family members. Children belong to the *'aiga,* not the biological parents, and are often adopted or borrowed by relatives.

The Samoan language has a special vocabulary of respectful words that are used at official *fono* meetings and at any time when talking to a *matai*.

### Tonga

Like most South Pacific islanders, Tongans have a deep sense of generosity, hospitality, reciprocity and community. However, tourists are less customary here than in Rarotonga and Samoa, and they may initially be greeted with some reserve. This reserve is also related to traditions surrounding respect and hierarchy.

Effectively, Tonga has three social tiers: royalty, nobility and commoners. Commoners are required to address royalty in a special language and can only approach the monarch while crawling on their hands and knees (though you won't see this in practice if the king is parading along the streets). This deference is further evident in public life: direct eye contact is disrespectful and people generally stoop or duck when passing a person of higher status. Saving face is all-important, and Tongans do not like to disappoint or say no to anyone. Don't be surprised if you fail to receive straight answers, or are presented with directions and itineraries that go awry.

Several missionaries recounted that one of the traditional greetings in the Cook Islands was to tip back the head, slightly elevating the eyebrows at the same time. Look out for it – it's still a relatively common gesture in a culture where body language is very important.

## The Importance of Religion

Sunday in the Cook Islands, Samoa and Tonga is virtually mandated as a time for reflection and relaxation. Take the time to slow down, attend a church service – bring along your best singing voice – and learn about the importance of Christianity across the Pacific.

### The Cook Islands

Few people today remember much about the pre-European religions of Polynesia, with its sophisticated system of 12 heavens and 70-plus gods.

However, despite the Cook Islands today being overwhelmingly and enthusiastically Christian, echoes of the ancient religion are still evoked in many traditional ceremonies. The investiture of a new *ariki* (high chief) involves chants to Tangaroa and other pagan deities.

The major local denomination is the Cook Islands Christian Church (CICC). Founded by the first London Missionary Society (LMS) missionaries in the early 1820s, its blend of Church of England, Congregational, Baptist and Methodist teachings attracts about 70% of the Cook Islands' faithful. The remaining 30% of Cook Islands churchgoers are split between Roman Catholics, Seventh-Day Adventists, Jehovah's Witnesses, Pentecostals and followers of the Church of the Latter-day Saints.

Visitors are welcome to attend a Sunday service, and it's a fantastic way to immerse yourself in Cook Islands culture. The service is usually in the local tongue, although if there are any *papa'a* (foreigners) present there will be a token welcome in English and parts of the service may be in English as well.

Derek Freeman ignited a major controversy when in 1983 he published his look at the gloomy side of life in Samoa, entitled *Margaret Mead and Samoa: The Making and Unmaking of an Anthropological Myth.*

### Samoa

Samoan churches don't just physically dominate the villages; they're a vital part of the social glue that holds everything together. Everyone dresses up in their Sunday best and goes to church at least once on the week's holiest day.

The village *pese* (choirs) practise two or three times a week (with fines for being late or absent), church youth groups organise dance competitions and sports events, and women's groups raise money by running bingo nights and aerobics classes in the church hall. Sunday school for the children is taken seriously, with a panel of teachers and annual exams. Families compete with each other to donate the most money to the church, and the amount given by each family is called out and written down during the service. Families often give more than they can afford (up to 30% of their income) to maintain their social standing. Some give and expect to receive back good health and other blessings in answer to their prayers.

### Tonga

Tongans invest great energy and creativity into decorating graves. Visitors passing cemeteries will spy embroidered quilts, beer bottles, plastic flowers, pictures of Jesus Christ, shells, rocks and soft toys adorning burial sites.

Tongans are extremely religious, and 99% of the country's population identifies with a wide range of Christian faiths. Minority religions represented include Baha'i, Islam and Hinduism. Missionaries in Tonga are prevalent and mostly well respected, and local church delegates are frequently on missions around the Pacific. Churches rely on donations and fundraising both in Tonga and overseas, and this often places a hefty financial burden on Tongan families. Many families end up taking out loans or selling heirlooms in the markets around the time of annual church donations.

Many premissionary superstitions linger, such as fear of *tevolo* (devils), and graveyard protocol retains the trace of ancient rituals. One belief is that if a family member is suffering from a terminal or chronic illness, it is because the bones of ancestors have been disturbed. Many Tongans will return to family burial sites, dig up remains and rebury old relatives to remedy their own ill health. *Faito'o* (traditional Tongan medicine) is also widely practised in every village, and is often a preferred alternative to Western healthcare.

## Family First

While relocation to Auckland, Sydney or Los Angeles can slowly weaken intergenerational ties, family remains profoundly important in these island cultures and children are highly prized. Child-rearing is a communal responsibility – you might be wondering where your toddler has got to when he or she turns up carried on the hip of a motherly eight-year-old. Kids are quickly absorbed into games with local children and fun has no language barrier.

### The Cook Islands

Every Cook Islander is part of a family clan that is connected in some way to the ancient system of chiefs – a system that has survived for centuries in an unbroken line. Most people can relate their genealogy over several generations – often in truly bewildering detail – and it's more than just

#### CANNIBALISM IN THE COOKS

Like many other South Pacific islanders, Cook Islanders practised cannibalism, but there's debate about exactly how widespread it was, and according to oral history the practice was only commonplace under certain chiefs. Cannibalism was usually enacted as a mark of victory in war or as a fearsome punishment. The practice ceased in the Southern Group of the Cooks with the advent of Christianity, although it had apparently already been outlawed by Mangaian chiefs by the time the missionaries arrived.

The favoured method, according to the missionary William Wyatt Gill, was to skewer the unfortunate victim on a long spear, and then barbecue them over an open fire to remove the hair. The body was then steamed in an underground oven and distributed among the warriors of the tribe (women and children were never allowed to join in). The intestines and thighs were the choicest cuts, but diners weren't overly fussy, and the only body parts remaining at the end of the feast were the bones and nails.

## CONVERSATION & ETIQUETTE

Want to get chatting with the locals? A good conversation starter is often sports such as rugby or netball: 'Can the Cooks/Samoa/Tonga knock over the Kiwis at the next Commonwealth Games?' Given that many islanders travel around the world, they may want to talk about where you're from and they're almost guaranteed to have a relative who moved to Auckland, Sydney or Utah. Here are a few simple rules that will help ingratiate you with your hosts in traditional villages:

- Remove your shoes when entering a home.
- Sit cross-legged on the floor, rather than with your feet pointing out.
- Avoid entering a house during prayers.
- Avoid walking between two people in conversation.
- Avoid extended direct eye contact at first meetings.
- Try to remain on a lower level than a chief to show respect.

a matter of family pride. The traditional systems of land tenure and title inheritance rely entirely on family genealogy. As Cook Islands families are often huge, with astonishingly complicated connections, crossovers and intermarriages, it pays to know exactly how you fit into the family tree. Extended families are an everyday feature of most Cook Islanders' lives, and you'll often find children living with their grandparents or aunts and uncles. Long-term adoption between families is fairly commonplace.

### Samoa

Family life is at the heart of *fa'a Samoa*. Parents and other relatives treat babies very affectionately, but when they reach three years old they are pushed away and made the responsibility of an older sibling or cousin. *Fa'aaloalo* (respect for elders) is the most crucial aspect of *fa'a Samoa,* and children are expected to obey not just their parents, grandparents, uncles and aunts but also the *matai* and other adults in their village. Any disobedience or answering back is sternly punished. Children are regularly reminded of the Samoan proverb, 'the path to power is through *tautua* (service)'. To many Samoan children, however, this service can seem like never-ending servitude to family, village and church. Most parents are strict and force their children to attend church, run errands and do household chores, and often school and homework are not the number-one priority.

### Tonga

Family is the central unit of Tongan life. An average family unit may comprise adopted children, cousins and other distant relatives, alongside the usual smattering of siblings and grandparents. Chores are distributed according to gender: men tend the *umu* (underground earth oven), grow and harvest food, collect and husk coconuts, and perform all manual labour. The women clean, wash clothes, prepare and cook food, and take on the lion's share of child-minding responsibilities. The patriarch is generally the head of the family, and land passes down from a father to his eldest son. However, women possess high (even superior) status in other facets of family life. For example, a brother's *fahu* (oldest sister) will be accorded the highest level of respect at all formal and informal occasions, from funerals to weddings and births.

Tongan society is devoid of materialism; possessions are communal and 'borrowing' is a way of life. Visitors staying with a Tongan family might find that some of their belongings are borrowed. Raising the issue with your hosts is best done with a sense of humour and the understanding that this is how society here operates.

# Myths & Legends

**Pre-Christian religion was remarkably consistent across the islands scattered over the vast expanse of Polynesia. Gods such as Vatea, Tangaroa, Rongomatane and Tane, and demigods such as Maui and Rata, were known to Polynesians everywhere from Hawai'i to Easter Island to New Zealand (NZ). Often the names changed slightly through dialectical differences, but the Polynesian celestial pantheon is largely familiar and consistent across the Pacific.**

*Cook Islands Custom*, by William Wyatt Gill (first published in 1892), contains first-hand accounts of many traditional Cook Islands customs, including birth and marriage practices, magic rituals and funeral rites.

It was the prodigious navigation and voyaging feats of the Polynesians in their long *vaka* (outrigger canoes) that made such homogeneity of religion possible. All myths and legends were passed orally from generation to generation and, as with any oral storytelling, quirks and regional variations have crept in across the centuries.

## Tangaroa the Creator

Tangaroa was the original 'creator' deity across much of the Pacific, and he is still referred to by this name in the Cook Islands and NZ. Worshipped as the father of the gods and the god of fertility, his other monikers include Kanaloa (Hawai'i), Tangaloa (Tonga) and Tagaloa (Samoa). Tangaroa's children were so-called 'departmental' gods, responsible for fields such as the forests (Tane) and agriculture (Rongo).

With characteristic Tongan humility, some Tongan legends say that the islands of Tonga were woodchips left over from the gods' workshop. In another tale, Tangaloa fished the islands from the sea with a hook made from tortoiseshell and whalebone. Perhaps not adept with the fishing rod, his line snagged on the island of Nuapapu, scattering into the sea the bits of land now known as the Vava'u Group.

### THE TURTLE & THE SHARK

One of Samoa's most famous legends began on the island of Savai'i. During a devastating famine, a blind old woman and her granddaughter threw themselves into the ocean so they would not be a burden on their selfish and unwelcoming family. Cast into the waves, with only the sea to protect them, they miraculously transformed into a turtle and a shark, and they set about finding another village to welcome them elsewhere in Samoa. Many times they turned themselves back into grandmother and granddaughter to approach a village, but many times they were spurned and forced to return to the ocean as a turtle and a shark.

Finally, the village of Vaitogi – now in American Samoa – accepted them, and it welcomed them to their community on the high cliffs above a rugged black-lava coastline dotted with surging blowholes. But after so long living in the sea, the old lady and her granddaughter missed the ocean, and they decided to return there and live beneath the rocks near the village. Now, when a special song is sung – one version of the legend states that it must be sung by the villagers of Vaitogi – a shark and a turtle appear, and the old lady and her granddaughter continue to thank the people of Vaitogi for their compassion and generosity.

Tagaloa (or Tangaloa) is known as the supreme being throughout Samoa and Tonga, but in other parts of the Pacific oral storytelling has varied the script. In the Cook Islands (and NZ), Tangaroa is not the father of the gods, but one of the kids. He is, though, the most important of the departmental gods, even more important than his father, Vatea, and mother, Papa. Tangaroa is the god of the seas here – pretty key in cultures where the ocean is so vital to survival.

Carvings of Tangaroa were super-popular in the Cook Islands in pre-Christian times, and they remain the most common carvings on the islands today (check him out: it's easy to see why Tangaroa was the god of fertility).

### A Mangaian Variation

Only on Mangaia, southeast of Rarotonga, did Tangaroa lose his position as the pre-eminent god. On Mangaia, they say, when Tangaroa's parents discussed their children's inheritance, Vatea wanted to give all the food to his first-born, Tangaroa. But his wife, Papa, suggested giving Tangaroa only the 'chiefly' food; ie only the food that was red. Vatea thought this was a fine salute to his favoured son, but the red food turned out to form only a tiny heap; Rongo's share, by contrast, was so plentiful that his huge pile of food kept falling over! Papa was happy, because although she was forbidden to eat with her first-born by the complex rules of *tapu* (the laws that define what is sacred and what is not), she was permitted to share Rongo's huge stash. Tangaroa, unsurprisingly, was not happy and stormed off to sea, leaving Rongo to rule Mangaia. Ever after, when human sacrifices were made to appease Rongo, a piece was always thrown aside for the hungry Papa.

## Maui the Trickster

Between gods such as Tangaroa and heroes such as Tangi'ia, there is a continuum of demigods. Of these, Maui Potiki is the most famous. A trickster cross between Prometheus and Brer Rabbit, Maui achieved his great feats (such as slowing the sun, bringing fire to people and creating the first coconut) not through the use of force but by cleverness and trickery.

According to Polynesian mythology, black pearls from the Northern Group of the Cook Islands and Tahiti were given by Tangaroa to Tane. Using the lustre of the pearls, Tane was able to illuminate heaven.

Maui's most famous achievement, remembered in legends all over the Pacific, was to fish an entire island out of the sea. NZ Maori say it was the North Island of their country, but in the Cook Islands they say it was the twin islands of Manihiki and Rakahanga.

Long ago, three brothers, all named Maui, held a fishing competition near an underwater coral outcrop. The first two caught only everyday fish, but Maui Potiki (Maui the Last Born) had arranged things beforehand with a woman, Hine i te Papa, who dwelt on the seabed. She hooked Maui Potiki's fish hook into the coral outcrop and Maui was able to pull it up above the surface to form a large island. Maui Potiki, ecstatic, jumped onto his catch and taunted his brothers about his fishing prowess.

However, if you know anything about Polynesian legends, you'll know that something always goes wrong. In this case, a Rarotongan named Huku had already discovered the underwater coral outcrop, and he returned at once to demand 'his' island. Maui Potiki was a trickster, not a fighter; he sprang into the air to escape, unfortunately breaking the island into two pieces as he leapt. Huku was left in possession of the two islands, which he named Rakahanga and Manihiki.

Yet another variation tells us that Tonga was the product of a successful fishing trip by Maui. Fishing with a hook borrowed from an old man called Tonga, Maui plucked all the islands from the ocean one by one, and called the largest Tonga to honour the old man and his miraculous hook. Many centuries later, it's little wonder that Polynesians are so keen on fishing as they try to discover their inner Maui.

To fast track a summation of the mythology of Oceania, see www.janeresture.com/oceania_myths/mythology.htm (just ignore the ads). Learn about Atonga, the half-human, half-spirit hero of Samoan myth, or Mahuika, the goddess of fire and earthquakes.

# The Arts

**These Polynesian island nations are rich in artistic heritage and endeavour, with exquisite traditional arts and crafts still produced to the highest standards, and customary dance and music performed with gusto. What's equally interesting is how these traditions have morphed into the new century, not only surviving, but thriving.**

## Traditional Dance & Music

### Dance

Traditional dance is super-popular across the Cook Islands, Samoa and Tonga. For a ritzy showcase of the local talent attend an 'island night', which combines a traditional feast with music and dance. Wallflowers, be warned: a feature of almost every island night is dragging some unsuspecting visitors up on stage to perform. Don't be shy – you'll get a lot more out of the evening if you just lose your inhibitions and shake your thang.

Cook Islanders' dancing is wonderfully suggestive and sensuous, and unsurprisingly this met with stern disapproval from the first European visitors. Each island also has its own songs, chants and dance variations.

Dance in Tonga is also an impressive sight, and is performed regularly for special occasions and feasts. Most Tongan dances are performed in groups, like the *lakalaka,* a formal, standing dance that can require the participation of an entire village. The *ma'ulu'ulu* is performed for festive and state occasions. Men also occasionally perform the *kailao* (war

#### SIA FIGIEL: AUTHOR

Samoan poet and novelist Sia Figiel is the recipient of the Commonwealth Writers Prize for her book *Where We Once Belonged*.

**What are your favourite books by South Pacific writers?**

If I had room in my suitcase for *one* book, *Tales of the Tikongs* (Epeli Hau'ofa) would be it! *Tales* is Epeli's masterpiece. It's a fabulous satirical look at island living that had me laughing hysterically from page one. An absolute must from our most gifted and sagacious storyteller.

Then there's *Sons for the Return Home* (Albert Wendt), the book that made me want to be a writer. Published over 40 years ago, it's an intimate history of Samoans and Pacific people that continues to be relevant today. It's an in-depth look into the Pacific migrant experience and the complexities of love, racism and cultural identity in a new country – then how that identity is changed upon return to the motherland. Compelling and provocative!

**And your novels?**

I wrote the first line to *Where We Once Belonged* on a napkin while travelling between Prague and Berlin. That was almost 20 years ago. It's an intimate look at what our lives were like in Samoa in the '70s. I've only reread the whole thing once, about five years ago, and I was overwhelmed by its understanding of *alofa* – that love really is what glues Samoan and Pacific peoples across this vast ocean.

### TOP READS BY TONGAN & SAMOAN WRITERS

- *Tales of the Tikongs*, by Epeli Hau'ofa (1983). An utterly entertaining read, Epeli's masterpiece is a satirical look at Tongan island life.
- *Sons for the Return Home*, by Albert Wendt (1973). A personal history of the Samoans, exploring the migrant experience and the nuances of cultural identity in a new country (and how that identity changes upon returning home).
- *Where We Once Belonged*, by Sia Figiel (1999). An intimate look at Samoan life in the 1970s.

dance), a dramatic display with wooden clubs, rapid pacing, war cries and fierce drumming. Oiled skin also facilitates *fakapale* (the traditional tipping of Tongan dancers): spectators slap one- and two-*pa'anga* notes on the bodies of performers to show respect and express gratitude. Visitors are expected to do the same.

In Samoa, the most popular dance is the *fiafia*, in which drummers keep the beat while singers, usually sitting on the floor, sing traditional songs. A *fiafia* traditionally ends with the *siva*, a languid dance performed by the village *taupou* (usually the daughter of a high chief). Larger hotels and resorts put on lavish *fiafia*, which always end with an exciting, though not traditional, fire dance.

## Music

Music and singing are vital cultural traditions across the Pacific. The close-harmony singing of church services in the Cook Islands, Samoa and Tonga is moving and memorable, and Polynesian string bands featuring guitars and ukuleles are a regular feature at restaurants and hotels on Rarotonga and Aitutaki.

In Samoa, musical highlights include the vibrant drumming that accompanies *fiafia* nights and the soaring harmonies of church choirs.

Visitors in search of Tonga's famed a cappella music should go to the nearest church. Practice sessions are always held on Sunday evenings, and occasionally during the week. As well as church music, string bands with guitars and ukuleles are well loved in Tonga, and often feature at parties, feasts, kava clubs and bars. Traditional instruments, such as the *fangufangu* (nose flute), *mimiha* (pan pipes), *nafa* (skin drum) and *kele'a* (conch shell blown as a horn), are often used on significant occasions.

The Cook Islands ukulele is traditionally made from coconut shells and carved wood (usually wild hibiscus or mahogany). It's noticeably smaller and tuned to a higher pitch than ukuleles in Tahiti and Hawai'i.

# Traditional Arts & Crafts

## Architecture

In the Cook Islands, houses and other buildings were made of natural materials that decayed rapidly, so only a few buildings of traditional construction remain on any of the islands in the Southern Group. Woodcarving was only rarely used in houses, although some important buildings, including some of the first locally built mission churches, had carved and decorated wooden posts.

The best example of traditional Samoan architecture is the *fale* (home or meeting hall), which also features in Tonga. *Fale* are oval structures without walls, to maximise the cool breezes inside. The thatched coconut-frond roof is lashed to wooden rafters with *sennit* (coconut-husk string) and supported by wooden posts. The floor consists of a platform of wood, coral, rock or pebbles covered with woven pandanus mats. The entire house is one room, and without exterior or interior walls privacy is impossible. Chickens, dogs and even pigs sometimes have to be chased out.

## Canoes

In the Cook Islands, *vaka* (canoes) were carved with great seriousness and ceremony in pre-European times. Not only did the canoes have to be large and strong enough for long-distance ocean voyages, they had to be made in accordance with strict religious rules. *Ta'unga vaka* (experts not only in canoes and woodcarving but also in spiritual matters) had to guide every step of the process.

None of those pre-European canoes survive today, but you can often see modern reconstructions at Avana Harbour on Rarotonga. These modern *vaka,* sailing from island to island using traditional navigation methods, have helped fine-tune many theories about ancient Polynesian settlement. On a smaller scale, Mitiaro's outrigger fishing canoes are some of the most beautiful canoes made today.

*Pacific Tapa*, by Roger Neich and Mick Pendergrast, is a useful illustrated booklet on tapa styles right across the South Pacific from the Solomon islands to Tahiti.

## Siapo & Tapa

The bark cloth known as *siapo* in Samoa and tapa or *ngatu* in Tonga is made from the inner bark of the Chinese paper mulberry tree. The bark has to be soaked, scraped and flattened before being stamped with traditional patterns or painted freehand. Geometric designs represent fishing nets, pandanus leaves, birds and starfish. Originally used as clothing, *siapo* and tapa are still used in customary gift exchanges.

In Samoa, you can sometimes see *siapo* production in Palauli village on the south coast of Savai'i, and don't miss the exquisite *siapo* wallpaper in Robert Louis Stevenson's former home overlooking Apia.

While tapa is the name commonly used overseas to describe Pacific bark cloth, in Tonga the elaborately decorated finished product is actually called *ngatu*. The longest and most elaborate pieces of *ngatu* are reserved for the most important occasions.

Patterns often represent animals and traditional flowers, and some designs also commemorate historical events, like the installation of electricity or the passing of Halley's Comet. Designs are hand-painted using a dried piece of pandanus fruit as a paintbrush, and paints tend to be earthy reds, browns and black. The inner bark of the *tongo (*mangrove tree) is used to make a glossy red-brown dye and burnt candlenuts are used to make a black dye.

Traditional Samoan tattooing has gained recent exposure via some high-profile sportsmen with Samoan heritage. Check out the amazing tatts on Australian footballer Tim Cahill, New Zealand rugby renegade Sonny Bill Williams and wrestler-turned-actor Dwayne 'The Rock' Johnson.

## Tattooing

Across Polynesia, islanders of both sexes were tattooed to mark the onset of puberty and arrival into adulthood, and later to signify status within their tribal groups. While tattoos became popular with passing European sailors in the 19th century, Christian missionaries discouraged or forbade tattooing.

In Samoa and Tonga, tattoos were elaborate designs worn on the buttocks and hips, using natural pigments pounded into the skin with shell or bone tools. Samoan *tofuga* (tattooists) remain strongly traditional. A tattoo boom here (and throughout the West) has seen full arm and leg designs becoming popular, and even the full-body patterns are the order of the day. Tongan *tatatau* (tattoos) were thought to be almost extinct until there was a revival in the early 2000s.

## Weaving

Pandanus mats are the most highly regarded examples of Tongan weaving, but weavers also make *kato* (baskets), belts and hats. Historically, traditional Tongan boat sails were woven from pandanus leaves, and ropes were made from the interwoven fibres of coconut husks.

Different varieties of pandanus plant are used for different colours and textures. The *kie* pandanus is used for the finest mats, which are creamy white in colour. Leaves are buried in mud for several days to

Traditional woodcarving, Rarotonga

*Pacific Pattern*, compiled by Susanne Küchler and Graeme Were, is a beautiful photographic collection of textiles, textures and materials from all over the Pacific. It includes a detailed section on Tongan art techniques.

make black pandanus, while bronze colours require an involved process of smoking over a fire.

Everyday *fala* (mats) are woven out of pandanus strips about 1cm to 1.5cm wide. Chiefly mats are known as *fala 'eiki* and are double woven with one coarse and one fine side. Many floor mats are patterned with diamond or floral designs.

In Samoa, *ie toga* (fine mats crafted from pandanus) take months of painstaking work. Woven from pandanus leaves split into very narrow widths, *ie toga* can resemble fine linen or silk. They're now only made in Samoa, and a few are sometimes available to buy at the market in Apia. Along with other woven mats, *ie toga* are a traditional currency, while *siapo* and oils are exchanged at Samoan weddings.

## Woodcarving

Figures of gods carved from wood were among the most widespread art forms in the Cook Islands and were particularly common on Rarotonga. These squat figures were usually dedicated to a specific god (Tangaroa, the god of sea, fishing and fertility, was a particularly popular subject). Staff gods (wooden staffs with figures carved down their lengths), war clubs and spears were other typical Rarotongan artefacts. You can view examples in the National Museum in Avarua.

Carving and wood turning have a more functional than decorative purpose in traditional Tongan society. *Tufunga* (specialist carvers) were always men. They made *kali (*neck rests), *kumete* (kava bowls), canoe paddles, *fue* (fly whisks), *kolo* and *povai (*war clubs) and, sometimes, figurative sculptures.

A superbly illustrated book, *Samoan Art & Artists*, by Sean Mallon, covers every artistic genre from architecture to weaving, and contains interviews with contemporary Samoan artists on and off the islands.

# Food & Drink

**The food of Rarotonga, Samoa and Tonga is sturdy and filling: don't expect to scale back the calories here! And don't worry about the indignity of piling your plate too high or going back for seconds – the more you eat, the more the islanders will love you for it. Expect lots of fish, chicken and pork, plus tropical fruit and some excellent South Seas beers to sluice it all down.**

## What to Eat

Most of the edible plants that now grow in abundance throughout the Pacific were originally introduced from Asia and the East Indies – but *kumara* (sweet potato) is actually South American, suggesting that Polynesian settlers travelled on to South America after settling the South Pacific.

### Fruit & Vegetables

With a temperate climate and often rich volcanic soil, things grow easily across the Pacific. On Rarotonga, look forward to papayas, mangoes and oranges. In Samoa, locally grown tropical fruit includes bananas, papayas, guavas, passion fruit, pineapples and *vi* (Tahitian apples); mangoes are available from late September. Across the islands of Tonga, seasonal fruit includes bananas, bush oranges, almonds, papayas, pineapples, guavas, passion fruit and watermelons. Across the region, starchy staples include breadfruit, and root vegetables such as yams, sweet potatoes and *cassavas*.

### Seafood

The Cook Islands offers a huge variety of seafood, and most Rarotongan restaurants offer a 'catch of the day', usually a deep-sea fish such as *mahimahi,* wahoo, swordfish or tuna. In Samoa, marine delicacies include tuna and shark, and lagoon species including parrotfish, perch, lobster, squid, octopus, crabs and *limu* (a crunchy seaweed). Tongan seafood highlights include local lobster, snapper, tuna and *mahimahi.*

### Traditional Foods & Celebrations

One of the best ways to sample local Pacific cuisine is to stay in a village, be invited into a home or take part in an *umu* feast (known as an *umukai* in the Cook Islands). An *umu* is a traditional Polynesian earth oven harnessing hot rocks to steam the food. It's used for feasts and celebrations or the weekly community get-together for a leisurely Sunday lunch after church. Typical *umu* foods include chicken and fish, or more prestigious roast suckling pig.

The Cook Islands banana is smaller and sweeter than the ones you might be used to back home, while the Cook Islands orange is actually green-skinned – a fact that made it rather unpopular on the international market, and ultimately contributed to the collapse of the island's orange industry.

Accompanying dishes include cooked green bananas, taro and yams, and corned beef fried with onions. Other dishes incorporate coconut cream, including the tasty Samoan delicacies *palusami* (young taro leaves baked in coconut cream), *oka* (marinated raw fish, known as *ika mata* in the Cook Islands), *supo esi* (papaya pudding) and *fa'ausi talo* (taro in coconut cream). In Tonga, a popular *umu* dish is *lu.* Infused with a smoky flavour, taro leaves are wrapped around corned beef, *sipi* (mutton), fish or chicken, and then mixed with coconut milk and onion. In the Cook Islands, other local specialities include *firi firi* (Tahitian-style doughnuts), *rukau* (steamed taro leaves), *poke* (banana with arrowroot and coconut) and *mitiore* (fermented coconut with onion and seafood).

You'll usually find all of these dishes at Rarotonga's weekly Punanga Nui Market. Inexpensive Tongan market foods include *faikakai* (pudding with a coconut syrup) and *keke* (deep-fried cakes flavoured with banana).

# What to Drink

## Nonalcoholic Drinks

Across the Pacific you can often buy green coconuts from the roadside or at local markets. Fresh fruit juices and smoothies are another refreshing tropical treat.

In the Cook Islands, coffee is grown and roasted on Rarotonga and 'Atiu, and on Tonga, locally produced Royal coffee is popular. But the quality of the brew can be questionable: interpretations of Italian-style espresso are sometimes rather abstract – weak and milky is the norm. For a stiff double shot, head for the resort restaurants or expat-run cafes in urban areas. The further you get from the major towns, the more likely it is that it'll be instant coffee in your cup.

In Samoa, local beverages include *koko Samoa* (a chocolate drink made with locally grown and roasted cocoa beans) and creamy *vaisalo* (made from fresh coconuts and thickened with starch).

Tongans enjoy a great non-alcoholic cocktail called *'otai.* Made from fresh coconut milk, it's combined with a small amount of sugar and shredded watermelon or mango.

## Alcoholic Drinks

Local beers to look for include Popoa in Tonga, Vailima in Samoa and Matutu in the Cook Islands. Liqueurs, wine and vodka made from local fruit are sold on Rarotonga, and visitors to 'Atiu should check out a *tumunu* (bush-beer drinking session), the Cook Islands equivalent of kava-drinking ceremonies in Tonga and Samoa. Wine – mostly imported from New Zealand or Australia – is available in most large towns, but it's usually expensive.

*Kava, the Pacific Elixir*, by Vincent Lebot, Mark Merlin and Lamont Lindstrom, is an exhaustive study of the South Pacific's oldest beverage. Fans of the wonder root should also check out www.kavaroot.com.

# Where to Eat & Drink

## Cafes & Restaurants

The Cook Islands – especially Rarotonga – has a diverse and cosmopolitan dining scene. Most Rarotongan restaurants prepare food to a high standard, courtesy of the tourist industry and the large number of local chefs trained overseas. Regular 'island nights' at Cook Islands resorts are a good opportunity to try local flavours. Aitutaki also features island nights and a couple of decent restaurants, but on other islands in the Cooks, dining options are more limited.

In Samoa and American Samoa, Apia and Pago Pago respectively have a range of restaurants, but outside these towns options for dining out are limited. Samoans don't eat out much, so most menus cater for Western tastes, with seafood, steak, pizza and pasta, and some Apia hotels put on island-style buffets.

### ETIQUETTE & FOOD SAFETY

- Tipping is not customary in the Cook Islands, Samoa or Tonga.
- Meals are often preceded by a short grace.
- Food is seen as something to be shared: village families are hospitable and may invite you home for a meal.
- If you stay with a village family, reciprocate by buying a sack of rice or tins of corned beef at the local store.
- On outer islands, meals are sometimes eaten in the traditional way – ie without cutlery – but most people will understand if you prefer to use a knife and fork.
- Be wary of dishes marinated in coconut cream, especially in markets and at village meals. Dishes are often prepared the day before and coconut cream can spoil quickly.
- Be wary of eating reef fish (parrotfish, snapper etc), as some islands have a problem with *ciguatera* poisoning. Stick to deep-sea fish (tuna, *mahimahi*, wahoo). These are generally the only fish served in restaurants.

Challenging regional favourites to try include *mitiore* (fermented coconut served with crab or shellfish; Cook Islands), *palolo* (salty blue reef worms served on toast; Samoa) and *sea* (an incredibly salty, oyster-like delicacy of sea-slug innards that leaves a metallic aftertaste; Samoa).

In Tonga there are Western-style cafes, restaurants and bars on Tongatapu and Vava'u, but options are limited (or nonexistent) on Ha'apai, 'Eua and the Niuas.

## Self-Catering & Markets

Supermarkets on Rarotonga are well stocked, but outer-island grocery stores are more limited. Rarotonga's Saturday-morning Punanga Nui Market is excellent for fresh produce, traditional foods and an expanding range of local gourmet goodies. Informal stalls around the island also sell fresh fruit and vegetables. Fresh seafood is easily purchased on Rarotonga, and Aitutaki has a weekly market. Fish and seafood are sold in most Rarotongan supermarkets, but on the outer islands you'll have to catch your own or buy from local fishers.

In Tonga, markets can be found in Nuku'alofa, Pangai and Neiafu, but on outer islands the availability and diversity of fresh produce can be erratic. Most villages have *fale koloa* (corner shops) and major towns have supermarkets.

Apia in Samoa has a small fish market (go as early as possible), but elsewhere it's difficult to buy fresh seafood to cook up yourself. Supermarkets in Apia and Pago Pago (American Samoa) are well stocked, but high transport costs to the islands can make some items more expensive than you might expect. Every village has a store, but they only stock the basics.

Outside of supermarkets on Rarotonga and in Nuku'alofa, Apia and Pago Pago, it's always worth checking the use-by dates on packaged or canned food, especially in smaller village shops with a low turnover of goods. Prices on outer islands are high, so it's worth stocking up at main-island supermarkets (but be aware that weight limits for baggage on short flights to smaller islands can be restrictive).

To recreate Pacific cuisine when you get back home, check out traditional Cook Islands recipes at www.ck/food or some Samoan favourites at www.samoafood.com.

## Vegetarians & Vegans

Restaurant menus on Rarotonga are dominated by fish, seafood and meat dishes, though there are usually a few meat-free salad and pasta options.

Vegetarians may struggle with traditional Tongan food, where nearly every dish involves meat. Even if you request meat-free food from stalls, takeaway stands and locally run restaurants, your food is likely to be cooked alongside meat products.

In Samoa, you can buy *palusami* and fresh fruit and vegetables in the Apia market. If you're accommodated in a homestay, tell your hosts you're vegetarian to avoid any awkward moments.

### KAVA CULTURE

Known as kava in Tonga and *'ava* in Samoa, the muddy and peppery drink made from the dried root of the kava plant is popular across the South Pacific. Although not alcoholic, kava is both anaesthetic and analgesic, high in fibre, low in calories, and serves as a mild tranquiliser, antibacterial agent and diuretic. Unfortunate side effects for committed drinkers are yellowing skin, excessive fatigue and a decreased red blood cell count.

In Samoa, *'ava* is usually reserved for special occasions and restricted to *matai* (chiefs), but a big wooden bowl of the drink is often available at the market in Apia.

Tongans prefer to drink home-grown kava. The best kava is said to come from the volcanic islands of Tofua in Ha'apai and Tafahi in the Niuas.

Kava is used in both formal and informal settings in Tonga. It is drunk before and after church on a Sunday, during the conferment of nobility, at village meetings and in the negotiations of contracts and other agreements. Most villages have at least one kava club *(kava kulupu)*, and big, intervillage kava parties are a common fundraiser.

Locally, only men visit kava clubs, but male and female visitors are usually welcome. You may be formally invited, or just ask a local taxi driver to take you. If you're lucky, you might be invited to join kava circles, which sometimes happen at local bars.

# Survival Guide

# Transport

## GETTING THERE & AWAY

Flights, cars and tours can be booked online at lonelyplanet.com/bookings.

## Entering the Region

Unless you're hoisting the spinnaker on a yacht or kicking back on a cruise ship, getting to this part of the South Pacific will mean a long-haul flight, usually via a gateway city such as Auckland, Brisbane, Sydney, LA or Honolulu.

### Passport

There are no passport restrictions when visiting these South Pacific countries – everyone is welcome!

## Air

Due to vast expanses of open ocean and the relatively small numbers of travellers visiting the region, just getting to Rarotonga, the Samoas and Tonga can be an adventure! This is a very remote part of the world.

The main gateway airports are in Australia, New Zealand (NZ) and the US – you'll have to get to one of these spots to be able to fly into the Cook Islands, the Samoas or Tonga.

There are also several smaller local airlines operating within this part of the South Pacific, but not all of these fly directly to all countries – you may find yourself having to detour through Auckland airport to get from one country to the next (not really a hassle – just a bit time consuming).

### Airlines

Airlines winging into the region include the following:

**Air New Zealand** (www.airnz.co.nz) Flies into Rarotonga from Auckland, Sydney and LA; and from Auckland to Samoa and Auckland to Tonga.

**Air Rarotonga** (www.airraro.com) Flies between Rarotonga and Tahiti.

**Air Tahiti** (www.airtahiti.com) Flies between Tahiti and Rarotonga.

**Fiji Airways** (www.fijiairways.com) Flies a number of international routes into Fiji, with connections to Samoa and Tonga. Also flies directly between Samoa and Honolulu.

**Hawaiian Airlines** (www.hawaiianair.com) Connects west-coast US cities (and New York) through Honolulu to American Samoa.

**Inter Island Airways** (www.interislandair.com) Flies between American Samoa and Samoa.

**Jetstar Airways** (www.jetstar.com) Flies into the Cook Islands from NZ.

**Polynesian Airlines** (www.polynesianairlines.com) Flies between Samoa and American Samoa.

**Virgin Australia** (www.virginaustralia.com) Flies to Tonga

### CLIMATE CHANGE & TRAVEL

Every form of transport that relies on carbon-based fuel generates $CO_2$, the main cause of human-induced climate change. Modern travel is dependent on aeroplanes, which might use less fuel per kilometre per person than most cars but travel much greater distances. The altitude at which aircraft emit gases (including $CO_2$) and particles also contributes to their climate change impact. Many websites offer 'carbon calculators' that allow people to estimate the carbon emissions generated by their journey and, for those who wish to do so, to offset the impact of the greenhouse gases emitted with contributions to portfolios of climate-friendly initiatives throughout the world. Lonely Planet offsets the carbon footprint of all staff and author travel.

from Auckland and Sydney; Samoa from Auckland, Sydney and Brisbane; and Rarotonga from Auckland and Christchurch.

### Tickets

Unless you've got a berth on a boat, transport to and between these South Pacific islands is almost exclusively by plane – plan and book in advance. Many people come to the Pacific as a stopover on round-the-world (RTW) tickets – such as those offered by Star Alliance (www.staralliance.com) and OneWorld (www.oneworld.com) – or you might consider a Circle Pacific ticket that allows South Pacific stops when travelling between Pacific Rim countries (the USA, South America, Southeast Asia, NZ and Australia).

### GETTING BETWEEN ISLANDS

Because of the lack of flights connecting the countries in the area (there are no flights between Samoa and Tonga, Tonga and Rarotonga, and Rarotonga and Samoa), most visitors choose to go to just one country in this region on a single trip.

If you do want to fly into all three nations on your South Seas jaunt, you'll need to jet into and out of Auckland a couple of times – which is by no means problematic; it just entails traversing a few more kilometres of sky.

The exception to this is that it is easy enough to get between the two Samoas, either by air or by boat, and visit them both in one hit.

**Rarotonga** Direct flights from NZ, Australia, USA and Tahiti.

**Samoa** Direct flights from NZ, Australia, Fiji and American Samoa.

**American Samoa** Direct flights from Hawai'i and Samoa.

**Tonga** Direct flights from NZ, Australia and Fiji.

## Sea

Climbing aboard a cargo ship, cruise liner or ocean-going yacht is a terrific way to see the sea.

### Cargo Ship

Cargo and dual-purpose cargo/passenger ships sail between Samoa and Tokelau, and Samoa and the Cook Islands. There's also a car ferry operating between Samoa and American Samoa.

### Cruise Ship

If you can manage to fight your way free of the prepackaging and get a little solo shore time, cruise ships can be a handy way to access this part of the South Pacific without any hassle. So if you've got the time, the cash and the inclination, go for it!

Cruise companies include the following.

**Crystal Cruises** (www.crystalcruises.com) LA to Sydney via American Samoa, Samoa and other islands.

**P&O Cruises** (www.pocruises.com.au) Major global player, with South Seas cruises from Australia and NZ.

**Princess Cruises** (www.princess.com) South Pacific cruises departing Australia (Sydney, Brisbane and Melbourne).

### Yacht

Harnessing the South Pacific trade winds and sailing from one island idyll to the next – what a dream! Prerequisites: time, money, yacht (or a friend with one). Most island groups here have reef-protected lagoons or lee-side moorings, and there are usually some nocturnal high jinks to be had ashore wherever yachties pull in for the night (Neiafu in Tonga springs to mind).

#### RED TAPE

You must enter a country at an official 'port of entry' (usually the capital). If this means sailing past a dozen beautiful outlying islands on the way to an appointment with an official in a dull capital city, bad luck. When you arrive, hoist your yellow quarantine flag (Q flag) and wait for the appropriate local official to contact you. Often you are expected to alert them by VHF radio (usually on channel 16). Ask customs officials at the port of entry about requirements for visiting other islands in the country. If you're the skipper, bear in mind that you are legally responsible for your crew's actions as well as your own.

## Tours

South Pacific package tours (p32) from travel agents often stray onto the 'uncool' side of the ledger, but they can be awesome value, including flights, transfers and accommodation. You might also consider specialist dive-tour agencies or other activity-based tours, which typically include flights, accommodation and activities. It's also often possible to book a package tour, then extend your stay with independent travel.

# GETTING AROUND

## Air

Clambering into a light aircraft is the primary way of getting from A to B in this part of the South Pacific. Don't expect cabin crew, complimentary meals or even a strip of tarmac in some cases (these small aircraft often land on grass airstrips on remote islands, where the terminal is a tin shed and a person with a mobile phone). Some interisland flights might operate just once or twice a week and can be heavily booked, so secure your seats well in advance.

### Airlines

The following carriers fly within Rarotonga, Samoa and Tonga.

**Air Rarotonga** (www.airraro.com) The Cook Islands' domestic carrier.

**Inter Island Airways** (www.interislandair.com) Flights within and between Samoa and American Samoa.

**Manu'a Airways** (www.manuaair.com) New in American Samoa in 2016, with flights between Pago Pago and Ofu and Ta'u islands, and between Ofu and Ta'u islands.

**Real Tonga** (www.realtonga.to) Tonga's domestic carrier, servicing the country's four main island groups – Tongatapu, Ha'apai, 'Eua and Vava'u. Also has occasional flights to the Niuas.

## Boat

There are a few possibilities for those romantics taken with the idea of exploring the Pacific by sea. It's certainly much slower than flying and not necessarily any cheaper – but adventure is more important than any of that!

### Cargo Ship

If you've got lots of time and don't mind roughing it, check the local supply-ship schedules. Some cargo vessels carry passengers and travel between far-flung island groups – many of which are not serviced by air. Schedules are notoriously flexible, with weather, sea and ship conditions playing a big part in whether boats turn up as planned. Cargo ships seldom arrive early, often arrive late and sometimes don't turn up at all.

### Ferry

Within these countries, passenger ferries ply the waters between various island groups and are a scenic and affordable (if not speedy or particularly comfortable) way to get from one island to the next. Tonga is a good example, with regular scheduled ferries (doubling as supply boats) chugging between the capital, Nuku'alofa, and the 'Eua, Ha'apai and Vava'u island groups.

## Local Transport

### Bicycle

On flat islands in the region, renting a bicycle can be an excellent way to get around. Most rental bikes won't come with a helmet or lock unless you ask for them – and be aware that maintenance often isn't a high priority. Watch for poor road surfaces, and check your travel insurance for disclaimers about hazardous activities. If you're bringing your own bike, ask the airline about costs and rules regarding dismantling and packing the bike.

### Boat

Within these countries, ferries and cargo boats are often the only way to get to some outer islands. Over shorter distances, sometimes it'll come down to negotiating with the local fishers to get you there.

### Bus

Larger islands in the region usually have some kind of bus service. However, public transport here couldn't be described as ruthlessly efficient. Buses are often privately (or sometimes family) owned, and it's not unusual for owner-drivers to set their own schedules. Formal bus stops may or may not exist – if not, just wave your arms around as a bus approaches. If there aren't many people travelling on a particular day, buses may stop altogether. Build flexibility into your plans.

### Car & Motorcycle

The larger islands in the region have car- or motorcycle-hire companies, either big international branches (Avis, Hertz etc) or locally run outfits. Bring your International Driving Permit and your licence from your home country.

#### INSURANCE

Make sure you get the rules and conditions of your insurance explained to you before you drive away. Check your own travel-insurance policy too; some policies do not cover damage on unsealed roads, windscreens, tyres or riding a motorcycle.

#### ROAD RULES & CONDITIONS

Driving is on the right-hand side of the road in the Cook Islands, Tonga and Samoa, and on the left-hand side in American Samoa. Roads in rural areas may be no more than dirt tracks used mostly for foot traffic – conditions can be dreadful if there has been recent cyclone or flood damage. Be super-watchful for kids and animals on the road, especially near villages. When you rent a car, ask about petrol availability if you're heading off the main routes. And don't park under coconut trees!

### Hitching

In many parts of the Cooks, Tonga and the Samoas, hitching is an accepted way of getting where you're going and is practised by locals and tourists alike.

The main difficulty with hitching on the South Pacific islands is that rides tend to be short, perhaps only from one village to the next – it could take you a while to travel longer distances. But hitching can be a great way to meet locals and is an option for getting around when the buses

## POLYNESIAN TIME WARP

Sit down, put your thinking cap on, and ponder this. When it is midday on Sunday in Apia, Samoa, it's exactly the same time (midday) in Pago Pago, American Samoa – only it's Saturday. Sort of makes sense, right? Everyone has heard of the International Date Line (IDL), but if Samoa and American Samoa are on opposite sides of the IDL, how can the time be the same? Shouldn't they be in different time zones?

Looking at a map you'll notice that the IDL isn't exactly straight; in fact, it has some major kinks. The theory was good at the 1884 International Meridian Conference in Washington when it was decided to put the imaginary IDL at the meridian of 180° longitude, exactly halfway around the world from the Greenwich meridian (0 °) – but it was also agreed that the IDL 'should not interfere with the use of standard or local time where desirable'.

Fiji didn't want to be split into two different days, it wasn't desirable for the Aleutian Islands to be a day ahead of Alaska – and the Tongan king didn't want to be a day behind South Pacific 'big boys' Australia and New Zealand (NZ). So the line was drawn arbitrarily east of Tonga and Samoa.

To make things really confusing, eight years later, in 1892, American traders persuaded the Samoan king to adopt the American date, resulting in a further kink in the date line – putting Samoa (which wasn't divided into two countries at that stage) and Tonga on different sides of the line (even though they were in the same time zone!).

Then, 119 years later, Samoa decided to shift back to west of the date line by skipping Friday 30 December 2011. The IDL now passes between Samoa and American Samoa, with American Samoa remaining aligned with the American date.

Samoa made the change because Australia and NZ have become its biggest trading partners, and also have large communities of expatriate islanders. Being almost a complete day behind made business difficult – having weekends on different days meant only four days of the working week were shared.

Keep this in mind when you are booking flights. Samoa and Tonga are west of the IDL, and the Cook Islands and American Samoa are east of it. Heading west to east, you'll pick up an extra day. Heading east to west, you'll lose one. You might only be sitting on the plane for 35 minutes from American Samoa to Samoa, but officially it's taking 24 hours 35 minutes for you to get there!

aren't running. You might be expected to pay a small fee for a ride, so offer what you think the ride is worth – although offers of payment will often be refused.

Keep in mind that hitching is never entirely safe. If you do choose to hitch it's safer to travel in pairs. Solo-travelling women should definitely seek alternative conveyances.

### Taxi

Taxis around these parts are a motley crew, ranging from company-owned and well-maintained minivans to rickety rust buckets someone's uncle runs as a cab when he's not fishing. Either way, you can expect plenty of conversation with the driver, often extending to an invitation to call them directly tomorrow/next week/next month when you need a taxi again. Meters aren't always present (and it's a good idea to discuss price before you start driving, even if they are). Have the specific address of your destination ready to go, too, so you don't end up at the driver's sister's guesthouse instead of the one you've booked.

# Health

## RECOMMENDED VACCINATIONS

For all countries in the region, vaccinations are recommended for hepatitis A, hepatitis B and typhoid fever. A current influenza shot is also recommended. And check how long it's been since you had a tetanus booster (once every 10 years is the going rate).

Most travellers who come to Rarotonga, Samoa or Tonga won't experience anything worse than an upset stomach or a hangover. But if you have an immediate and serious health problem, visit the nearest public hospital or call into a pharmacy for advice. These regions have no malaria, rabies or crocodiles: the main danger is from mosquito-borne dengue fever.

# BEFORE YOU GO

- A signed and dated letter from your physician describing your medical conditions and medications, including generic names, is a good idea.
- Bring medications in their original, clearly labelled, containers.
- See your dentist before a long trip.
- Carry a spare pair of contact lenses and glasses; take your optical prescription with you.

## Insurance

A comprehensive travel- and health-insurance policy is essential for the region. Check whether you're covered for 'dangerous' activities (surfing, snorkelling, diving etc) and make sure your policy has provision for evacuation. Under these circumstances, hospitals will accept direct payment from major international insurers, but for all other health-related costs cash up front is usually required.

Worldwide travel insurance is available at www.lonelyplanet.com/travel-insurance. You can buy, extend and claim online anytime – even if you're already on the road.

# IN RAROTONGA, SAMOA & TONGA

## Availability & Cost of Health Care

The further you get from population centres, the more basic the services and facilities. Cost varies between countries but is generally similar to Australia.

**Cook Islands, Samoa & Tonga** Specialised services may be limited, but private general practitioners, dentists and pharmacies are present.

**American Samoa** There are doctors in private practice and standard hospital and laboratory facilities with consultants in the major specialities. Private dentists, opticians and pharmacies are also available.

## Diseases

### Dengue Fever

**Risk** All countries, especially in the hotter, wetter months.

**Symptoms & treatment** Mosquito-borne dengue fever causes a high fever, headache and severe muscle pains. A fine rash may also be present. Self-treatment includes paracetamol (do *not* take aspirin), fluids and rest. Danger signs are prolonged vomiting, blood in the vomit, a blotchy, dark-red rash and/or bruising.

### Eosinophilic Meningitis

**Risk** Cook Islands, Tonga.

**Symptoms & treatment** An illness manifested by scattered abnormal skin sensations, fever and sometimes meningitis symptoms (headache, vomiting, confusion, stiffness of the neck and spine). Eosinophilic meningitis is caused by a microscopic parasite – the rat lungworm – that contaminates raw food. There is no proven treatment, but symptoms may require hospitalisation. For prevention, pay strict attention to advice on food and drink.

### Leptospirosis

**Risk** American Samoa, possibly elsewhere.

**Symptoms and treatment** Also known as Weil's disease, leptospirosis produces fever, headache, jaundice and, later, kidney failure.

It's caused by the spirochaete organism found in water contaminated by rat and pig urine. Often confused with dengue fever, this disease is the more serious of the two. The organism penetrates skin, so swimming in flooded areas is a risk. If diagnosed early, it's cured with penicillin.

# Traveller's Diarrhoea

Diarrhoea is caused by viruses, bacteria or parasites present in contaminated food or water. In temperate climates the cause is usually viral, but in the tropics bacteria or parasites are more usual.

If you get diarrhoea, be sure to drink plenty of fluids, preferably an oral rehydration solution (eg Diarolyte, Gastrolyte). If you start passing more than four or five stools a day, you should take antibiotics (usually a quinolone drug) and an antidiarrhoeal (eg Loperamide). If diarrhoea is bloody, persists for more than 72 hours or is accompanied by fever, shaking, chills or severe abdominal pain you should seek medical attention.

# Environmental Hazards

## Bites & Stings

### CONE SHELLS

Avoid handling these poisonous shells, which abound along shallow coral reefs. Stings cause local reactions, but nausea, faintness, palpitations or difficulty breathing are signs that medical attention is needed.

### DOGS

Dogs have free rein across these island groups, but their bark is generally worse than their bite. Play it safe on the streets: cross the road to avoid packs and don't try to pat or befriend wandering mutts.

### JELLYFISH

If you see these floating in the water or stranded on the beach, play it safe and stay on dry land. The sting is very painful and is best treated with vinegar or ice packs. Do not use alcohol.

### SEA SNAKES

Sea snakes may be seen around coral reefs. Unprovoked, sea snakes are extremely unlikely to attack – and their fangs will not penetrate a wetsuit.

### SHARKS

Sharks do swim around these warm tropical waters, but they rarely pose a threat to humans. Whitetip and blacktip reef sharks are too small to do any damage, but grey reef, tiger and bull sharks occasionally get nippy. If you're in the sea, remember that so are they.

## Coral Ear

This is a fungal infection caused by water entering the ear canal. Apart from diarrhoea it is the most common reason for tourists to consult a doctor: it can be very painful and spoil your holiday. Self-treatment with an antibiotic-plus-steroid eardrop preparation (eg Sofradex, Kenacomb Otic) is very effective. Stay out of the water until the pain and itch have gone.

## Diving Hazards

Because the region has wonderful opportunities for scuba diving, it's easy to get overexcited and neglect strict depth and time precautions. If you're inexperienced, make sure you're diving with a licensed operator who knows what they're doing and has a realistic understanding of your limits.

## Fish Poisoning

*Ciguatera* poisoning is characterised by stomach upsets, itching, faintness, slow pulse and bizarre inverted sensations – cold feeling hot and vice versa. *Ciguatera* has been reported in many carnivorous reef fish, including red snapper, barracuda and even smaller reef fish. There is no safe test to determine whether a fish is poisonous or not, although it is reasonable to eat what the locals are eating. Deep-sea tuna is perfectly safe.

Treatment consists of rehydration; if the pulse is very slow, medication may be needed. Healthy adults will make a complete recovery, although disturbed sensation may persist for some weeks – sometimes much longer.

## Heat Sicknesses

Sunburn is an obvious issue, so use sunscreen liberally. It's also important to stay hydrated; heat exhaustion is a state of dehydration associated with salt loss.

Heatstroke is more dangerous and happens when the cooling effect of sweating fails. This condition is characterised by muscle weakness and mental confusion. Skin will be hot and dry. If this occurs, 'put the fire out' by cooling the body with water on the outside and cold drinks on the inside, and seek urgent medical help.

## Staph Infection

Infection of cuts and scrapes is very common, and cuts from live coral are particularly prone to infection. Cleanse the wound thoroughly (getting out all the little bits of coral or dirt if needed), apply an antiseptic and cover with a dressing. Change the dressing regularly, never let it sit wet and check often for signs of infection.

### TAP WATER

To steer yourself clear of diarrhoea, avoid tap water unless it has been boiled, filtered or chemically disinfected (with iodine tablets), and also avoid ice unless you've made it yourself from bottled water. This is a sensible overall precaution, but the municipal water supply in capital cities in the region can be trusted.

# Language

## RAROTONGAN

Rarotongan (or Cook Islands Maori, as it's also known) is a Polynesian language similar to New Zealand Maori and Marquesan (from French Polynesia). There are minor dialectal differences between many of the islands, and some northern islands have their own languages. English is spoken as a second (or third) language by virtually everyone.

Cook Islands Maori was traditionally a spoken language, with no written form. The language, in its Rarotongan guise, was first written down by missionaries in the 1830s.

Most consonants are pronounced as they are in English, although the letter *v* is pronounced closer to the English 'w' sound on many islands. The letters *ng* are pronounced the same as in the English word 'singing', but in Rarotongan often occur at the beginning of a word (eg Nga, Ngatangi'ia). The glottal stop (like the pause in the middle of 'uh-oh') replaces the 'h' or 'f' sounds of similar Polynesian languages and is represented in writing by an apostrophe ('): for example, the Tahitian word for 'one', *tahi* (pronounced ta-hee), is *ta'i* (pronounced ta-ee) in Rarotongan. Vowels have long and short variants, and using the wrong one can result in a completely different meaning. Long vowels are sometimes written with a stroke above the letter, eg *ā*.

| | |
|---|---|
| **Hello.** | *Kia orana.* |
| **Goodbye.** (if staying) | *'Aere ra.* |
| **Goodbye.** (if leaving) | *'E no'o ra.* |
| **See you again.** | *Ka kite.* |
| **How are you?** (to one person) | *Pe'ea koe?* |
| **How are you?** (to two people) | *Pe'ea korua?* |
| **How are you?** (to more than two people) | *Pe'ea koutou?* |
| **I'm fine.** | *E meitaki au.* |
| **I'm hot/cold.** | *E vera/anu au.* |
| **Please.** | *'Ine.* |
| **Thank you (very much).** | *Meitaki (ma'ata).* |
| **Welcome!** | *Turou!* |
| **Good luck!** (a toast) | *Kia manuia!* |
| **Yes./No.** | *Ae./Kare.* |
| **Maybe.** | *Penei ake.* |

| | |
|---|---|
| **I/me** | *au* |
| **my** | *taku* |
| **you** (one person) | *koe* |
| **you** (two people) | *korua* |
| **you** (three or more) | *koutou* |
| **him/her/he/she** | *'aia* |
| **we** (two) | *taua/maua* |
| **we** (three or more) | *tatou/matou* |
| **they** (two) | *raua* |
| **they** (three or more) | *ratou* |

| | |
|---|---|
| **What's your name?** | *Ko 'ai to'ou ingoa?* |
| **My name is ...** | *Ko ... toku ingoa.* |
| **Where are you from?** (to one person) | *No 'ea mai koe?* |
| **I'm from ...** | *No ... mai au.* |
| **Where are you going?** (to one person) | *Ka 'aere koe ki'ea?* |

### WANT MORE?

For in-depth language information and handy phrases, check out Lonely Planet's *South Pacific Phrasebook*. You'll find it at **shop.lonelyplanet.com**, or you can buy Lonely Planet's iPhone phrasebooks at the Apple App Store.

### NUMBERS – RAROTONGAN

| | |
|---|---|
| 1 | *ta'i* |
| 2 | *rua* |
| 3 | *toru* |
| 4 | *'a* |
| 5 | *rima* |
| 6 | *ono* |
| 7 | *'itu* |
| 8 | *varu* |
| 9 | *iva* |
| 10 | *ta'i-nga'uru* |
| 11 | *ta'i-nga'uru ma ta'i* |
| 20 | *rua-nga'uru* |
| 100 | *ta'i-anere* |
| 101 | *ta'i-anere ma ta'i* |
| 200 | *rua 'anere* |
| 1000 | *ta'i-tauatini* |

| | |
|---|---|
| **I'm going to ...** | *Te 'aere nei au ki ...* |
| **Where are you going?** (to two people) | *Ka 'aere korua ki'ea?* |
| **We're going to ...** | *Te 'aere nei maua ki ...* |
| **Who is that person?** | *Ko 'ai tena tangata?* |
| **That's my (son).** | *Ko toku (tamaiti) tena.* |

| | |
|---|---|
| **baby** | *pepe* |
| **boy/son** | *tamaiti* |
| **brother** | *tungane* |
| **child/children** | *tama/tamariki* |
| **father** | *papa/metua tane* |
| **friend** | *'oa/taeake* |
| **girl/daughter** | *tama'ine* |
| **man/husband** | *tane* |
| **mother** | *mama/metua va'ine* |
| **person/people** | *tangata* |
| **sister** | *tua'ine* |
| **woman/wife** | *va'ine* |

| | |
|---|---|
| **beautiful** | *manea* |
| **language** | *reo* |
| **many** | *rau* |
| **speak/word** | *tuatua* |
| **that** | *tena* |
| **that over there** | *tera* |
| **this** | *teia* |
| **ugly** | *vi'ivi'i* |
| **understand** | *marama* |

| | |
|---|---|
| **Do you understand Maori?** | *E marama ana koe i te reo Maori?* |
| **I don't understand.** | *Kare au i marama.* |
| **I don't understand Maori.** | *Kare au e marama i te reo Maori.* |
| **What's the Maori word for ...?** | *E a'a te tuatua Maori no te ...?* |
| **How do you say ...?** | *Ka 'aka pe'ea au me tuatua ...?* |
| **Please speak slower.** | *E tuatua marie koe, 'ine.* |
| **What's this?** | *E aka teia?* |
| **How much is it?** | *'E a'a te moni i teia/te ra?* |
| **I'd like to buy ...** | *'Inangaro au i te 'oko ...* |
| **I'm just looking.** | *'Akarakara 'ua nei au.* |

| | |
|---|---|
| **beach** | *tapa ta'atai* |
| **church** | *ekalesia/'are pure* |
| **house** | *'are* |
| **island/lagoon islet** | *motu* |
| **lagoon/lake** | *roto* |
| **land** | *'enua* |
| **mountain** | *maunga* |
| **ocean** | *moana* |
| **reef** | *akau* |
| **sky** | *rangi* |
| **store/shop** | *toa* |
| **town** | *taoni* |
| **village** | *tapere* |

## SAMOAN

Samoan is the main language spoken in Samoa and American Samoa, although most people also speak English. Samoan is a Polynesian language similar to Maori, Tongan, Hawaiian and Tahitian.

Most consonants in Samoan are pronounced the same as their English counterparts. The glottal stop (the sound heard in the middle of 'uh-oh', represented in writing by an apostrophe) replaces the *k* of many other Polynesian languages, *s* replaces *h*, and *l* replaces *r*. Therefore, the Tahitian word for 'one', *tahi*, is *tasi* in Samoan, *rua* (two) is *lua*, and *ika* (Rarotongan for 'fish') is *i'a*. In Samoan the letter *g* is pronounced as a soft 'ng' sound (*palagi*, for example, is pronounced pa-lung-i). Vowels can be long or short, depending on whether or not they are stressed, but the actual difference in sound between them is very slight to the untrained ear. A long vowel is conventionally indicated by a line above it (eg *ā*) and is pronounced as a long version of its short counterpart. Stress in Samoan is normally placed on the second-last syllable.

| | |
|---|---|
| **Hello.** | *Malo.* |
| **Goodbye.** | *Tofa soifua.* |
| **Bye.** | *Tofa./Fa.* |
| **How are you?** | *'O a mai 'oe?* |
| **I'm fine, thanks.** | *Manuia lava, fa'afetai.* |
| **Please.** | *Fa'amolemole.* |
| **Thank you (very much).** | *Fa'afetai (tele).* |
| **Welcome.** | *Afio mai.* |
| **Excuse me.** | *Tulou.* |
| **I'm sorry.** | *Ua ou sese.* |
| **Forgive me.** | *Malie.* |
| **Yes.** | *Ioe.* |
| **No.** | *Leai.* |
| **Maybe.** | *Masalo.* |

| | |
|---|---|
| **What's your name?** | *O ai lou igoa?* |
| **My name is ...** | *O lo'u igoa o ...* |
| **Where are you from?** | *Fea lou atunu'u?* |
| **Where are you going?** (often used as a pleasantry) | *Alu i fea?* |
| **Are you married?** | *Ua fai se aiga?* |
| **How many children do you have?** | *E to'afia tama'iti?* |
| **How old are you?** | *Fia ou tausaga?* |
| **I'm ... years old.** | *Ua ... o'u tausaga.* |
| **Do you like ...?** | *E te manao i le ...?* |
| **I like it very much.** | *O lo'u vaisu.* |
| **May I?** | *E mafai?* |
| **It's all right./ No problem.** | *Ua lelei.* |

| | |
|---|---|
| **(little) boy** | *tama('iti'iti)* |
| **boyfriend** | *uo tama* |
| **(little) girl** | *teine('iti'iti)* |
| **girlfriend** | *uo teine* |
| **family** | *'aiga* |
| **father** | *tama* |
| **man** | *tamaloa* |
| **mother** | *tina* |
| **white person** | *palagi* |
| **woman** | *fafine* |

| | |
|---|---|
| **bad** | *leaga* |
| **beautiful** | *manaia* |
| **fine** | *manuia* |
| **good** | *lelei* |
| **happy** | *fiafia* |
| **journey** | *malaga* |
| **love** | *alofa* |

## NUMBERS – SAMOAN

| | |
|---|---|
| 1 | *tasi* |
| 2 | *lua* |
| 3 | *tolu* |
| 4 | *fā* |
| 5 | *lima* |
| 6 | *ono* |
| 7 | *fitu* |
| 8 | *valu* |
| 9 | *iva* |
| 10 | *sefulu* |
| 11 | *sefulu tasi* |
| 20 | *lua sefulu* |
| 100 | *selau* |
| 101 | *selau ma le tasi* |
| 200 | *lua selau* |
| 1000 | *afe* |

| | |
|---|---|
| **Do you speak English?** | *Ete iloa Nanu?* |
| **I don't speak ...** | *Ou te le tautala ...* |
| **I understand.** | *Ua ou mala-malama.* |
| **I don't understand.** | *Ou te le mala-malama.* |
| **How do you say ...?** | *E faapefea ona ...?* |
| **Please write it down.** | *Fa'amolemole tusi i lalo.* |
| **How much is it?** | *E fia le ta'u?* |
| **I'd like to buy it.** | *Ou te fia fa'atauina.* |
| **It's too expensive.** | *Taugata mo a'u.* |

| | |
|---|---|
| **beach** | *matafaga* |
| **bird** | *manulele* |
| **chicken** | *moa* |
| **entrance** | *ulufale* |
| **exit** | *ulufafo* |
| **fish** | *i'a* |
| **flower** | *fuamatala* |
| **house** | *fale* |
| **island** | *motu* |
| **lake** | *vaituloto* |
| **mosquito** | *namu* |
| **pig** | *pua'a* |
| **rain** | *timu* |
| **sea** | *sami* |
| **sun** | *la* |
| **village** | *nu'u* |
| **wind** | *savili* |

| | |
|---|---|
| **Where is (the/a) ...?** | *O fea (le/se) ...?* |
| **church** | *falesa* |
| **city centre** | *nofoaga autu o le a'ai* |
| **hospital** | *falemai* |
| **market** | *maketi* |
| **store** | *faleoloa* |

## TONGAN

Tongan is a Polynesian language from the Austronesian language family. Its closest relatives are the other Polynesian languages such as Samoan, Hawaiian, Maori and Tahitian. It's the official language of Tonga, alongside English, and the language most often used in everyday communication. On major islands (Tongatapu, Vava'u), almost everyone speaks English as a second language.

The same variety of Tongan is spoken on all the islands in Tonga, with the exception of Niuafo'ou, the most northwesterly island, where a dialect that's closer to Samoan is spoken.

It's worth listening to the way native speakers pronounce vowels because vowel length can affect the meaning of some words. You may see vowels written with a macron (eg *ā*), which indicates that they are long. The long sound is simply an extended and accented (stressed) version of the short vowel. The glottal stop, represented in writing by an apostrophe ('), is similar to the sound heard in the middle of 'uh-oh', and can also change the meaning of words: for example, *hau* means 'earring', but *ha'u* means 'come here'. Note also that the letters *ng* are pronounced as in 'singer', the letter *p* represents a sound midway between the 'p' in 'park' and the 'b' in 'bark', while *t* is pronounced midway between the 't' in 'tip' and the 'd' in 'dip'.

Stress falls on the second-last syllable in most words, unless there's a long vowel, in which case that syllable receives the stress.

| | |
|---|---|
| **Hello.** | *Malo e lelei.* |
| **Goodbye.** (if staying) | *'Alu a.* |
| **Goodbye.** (if leaving) | *Nofo ā.* |
| **How are you?** | *Fefe hake?* |
| **I'm fine, thanks.** | *Sai pe, malo.* |
| **Please.** | *Faka molemole.* |
| **Thank you (very much).** | *Malo ('aupito).* |
| **You're welcome.** | *'Io malo.* |
| **Welcome.** | *Talitali fiefia.* |
| **Excuse me.** | *Kataki.* |
| **I'm sorry.** | *Faka molemole'iau.* |
| **Yes.** | *'Io.* |
| **No.** | *Ikai.* |
| **Maybe.** | *Mahalo pe.* |
| **What's your name?** | *Ko hai ho hingoa?* |
| **My name is ...** | *Ko hoku hingoa ko ...* |
| **Where are you from?** | *Ko ho'o ha'u mei fe fonua?* |
| **I'm from ...** | *Ko 'eku ha'u mei ...* |
| **Are you married?** | *Kuo ke'osi mali?* |
| **How old are you?** | *Koe ha ho ta'u motua?* |
| **I'm ... years old.** | *'Oku 'ou ta'u ... ta'u motua.* |
| **I'm a (tourist/ student).** | *Ko 'eku ha'u (eve'eva/ taha ako).* |
| **Do you like ...?** | *'Oku ke sai'ia 'ihe ...?* |
| **I don't like ...** | *'Oku ikai teu sai'ia ...* |
| **I like it very much.** | *'Oku 'ou sai'ia 'aupito.* |
| **Just a minute.** | *Tali si'i.* |
| **May I?** | *Faka molemole kau?* |
| **It's all right./ No problem.** | *'Io 'oku sai/sai pe ia.* |

| | |
|---|---|
| **boy** | *tamasi'i* |
| **girl** | *ta'ahine* |
| **man** | *tangata* |
| **woman** | *fefine* |

### NUMBERS – TONGAN

There are several numbering systems in Tongan. The system used depends on what is being counted. For most items, the standard system (given here) can be used, but if you wish to count certain culturally significant items such as coconuts, yams or fish, you'll need to learn the appropriate terms.

| | |
|---|---|
| **1** | *tahs* |
| **2** | *ua* |
| **3** | *tolu* |
| **4** | *fā* |
| **5** | *nima* |
| **6** | *ono* |
| **7** | *fitu* |
| **8** | *valu* |
| **9** | *hiva* |
| **10** | *hongofulu* |
| **11** | *taha-taha* |
| **20** | *ua-noa* |
| **100** | *teau* |
| **101** | *teau mā taha* |

| | |
|---|---|
| **bad** | *kovi* |
| **big** | *lahi* |
| **bigger** | *lahi ange* |
| **cheap** | *ma'ama'a* |
| **cheaper** | *ma'a ma'a ange* |
| **expensive** | *mamafa* |
| **good** | *lelei* |
| **less** | *si'i* |
| **more** | *lahi* |
| **pretty** | *faka 'ofa 'ofa* |
| **small** | *si'i si'i* |
| **smaller** | *si'i si'i ange* |

| | |
|---|---|
| **Do you speak English?** | *'Oku ke lava 'o lea faka palangi?* |
| **Does anyone speak English?** | *'Oku 'iai ha taha'oku lea faka palangi?* |
| **I understand.** | *'Oku mahino kiate 'au.* |
| **I don't understand.** | *'Oku ikai ke mahino kiate 'au.* |
| **How do you say ...?** | *Koe ha ho lea ...?* |
| **What is this called?** | *Ko 'e ha hono hingoa 'o 'e me'a ko 'eni?* |
| **How much is it?** | *Fiha hono totongi?* |
| **I'd like to buy it.** | *'Oku ou fie fakatau ia.* |
| **It's too expensive.** | *Fu'u mamafa kiate au.* |
| **Where is ...?** | *Ko fe'ia a'e ...?* |

| | |
|---|---|
| **bank** | *pangike* |
| **beach** | *matatahi* |
| **bridge** | *hala kavakava* |
| **church** | *fale lotu* |
| **city centre** | *i loto kolo* |
| **embassy** | *'api 'oe 'amipasitoa* |
| **hospital** | *fale mahaki* |
| **island** | *motu* |
| **lake** | *ano vai* |
| **market** | *maketi* |
| **ocean (deep)** | *moana* |
| **palace** | *palasi* |
| **post office** | *positi 'ofisi* |
| **rain** | *'uha* |
| **restaurant** | *fale kai* |
| **ruins** | *maumau* |
| **sea** | *tahi* |
| **street/road** | *hala* |
| **suburb** | *lotokolo* |
| **sun** | *la'a* |
| **telephone office** | *fale telefoni* |
| **tourist office** | *'ofisi taki mamata* |
| **tower** | *taua* |
| **village** | *kolo si'i si'i* |
| **wind** | *matangi* |

# GLOSSARY

**'aiga** – see *kainga* (Samoa)

**'ava** – see *kava* (Samoa)

**ariki** – paramount chief; members of a noble family

**atoll** – low-lying island built up from successive deposits of coral

**aualuma** – society of unmarried women (western Polynesia)

**aumaga** – society of untitled men who do most of the fishing and farming (Samoa and Tokelau)

**Austronesians** – people or languages from Indonesia, Malaysia and the Pacific Islands

**barrier reef** – a long, narrow coral reef lying offshore and separated from the land by a lagoon of deep water that shelters the land from the sea

**blackbirding** – a 19th-century recruitment scheme little removed from outright slavery

**bonito** – blue-fin tuna

**'ei** – necklace (Cook Islands)

**fa'a** – see *faka*

**fa'afafine** – see *fakaleiti* (Samoa)

**faka** – according to (a culture's) customs and tradition, eg *fa'a Samoa* or *faka Pasifika*

**fakaleiti** – man who dresses and lives as a woman (Tonga)

**fale** – house with thatched roof and open sides, but often used to mean any building

**fale fono** – meeting house, village hall or parliament building

**fale umu** – kitchen huts

**fare** – see *fale*

**fiafia** – dance performance (Samoa)

**fono** – governing council (Polynesian)

**heilala** – Tonga's national flower

**ika** – fish

**kai** – food

**kainga** – extended family (Polynesia)

**kava** – mud-coloured, mildly intoxicating drink made from the roots of the *Piper methysticum* plant

**kikau** – thatch-roofed

**kirikiti** – cricket with many players on each side (French Polynesia, Samoa, Tokelau, Tuvalu, and Wallis and Futuna)

**koutu** – ancient open-air royal courtyard (Cook Islands)

**kumara** – sweet potato

**Lapita** – ancestors of the Polynesians

**lava-lava** – sarong-type garment; wide piece of cloth worn as a skirt by women and men

**lei** – necklace (Samoa)

**LMS** – London Missionary Society

**mahimahi** – dolphin fish

**maire** – aromatic leaf (Cook Islands)

**makatea** – geological term for a raised coral island; coral coastal plain around an island

**malae** – see *marae*

**mana** – personal spiritual power

**Maori** – indigenous people (Cook Islands, Society Islands)

**marae** – community village green (western Polynesia); pre-Christian sacred site (eastern Polynesia); ceremonial meeting ground (Cook Islands)

**matai** – senior male, political representative of a family (Samoa, Tokelau and Tuvalu)

**mataiapo** – see *matai* (Cook Islands)

**motu** – island, islet

**niu** – coconut

**nuku** – village (Polynesian)

**pa'anga** – the currency of Tonga

**PADI** – Professional Association of Dive Instructors

**palagi** – see *palangi*

**palangi** – White person (Samoa)

**Papuans** – ancient people who are among the ancestors of modern Melanesians

**pareu** – see *lava-lava* (Cook Islands)

**pe'a** – male tattoos (Samoa)

**peka** – bat, small bird

**Polynesia** – the huge triangle of ocean and islands bounded by Hawai'i, New Zealand and Easter Island; includes the Cook Islands, French Polynesia, Niue, Pitcairn Island, Samoa, American Samoa, Tokelau, Tonga, Tuvalu, and Wallis and Futuna; the name is Greek for 'many islands'

**pulenu'u** – head man, village mayor

**rangatira** – chief, nobility (Polynesia)

**sa** – sacred, forbidden; holy day, holy time (Samoa and Tuvalu)

**siapo** – tapa; bark cloth (Samoa)

**ta'ovala** – distinctive woven pandanus mats worn around the waist in Tonga

**tapa** – bark cloth with designs printed in black and rust

**tapu** – sacred, prohibited

**taro** – plant with green heart-shaped leaves, cultivated for both its leaf and edible rootstock

**tatau** – tattoo

**taupou** – title bestowed by high-ranking chief upon a young woman of his family (Polynesia)

**tivaevae** – colourful intricately sewn appliqué works (Cook Islands)

**to'ona'i** – Sunday lunch (Samoa)

**tufanga** – priest, expert (Polynesia)

**tufuga** – see *tufanga* (Samoa)

**tumunu** – hollowed-out coconut-tree stump used to brew bush-beer; also bush-beer drinking sessions

**umu** – earth oven

**umukai** – feast of foods cooked in an *umu*

**USP** – University of the South Pacific

**va'a** – see *vaka*

**vaka** – canoe

# Behind the Scenes

## SEND US YOUR FEEDBACK

We love to hear from travellers – your comments keep us on our toes and help make our books better. Our well-travelled team reads every word on what you loved or loathed about this book. Although we cannot reply individually to your submissions, we always guarantee that your feedback goes straight to the appropriate authors, in time for the next edition. Each person who sends us information is thanked in the next edition – the most useful submissions are rewarded with a selection of digital PDF chapters.

Visit **lonelyplanet.com/contact** to submit your updates and suggestions or to ask for help. Our award-winning website also features inspirational travel stories, news and discussions.

Note: We may edit, reproduce and incorporate your comments in Lonely Planet products such as guidebooks, websites and digital products, so let us know if you don't want your comments reproduced or your name acknowledged. For a copy of our privacy policy visit lonelyplanet.com/privacy.

## OUR READERS

**Many thanks to the travellers who used the last edition and wrote to us with helpful hints, useful advice and interesting anecdotes:** Chris Evans, Inano McMurchy, Iris Hüll, Jim Green, Judy Chappell, Kaori Hashimoto, Katherine Lynch, Logan McDaneld, Steve Waters.

## AUTHOR THANKS

### Brett Atkinson

*Meitaki ma'ata* to all the friendly Cook Islanders I met on my travels, especially Christian Mani, Nane Teokotai Vainepoto Papa and Daniel Fisher at Cook Islands Tourism in Avarua. On 'Atiu thanks to Mata Arai, Roger Malcolm, and Mareta Atetu, and to Tangata and Teata Ateriano on Ma'uke. Final thanks to Carol for sharing this latest South Pacific adventure with me – especially the mammoth tuna sandwiches, bush-bashing excitement and lazy sunset cocktails.

### Charles Rawlings-Way

Huge thanks to Tasmin for the gig: it had been far too long since I'd experienced the South Pacific any closer than 39,000 feet above the waves. Thanks also to the all-star in-house LP production staff in London and Melbourne, and kudos to my island-addled crew of co-authors (dirty job, someone's gotta do it, etc). Special praise and adoration as always to Meg and our daughters Ione and Remy, who held the fort at home while I reported in from sundry remote islands with stories of coral reefs, sunsets and cold beer.

### Tamara Sheward

*Fa'afetai tele* to the wonderful folks of the erstwhile Navigator Isles for all of their invaluable guidance and assistance while researching and travelling for this book. Among hundreds of others, garlands must go to Maria, Sophie, Jay and Killi in Samoa, and Fanua, Cita, Tom and Howard in American Samoa. Frangipanis and South Sea smooches to my two crazy coconuts, Dušan and Masha.

## ACKNOWLEDGEMENTS

Climate map data adapted from Peel MC, Finlayson BL & McMahon TA (2007) 'Updated World Map of the Köppen-Geiger Climate Classification', Hydrology and Earth System Sciences, 11, 163344.

Cover photograph: Humpback whale, Tonga. Maria Teresa Lara/500px ©

## THIS BOOK

This 8th edition of Lonely Planet's *Rarotonga, Samoa & Tonga* guidebook was researched and written by Brett Atkinson, Charles Rawlings-Way and Tamara Sheward. The previous edition was written by Craig McLachlan, Brett Atkinson and Celeste Brash. This guidebook was produced by the following:

**Destination Editor** Tasmin Waby

**Coordinating Editor** Sarah Bailey

**Product Editors** Grace Dobell, Alison Ridgway

**Senior Cartographers** Diana Von Holdt, Corey Hutchison

**Book Designer** Wibowo Rusli

**Assisting Editors** Janet Austin, Katie Connolly, Andrea Dobbin

**Cover Researcher** Naomi Parker

**Thanks to** Dan Corbett, Joel Cotterell, Laura Crawford, David Hodges, Lauren Keith, Kirsten Rawlings, Sarah Reid

# Index

Map Pages **000**
Photo Pages **000**

## Y

# Map Legend

## Sights

- Beach
- Bird Sanctuary
- Buddhist
- Castle/Palace
- Christian
- Confucian
- Hindu
- Islamic
- Jain
- Jewish
- Monument
- Museum/Gallery/Historic Building
- Ruin
- Shinto
- Sikh
- Taoist
- Winery/Vineyard
- Zoo/Wildlife Sanctuary
- Other Sight

## Activities, Courses & Tours

- Bodysurfing
- Diving
- Canoeing/Kayaking
- Course/Tour
- Sento Hot Baths/Onsen
- Skiing
- Snorkelling
- Surfing
- Swimming/Pool
- Walking
- Windsurfing
- Other Activity

## Sleeping

- Sleeping
- Camping

## Eating

- Eating

## Drinking & Nightlife

- Drinking & Nightlife
- Cafe

## Entertainment

- Entertainment

## Shopping

- Shopping

## Information

- Bank
- Embassy/Consulate
- Hospital/Medical
- Internet
- Police
- Post Office
- Telephone
- Toilet
- Tourist Information
- Other Information

## Geographic

- Beach
- Gate
- Hut/Shelter
- Lighthouse
- Lookout
- Mountain/Volcano
- Oasis
- Park
- Pass
- Picnic Area
- Waterfall

## Population

- Capital (National)
- Capital (State/Province)
- City/Large Town
- Town/Village

## Transport

- Airport
- Border crossing
- Bus
- Cable car/Funicular
- Cycling
- Ferry
- Metro station
- Monorail
- Parking
- Petrol station
- Subway station
- Taxi
- Train station/Railway
- Tram
- Underground station
- Other Transport

*Note: Not all symbols displayed above appear on the maps in this book*

## Routes

- Tollway
- Freeway
- Primary
- Secondary
- Tertiary
- Lane
- Unsealed road
- Road under construction
- Plaza/Mall
- Steps
- Tunnel
- Pedestrian overpass
- Walking Tour
- Walking Tour detour
- Path/Walking Trail

## Boundaries

- International
- State/Province
- Disputed
- Regional/Suburb
- Marine Park
- Cliff
- Wall

## Hydrography

- River, Creek
- Intermittent River
- Canal
- Water
- Dry/Salt/Intermittent Lake
- Reef

## Areas

- Airport/Runway
- Beach/Desert
- Cemetery (Christian)
- Cemetery (Other)
- Glacier
- Mudflat
- Park/Forest
- Sight (Building)
- Sportsground
- Swamp/Mangrove

# OUR STORY

A beat-up old car, a few dollars in the pocket and a sense of adventure. In 1972 that's all Tony and Maureen Wheeler needed for the trip of a lifetime – across Europe and Asia overland to Australia. It took several months, and at the end – broke but inspired – they sat at their kitchen table writing and stapling together their first travel guide, *Across Asia on the Cheap*. Within a week they'd sold 1500 copies. Lonely Planet was born.

Today, Lonely Planet has offices in Franklin, London, Melbourne, Oakland, Dublin, Beijing and Delhi, with more than 600 staff and writers. We share Tony's belief that 'a great guidebook should do three things: inform, educate and amuse'.

# OUR WRITERS

**Brett Atkinson**

From his home in Auckland, Brett has travelled to many of the islands in his South Pacific backyard. For this extended research trip to the Cook Islands, he snorkelled and scootered around Aitutaki, drank bush beer and organic coffee on 'Atiu, and explored Rarotonga on two and four wheels with his wife, Carol. Brett has covered more than 50 countries as a guidebook author and travel and food writer. See www.brett-atkinson.net for his most recent work and upcoming travels.

**Charles Rawlings-Way**

As a likely lad, Charles suffered in school shorts through Tasmanian winters: ice on the Hobart puddles, snow on Mt Wellington... He dreamed of one day exploring tropical isles with a more humane climate. After dropping a windsurfer mast on a Texan tourist's head in Fiji in 1985 and chasing rats around an Aitutatki guesthouse in 2005, a trip to see what Tonga had to offer was well overdue. Charles has penned 30-something Lonely Planet guidebooks, and remains pathologically fixated on the virtues and vices of travel.

**Tamara Sheward**

Despite a hearty dislike of heat and humidity – not to mention that pesky mango allergy – Tamara not only lives in the tropics, but enjoys travelling them extensively. While researching the South Pacific, she rode in 50-plus boats, 14 aeroplanes, umpteen rattly open-air buses and one submarine; alas, no similar tally was kept on kava and coconut consumption. In addition to the islands in this book, Tamara has covered an incongruous miscellany of countries for Lonely Planet, including Serbia, northern Australia, Bulgaria and Russia.

**Published by Lonely Planet Global Limited**
CRN 554153
8th edition – December 2016
ISBN 978 1 78657 217 2

10 9 8 7 6 5 4 3 2 1
Printed in China